June 3–5, 2015
Brussels, Belgium

I0038011

Association for Computing Machinery

Advancing Computing as a Science & Profession

TVX 2015

Proceedings of the ACM International Conference on

Interactive Experiences for TV and Online Video

Sponsored by:

ACM SIGCHI

Supported by:

ifip, iMinds, SBS Belgium, and Telenet

**Association for
Computing Machinery**

Advancing Computing as a Science & Profession

The Association for Computing Machinery
2 Penn Plaza, Suite 701
New York, New York 10121-0701

Notice to Past Authors of ACM-Published Articles
ACM intends to create a complete electronic archive of all articles and/or other material previously published by ACM. If you have written a work that has been previously published by ACM in any journal or conference proceedings prior to 1978, or any SIG Newsletter at any time, and you do NOT want this work to appear in the ACM Digital Library, please inform permissions@acm.org, stating the title of the work, the author(s), and where and when published.

ISBN: 978-1-4503-3526-3 (Digital)

ISBN: 978-1-4503-3867-7 (Print)

Additional copies may be ordered prepaid from:

ACM Order Department
PO Box 30777
New York, NY 10087-0777, USA

Phone: 1-800-342-6626 (USA and Canada)
+1-212-626-0500 (Global)
Fax: +1-212-944-1318
E-mail: acmhelp@acm.org
Hours of Operation: 8:30 am – 4:30 pm ET

Printed in the USA

Welcome from the General Chairs

It is our great pleasure to welcome you to Brussels for the second edition of the *ACM International Conference on Interactive Experiences for Television and Online Video – ACM TVX2015*. It is an honour for the Digital Society Department of iMinds to have been selected to host this leading conference in the heart of Europe.

iMinds is Flanders' digital research center and business incubator, established by the Flemish government in 2004. Building on the strength of our 850+ top researchers located at 5 Flemish universities, we introduce digital innovation in 5 key markets (ICT, Media, Health, Smart Cities and Manufacturing). We collaborate with research partners to convert digital knowhow into real-life products and services that change people's lives for the better. Key asset is our agile, open research mind set and proven methodology. As a business incubator, iMinds also guides researchers, young entrepreneurs and start-ups in the successful market introduction of their ideas.

iMinds' Digital Society Department consists of three research groups at as many universities in Flanders, Belgium: the Centre for User Experience Research (CUO) at the University of Leuven (KU Leuven), Studies on Media and Information Technologies (SMIT) at Vrije Universiteit Brussel (VUB), and Media and ICT (MICT) at the University of Ghent (UGent). These three research groups combined have an extensive track record in research on the design and use of television and online video experiences, and are pleased to be part of a conference that is so close to many of its core research activities.

This conference would not be possible without the practical and financial support from different supporters. First of all, we would like to thank you for registering for and attending the conference, as you are an important part of our community and making these events possible. We would also like to thank all members of the organizing committee, who have been working very hard during more than a year to prepare the conference. Finally, we want to thank our sponsor, ACM SIGCHI, and our generous corporate supporters, iMinds, SBS and Telenet who provided the much welcomed support for making this conference an enjoyable experience.

We wish you have a great conference and hope that you will enjoy your stay in Brussels!

David Geerts
ACM TVX2015 General Chair
iMinds / KU Leuven

Lieven De Marez
ACM TVX2015 General Chair
iMinds / UGent

Caroline Pauwels
ACM TVX2015 General Chair
iMinds / VUB

Welcome from the Program Chairs

We are very pleased that we can present to you an exciting program for ACM TVX 2015, which has been put together based on many submissions from all around the globe.

As the leading international conference for presentation and discussion of research into interactive experiences for online video and TV, the conference brings together international researchers and practitioners from a wide range of disciplines, ranging from human-computer interaction, multimedia engineering and design to media studies, media psychology and sociology, to present and discuss the latest insights in the field. ACM TVX2015 presents research on content production, systems & architectures, interaction technologies & techniques, experience design & evaluation, media studies, empirical methods, data science, business models & marketing and innovation & visions.

The call for papers attracted submissions from Asia, Canada, Europe, the United States and South America. Fifty full and short papers were submitted and subjected to a thorough double-blind review process. Each paper was assigned to an Associate Chair (AC) who recruited at least three reviewers per paper and wrote a meta-review summarizing the main points of each review. The review process included a rebuttal period, giving authors the chance to respond to reviewers' comments. During the TPC meeting on March 6, 2015, in Leuven, Belgium, each paper was discussed in depth and the final decision of which papers to accept was made, resulting in a high-quality program of twelve accepted full and short papers and an acceptance rate of 24%. Work in Progress papers were also reviewed by at least three reviewers per paper, of which 13 were accepted (50% acceptance rate) and will be presented as a poster during the conference. Full papers, short papers and Works in Progress are part of the main proceedings and will be included in the ACM Digital Library.

In addition to these submissions, there were several other categories that received submissions, resulting in 3 workshops, 3 courses, 6 Doctoral Consortium papers, 9 TVX in Industry presentations, and 13 demos, which are all made available in the adjunct proceedings.

Finally, we also encourage attendees to attend the keynote:

Empowering storytellers with social media, Jacob Shwirtz (Endemol Beyond USA)

Putting together the program of *ACM TVX2015* was a team effort. We would therefore like to thank the authors for providing the content of the program, the reviewers who worked very hard in reviewing papers and providing feedback for authors, and the AC's who managed the whole review process for each paper.

We hope that you will find this program interesting and thought-provoking and that the conference will provide you with a valuable opportunity to share ideas with other researchers and practitioners from institutions around the world.

Frank Bentley　　　　　　　　**Christian Timmerer**
ACM TVX2015 Program Chair　　*ACM TVX2015 Program Co-Chair*
Yahoo　　　　　　　　　　　*Alpen-Adria-Universität Klagenfurt*

Table of Contents

Opening Keynote Address
Session Chair: David Geerts *(KU Leuven)*

Social Experiences and Awareness
Session Chair: Santosh Basapur *(Illinois Institute of Technology)*

Experiencing Live Events
Session Chair: Wendy Van den Broeck *(iMinds-SMIT-VUB)*

Context-aware Systems
Session Chair: Rene Kaiser *(Joanneum Research)*

Multi-screening
Session Chair: Omar Niamut *(TNO)*

Design for User Experience and Engagement

Session Chair: Marian Ursu *(University of York)*

Works in Progress (poster presentations)

Session Chair: Blake Ryu Hokyoung *(Hanyang University)*

Course Overviews

Workshop Summaries

Closing Keynote Address
Session Chair: David Geerts *(KU Leuven)*

TVX 2015 Conference Organization

General Chairs: David Geerts *(iMinds / KU Leuven, Belgium)*
Lieven De Marez *(iMinds / UGent, Belgium)*
Caroline Pauwels *(iMinds / VUB, Belgium)*

Program Chairs: Frank Bentley *(Yahoo, USA)*
Christian Timmerer *(Alpen-Adria-Universität Klagenfurt, Austria)*

Work in Progress Chairs: Hokyoung Blake Ryu *(Hanyang University, Korea)*
Jeroen Vanattenhoven *(iMinds / KU Leuven, Belgium)*

Workshop Chairs: Rene Kaiser *(Joanneum Research, Austria)*
Noor Ali-Hasan *(Google, USA)*

Course Chairs: Pedro Almeida *(University of Aveiro, Portugal)*
Santosh Basapur *(Illinois Institute of Technology, USA)*

Doctoral Consortium Chairs: Marian Ursu *(University of York, UK)*
Teresa Chambel *(University of Lisbon, Portugal)*

TVX in Industry Chairs: Katia Aerts *(VRT, Belgium)*
Mike Matton *(VRT, Belgium)*

Demo Chairs: Tom Bartindale *(Newcastle University, UK)*
Rinze Leenheer *(iMinds / KU Leuven, Belgium)*

Inclusion and Accessibility Chairs: Reuben Kirkham *(Newcastle University, UK)*
Tom Evens *(iMinds / UGent, Belgium)*

Local Production Chair: Jonathan Huyghe *(iMinds / KU Leuven, Belgium)*

Steering Committee: Pablo Cesar *(CWI, The Netherlands)*
Santosh Basapur *(Illinois Institute of Technology, USA)*
Konstantinos Chorianopoulos *(Ionian University, Greece)*
David Geerts *(iMinds / KU Leuven, Belgium)*
Hendrik Knoche *(Aalborg University, Denmark)*
George Lekakos *(Athens University of Economics and Business, Greece)*
Artur Lugmayr *(Curtin University, Australia)*
Marianna Obrist *(University of Sussex, UK)*
David A. Shamma *(Yahoo Research, USA)*

Technical Program Committee
(Associate Chairs):   Petter Bae Brandtzaeg *(SINTEF, Norway)*
Cyril Concolato *(Telecom ParisTech, France)*
Mike Darnell *(Samsung Information Systems America, USA)*
Marco de Sá *(Twitter, USA)*
Sebastian Egger *(Austrian Institute of Technology, Austria)*
Benjamin Falchuk *(Applied Communication Sciences, USA)*
Michail Giannakos *(NTNU, Norway)*
David Green *(Newcastle University, UK)*
Rodrigo Laiola Guimarães *(IBM Research, Brazil)*
Diego Martinez Plasencia *(University of Bristol, UK)*
Donald McMillan *(Mobile Life Centre, Sweden)*
Britta Meixner *(University of Passau, Germany)*
Frank Nack *(University of Amsterdam, NL)*
Omar Niamut *(TNO, The Netherlands)*
Alexander Raake *(TU Berlin, Germany)*
Mark Rice *(Agency for Science, Technology and Research, Singapore)*
Teresa Romão *(Universidade Nova de Lisboa, Portugal)*
Alan Said *(Recorded Future, Sweden)*
Raimund Schatz *(Forschungszentrum Telekommunikation Wien, Austria)*
Dimitri Schuurman *(iMinds-MICT-Ghent University, Belgium)*
Wendy Van den Broeck *(iMinds-SMIT-VUB, Belgium)*

TVX 2015 Sponsor & Supporters

Sponsor:

In cooperation with:

Supporters:

Empowering Storytellers with Social Media

Jacob Shwirtz
Endemol Beyond
New York, New York, USA

Abstract

From entertainment to news to corporate marketing, social media has infused, informed and revolutionized the way creators are reaching their audience.

In this discussion we will explore the core impact of social media as a storytelling medium, how standard operating procedures and strategies have changed, delve into case studies and how we chart a path forward.

When viewed through the lens of storytelling, social media becomes a wildly exciting domain for innovative creators to push boundaries, invent new genres of content and connect with audiences in ways never before possible.

Case studies considered will span everything from traditional talent making the move to the Internet, digital-native talent, already-successful and new TV programs and web series, as well as legacy content finding new life and audiences online.

ACM Classification
H.5.1 [Information Interfaces and presentation]: Multimedia information systems – audio, video

Author Keywords: television; storytelling; social media; transmedia

Short Bio
Jacob Shwirtz has been a part of the Endemol Beyond USA since its launch in November 2013 as Chief Social Media Officer, where he has been responsible for creating and implementing forward-looking strategies that maximize the potential of social media as a global storytelling platform, using new methods and genres of content creation for distribution and monetization.

Prior to joining Endemol Beyond USA, Shwirtz served as social TV lead for Viacom and, previously, he launched dozens of initiatives that blended linear and digital for MTV and VH1. As a digital entrepreneur, Shwirtz co-created TweetBookz, offering personalized coffee table books of tweets. In 2012, Shwirtz was named as one of the top 10 social media mavens in media by Multichannel News.

TVX 2015, June 3–5, 2015, Brussels, Belgium.
ACM 978-1-4503-3526-3/15/06.
http://dx.doi.org/10.1145/2745197.2749467

Experiencing Liveness of a Cherished Place in the Home

Jinyi Wang
Mobile Life
@ Stockholm University
Borgarfjordsgatan 12
164 07, Kista, Sweden
jinyi@mobilelifecentre.org

Mudassar Ahmad Mughal
Mobile Life
@ Stockholm University
Borgarfjordsgatan 12
164 07, Kista, Sweden
mamughal@dsv.su.se

Oskar Juhlin
Mobile Life
@ Stockholm University
Borgarfjordsgatan 12
164 07, Kista, Sweden
oskarj@dsv.su.se

ABSTRACT

Liveness, as discussed in HCI and in media studies, focuses on an intriguing and beloved experiential quality that can influence new forms of video applications. We suggest a shift from accounts of liveness in "events" to liveness in ambient media for home décor by designing a system called TransLive that exploits the "magic" of mediatizing the "now" at a distant and cherished place. We present an interview study including four families, who experienced the system for two weeks each in a concept apartment setting. It shows how immediacy and unpredictability provide compelling experiences. Authenticity and engagement, which are previously considered as inherent qualities in live media, instead occur in the context of use. Finally, the experience of transcendence triggered by slow and continuous video streams open up a new design space of liveness. Thus, not only do we take inspiration from liveness theory, but we also need to redefine it.

Author Keywords

Liveness; mobile webcasting; ambient media; design; home

ACM Classification Keywords

H.5.2. [Information interfaces and presentation (e.g., HCI)]: User Interfaces.

INTRODUCTION

Liveness is important for people who experience it, as the "now" brings a "magical" quality [34]. Understanding the intriguing, but somewhat escaping, characteristic of it has been a longstanding concern in the field of media studies [11]. Different from traditional media, e.g. live programs on TV, the advances of mobile cameras and sensors make live contents more accessible for both consumption and production, which opens up new territory for personalized liveness experiences [4,27]. The field of Human Computer Interaction (HCI) shows an increasing interest in the

experiences of liveness [19], which promises to open up new design spaces where the experiencers are offered with "the real sense of access to an event in its moment by moment unfolding" [34].

For example, there are potentials to design for liveness experiences beyond the understandings of it articulated in contemporary theoretical accounts, e.g. if taking away its "event" character and situating liveness in the ambience. Notably, the concept of "liveness" inspires emergence of new applications in a different way than the concept of "real time". The former emphasizes experiential qualities, and the latter highlights time constraints, i.e. between an action and system response. Liveness is an interesting concept since appreciating the "now" is a heterogeneous experience, rather than a distinct time measure. Live is also interesting as a media broadcast format and viewing practice, which evokes conglomerated experiences such as immediacy and authenticity.

We report the findings from the initial user study of TransLive, a system we have designed and developed that situates the liveness experiences in a domestic environment and positions ambience and aesthetics in the centre (see Accompanying Video). TransLive was deployed in the context of a "concept apartment", i.e. an ordinary apartment in a residential building furnished and maintained by the research department at a European furniture manufacturer. We interviewed four adult individuals, each of whom lived in the concept apartment with their family and experienced the system for two weeks. We found liveness, understood as experiences of *immediacy* and *unpredictability*, provided compelling experiences. The study extends the understanding of liveness experiences by showing that continuous live content presented in an ambient and aesthetical way may encourage a new type of *engagement* given the context of use; and that *authenticity* is not an inherent quality in the live media, but occurs through the actions of acquiring authenticity. We also discovered *transcendence* as a quality of liveness, unarticulated in previous research, which seems to bring an important experience in the everyday life.

In the following, we motivate the attention to liveness by drawing a technological landscape where it becomes a relevant and timely concept, and look at how liveness experiences are discussed within HCI in relation to terminologies well developed in media studies. Then we describe in detail our study and findings, which leads to the discussion of a more nuanced understanding of liveness.

MOTIVATION AND BACKGROUND

Real time video, distributed over mobile networks, becomes increasingly abundant and cheap, making the combination of mobile webcasting and ambient video possible. The ubiquity of camera phones and consumer-level digital cameras have brought a great anticipation in public discourse of how new live video services and new forms of use would emerge and become everyday practice among non-professionals [1,35]. Previous research has identified a number of general characteristics that make video production challenging and hampers its use, such as required editing, difficulties in finding and capturing relevant content [22,25,38]. With real time mobile webcasting, these problems are emphasized further [22,23]. In all, the use of mobile webcasting is in its infancy and new ways of viewing live videos are emerging.

One way is to present real time videos in ambient format in domestic settings, as the combination of liveness and ambience may open up new spaces for producing and experiencing live videos. Ambient video [5] is defined as a form of art presented on high-resolution screens [4,6] showing continuous, slow and aesthetically interesting content such as the changes occurring in sceneries of nature [6], which is only viewed casually.

Liveness in Media Studies and in HCI

The focus on liveness, in the suggested format presented above, is influenced and motivated by its long-standing and continuous success in traditional TV and radio. As the media theorist Scanell argues, there is a "magical" quality in the temporal now of live broadcasts [34].

In recent years, there has also been a concern within HCI to account for liveness experiences [19]. Various accounts of liveness are emerging but somehow scattered. Technical research (e.g. [21,28,29]) is usually occupied with achieving media presentation occurring as close in time to the captured content as possible i.e. "real time". Works in art, music and performance have investigated various experiences associated with such temporal adjacency, beyond the studies of live webcasting of video (e.g. [18,20,37]). Design-oriented research projects touch upon liveness experiences without explicitly stating it (e.g.[13,15]). Given this interest, we are motivated to align and articulate liveness experiences existing in HCI research with the theoretical concepts that are well established in the area of media studies, in order to investigate its potentials in design. In the following, we account for liveness in relation to a set of experiential qualities conceptualized in media studies, namely *immediacy, unpredictability, engagement* and *authenticity*.

Immediacy: Liveness is considered as an immediate experience, as it occurs in the "now" [2]. It works as an extension of human vision, enabling instant access to distant events as they unfold. Research in HCI is interested in the topic, although conceptualising it in various ways. Video chat is seen to have the quality of liveness, as it allows immediate connection with families and friends remotely [30]. In the study of the photograph app Instagram, Weilenmann et al. discuss how immediacy, or real-time distribution, makes it different from other photo-sharing services [39]. A design project pushes the liveness experiences of photo-sharing further by instantly and continuously displaying all the published Instagram photos from a chosen area in a city [42]. Real time data is also used for creating liveness experiences, e.g. the so called "Threshold Devices" gather real time data from a home's surroundings, such as blowing wind and passing-by airplanes, and present them in an aesthetic way in the homes [13]. Immediate access to information surrounding the home, enable the inhabitants to experience liveness from the outside. In all, immediacy, or the sense of now, is essential for various liveness experiences.

Unpredictability: Live content potentially generates experiences of the unexpected as a combination of unpredictability and spontaneity [2]. There is an anticipation that something unplanned might happen in the viewing experience of liveness. Hook et al. investigates a non-mediated event, where the performers and the audience are co-located, and how the liveness experience is diminished if part of the creative work is pre-manufactured in advance of a performance [18]. For example, co-present experiences of "laptop"-generated VJ performances feel less "live" than traditional live concerts. Liveness includes some sort of improvisation, responsivity and uniqueness [7,26]. The unexpected character of liveness was also discussed in Gaver's design of the Video Window, in which he attached a camera on the outside wall of his home that was continuously streaming the video to a monitor on his bedroom wall [16]. He described extensively how unanticipated weather changes, e.g. raindrops or snowflakes landing on the camera, brought aesthetically pleasing experiences in viewing the live video [16]. The unpredictability is thus crucial for liveness experiences.

Engagement: Liveness often comprises *engagement* among viewers such as during concerts, performances and sports events. The audience have an emotional connection, i.e. an "despatialised simultaneity" with the event and its participants [36]. The presence of the audience also creates the sense of liveness, as a performer's awareness of the audience is often fundamental to the flow of the performance [33]. In an interactive dance performance, the researchers even involved the audience in the creation of the liveness experiences [12]. The interactive performance can only be fully experienced when the audience's active engagement is achieved [12]. The understanding of liveness in relation to engagement appears to emphasize its "event" character, where co-presence and co-location is key to the experiences. This view indicates that the level of engagement is high. It implies to fully engage in liveness experiences is something special that stands out from "everyday life".

Authenticity: Liveness is also associated to experiences of trust and authenticity. It seems that liveness comprises an experience of realism, i.e. as being there while something is really happening. The almost immediate transmission decreases the possibilities to manipulate the media through post-processing, or censoring content. However, the structure of the camera and production setup means that there are ways that the media content can be pre-computed into the system to give a viewpoint that is not quite as neutral as it may appear (see [27]). In HCI, the relation between liveness and authenticity has been a concern. It is argued that co-present performers and audiences at a live event provide inherent authenticity, which might be lost if it is mediated. Co-present mediatization could be interesting if it increases engagement by parallel activities [6]. Jacobs et al. discuss the balance of data authenticity and audience engagement in liveness [20]. In a study of an interactive artwork, an audience was presented with scientific climate change data through live connection between two remote forests. The artists gained the public's trust by creating various "smoke and mirrors" effects [20]. Research in HCI recognizes authenticity as an important aspect of liveness experiences mediated through technology. But the detailed ways in which such experiences occur lack in articulation. The ubiquity of mobile cameras, sensors and networks makes real time media more ubiquitous. Thus, there is a need for an increased understanding of how this map to authenticity in liveness experiences.

In sum, the "magic" of liveness has already been identified within the studies of traditional broadcast media. With the emergence of technology for personalized media production and consumption, so has the interest in liveness experiences increased within HCI. The latter interest is both recent and fragmentary, which motivates further investigation.

METHODOLOGICAL APPROACH AND SETTING

This paper focuses on understanding people's experiences with liveness through an interview study of the TransLive system. The system per se was created as a way to explore the opportunities to extend liveness as design space beyond the "event" [31]. It was generated following the Research through Design (RtD) approach [41] in order to investigate liveness experiences through design instantiations. RtD has become a widely adopted approach within HCI as it embraces the practice-based nature of design investigation [14,40], where the knowledge should be "generative and suggestive" [14]. By adopting RtD, our approach can be seen as twofold: 1) the practice-based design exercise that examines the idea of combining personalized mobile webcasting and its representation in an aesthetical and ambient way; and 2) the focus on liveness experiences that opens up the design space of bringing the "magical" quality

of liveness in the everyday. The home is then an instance of the "everyday" as opposed to the "event".

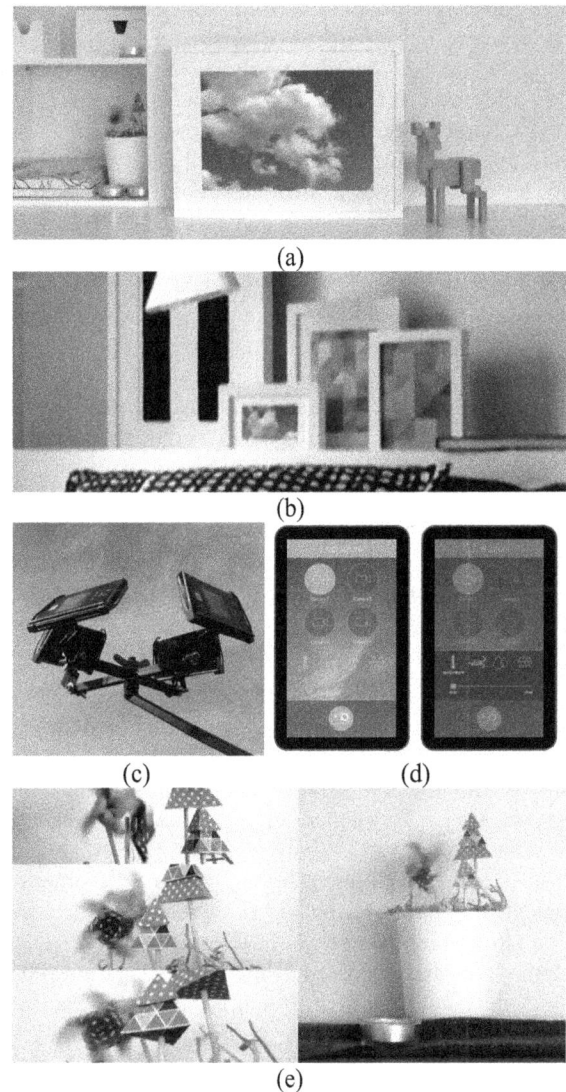

Figure 1. (a) Large Display (b) Small Display (c) Mobile Cameras (d) TransLive App (e) Windmill Ornament

TransLive

We refer to a cherished place as a geographical location to which one has a strong emotional attachment. TransLive is a system that intends to bring the sense of such a place into the home by presenting the views and the weather live in an ambient and aesthetic way that fosters reveries. The design process includes three ethnography studies of people's love for their cherished places, the design vision emerged from the fieldwork, technology context and aesthetics in home, and an iterative process from ideation, prototyping and pilot tests, to the resulting system (details of the design process have been reported in [31]). A set of artefacts, collectively seen as the interface of TransLive, are designed and built to support the live connection to the cherished places (see Accompanying Video). The interface consists of four *small displays* and a 20-inch *large display* attached in wooden painting frames, as well as a handcraft *windmill ornament*. The four small displays (Figure 1-b) show the real time videos streams captured by four water-resistant mobile phone cameras installed at the cherished place. The mobile phones are attached to a flexible stand that we designed and built in order to make the cameras angles adjustable (Figure 1-c). The large display (Figure 1-a), connected to a server, shows a selected live stream video and allows the weather from the cherished place to influence its visual style. For example, the changing wind speed makes the video appear blurry, which mimics a camera lens trying to find its focus in the blowing wind. The weather data, e.g. temperature, wind speed and direction, are captured by a weather station co-located with the mobile cameras. Both the video and the weather data were sent to the home via 4G networks to ensure high quality and smooth transmission. We also developed an Android app (Figure 1-d) for selecting the video and weather visualization. The *windmill ornament* spins in relation to the wind from the cherished place (Figure 1-e). A hidden fan, blowing to the windmill, is installed in the bottom of the windmill, connected to an Arduino Yun component and driven by the wind speed data from the weather station.

Interview Study

The system prototype was deployed in the context of a "concept apartment", which is maintained by an international furniture company in order to evaluate novel concepts with potential users in a domestic environment for long-term use. It is situated at an ordinary apartment in a residential building in the city of Malmö in Sweden. The 100-square-meter apartment has three rooms. Its interior is designed and furnished by the designers in the company with a strong brand identity. An interior designer from the company was also involved in the implementation process and acted as a stakeholder of both the company and future dwellers. The concept apartment context provided us, with our limited resources, an opportunity to evaluate the system with multiple families for a longer time. Ideally the participants should have installed the cameras and weather station at their cherished place by themselves. However, the current system implementation was still difficult to install and configure. Therefore, we asked where the participants' cherished places were and installed the input for them. The provision of a concept apartment allowed us to install the ambient displays and set up the configurations for one time although testing it with multiple families, which saved our time and resources. Even though the set-up provides initial user feedback, a concept apartment is not the participants' real home. To accommodate for this difference, the interior was designed to be casual and comfortable. Furthermore, TransLive was only one of three unrelated prototypes evaluated in the lab at the same time. This situation had put high requirement on the design and deployment [31]. It also limited the time and attention we could acquire from the participants.

We have predominantly considered adult individuals living with their family as main participants, instead of considering all family members as participants. Still, we recognize cherished personal belongings may relate to the families and have an impact on family lives [10]. The same applies to a personal cherished place when presented as a digital artefact in the home. Four participants were recruited by the property management company via posters in the neighbourhood, where the concept apartment was located. They were respectively invited to stay in the concept apartment with their family for two weeks during April to June 2014. Selecting four out of totally five adults provides a sufficient sample in the early phase.

Before arriving at the concept apartment, the participants were interviewed about their cherished places, where it was located and their feelings thereof. We then installed the mobile cameras and the weather station as close as possible to this place. The videos and weather data were then presented through the TransLive interface. The families were informed of the study and had full control over the usage of the system. As the idea was to design for ambient experiences that allow varied attentions, we chose not to request the participants to pay special attention to the displays or to keep a record of their experiences with the system on a regular basis. Instead, the focus was on how they experienced TransLive and what it might bring to their everyday lives. In the following, we briefly describe the respondents and their families with fictional names for anonymity concern.

Ron's Family: Ron moved to Malmö from Wales more than 12 years ago. He is a 43 year-old single father and lives with his 5-year old son. He has two teenage sons who stay with him every other week. Ron chose Beijers Park in Malmö as his cherished place, as he had "been there so many times in the past 12 years of living here". Thus, we contacted a company nearby and installed the cameras and weather station on their balcony facing Beijers Park direction. The installation was completed before Ron and his younger son moved in to the concept apartment.

Mia's Family: Mia is 33 years old and a single mother, living with her 5-year old son in Malmö city. She is from Sweden, but she has close relatives abroad. Mia also selected "Beijers Park" as her cherished place. Thus we kept the cameras and weather station in the same location.

Jane's Family: Jane is a 35 years old single mother living with her 9 years old son. She has two teenage children, who stay with her every second week. She is from Sweden and has many friends in the city. She loves the ocean and her cherished place is a harbour called "Västra hamnen", located west of Malmö. Before Jane and her son moved in the concept apartment, we reinstalled the cameras and weather station on the roof of an 8-floor building beside her selected location. During her stay in the concept apartment, Jane had her teenage children staying with her, occasionally had some friend visiting and organised a party in the apartment.

Ben's Family: Ben is 58 years old and living with his wife. They moved to Sweden and Malmö decades ago. Their children and grandchildren visit them every day. Ben also said that his cherished place was Västra Hamnen, where he often took the ferries and went for walks with his wife. We kept the cameras and weather station at the same location.

Data Collection and Analysis
On the last day of each family's two-week stay in the concept apartment, one interviewer visited the family to conduct a one-hour semi-structured interview with the main respondent. We adopted a semi-structured interview approach, as it is a commonly adopted approach in studying technology in the homes [17]. It is beneficial for making both experiences and interactions available at an early stage while preserving users' privacy. The interview questions focused on two themes: 1) the use of the system, e.g. when they looked at the displays and for how long, and if they discussed it with others at home; 2) the experiences, e.g. feelings and thoughts while seeing the cherished place from the displays, and if they remembered particular moments.

The interviews were audio-recorded with the participants' consent. The same routine was repeated for the four families. The first interview with Ron was done in English. The other three interviews were done in Swedish. We transcribed the interviews and translated the Swedish interviews to English. After transcribing and translating the interviews, a set of aggregated categories that brought out salient characteristics in the materials was developed. The aggregation was conducted following a qualitative approach [9,32], whereby themes were developed by attending to individual answers and comments, as well as to theoretical concepts of liveness.

FINDINGS
The analysis is focused on viewers' experiences related to previous liveness theory, as well as on particular experiences of TransLive as a form of ambient media.

The Instant Access to the Cherished Place
The TransLive system provided the participants with access to a remote and cherished place. It offers, similar to live television [2], an extension of human vision and provides viewers with instant access to the distant events as they unfold. All respondents appreciated seeing things unfolding as they occur. Different from engaging live TV from e.g. a sports event, the sense that something ordinary is happening and constantly changing seems to bring a calmly pleasant feeling. Both Mia and Jane described such experience as "*pleasant*" and "*nice*". Ben stated that it was "*a pleasure*", and he felt in "*a relaxed mood*" when looking at the displays, since the view of the sky and clouds were changing. For example, Ron enjoyed watching the shift of time between day and night. He liked "*(to) see changes in the daytime and night time, and even three o'clock in the*

morning when it's quiet, it would bring the air". The participants also enjoyed looking at people, cars, boats and planes as they moved. Mia mentioned that her son enjoyed watching passing airplanes. Ben liked to watch "*cars and drivers, when they drive*". He enjoyed looking at people, which made him feel "*myself being there*". Jane enjoyed "*a feeling that something is happening.*" And she commented, "*It's for real, it's live and it really exciting, because you know for yourself that it is something going on live that you are filming now*".

The instant access to the unfolding events also enabled the participants to encounter moments of surprise, which were essentially just small happenings that brought a sense of the dynamics of the world. Most of the participants referred to such occasions. For example, Ben recalled that "*I was looking* [at the display, authors' comment] *yesterday and then there was a boat passing by. You could see it on the screen there!*" And Mia commented on how her five-year-old son liked to watch when airplanes and birds went by. Jane enjoyed looking at the boats by the harbour and had a growing attachment to it, "*I was like, what has it* [the boat, our comment] *been doing there for so many days?*" One morning, she found it was gone and shouted out loud, "*wow, check this out kids, come and see, the boat is gone! It moves!*" She also recalled, "*One day, it was such a beautiful day, no clouds, really beautiful, and you could see the sun there in the camera, it was really nice*".

The excitement of looking at something unexpected was also observed during the interviews per se. As the system was running during the interviews in the concept apartment, several participants were distracted by unexpected events on the displays. They interrupted the interviews and asked the interviewer to look at the displays. For example, Ben turned to the display and shouted out loud "*A bird!*" while answering a question. Ron suddenly pointed to the cloud on the display, "*It's nice, looking at that now! You can count how long it takes to move, that's quite interesting, isn't it! ... You can look at the screen now for a while to see, you now like, how long it will take for this little cloud to move, you know here, to move off the screen.*" Later during the interview, Ron saw a bird, and the excitement was triggered again, "*Oh, there's a bird there!... That's great! I like that. I could sit here and count them. It only seems to be one at a time that goes by. Usually, there's a flock of them in there!*" The participants seemed to enjoy viewing something unexpected on the display. Such enjoyment was provided by the experience of "now" and "unexpected", and the live content on the display had a quality of uniqueness compared to recorded videos. This finding is in line with media theory that liveness has a magic quality enabled by immediacy and the "unexpected".

In sum, the experience of the immediacy, i.e. looking at something perceived as happening "now", as well as the thrill of the unexpected seemed to transport itself from event-based live broadcasts to that of an ambient media.

Sporadic Engagement

In previous articulations of liveness, it has been noted that the viewers are getting very engaged. Their focus and attention shift from the everyday to the broadcasted event. TransLive on the other hand envisions interaction with live broadcast that blends in everyday life, individually or with families and friends. The live connection to a cherished place is intended to become a subtle, ambient and pleasant element in the everyday life at home, and both individual and social viewing practices point towards that direction:

Individual viewing practices: All individual participants seemed to have paid varied attentions to the displays at different times of the day. Ron commented that the big display in the hallway caught his eyes every time he came in and went out of the apartment, especially when the light switches were off. Similarly, Mia enjoyed the display particularly in the evenings and nights when the lights were down, and she described this experience as "cosy". Both Jane and Ben commented that they liked looking at the clouds from the displays when they just got up in the morning. The duration of watching the screens varied too. Mia and Jane glanced at the display for just a few seconds when they passed by, while Ben enjoyed looking at the display for a few minutes and Ron preferred being able to look at the display constantly when he could sit down and relax. Ben's son came to visit while the interview was taking place; he described nicely the varied attentions the display afforded, *"when you are going to the toilet or the kitchen, you pay attention to it (the big display hanging on the wall in the hallway), but it doesn't draw your gaze, as soon as you start looking at it, you start thinking, oh, I want to be by the ocean now!"*

Looking together: All participants reported looking at the displays and talking about the views with their family members or friends, e.g., Jane said *"I showed all my friends when they were here, and they got really 'wow'! They were like, is it live, where is it, how does it works... They thought it was awesome to have such a thing at home."*

In sum, the TransLive system enabled a less engaged orientation to the media, as compared to live TV broadcasts of events, which could be described as "sporadic" [13]. The participants often paid varied attentions to the displays rather than being fully immersed during the viewing. They instead conducted repetitive and glance-based viewing. This type of interaction seems to encourage participants to embrace the liveness experiences in the everyday life over a long term. The system became part of their daily life in the sense that the families and friends of the participants were often involved in the interactions and the live content became a topic of conversation. In all, TransLive pointed to a new direction for designing liveness experiences, which allows for varied attentions, encourages sporadic interactions and enhanced the "low" but long-term engagement, which, in turn, enriches a new type of liveness experience.

Authenticity

In previous theory, liveness has been said to comprise trust and authenticity. However, the experience of TransLive engendered rather mixed experiences of this sort. Some did perceive the video streams as real rather than edited and the weather data as genuine even though they were interpreted and represented in an uninformative manner. Ben reported that he checked the weather through the displays before going out, *"the weather outside, if I want to know I look at the screen".* Similarly, Jane perceived the spinning windmill as an indication of the wind speed outside. She said that she had the windmill on *"to get a feeling, to see the weather and the wind and so, if you should put on your jacket and so, or maybe I will not take my bike, because it's so windy".* She added *"I showed all my friends (the system) when they were here, and they got really wow, so before you walk out you can have a look at the weather".*

Other participants displayed a degree of distrust of the authenticity of the media. Mia, Ron and Jane all commented that the media might be produced on other places than their individual cherished places. Ben presumed the cameras could have been installed in the cherished places picked by previous families who also participated in the study, *"I have been here since the fourteenth of this month, and maybe it* [the installation of the cameras, authors' comment] *was from the other people living here?"* Sharing the same concern, Ron repeatedly asked the interviewer if the camera was actually in his chosen park, in spite of the interviewer had confirmed so.

In all, authenticity is viewed as a given feature of liveness experiences in media studies. However, the study revealed some degree of complexity and paradox in relation to authenticity, i.e. the participants trusted streaming videos and weather data as authentic, but also expressed uncertainties towards the camera locations. The view of live as inherently authentic is here challenged by the emerging format of live content.

Authentication Work

Since the viewers did not experience the media as authentic from start, it was obvious to observe the ways in which they approached the media to investigate its trustfulness. The participants displayed a set of strategies, which we term "authentication work", to examine the authenticity of the media.

Matching the digital with physical: The participants tried to match the digital content shown in the live video with the physical world as a means to investigate its authenticity. Such matching included identifying physical landmarks in the videos, and observing the synchronization of the video content and the physical world. Ron and Ben suggested providing recognizable visual references to identify the camera locations. Ben suggested pointing a camera to the landmark, "bo01 tower", at his cherished place. Ron suggested displaying some scenic features, e.g. *"the grass and the river, the little pond there"* in his cherished place to increase his trust. Jane commented the display showing the harbour felt *"more real"*. She also compared the sky from her balcony with what was shown on the big display, and the similarity between them had reassured her that the location of the camera was close to her chosen location: *"I sat on the balcony with a friend, and then it was this strange weather, suddenly it was sunny then it became cloudy a few times. I went here (to the big display in the hallway) and had a look at that screen, aha, it's going to be like that, there's a lot of clouds!"*

Witness and authority: The need for reassurance was expressed by Jane's friends too when they had a party in the apartment. Jane shot a video with her mobile phone when she was telling her friends about the system. Her friends (about 15 people) asked again and again, *"Is it real?" "Is it now?" "Is it live?"* and *"is it in Malmö?"* She confirmed all the questions with confidence and showed the other camera views by switching them via the mobile phone app. Her reassurance was met with a shared "wow"-expression from the audience. Authenticity, in this case, is then achieved through some kind of "witness" or "authority", which is also discussed by Jacob et al.[20]. Jane's friends' inquiry about the state of media and Jane's response and then her friend's satisfaction, as discussed above, is tantamount to seeking testimony from a trustworthy eye witness and/or an authority.

Involvement in production: Some participants commented their involvement in the media production, i.e. to install the mobile cameras themselves, could be a way to increase the turst. We designed and built a flexible camera stand with that exact purpose in mind and intended to involve the participants in the installation. Due to technical and logistic constrains, we could not involve them in installing the cameras and weather station. However, the participants' comment confirms our idea of supporting personalized media production. And it also points out that authenticity can be achieved by involvement in media production.

In sum, the participants tried to get to the "truth" by requiring landmarks for identification; by checking the synchronization of the weather from the displays and from the outside; and by inquiring trusted "authorities" or reveal that authenticity should not be taken as given. Instead, authentication works should be considered and possibly designed for.

Transcendence in Time and Space
The views from the displays seemed to have the power to take the viewers' minds from the immediate domestic environment to the remote cherished places, or simply from *here and now* to *there and beyond*. As Jane put it: *"you are inside, but...you are taking part of the outside."* But the experience is more than being able to look outside. Looking at the displays seemed to trigger the viewers' memories, imaginations and dreams, e.g. good memories from the past, or something they used to do or could do, or the longing for the next trip. Ron described his experience as *"(being) drifted away and thinking about home"*. Similarly, Mia imagined installing the cameras and weather station close to her beloved relatives in another country, so that she could see

their place and the weather. With enthusiasm, Jane commented, *"(I) start thinking of flying! I want to fly where you see clouds."* Ben said he started imaging when seeing the images and the imagination felt like coming from inside. He further described the experiences, which demonstrated how his mind drifted away from the display, *"I feel like I go inside the boat and inside the sea, because I like it, the clouds and the sea. Every two or three weeks I go to Helsingør. I see the clouds in the sea, and the boats, I like this. I take my wife. I want to go to Helsingør by boat, sometimes in my car. Sometimes I leave it in the parking lot, and we shop and eat."* Ben's son also recalled that *"once I saw it (the display) briefly, then I thought about airplanes. When it's cloudy and blue, you think about an airplane up there in the sky."*

The accounts for liveness experiences in media studies tend to focus on highly engaging experiences of an event. At the same time, such experiences can be somewhat passive drawing on consumption of the live events. In our study, the participants seemed to have experienced their minds actively drifting beyond the content of the displays to different locations in time and space. This experience echoes a type of transcendence, which happens in environments that are familiar and considered with more affection or feelings of belonging [37], in other words, the cherished places. The drifting minds also indicated a sense of ease and effortless attention with less intense focus or engagement, similar to the transcendent experience when people are in nature. Liveness in previous research is understood as a means to induce the experience of an event as it is, whereas we extend this understanding by showing that TransLive triggers viewers' imagination and enables them to transcend their mind's eye through time and space.

DISCUSSION
We took a qualitative approach and presented detailed descriptions of a small number of families' experiences of the TransLive system for two weeks. Such limited approach still enabled us to obtain some insights into the participants' experiences over time and focus on articulating a nuanced understanding of the use of mobile webcasting in particular, and of liveness experiences in general. The understandings of liveness through our study showed both similarities and differences compared to previous research in media theory. Therefore, our approach does not only take inspiration from the theory, but also revisits and develops it. In the following, we reflect on immediacy, the liveness concept and broadly discuss a more nuanced understanding of liveness experiences.

Restating the "Magic" in an Ambient Setting
Overall, our study of TransLive supported our idea of combining personalized mobile webcasting with its representation in an aesthetical and ambient way. The results indicated that the viewers' acquired liveness experiences of a cherished place in a domestic environment. The participants appreciated the connection with their cherished place and valued its immediacy and unpredictability. The sense of

mediated sceneries happening "now" was positively regarded. Similarly, the system provided unexpected and unanticipated experiences of e.g. a boat leaving the harbour or a bird flying by. In a broad sense, our orientation to liveness, including immediacy and reality, seems both valuable and fundamental for the experiences. Existing approaches to experience liveness through user-generated webcasting could be extended beyond mediatizing events, to account for content of ambient nature. It may inspire further design-oriented research with similar topics in HCI.

Real Time vs. Liveness
Since the concept of immediacy is fundamental to liveness, we need to consider why it is not enough to investigate the potential of getting inspiration and understanding the implications of "real time" applications. Some of the attention to liveness concept in HCI has also focussed narrowly on the benefits of immediacy [38], which is very close to conflating the concept with the notion of "real time". The concept of real time pinpoints measurable temporal differences between an action and system responses, whereas the experiences related to liveness are less easy to articulate. It seems to require a broader set of characteristics i.e. a *conglomerate*, as the same as it seems diffuse and *heterogeneous*. Appreciating the "now" is a *heterogeneous* experience, rather than a distinct time measure. The experience of "now" is plastic and might refer to a second, today or a year, or to mobility. The users of TransLive seem to experience immediacy when they identified movements of a boat or a bird, although with very different understandings of what "now" referred to. Live is also a media broadcast format and viewing practice, which evokes *conglomerate* experiences such as both immediacy and authenticity.

In media theory, liveness has been specifically associated with authenticity and something being "real". In HCI, it has been noted that the liveness experience decreases if the media, such as in a VJ-performance, is understood as pre-manufactured [18], disregarding how "real time" the digital animation might be. Liveness is still interesting, despite its somewhat evading meaning, since it is the experience that we intent to design for.

Redefining the Liveness Theory
Although the liveness concept is inspiring, we should not just accept it as is. We need to ensure that when we apply it to new domains, we also rethink the aggregated concept of liveness. In specific, our study reveals a need to revisit how existing categorisations such as that of the experiences of *engagement* and *authenticity* as part of the liveness conglomeration.

Sporadic Engagement: In media theory it is stated that live content is particularly engaging, which implies some sort of focused interaction between the viewer and the mediatized content. In our case, liveness content is accommodated in a domestic environment. It requires its physical form to be unobtrusive, in the sense that it doesn't grab attention and it blends in the surroundings aesthetically. The media representing the content should afford both glance-based and highly focused engagement. In our study, the participants enjoyed the location of displays in the hallway, which allowed them to experience the media upon passing by in-between rooms, and entering or exiting the apartment. But when the interaction was extended, the displays needed to be placed where the inhabitants hold their view for a prolonged duration, such as at the TV screen. Then the concept of locating the screens at the same place as other picture frames became problematic. Although the participants were engaged, it was in a very different sense that being highly aroused for a short period. We therefore understand engagement as blended into everyday life in the homes, in a way that allows varied attention. We also found the viewers having a tendency of sporadic and prolonged engagement over days and weeks with the system. Thus we refer to such engagement as "sporadic engagement", and we argue for a broader conceptualisation of engagement of liveness that includes sporadic engagement. The design of liveness experiences in everyday settings can encourage such engagement that is both sporadic and prolonged.

Authenticity work: The concept of *authenticity*, as discussed in media theory, also needs a revisit. Previous related works tend to see authenticity as a given feature in real time broadcasts. In our study, several participants raised a concern whether the media was live. At the same time, we identified practices through which the experience of authenticity increased e.g. matching, witnessing and producing. The uncertainties expressed by the participants, and the visible authentication work, pinpointed the fact that authenticity should not be taken as a given characteristic of real time media or live broadcasts, when designing for such experiences, especially in the era of "democratized" media production. The design of liveness experiences also needs to account for the authentication work. With the increase of user generated live content, we need to recognize that the questions of trustworthiness are much less settled compared to traditional TV and radio broadcasts. We also see an opportunity to design for authenticity work in order to embrace and expand liveness experiences.

In media studies, both engagement and authenticity have been conceptualised and understood as emerging out of the broadcast content, which is independent of the viewing context. In our study, we identify a form of sporadic engagement and authenticity work by focussing both on the content and the context of use. Both these extensions are of relevance to provide a nuanced understanding of liveness experience. A broader conceptualisation may also lead to an extended variation of liveness in design.

Extending the Scope of Liveness Experiences
We identified a type of experience, namely transcendence, which has not been accounted for in theoretical conceptualisations of liveness. The participants not only enjoyed being able to see views of a cherished place, but also surpassed those views in their mind's eye. When looking at

the clouds and the sky above their requested cherished place, they started thinking about good memories, other places far away, or plans for the future. In other words, they transcended the mediated connection to a remote place. The experiences of transcendence triggered by the surrounding objects are previously identified in other areas. Bachelard describes such experience as, "(the mind) flees the object nearby and right away it is far off, elsewhere, in the space of *elsewhere*" [3]. Katz [24] discusses another form of transcendence, which also seems relevant in the generation of liveness experiences. He describes how anger in road traffic is created partly when a driver transcends the available social situation and infers other problematic contexts (e.g. unemployment) that are not available to other drivers. In our study, liveness "transported" the participants' minds away from the mediated cherished place to elsewhere in time and space. Drawing on Katz, this activity contributes to emotion, and the system then contributes to making transcendence possible. Importantly, it does not happen in the system or in the mediated content, but as an associated activity by the viewer. In all, we argue recognizing transcendence emerged from liveness could inspire a new design space.

Design Implications
Although our focus is to develop a nuanced understanding of liveness on a theoretical level, some design implications emerged from the study. Firstly, more attention is needed on the design for authenticity works, e.g. to provide the users with logs or GPS data of the cameras. Secondly, sporadic engagement can be further encouraged to enrich the daily lives at home, e.g. different designs of ambient media and live content in forms of slow art. Furthermore, customization can be further developed, e.g. to enable close-ups or wider viewing angles.

Reflection on Methodology
Although open-ended design study, often referred to as field trial, is a commonly used method in HCI, it is also an approach that makes it hard to distinguish whether the results are derived out of experiencing the system, the positive experience of trying out something new, or the orientation to pleasing the evaluators by providing positive judgments [8]. Two weeks of experiencing the system may decrease some of the novelty factors, but the result must still be handled with caution. Furthermore, this initial user study is intended to generate more specific research questions. As discussed by Gaver, the aim of a study, in an early stage where the ambiguity and uncertainty is high and valuable, is to collect results that are suggestive and generative [14]. In this case, the design concept seems intriguing and suggests new design space for liveness experiences. However, it doesn't address specific questions such as if user experiences of live streaming change in between transmissions with high frame rate, e.g. video, and low frame rate, e.g. static image.

CONCLUSION
Our research aim has the ambition to both describe the liveness experience and inspire design. We share the interest in liveness with media studies that has identified the attractiveness of "live" in the context of traditional TV and radio broadcasts, which in turn led us to the elaborated conceptualisation described in this paper. We also share the interest with emerging research in HCI that identifies liveness experiences, e.g. as part of interactive art and performance. But since the use of the term "liveness" seems scattered in this area, we suggest a comprehensive approach that articulates media conceptions in a broad sense.

This paper presents an initial user study of TransLive, a system connecting people with their cherished places. The findings support our idea of combining personalized mobile webcasting and its materialization in an aesthetical and ambient way in the home. Our study underscores experience of immediacy and appearance of the unexpected as compelling. It extends the understanding of liveness by arguing for its experience in conjunction with sporadic engagement and authenticity work. We also identified how the experience of transcendence blends into liveness, which points to a potential new direction in design.

In all, we suggest that research in HCI, which e.g. addresses the emergence of real time video applications, benefits from elaboration of liveness in media theory for two reasons. First, liveness captures important aspects of a "magical" experiential quality. Second, it supports forming a domain and research community including traditional media and new variations of them, which draw on mobile technology and user-generated content. An alternative would be to scale down the scope of conceptualisations. This however would lead us to define the "magic" as being "real time". Such articulation could account for important aspects of the favoured experiences but risk being too abstract to inspire new design. At the same time, we also need to acknowledge the need to revisit and extend the concept of liveness.

REFERENCES
1. Al-Ani, B., Mark, G., Chung, J., and Jones, J. The Egyptian Blogosphere: A Counter-narrative of the Revolution. *In Proc. CSCW'12*, ACM (2012), 17–26.
2. Auslander, P. *Liveness: Performance in a mediatized culture.* Routledge, 2008.
3. Bachelard, G. *The Poetics of Space.* Beacon Press,1994.
4. Bizzocchi, J. The magic window: the emergent aesthetics of high-resolution large-scale video display. . *In Proc. ICPS'03,* (2003), 1–4.
5. Bizzocchi, J. Ambient Video. *In Proc.ACE'06*, (2006)
6. Bizzocchi, J. Winterscape and ambient video: an intermedia border zone. *In Proc.MM'08*, ACM (2008), 949–952.
7. Bowers, J., Taylor, R., Hook, J. et al. HCI: Human-computer Improvisation. *In Proc.DIS'14*, ACM (2014), 203–206.
8. Brown, B., Reeves, S., and Sherwood, S. Into the Wild: Challenges and Opportunities for Field Trial Methods. *In Proc.CHI'11*, ACM (2011), 1657–1666.

9. Creswell, J.W. *Qualitative inquiry and research design: Choosing among five approaches.* Sage publications, 2012.

10. Csikszentmihalyi, M. and Halton, E. *The Meaning of Things: Domestic Symbols and the Self.* Cambridge University Press, 1981.

11. Engström, A. and Perry, M. "Liveness" in live TV: production, experience and future design. *In Proc. CHI'11 EA,* ACM Press (2011).

12. Friederichs-Büttner, G., Walther-Franks, B., and Malaka, R. An Unfinished Drama: Designing Participation for the Theatrical Dance Performance Parcival XX-XI. *In Proc.DIS'12,* ACM (2012), 770–778.

13. Gaver, W., Boucher, A., Law, A., et al. Threshold Devices: Looking out from the Home. *In Proc.CHI'08,* ACM (2008), 1429–1438.

14. Gaver, W.What should we expect from research through design? *In Proc. CHI '12,* (2012), 937 - 946.

15. Gaver, W., Bowers, J., Boehner, K., et al. Indoor weather stations: investigating a ludic approach to environmental HCI through batch prototyping. *In Proc.CHI '13,* ACM (2013), 3451–3460.

16. Gaver, W. The video window: my life with a ludic system. *Personal and Ubiquitous Computing 10,* 2-3 (2005), 60–65.

17. Harper, R. *The Connected Home: The Future of Domestic Life: The Future of Domestic Life.* Springer, 2012.

18. Hook, J., McCarthy, J., Wright, P., and Olivier, P. Waves: Exploring Idiographic Design for Live Performance. *In Proc.CHI'13,* ACM (2013),2969-2978.

19. Hook, J., Schofield, G., Taylor, R., et al. Exploring HCI's Relationship with Liveness. *In Proc. CHI'12 EA,* ACM (2012), 2771–2774.

20. Jacobs, R., Benford, S., Selby, M., et al. A Conversation Between Trees: What Data Feels Like in the Forest. *In Proc.CHI'13,* ACM (2013), 129–138.

21. Joshi, N., Kar, A., and Cohen, M. Looking at You: Fused Gyro and Face Tracking for Viewing Large Imagery on Mobile Devices. *In Proc.CHI'12,* ACM (2012), 2211-2220.

22. Juhlin, O., Engström, A., and Reponen, E. Mobile Broadcasting: The Whats and Hows of Live Video As a Social Medium. *In Proc.MobileHCI'10,* ACM (2010), 35–44.

23. Juhlin, O., Zoric, G., Engström, A., et al. Video interaction: a research agenda. *Personal and Ubiquitous Computing 18,* 3 (2014), 685–692.

24. Katz, J. *How emotions work.* University of Chicago Press, 1999.

25. Kirk, D., Sellen, A., Harper, R., et al. Understanding Videowork. *In Proc.CHI'07,* (2007), 61–70.

26. Leong, T.W. and Wright, P.C. Revisiting Social Practices Surrounding Music. *In Proc.CHI'13,* ACM (2013), 951–960.

27. MacNeill, M. Networks: producing Olympic ice hockey for a national television audience. *Sociology of Sport Journal 13,* 2 (1996), 103–124.

28. Maleki, M.M., Woodbury, R.F., and Neustaedter, C. Liveness, Localization and Lookahead: Interaction Elements for Parametric Design. *In Proc.DIS'14,* ACM (2014), 805–814.

29. Maloney, J.H. and Smith, R.B. Directness and Liveness in the Morphic User Interface Construction Environment. *In Proc.UIST'95,* ACM (1995), 21–28.

30. Massimi, M. and Neustaedter, C. Moving from Talking Heads to Newlyweds: Exploring Video Chat Use During Major Life Events. *In Proc.DIS'14,* ACM (2014), 43–52.

31. Mughal, M.A., Wang, J., and Juhlin, O. Juxtaposing Mobile Webcasting and Ambient Video for Home Décor. *In Proc.MUM'14,* ACM (2014), 151-159.

32. Patton, M.Q. *Qualitative evaluation and research methods .* SAGE Publications, inc, 1990.

33. Reeves, S., Benford, S., O'Malley, C., and Fraser, M. Designing the Spectator Experience. *In Proc.CHI'05,* ACM (2005), 741–750.

34. Scannell, P. Radio, Television, and Modern Life: a phenomenological approach. (1996).

35. Shirky, C. *Here comes everybody: The power of organizing without organizations.* Penguin, 2008.

36. Thompson, J.B. *Media and modernity: A social theory of the media.* John Wiley & Sons, 1995.

37. Unander-Scharin, C., Unander-Scharin, A., and Höök, K. The Vocal Chorder: Empowering Opera Singers with a Large Interactive Instrument. *In Proc.CHI'14,* ACM (2014), 1001–1010.

38. Vihavainen, S., Mate, S., Liikkanen, L., and Curcio, I. Video As Memorabilia: User Needs for Collaborative Automatic Mobile Video Production. *In Proc.CHI'12,* ACM (2012), 651–654.

39. Weilenmann, A., Hillman, T., and Jungselius, B. Instagram at the Museum: Communicating the Museum Experience Through Social Photo Sharing. *In Proc.CHI'13,* ACM (2013), 1843–1852.

40. Ylirisku, S., Lindley, S., Jacucci, G., et al. Designing web-connected physical artefacts for the 'aesthetic' of the home. *In Proc. CHI '13,* ACM (2013), 909.

41. Zimmerman, J., Forlizzi, J., and Evenson, S. Research through design as a method for interaction design research in HCI. *In Proc. CHI'07,* ACM (2007), 493- 502

42. Instant Peeping. http://instantpeeping.dareville.com/

Audience Silhouettes: Peripheral Awareness of Synchronous Audience Kinesics for Social Television

Radu-Daniel Vatavu

University Stefan cel Mare of Suceava

Suceava 720229, Romania

vatavu@eed.usv.ro

ABSTRACT

We introduce *audience silhouettes* for TV, which are visual representations of viewers' body movements displayed in real-time on top of television content. With their minimal visual cues and their ability to convey presence and to leverage interactions via non-verbal *kinesics*, audience silhouettes are strong candidates for implementing Oehlberg et al.'s theater metaphor of an unobtrusive social TV system [37]. In a user study, we found our participants connecting well to the on-screen silhouettes, while their television watching experience was perceived more enjoyable. We also report viewers' body movement behavior in the presence of on-screen silhouettes, which we characterize numerically with new measures (*e.g.*, average body movement) and we report experimental findings; *e.g.*, we found that the number of silhouettes influences viewers' body movements and the body postures they adopt and that women produce more body movement than men.

Author Keywords

Television; Kinect; audience silhouettes; social TV; motion capture; whole body gestures; peripheral awareness; user study; user experience; SUS; augmented TV; kinesics.

ACM Classification Keywords

H.5.1 Multimedia Information Systems: Artificial, augmented, and virtual realities; H.5.2. User Interfaces: Input devices and strategies (*e.g.*, mouse, touchscreen).

INTRODUCTION

Social television watching at distance is supported today by a variety of smart devices and social networks. Many studies have revealed viewers' desire to feel connected, either to family and friends or to a larger community interested in the same TV shows [4,17,39]. However, despite numerous research on leveraging audience interactions with text and audio chat during synchronous television watching [19,25,28], little work has addressed non-verbal body communication, *i.e.*, kinesics, for iTV. Body movement can provide rich informational cues about one's intents or emotions [7,32,34], but today's social

Figure 1. Audience silhouettes are body profiles of remote viewers displayed on top of TV content. Silhouettes do not disclose a person's fine traits, such as face or clothes (as video does), but instead they communicate presence and expressive body movement with minimal visual cues; *e.g.*, color gradients assist the perception of depth and body movement.

iTV systems offer no availability for transmitting these cues, other than through fully-disclosing video or artificial avatars with little expressive resources [14,36]. Moreover, this challenge has existed in the research agenda of social television for quite a while, *i.e.*, delivering *"presence awareness that aids communication flow"* [11] (p. 8), and Oehlberg et al. [37] imagined the *theater metaphor* to depict an unobtrusive social TV system, yet to be implemented at its full potential. In this work, we make one step further toward Oehlberg et al.'s vision by introducing *audience silhouettes*, which are body profiles of remote viewers watching the same show; see Figure 1. Audience silhouettes do not disclose a person's fine traits, such as face or clothes (as video does), but instead they communicate presence and expressive body movements in real-time.

Our contributions are as follows: (1) we introduce the concept of *audience silhouettes* to support real-time non-verbal communication during social television watching; (2) we evaluate viewers' perceptions of audience silhouettes, and we report findings on the *peripheral awareness* of kinesics; *e.g.*, our participants felt connected to silhouettes, which made the TV watching experience more enjoyable; (3) we introduce new measures to characterize viewers' body movements in relation to audience silhouettes; *e.g.*, we found that the number of silhouettes affects body movement and adopted body postures; and (4) we introduce Motion-Amount Images to visualize and interpret body movements. As we have barely scratched the potential of real-time kinesics for social iTV in this work, we hope that this first exploration of audience silhouettes will inspire the community to explore kinesics further for designing enriched experiences for social interactive television.

RELATED WORK

In this section we discuss related work on designing systems to enrich user experience during television watching, we review prior work on designing for social television, and we connect to existing research in kinesics and body gestures.

Social television watching at distance

The social aspect of watching television by viewers that are geographically located at distance has been supported with communications technology. Over time, television-mediated interpersonal communication has employed many modalities, such as text, audio, and voice chats, emoticons and avatars, as well as combinations of these [14,19,26,36,40]. For example, Amigo-TV [14] is a system that combines broadcast television with communication between viewers implemented by transmission of speech, text, and emoticons to leverage a rich social experience during television watching; in Amigo-TV, viewers are represented by avatars. Nathan *et al.* [36] developed CollaboraTV, a system that supports both synchronous and asynchronous viewers under a unified interface; viewers are represented as iconic avatars forming a virtual audience at the bottom of the TV screen that can share text messages with localized speech bubbles and perform small animations (*e.g.*, avatars may raise their arms and produce the thumbs-up or thumbs-down gestures, or may turn around toward the viewer and show a happy emoticon face). Social TV and Social TV 2 [25,26] are interactive TV systems that display the watching status of remote viewers and allow sending lightweight text messages between viewers.

Text and audio have been widely researched for social iTV with findings that depend on the audience and usage context. For instance, in a controlled lab experiment involving 17 subjects, Geerts [19] found that voice chat was considered more natural and direct than text chat, but text was preferred by young viewers who had previously used it on computers. In an *in-situ* study with 5 male subjects, Huang *et al.* [28] found that their participants overwhelmingly preferred text to voice chat, but also that they often employed the system to communicate about topics not related to television content. Whatever the modality of mediating interactions, the challenge has always been to support viewers engaging in communication, while not obstructing television watching [11,37].

The iTV community has also looked at ways to better define, understand, and analyze the social dimensions of television watching in order to inform improved designs of social iTV systems and, consequently, deliver enriched user experience. For instance, Chorianopoulos [13] introduced *presence* and *type of communication* as two dimensions for analyzing the social aspects of television; in terms of presence, viewers can be collocated or at distance, while communication can be either synchronous or asynchronous. Oehlberg *et al.* [37] proposed design strategies for social interaction between distant viewers during television watching to prevent disruption of TV flow and to support fluent conversation between viewers, such as minimize disruptions in following content on the TV, isolate side conversations, and avoid drawing viewers' attention away from the TV screen. Cesar, Chorianopoulos, and Jensen [11] provided a relevant overview of the social and interaction

aspects of television. Geerts and De Grooff [21] remarked the lack of sociability heuristics for evaluating social TV systems, and introduced twelve guidelines to assist practitioners in this direction, such as allowing for both synchronous and asynchronous communication, exploiting viewing behavior to engage other viewers, guaranteeing personal and group privacy, and letting users share content in a flexible manner.

Recently, social television watching has been leveraged and boosted by secondary screen applications and by a variety of social networks. These instruments allow people to interact with each other using their mobile devices, either directly, *e.g.*, by means of live chat, or indirectly by posting and following posts about TV content on various social websites. While reviewing previous work on secondary screens, Cesar, Bulterman, and Jansen [10] identified four main motivations for their usage in an interactive television environment, which are control, enrich, share, and transfer of television content. In a different study, Courtois and D'heer showed that participants mostly used their tablet devices during television watching for social networking and content search [15].

Kinesics and body gestures

Kinesics represents the interpretation of non-verbal communication expressed with body movement, gestures, and facial expressions. While coining the term, Birdwhistell [7] also considered pre-kinesics (*i.e.*, the physiology of kinesics), micro-kinesics (*i.e.*, the study of *kines*, which represent particles of abstractable body movement), and social kinesics (*i.e.*, the use of body communication in social interaction). A large body of literature in psycholinguistics has shown that body gestures are deeply connected with language, speech, and thought [18,34], making them remarkable conveyors of information to listeners [32]. Moreover, gestures were found to facilitate the smoothness of interaction and to increase linking between interaction partners, *i.e.*, *the chameleon effect* [12], and to communicate attitudes and emotions both voluntarily and involuntarily [23]. Kleinsmith and Bianchi-Berthouze [33] compiled a survey of the literature concerned with the perception of affective body expression. Bianchi-Berthouze [6] investigated players' body engagement during whole-body gesture-controlled video games, for which she proposed a taxonomy of body movements and worked with a model describing the relationship between movement and type of engagement.

Designing augmented TV experiences with Kinect

We employ in this work the Microsoft Kinect depth sensor to capture audiences' body movements and to display them on top of television content. Our use of depth sensing and human motion capture technology for interactive TV applications is not new in the iTV community. In fact, researchers have employed Kinect to create novel interfaces for TV and home entertainment, such as controlling the TV set with the bare palm [16], entering text on TV [38], projecting video gaming content in the periphery of the TV set [30] and in the entire room [29]. Also, researchers have used Kinect to collect viewers' preferences for TV gestures [35,42,43]. In this work, we follow this practice and employ the Kinect sensor to capture viewers' silhouettes in their environment to deliver new, enriched social experiences for television.

PROTOTYPE

We implemented a prototype application that captures viewers' body silhouettes from the depth stream delivered by the Microsoft Kinect sensor[1], and displays them on top of television content. Other silhouettes, captured by distinct Kinect sensors installed in other locations are synchronously displayed on top of the same content (at about 13.5 fps for 3 active silhouettes, see the Results section). Silhouettes are not disclosing any traits of their viewers, such as face or clothes, as they are displayed using color gradients with darker colors showing more depth, see Figure 1 on the first page. The prototype was implemented in .NET 4.5 C# using the Microsoft Kinect SDK that distinctly marks body pixels inside depth frames, which makes user segmentation easy. In our implementation, we have followed Oehlberg et al.'s "Mystery Science Theater 3000" metaphor of an unobtrusive social TV system [37], for which the interface is a row of theater seats at the bottom of the TV screen. According to Oehlberg et al., such an interface would be less distracting than displaying full-bandwidth video of each viewer, but it would not convey as many social cues as video. Our prototype represents the reasonable compromise for conveying kinesics of remote viewers, while minimizing the resolution for human body representation and, consequently, minimizing bandwidth for video transmission.

USER STUDY

We conducted a study to understand the opportunity of audience silhouettes to enrich viewers' television watching experience as well as to collect user feedback in terms of perceived kinesics and overall body movement reaction and responsiveness with respect to the audience silhouettes concept.

Participants

Fifteen (15) participants volunteered for the study (7 were females) with ages between 19 and 28 years old (average age 22.4 years, SD=2.1 years). Ten (10) participants had a technical background, while the rest were non-technical. We made sure that our participants' age range (19−28 years) was reflective of today's owners of smart TV products. For instance, "The Connected Consumer Survey 2013: TV and video" of Analysis Manson Limited reports that people in the 18−34 age group are most likely to own a smart TV and also to make full use of it, e.g., to actually connect it to the Internet [1] (p. 31). Our participants reported watching TV content (either on the TV set or on some other device) for an average of 2.6 hours per day (SD=1.2 hours).

Apparatus

The audience silhouettes application prototype ran on a 3.2GHz Quad-Core PC with Windows 7, which was connected to the TV set (Sony BRAVIA, 40 inch/102 cm diagonal) running at full HD resolution 1920×1080 pixels. The Microsoft Kinect sensor was placed on top of the TV set, and depth video frames were captured at a resolution of 320×240 pixels, while the frame rate depended on the actual CPU load (with an average 13.5 frames per second). Participants' body silhouettes were recorded as binary files, with one file per each experimental condition (see next) and 180 files in total.

---

[1] http://www.microsoft.com/en-us/kinectforwindows/

Design

Our study was a within-subjects design with two factors:

1. AUDIENCE-TYPE, nominal variable having 4 conditions: NO-AUDIENCE (i.e., regular television watching with no silhouette feedback), SELF-AUDIENCE (i.e., only the viewer's body silhouette is displayed on screen), SINGLE-AUDIENCE (i.e., the viewer's body silhouette and one audience silhouette are shown), and MULTIPLE-AUDIENCE (i.e., two different silhouettes are shown on the TV screen next to the viewer's own silhouette). Figure 2 shows these conditions.

2. GENRE, nominal variable with 3 conditions: NEWSCAST, MOVIE, and SPORTS. Genres were informed by prior research that investigated the types of content that make people talk the most while watching TV and, consequently, are most suited for synchronous social iTV applications [20].

In our analysis, we also report and discuss results based on participants' GENDER, nominal factor with 2 conditions.

Task

Participants sat in a comfortable armchair at a distance of approximately 2 meters from the TV set. Each AUDIENCE-TYPE condition was presented to each participant for 3 minutes, with a total of 12 minutes of television watching per participant. We considered that this amount of time would be sufficient to capture participants' body movement behavior, knowing that prior investigations of people watching TV showed that engaged looks generally take between 6 and 15 seconds and that staring installs after 15 seconds of continuous TV watching [27]. The order of conditions was randomized across participants. Each condition showed a sequence from a larger video file with NO-, SELF-, SINGLE-, and MULTIPLE-AUDIENCE silhouettes displayed on top. Participants were told that friends of theirs were in a different room watching the same transmission in order to create the impression of a live audience. Instead, we played recordings of previously captured audience silhouettes in order to assure the same visual stimuli for each participant (i.e., the silhouettes we displayed always behaved in the same way at exactly the same time of the experiment). From this perspective, our experimental setup is actually a Wizard-of-Oz design [31]. The experimenter left the room while participants watched television to not influence their body behavior. Then, the experimenter returned and asked participants to fill a questionnaire, which is described in detail in the next section. The experiment took about 25 minutes per participant.

Measures

We employ both *objective* and *subjective* measures to characterize and analyze participants' behavior in relation to on-screen audience silhouettes and their displayed kinesics.

The objective measures are computed from the body movement data collected with the Microsoft Kinect sensor. Specifically, the Kinect sensor delivers depth frames of the scene that we recorded at a resolution of 320×240 pixels and a maximum frame rate of 30 fps. We extracted participants' body movements from the Kinect-delivered depth scene, which we recorded as a set of body postures P_i, $i = 1..T$ for the entire monitored time interval T, with each posture P_i representing a set of 3-D body points whose coordinates are expressed in

Figure 2. The four experimental conditions employed for the AUDIENCE-TYPE factor, from left to right: NO-AUDIENCE, SELF-AUDIENCE, SINGLE-AUDIENCE, and MULTIPLE-AUDIENCE. The participant's own silhouette is displayed in red colors at the bottom-left side of the TV screen.

meters in a system of reference centered on the Kinect sensor:

$$P_i = \{p_{i,j} = (x_j, y_j, z_j) \in \mathbb{R}^3 \mid j = 1..|P_i|\} \qquad (1)$$

where $|P_i|$ is the number of points constituting posture P_i.

Based on this representation for body posture and movement, we define and employ the following objective measures to characterize participants' body movement behavior during television watching in the presence of audience silhouettes:

1. BODY-MOVEMENT represents the average amount of movement performed by participants during the monitored time interval defined as the average of normalized symmetric differences between time-consecutive postures P_i and P_{i+w}:

$$\text{BODY-MOVEMENT} = \frac{w}{T} \cdot \sum_{i=1}^{T-w} \frac{|P_{i+w} \triangle P_i|}{|P_i| + |P_{i+w}|} \cdot 100\% \quad (2)$$

where w is a time window parameter for which we used 1 second (*i.e.*, w averages to 13.5 fps for our dataset). The symmetric difference $\triangle$ between two point sets means that we count all the pixels that are present in P_{i+w} but not in P_i and vice versa, after which we normalize the result by dividing it by the total number of points subjected to comparison, *i.e.*, the cardinals of sets P_i and P_{i+w}. We then compute BODY-MOVEMENT as the average of $\triangle$ differences between w-consecutive body frames. Due to this normalization process, we report BODY-MOVEMENT values as percentages, *e.g.*, an average of 12% of the participant's body pixels moved during a time duration of 60 seconds.

2. DISTINCT-POSTURES represents an indicator of the diversity of body postures produced by participants during the monitored time interval. To compute this measure, we apply the symmetric difference operator $\triangle$ (eq. 2) to all pairs of body postures for a participant in a trial and count how many postures are different by at least $\delta = 25\%$ difference (a threshold value that we derived experimentally by visually appreciating the difference in body postures):

$$\text{DISTINCT-POSTURES} = \frac{\left|\left\{(P_i, P_j) \mid \frac{|P_i \triangle P_j|}{|P_i| + |P_j|} \geq \delta\right\}\right|}{\frac{1}{2} \cdot T \cdot (T-1)} \cdot 100\%$$

$$(3)$$

where we enumerate all body posture pairs (P_i, P_j), $1 \leq i < j \leq T$. Due to the normalization process, we also express DISTINCT-POSTURES values as percentages, *e.g.*, a value of 36.1% means that 36.1% of all body posture pairs of the participant in a trial were composed of postures different by at least $\delta = 25\%$.

3. MOVEMENT-AMPLITUDE represents the space volume in which body movement occurs:

$$\text{MOVEMENT-AMPLITUDE} = \left(\max_{i=1,T} x_i - \min_{i=1,T} x_i\right) \cdot \quad (4)$$

$$\left(\max_{i=1,T} y_i - \min_{i=1,T} y_i\right) \cdot$$

$$\left(\max_{i=1,T} z_i - \min_{i=1,T} z_i\right)$$

As the Kinect sensor reports x, y, and z coordinates in meters, we report MOVEMENT-AMPLITUDE in m^3, *e.g.*, $1.8\ m^3$ would represent the space volume in which a participant moved during a total time of say 60 seconds.

These 3 quantitative measures capture various aspects of how people move in front of the TV. For instance, while BODY-MOVEMENT reports differences in movement from frame to frame and MOVEMENT-AMPLITUDE characterizes the space in which movement takes place, DISTINCT-POSTURES measures the uniqueness and distinctiveness of one's body postures. Although more measures can be imagined to further characterize body movement, we employ in this work the minimal set capable to validate our hypotheses numerically (see next section), while we hope that readers will be inspired to try out other measures as well (see the Future Work section).

We also employ a number of 9 subjective measures collected with questionnaires, mostly as Likert scale ratings denoting the degree of participants' agreement to various statements:

1. PERCEIVED-USEFULNESS, measured on a 5-point Likert scale as evaluation of the statement *"I find the concept of TV audience silhouettes an useful one."* The 5 levels of the Likert scale are (1 to 5): strongly disagree, disagree, neither agree nor disagree, agree, and strongly agree.

2. PERCEIVED-ENJOYMENT, measured on a 5-point Likert scale as degree of agreement with the statement *"I find the concept of TV audience silhouettes an enjoyable one."*

3. PERCEIVED-DISTRACTEDNESS, measured on a 5-point Likert scale as degree of agreement with *"I find the concept of TV audience silhouettes distracting me from watching the TV program."*

4. DESIRABILITY, measured with the Microsoft Reaction Cards method[2] [5]. Participants are asked to describe the audience silhouettes concept using any of a set of 118 words, such as *appealing, effortless, impressive, distracting*, etc.

---

[2]Permission is granted to use this Tool for personal, academic and commercial purposes. If you wish to use this Tool, or the results obtained from the use of this Tool for personal or academic purposes or in your commercial application, you are required to include the following attribution: "Developed by and © 2002 Microsoft Corporation. All rights reserved".

Participants can pick as many words as they deem relevant, after which they highlight the 5 most relevant words.

5. PERCEIVED-USABILITY, measured with the System Usability Scale (SUS) tool [9]. SUS consists of 10 statements for which participants rate their degree of agreement using 5-point Likert scales, and answers are aggregated into a score ranging from 0 (low usability) to 100 (perfect score).

6. PERCEIVED-CONNECTEDNESS, measured on a 5-point Likert scale as degree of agreement with *"I felt connected with the remote person while watching television."*

7. PERCEIVED-SOCIAL-DISCOMFORT, measured on a 5-point Likert scale as degree of agreement with *"I felt discomfort seeing the remote person while watching television."*

8. PERCEIVED-SOCIAL-EXPERIENCE, measured on a 5-point Likert scale as degree of agreement with the statement *"Watching TV with another remote person that I was able to see made my watching experience more enjoyable."*

9. PERCEIVED-KINESICS, measured on a 5-point Likert scale as degree of agreement with the statement *"I was able to understand well the body language of the other person."*

Hypotheses

We formulate the following hypotheses for our study:

H_1. AUDIENCE-TYPE will influence participants' body movement behavior.

H_2. The GENRE of displayed TV content will influence participants' body movement behavior.

H_3. Men and women will react differently to audience silhouettes in terms of their body movement behavior.

RESULTS

We collected a total number of 146,087 body postures from 15 participants representing 180 minutes of body movement data recorded at an average frame rate of 13.5 frames per second. In the following, we analyze participants' body movements with our quantitative measures and we look at participants' self-reported experience with TV audience silhouettes that we measured using SUS, report cards, Likert scale ratings, and comments elicited with open-ended questions.

Participants' body movements

We found a significant effect of AUDIENCE-TYPE on participants' average BODY-MOVEMENT ($\chi^2_{(3,N=45)}=30.408$, $p<.001$), which increased from 7.9% (SD=2.8%) for the NO-AUDIENCE condition to 8.2% (SD=3.4%) for SELF-AUDIENCE, 8.8% (SD=3.8%) for SINGLE-AUDIENCE, and reached the maximum value of 9.7% (SD=3.3%) when participants were subjected to the MULTIPLE-AUDIENCE condition; see Figure 3. Follow-up post-hoc Wilcoxon signed-rank tests showed significant differences (Bonferroni corrected at $p=.05/6=.0083$) only between MULTIPLE-AUDIENCE and all the other three AUDIENCE conditions. There were no significant differences detected between body movement collected during the NO-, SELF-, and SINGLE-AUDIENCE conditions. These results suggest that more on-screen silhouettes were able to influence participants' behavior to change significantly in terms of produced body movement, which can be interpreted

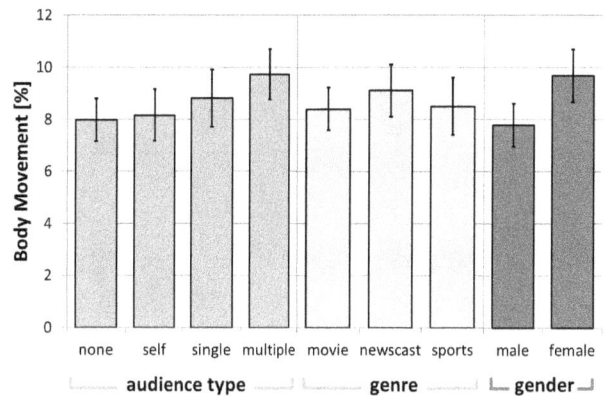

Figure 3. Participants' average percentages of BODY-MOVEMENT computed for the AUDIENCE-TYPE, GENRE, and GENDER experimental conditions. NOTE: error bars show 95% CIs.

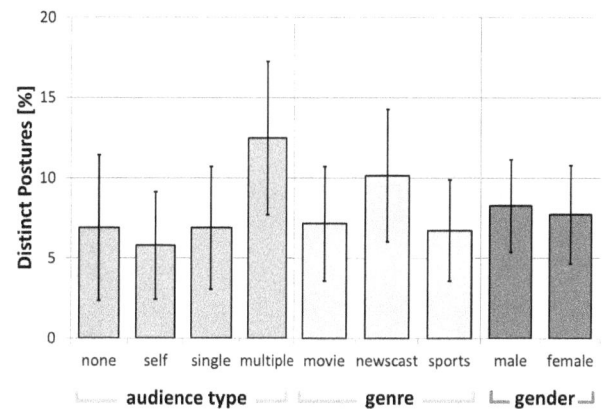

Figure 4. Participants' average percentages of DISTINCT-POSTURES computed for the AUDIENCE-TYPE, GENRE, and GENDER experimental conditions. NOTE: error bars show 95% CIs.

as greater involvement with the on-screen audiences. We detected no significant effect of GENRE on participants' BODY-MOVEMENT ($\chi^2_{(2,N=60)}=5.246$, *n.s.*), which shows that our selected genre content was not able to influence body behavior on its own. Note however that different results could be obtained by exposing participants to other TV content and genres that might possess different capabilities to trigger emotional response, not examined in this work. However, we found a significant effect of GENDER ($t_{(178)}=-3.907$, $p<.001$), showing that women produced significantly more body movement than men during television watching (9.7%, SD=3.4% versus 7.8%, SD=3.4%). This finding confirms for our specific television application scenario previous research results that showed women generally expressing more emotion than men in terms of their non-verbal behavior, such as smiles, laughs, head and body movement [24].

We found a significant effect of AUDIENCE-TYPE on participants' percentage of distinctly adopted body postures ($\chi^2_{(3,N=45)}=14.217$, $p<.01$). The maximum percentage of DISTINCT-POSTURES (12.5%, SD=16.4%) occurred for the MULTIPLE-AUDIENCE condition; see Figure 4. Follow-up Wilcoxon signed-rank tests showed significant differences (Bonferroni corrected at $p=.05/6=.0083$) only between the (MULTIPLE-AUDIENCE and NO-AUDIENCE) and (MULTIPLE-

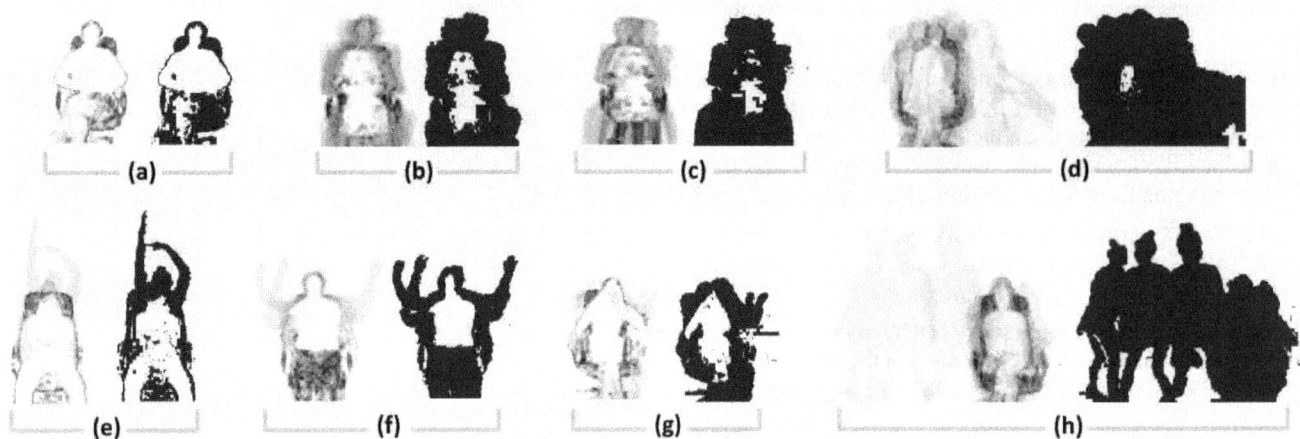

Figure 5. Examples of Motion-Amount Images (gray levels) and Motion-Energy Images (black & white) computed from one minute of recording. Note the various body behaviors of our participants, such as sitting and crossing legs (a), leaning left and right (b), swiveling (c), reaching for an object (d), trying to attract the attention of the on-screen silhouettes (e), (f), (g), and even standing up and walking around (h).

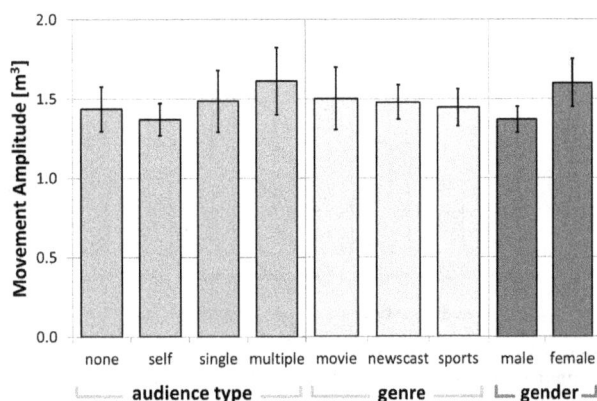

Figure 6. Participants' average MOVEMENT-AMPLITUDE computed for the AUDIENCE-TYPE, GENRE, and GENDER experimental conditions. NOTE: error bars show 95% CIs.

AUDIENCE and SELF-AUDIENCE) pairs of conditions. These results show again that our participants' body behavior was influenced more by the presence of more on-screen silhouettes. We detected no significant effects of GENRE on participants' DISTINCT-POSTURES ($\chi^2_{(2,N=60)}=1.636$, $n.s.$), and no significant effect of GENDER ($t_{(178)}=0.257$, $n.s.$).

We found no significant effect of AUDIENCE-TYPE nor GENRE on MOVEMENT-AMPLITUDE ($\chi^2_{(3,N=45)}=7.664$, $n.s.$, and $\chi^2_{(2,N=60)}=0.795$, $n.s.$ at $p=.05$). There was however a significant effect of GENDER ($t_{(178)}=-2.657$, $p<.01$), showing that women produced slightly (14%) more ample movements than men did (1.6 m^3, SD=0.7 m^3 versus 1.4 m^3, SD=0.4 m^3); see Figure 6.

These results validate hypotheses H_1 and H_3, but not H_2. To understand participants' body movements in more detail, we generated Motion-Energy Images (MEIs) and a variant of Motion-History Images (MHIs) [8] from our collected body posture data. Motion-Energy Images are black and white image representations of motion, which are computed as cumulative differences of motion occurring between consecutive

video frames [8] (p. 260). Motion-History Images are gray-level images that reflect the temporal aspect of motion as it unfolds in time with brighter colors showing motion that is more recent [8] (p. 260). Instead of depicting time, we used gray levels to illustrate the *amount* of body movement and, consequently, we compute Motion-Amount Images (MAIs). Note that while MEIs show *where* body movement occurred, MAIs reveal *how much* movement occurred at each point in the captured scene. Figure 5 shows MAI and MEI images computed for some of our participants. The Appendix (Figure 9) provides all the MAI images generated for all the 180 experimental recordings (=15 participants × 4 AUDIENCE-TYPEs × 3 GENREs) so that readers can form a better understanding of all our participants' body movement behavior.

Overall, we found participants producing a variety of body movements suggestive of their experience of watching and interacting with TV audience silhouettes, even if our setting was a laboratory-controlled one. (It is reasonably to assume that a larger variety of body movements will be produced in the familiarity of one's own living room, which is an investigation that we leave for future work.) For example, we observed that some participants did not bother at all interacting with the on-screen silhouettes, while they simply preferred to sit comfortably in the armchair, which is characteristic for the lean-back paradigm; see Figures 5a, 5b, and 5c. This behavior can be explained by participants actually focusing on the TV content and ignoring the audience or by deliberately self-restraining their body movements because of the unfamiliar laboratory environment. On the other hand, other participants felt more comfortable and we were able to see their willingness to interact and communicate with the on-screen audience silhouettes in a lean-forward way; see Figures 5e, 5f, and 5g for some examples of participants trying to attract the attention of the on-screen silhouettes. Indeed, when asked about their behavior vis-a-vis silhouettes, nearly all participants (14/15=93%) said they tried to interact with the on-screen silhouettes, from *a little* (12 out of 15 responses) to *a lot* (2 participants). Other body behavior included reaching for objects (Figure 5d) or even walking to the TV and back (Figure 5h).

Figure 7. Word clouds generated from our participants' word selections from the Microsoft Reaction Cards [5] to describe TV audience silhouettes. Left: word cloud generated from all participants' words ($N{=}249$). Right: word cloud generated from participants' selections of top-5 most relevant words that describe audience silhouettes ($N{=}60$). Note the high frequency of positive words, such as *creative, fun, friendly, entertaining, connected*, and *collaborative*. NOTE: word clouds were generated with the on-line tool available at http://www.wordle.net.

Perceived experience and self-reported feedback

Participants rated their experience using 5-point Likert scales; see Figure 8. Overall, participants agreed that audience silhouettes made them feel connected to the remote persons (median rating 4 - *agree*), connectedness which they felt to improve their watching experience (median rating 4) for a TV application they perceived as useful (median rating 4). Also, participants considered that they were able to understand well the body movements of the on-screen silhouettes (median rating 4), which did not cause discomfort during television watching (median rating 2, *i.e., disagree* with the discomfort statement). Mann-Whitney U tests did not detect any significant effect (at $p{=}.05$) of GENDER on any of these self-reported measures.

Figure 8. Median values ($N{=}15$) for participants' self-reported experience collected with 5-point Likert scales (1 to 5): *strongly disagree, disagree, neither agree nor disagree, agree*, and *strongly agree*.

We found significant positive correlations between perceived USEFULNESS and SOCIAL-EXPERIENCE (Spearman's $\rho_{(N=15)}{=}.637$, $p{=}.05$), between perceived DISTRACTEDNESS and SOCIAL-DISCOMFORT ($\rho_{(N=15)}{=}.662$, $p{=}.01$), as well as between perceived CONNECTEDNESS and KINESICS ($\rho_{(N=15)}{=}.720$, $p{=}.01$). These results show that participants that rated audience silhouettes as more useful, also felt that their television watching experience was more enjoyable, while participants that found silhouettes distracting also reported discomfort while watching TV with remote viewers. The degree of perceived connectedness to other viewers represented as silhouettes was higher when participants felt they understood the meaning of silhouettes' body movements (Spearman's $\rho_{(N=15)}{=}.720$, $p{=}.01$). We also found significant negative correlations between perceived USEFULNESS and DIS-

TRACTEDNESS ($\rho_{(N=15)}{=}{-}.641$, $p{=}.01$) and between USEFULNESS and perceived KINESICS ($\rho_{(N=15)}{=}{-}.534$, $p{=}.05$), the latter suggesting that less understanding of the silhouettes' body movements may have caused a low perceived usefulness of the audience silhouettes concept.

Next to collecting participants' degree of agreement with Likert scale statements, we also ran two usability tests for the audience silhouette concept by employing the System Usability Score tool [9] and the Microsoft Reaction Cards [5].

The average SUS usability score computed from participants' self-reported answers to all the 10 questions of the test [9] was 68.3 (SD=8.3, CI$_{95\%}{=}[63.8, 72.9]$). Note that SUS scores range in $[0, 100]$, with 100 representing a perfect usability result. Based on previous research employing SUS scores [2,3], our result is slightly above average, near the *good* threshold (that corresponds to SUS=70) in terms of the 7-point adjective ratings scale [2] (p. 121), and it falls within the *high acceptability* range proposed by Bangor *et al.* [3]. Men generally rated usability of audience silhouettes higher than women (70.0 versus 66.4), yet we found no statistically effect of GENDER on SUS ($U{=}19.5$, $Z{=}{-}1.004$, *n.s.* at $p{=}.05$)

Our participants used an average of 16.6 words (SD=7.3) from the Microsoft Reaction Cards [5] to describe their experience with audience silhouettes. Figure 7 shows two word clouds generated from all participants' word selections ($N{=}249$ words, Figure 7, left) as well as from their top-5 most relevant words ($N{=}60$, Figure 7, right). Note the high frequency of positive words, such as *creative* (14, almost all participants considered audience silhouettes to be creative), *fun* (12), *friendly* (11), *entertaining* (9), *connected* (8), *innovative* (8), *attractive* (8), and *collaborative* (8). Women used in average more words than men to describe audience silhouettes (19.7, SD=9.2 versus 13.9, SD=4.1), however we did not detect any significant effect of GENDER, as showed by a Mann-Whitney U test ($U{=}16.000$, $Z{=}{-}1.392$, *n.s.*).

Open-ended feedback and comments

Next to objective and subjective measures, we also collected participants' open-ended comments about audience silhouettes. By analyzing those comments, we were able to identify several common perceptions, such as (i) audience silhouettes can help viewers interact and communicate with each other using non-verbal behavior, (ii) they foster connectedness between remote persons, (iii) they may be used as indicators for TV content popularity (*i.e.*, what to watch?), and (iv) audience silhouettes may also interfere with one's privacy.

For example, the communication potential of audience silhouettes was repeatedly remarked by participants, *e.g.*, *"viewers can interact using non-verbal communication"* (P_1), silhouettes *"transmit emotions"* (P_3), *"help compare one's reaction to others"* (P_4), *"can replace verbal communication during television watching"* (P_4), they *"make television more interactive"* (P_6), *"help communication"* (P_7), and *"help interaction between viewers"* (P_{14}). Participants also remarked the capability of audience silhouettes to deliver the feeling of connectedness between remote individuals, *e.g.*, silhouettes *"reduce the feeling of loneliness when watching TV"* (P_1), *"it is comforting to know that my friends are all right"* (P_8), *"less loneliness when watching TV"* (P_8), *"I would feel more close to dear ones, making sure the other person is all right"* (P_{10}), *"watching movies becomes a social experience"* (P_{12}), *"helps with the feeling of loneliness while watching TV"* (P_{14}), silhouettes are a *"form of socialization"* (P_9) and a *"tool for socialization"* (P_{11}). Several participants suggested the use of audience silhouettes as indicators for the quality of TV content, *i.e.*, more silhouettes means more of their friends enjoying the show: *"the number of silhouettes are a recommender for that show"* (P_7), *"I can discover what others are watching, what are their preferences"* (P_{13}), *"useful feedback for evaluating the quality of a show"* (P_{13}). Some participants had privacy concerns in the case of a security breach in the system.

Eleven (11) of our participants (73%) said they would like to have the audience silhouettes application running on their home TVs, and 13 of them (87%) said they would recommend the audience silhouettes system to others.

CONCLUSION AND FUTURE WORK

We introduced in this work *audience silhouettes* as a practical technique to convey *peripheral awareness* of remote viewers and to leverage *kinesics* as a non-intrusive communication channel for viewers during television watching. Overall, our participants rated the concept favorably, a finding that we were able to verify with multiple usability metrics. Furthermore, we characterized participants' body movement responses in relation to the on-screen audience silhouettes, and we introduced a visualization technique to serve for future explorations in this line of work. The data that we collected enable us to believe that audience silhouettes can provide a simple and effective channel for presence and non-verbal communication over distance in the context of social television watching.

Future work will address *in-situ* studies (for which we expect more body movement reactions), solving technical issues for transmitting many silhouettes over the network without compromising video synchronization [22], and visualization enhancements (*e.g.*, color, depth granularity, etc.). Also, exploration of more body movement measures (*e.g.*, kinematic features relying on speed and acceleration, which we did not explore in this work) will likely reveal more findings about

how viewers engage with interactive television content. Predicting viewers' body behavior and engagement with television content with workable models [6] would be very valuable for designers of such iTV systems. Interactive TV systems will probably benefit of combining audience silhouettes with whole-body gesture recognition [41] that will offer users the opportunity for more control, from passive engagement (*i.e.*, using the silhouette only, as in this work) to gesture commands that invoke specific functions for iTV [42,43,46]. The effect of distributed visual attention on peripheral awareness of various audiences for multi-screen TV [44,45] is also an interesting research direction.

We believe that this work on audience silhouettes has barely scratched the opportunity of employing real-time kinesics for social TV watching, and we are eager to see how the community will employ our concept and techniques to design enriched social interactive television experiences for viewers.

ACKNOWLEDGMENTS
This work was supported by the liFe-StaGE project 740/2014, "Multimodal Feedback for Supporting Gestural Interaction in Smart Environments", co-funded by UEFISCDI & OeAD.

REFERENCES

1. Analysis Manson Limited. The Connected Consumer Survey 2013: TV and video
   `http://www.analysysmason.com/Research/Content/Reports/Connected-Consumer-TV-May2013-RDMB0/samples-TOC/` (last accessed march 2015).

2. Bangor, A., Kortum, P., and Miller, J. Determining what individual SUS scores mean: Adding an adjective rating scale. *Journal of Usability Studies 4*, 3 (2009), 114–123.

3. Bangor, A., Kortum, P. T., and Miller, J. T. An empirical evaluation of the system usability scale. *Int. Journal of Human-Computer Interaction 24*, 6 (2008), 574–594.

4. Basapur, S., Mandalia, H., Chaysinh, S., Lee, Y., Venkitaraman, N., and Metcalf, C. FANFEEDS: Evaluation of socially generated information feed on second screen as a TV show companion. In *Proc. of EuroITV '12*, ACM (New York, NY, USA, 2012), 87–96.

5. Benedek, J., and Miner, T. Measuring desirability: New methods for evaluating desirability in a usability lab setting. In *Proc. of the Usability Professionals Assoc. Conf.*, 2002 `http://www.microsoft.com/usability/uepostings/desirabilitytoolkit.doc`.

6. Bianchi-Berthouze, N. Understanding the role of body movement in player engagement. *Human Computer Interaction 28*, 1 (2013), 40–75.

7. Birdwhistell, R. Introduction to kinesics: An annotation system for analysis of body motion and gesture. Washington, DC: Foreign Service Institute, 1952.

8. Bobick, A. F., and Davis, J. W. The recognition of human movement using temporal templates. *IEEE TPAMI 23*, 3 (Mar. 2001), 257–267.

9. Brooke, J. SUS: A quick and dirty usability scale. In *Usability evaluation in industry*. Taylor & Francis, 1996.

10. Cesar, P., Bulterman, D. C., and Jansen, A. J. Usages of the secondary screen in an interactive television

environment: Control, enrich, share, and transfer television content. In *Proc. EuroITV'08* (2008), 168–177.

11. Cesar, P., Chorianopoulos, K., and Jensen, J. F. Social television and user interaction. *Computers in Entertainment 6*, 1 (May 2008), 4:1–4:10.

12. Chartrand, T., and Bargh, J. The chameleon effect: The perception-behavior link and social interaction. *J. of Personality and Social Psychology 76*, 6 (1999), 893–910.

13. Chorianopoulos, K. Content-enriched communication supporting the social uses of TV. *The Journal of The Communications Network 6*, 1 (2007), 23–30.

14. Coppens, T., Trappeniers, L., and Godon, M. AmigoTV: towards a social TV experience. In *EuroITV '04* (2004).

15. Courtois, C., and D'heer, E. Second screen applications and tablet users: Constellation, awareness, experience, and interest. In *Proc. of EuroITV '12* (2012), 153–156.

16. Dezfuli, N., Khalilbeigi, M., Huber, J., Müller, F., and Mühlhäuser, M. PalmRC: Imaginary palm-based remote control for eyes-free television interaction. In *Proc. of EuroITV '12*, ACM (New York, NY, USA, 2012), 27–34.

17. Doughty, M., Rowland, D., and Lawson, S. Who is on your sofa?: TV audience communities and second screening social networks. In *EuroITV '12* (2012), 79–86.

18. Feyereisen, P., and de Lannoy, J. *Gestures and Speech: Psychological Investigations*. Cambridge University Press, New York, 1991.

19. Geerts, D. Comparing voice chat and text chat in a communication tool for interactive television. In *Proc. of NordiCHI '06*, ACM (New York, USA, 2006), 461–464.

20. Geerts, D., Cesar, P., and Bulterman, D. The implications of program genres for the design of social television systems. In *Proc. of UXTV '08* (2008), 71–80.

21. Geerts, D., and De Grooff, D. Supporting the social uses of television: Sociability heuristics for social TV. In *Proc. of CHI '09*, ACM (New York, NY, USA, 2009), 595–604.

22. Geerts, D., Vaishnavi, I., Mekuria, R., van Deventer, O., and Cesar, P. Are we in sync?: Synchronization requirements for watching online video together. In *Proc. of CHI '11*, ACM (New York, NY, USA, 2011), 311–314.

23. Graham, J. A., and Argyle, M. A cross-cultural study of the communication of extra-verbal meaning by gestures. *Int. Journal of Psychology 10* (1975), 57–67.

24. Hall, J. A. *Nonverbal Sex Differences: Communication Accuracy and Expressive Style Paperback*. Johns Hopkins University Press, 1990.

25. Harboe, G., Massey, N., Metcalf, C., Wheatley, D., and Romano, G. The uses of social television. *Computers in Entertainment 6*, 1 (May 2008), 8:1–8:15.

26. Harboe, G., Metcalf, C. J., Bentley, F., Tullio, J., Massey, N., and Romano, G. Ambient social TV: Drawing people into a shared experience. In *CHI '08* (2008), 1–10.

27. Hawkins, R. P., Pingree, S., Hitchon, J., Radler, B., Gorham, B. W., Kahlor, L., Gilligan, E., Serlin, R. C., Schmidt, T., Kannaovakun, P., and Kolbeins, G. H. What produces television attention and attention style? *Human Communication Research 31*, 1 (2005), 162–187.

28. Huang, E. M., Harboe, G., Tullio, J., Novak, A., Massey, N., Metcalf, C. J., and Romano, G. Of social television comes home: A field study of communication choices and practices in TV-based text and voice chat. In *Proc. of CHI '09*, ACM (New York, NY, USA, 2009), 585–594.

29. Jones, B., Sodhi, R., Murdock, M., Mehra, R., Benko, H., Wilson, A., Ofek, E., MacIntyre, B., Raghuvanshi, N., and Shapira, L. Roomalive: Magical experiences enabled by scalable, adaptive projector-camera units. In *Proc. of UIST '14*, ACM (New York, NY, USA, 2014), 637–644.

30. Jones, B. R., Benko, H., Ofek, E., and Wilson, A. D. Illumiroom: Peripheral projected illusions for interactive experiences. In *Proc. of CHI '13* (2013), 869–878.

31. Kelley, J. F. An iterative design methodology for user-friendly natural language office information applications. *ACM Trans. on Inf. Sys. 2*, 1 (1984), 26–41.

32. Kendon, A. Do gestures communicate? A review. *Research on Language and Social Interaction 27* (1994), 175–200.

33. Kleinsmith, A., and Bianchi-Berthouze, N. Affective body expression perception and recognition: A survey. *IEEE Trans. Affect. Comput. 4*, 1 (Jan. 2013), 15–33.

34. McNeill, D. *Hand and Mind: What Gesture Reveals about Thought*. University Chicago Press, 1992.

35. Morris, M. R. Web on the wall: Insights from a multimodal interaction elicitation study. In *Proc. of ITS '12*, ACM (New York, NY, USA, 2012), 95–104.

36. Nathan, M., Harrison, C., Yarosh, S., Terveen, L., Stead, L., and Amento, B. CollaboraTV: Making television viewing social again. In *Proc. UXTV '08* (2008), 85–94.

37. Oehlberg, L., Ducheneaut, N., Thornton, J. D., Moore, R. J., and Nickell, E. Social TV: Designing for distributed, sociable television viewing. In *Proc. of EuroITV '06* (2006), 251–259.

38. Ren, G., and O'Neill, E. Freehand gestural text entry for interactive TV. In *Proc. of EuroITV '13* (2013), 121–130.

39. Schirra, S., Sun, H., and Bentley, F. Together alone: Motivations for live-tweeting a television series. In *Proc. of CHI '14*, ACM (New York, USA, 2014), 2441–2450.

40. Shamma, D. A., Bastea-Forte, M., Joubert, N., and Liu, Y. Enhancing online personal connections through the synchronized sharing of online video. In *Proc. of CHI EA '08*, ACM (New York, NY, USA, 2008), 2931–2936.

41. Vatavu, R.-D. Nomadic gestures: A technique for reusing gesture commands for frequent ambient interactions. *J. Ambient Intell. Smart Environ. 4*, 2 (Apr. 2012), 79–93.

42. Vatavu, R.-D. User-defined gestures for free-hand TV control. In *Proc. of EuroITV '12* (2012), 45–48.

43. Vatavu, R.-D. A comparative study of user-defined handheld vs. freehand gestures for home entertainment environments. *Journal of Ambient Intelligence and Smart Environments 5*, 2 (2013), 187–211.

44. Vatavu, R.-D. There's a world outside your TV: Exploring interactions beyond the physical TV screen. In *EuroITV '13*, ACM (New York, NY, USA, 2013), 143–152.

45. Vatavu, R.-D., and Mancas, M. Visual attention measures for multi-screen tv. In *Proc. of TVX '14*, ACM (New York, NY, USA, 2014), 111–118.

46. Vatavu, R.-D., and Zaiti, I.-A. Leap gestures for TV: Insights from an elicitation study. In *Proc. of TVX '14*, ACM (New York, NY, USA, 2014), 131–138.

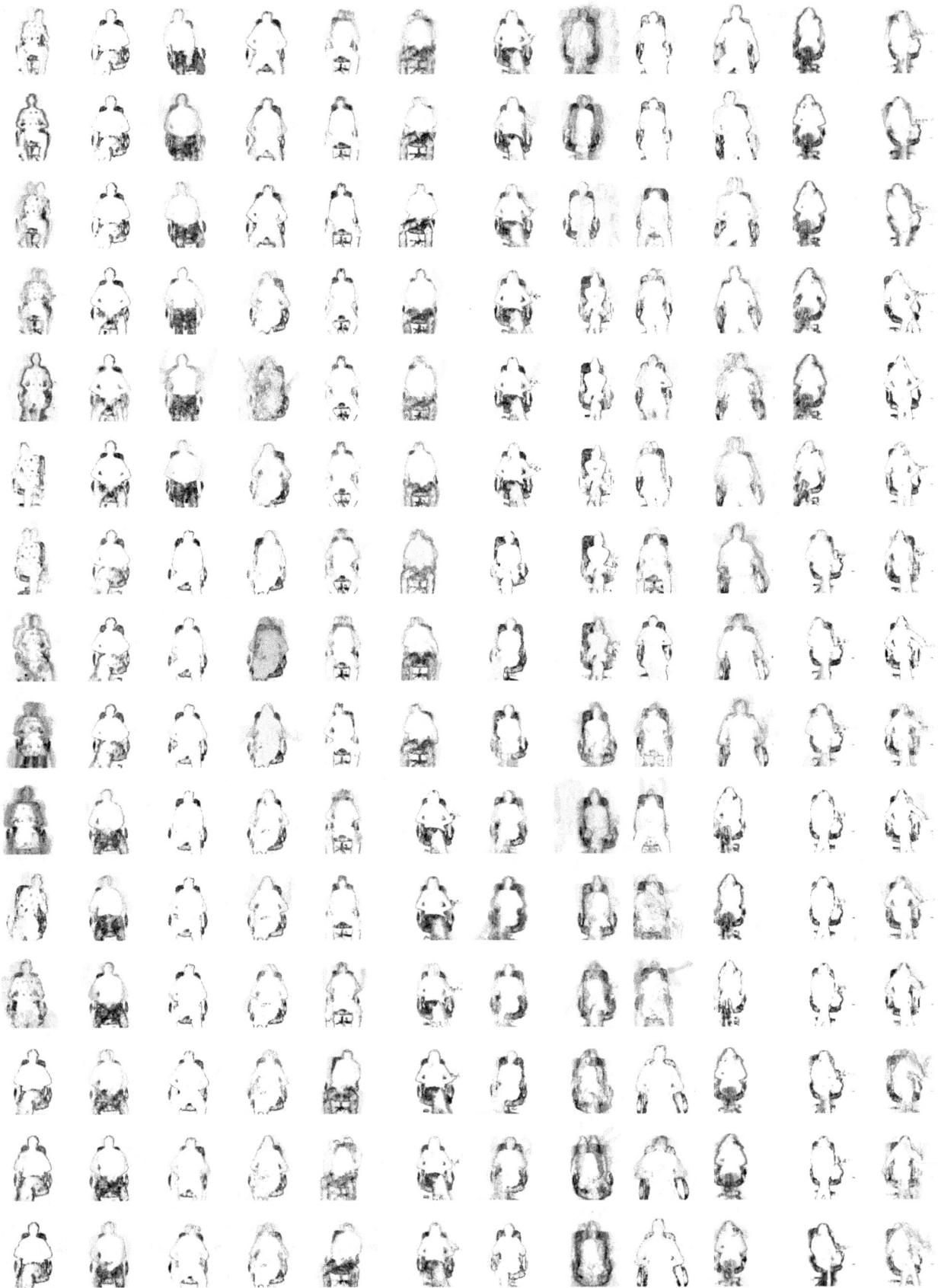

Figure 9. Motion-Amount Images for all the 180 experimental conditions (=15 participants × 4 AUDIENCE-TYPES × 3 GENRES).

It Takes Two (To Co-View): Collaborative Multi-View TV

Mark McGill†
m.mcgill.1@research.gla.ac.uk

John Williamson‡
jhw@dcs.gla.ac.uk

Stephen A. Brewster†
stephen.brewster@glasgow.ac.uk

† Glasgow Interactive Systems Group ‡ Inference, Dynamics and Interaction Group
School of Computing Science, University of Glasgow, Glasgow, G12 8QQ, Scotland, UK

ABSTRACT

This paper investigates how we can design interfaces and interactions for multi-view TVs, enabling users to transition between independent and shared activity, dynamically control awareness of other users activities, and collaborate more effectively on shared activities. We conducted two user studies, first comparing an Android-based two-user TV against both multi-screen and multi-view TVs. Based on our findings, we iterated on our design, giving users the ability to dynamically set their engagement with other users activity. We provide the foundations of a multi-user multi-view smart TV that can support users to transition between independent and shared activity and gain awareness of the activities of others, on a single shared TV that no longer suffers the bottleneck of one physical view. Through this we significantly improve upon a user's capability for collaborative and independent activity compared to single-view smart TVs.

Author Keywords

Multi-user; TV; Multi-view; Displays; Engagement;

ACM Classification Keywords

H.5.m. Information Interfaces and Presentation (e.g. HCI): Miscellaneous

INTRODUCTION

There has rarely been a technology of such prevalence as the TV. With over ~52.2 million [20] of them in the UK alone, they continue to be a central component in our home lives. A report by Ofcom [21] showed that 91% of UK adults view TV on the main set each week, and underlined the importance of the living-room TV specifically by stating that people were "increasingly reverting to having just one TV in their household - 41% of households in 2012 compared to 35% in 2002". The TV is often a social medium, with one survey suggesting that over 52% of live viewing and 56% of time-shifted viewing is shared, predominantly with one other person [26]. However, its use is often supplemented or entirely supplanted by other devices, for multi-tasking, co-viewing or private viewing of content. It is both this proliferation of TVs, and the rapid uptake of other devices (such as tablets and phones) which confirm a fundamental problem of the TV:

shareability. We use TVs because they offer large, accessible, HD displays which enhance our media experiences. However, this naturally disposes users against sharing the display: split-screen and picture-in-picture approaches force users to attend to distracting content they may not necessarily wish to, whilst compromising the existing experience through obscuring, downscaling, or compromising the aspect ratio of, the content being consumed. Additionally, they offer no privacy considerations. Personal devices circumvent these issues, guaranteeing the user full use of a semi-private display.

TVs also have issues regarding interactivity in shared contexts. Consumer approaches such as Chromecast[1] offload interaction from the TV display onto secondary devices, using the TV as a terminal for showing selected content or mirrored activity. These approaches allow for both independent (device-based) and shared (TV-based) activity, and some awareness of what others are doing. However, when second screening (using a secondary device alongside the TV) it can be problematic to actively or passively share activity with others [14], whilst interacting with others on the same TV display is often poorly facilitated [13] and potentially distracting, with no capability for truly independent views. Additionally, the phones, tablets or other devices being used are often inferior to the TV in some important respects, for example, in terms of size, casual accessibility to others in the room, and socialization, with users in their own private "digital bubble" [8]. Finally, not every user in the room may have a secondary device, or wish to use one instead of the TV; this leads to what one survey termed "digital divorce", whereby 24% of polled couples resorted to going into different rooms in order to watch TV separately [19].

These problems arose because of a fundamental limitation of the TV: it has one shared physical view. However, this technological limitation is being overcome, with existing consumer TVs capable of multiplexing many separate views in what is often termed "multi-view" [10]. These allow users the capability to consume content independent of others in the room, whilst retaining the same shared focal point e.g. one user might be watching sport whilst the other watches the news. However, we can imagine interactions that go beyond this e.g. allowing users to privately investigate details on a film they are watching, with the capability for others to switch over to see these details if they so wish, all without having to resort to a secondary devices. This paper examines how we can design interfaces and interactions for multi-view TV usage, enabling users to transition between independent and shared activity, dynamically control awareness of other

TVX'15, June 03 – 05, 2015, Brussels, Belgium
Copyright is held by the owner/author(s). Publication rights licensed to ACM.
ACM 978-1-4503-3526-3/15/06...$15.00
http://dx.doi.org/10.1145/2745197.2745199

---

[1] google.co.uk/chrome/devices/chromecast/

users' activities, and collaborate more effectively on shared activities. Our first study compares an Android-based two-user smart TV against both multi-screen and multi-view displays in a collaborative movie browsing task. Based on our findings, we iterate on our design, giving users the ability to transition between casual (viewing both views) and focused (viewing only one view) modes of usage, and dynamically set their engagement with other users' activities. This work provides a foundation for multi-user multi-view smart TVs that can support both collaborative and independent activity, and transitions between activities on a single shared TV.

BACKGROUND

Multi-View Displays

Multi-view displays are displays that are capable of providing two or more independent views to two or more users. There are a number of technologies that are capable of achieving this aim[4] e.g. Lenticular displays, using sheets of lenticular lenses atop a standard LCD screen allowing for different views based on gaze angle; Parallax-barrier or Masked Displays, employing masks (e.g. singular portholes[7]) in order to control what subpixels are viewed at a given angle. Today's state-of-the-art multi-view technologies are active-shutter displays, which have high refresh rate, low pixel-persistence[2] displays combined with "active shutter" glasses which can selectively reveal or mask frames as they are displayed. These displays offer platforms for developing gaze-angle agnostic multi-view interfaces, with low levels of crosstalk[3] whilst retaining high frame rates and image fidelity, albeit at the expense of brightness due to the amount of time the glasses are in their "shuttered" state. Active shutter displays are relatively commonplace currently, being used predominantly for consumer 3DTV. As such there are a number of multi-view capable 3DTVs on the market e.g. LG "dual-play"[4] and Samsung "Multi-View" displays[5] support either two-view/two-person gaming, or the capability to independently consume different media, with transitions managed via a physical switch on the 3D glasses. This synchrony between 3DTV and multi-view TV is likely to continue: consumer glasses-free 3DTVs demonstrated thus far rely on lenticular displays. As a consequence, displays capable of supporting a number of independent views based on gaze angle, without the need for glasses, might soon be a reality in consumer households.

Usage Versus Single And Multi-Display Groupware

Multi-view displays can be used by single users or groups and have a number of advantages over comparable smart TVs in each case. For example, in single-user scenarios they have been used to present different aspects of an interface based on view position, allowing users to move their head in order to peek at a menu [12]. In multi-user contexts, they have been

used to support single display privacyware [24], independent and collaborative activity on table-tops, e.g. Permulin by Lissermann *et al.*[10] which supported two users sharing a 120Hz two-view display, or Permulin's precursor[1], and independent views in groups such as in the case of C1x6[9] which employed multiple projectors in order to achieve a 12-view 360 Hz display allowing for 6 stereoscopic views.

It is in terms of multi-user use that multi-view displays have the most potential. In Single Display Groupware (SDG) and Multi-Display Groupware (MDG), multiple users have to either share display resources, or split attention across different displays. In SDG, they typically share use of the interface presented, e.g. [13], or partition the display in order to accommodate multiple interfaces or activities, e.g. [31]. In MDG they leverage additional displays in order to provide elements of task independence, perhaps moving activities to a secondary display, or a personal private display, or even having multiple shareable displays such that there are more display surfaces to present or interact on e.g. [18].

Multi-view displays have the potential to combine the advantages of both SDG and MDG. SDG provides a shared focus of attention and thus activity [5], which has been shown to significantly improve users' ability to collaborate [29]. MDG allows for task independence and selective or casual awareness. For example in Lunchtable [18] where group work could be spread between multiple displays, allowing for an element of independence, but with activity still be visible to the group as a whole. Multi-view displays have the capability for both independent operation and collaboration, with a shared focus of attention throughout. However, unlike in SDG and MDG, transitioning between independent and collaborative states, and gaining mutual awareness of the activity of others (e.g. through glancing, peeking, peripheral vision) must be explicitly designed for, as users no longer have the ability to manage their visual attention via gaze. This is a significant problem with respect to collaboration and coordination, as systems utilizing multi-view displays must actively communicate the requisite information to allow users to gain awareness of group activity.

Permulin[10] attempted to address this issue by providing a set of behaviours that enabled users to selectively gain a level of awareness of their partners' activities on a collaborative table-top. This was achieved through providing the ability to have both private views and a shared group view which could contain private information, as well as the ability to peek at a collaborators' private views to facilitate activity awareness. Permulin exemplified both why multi-view displays have great potential for collaboration. It provided a shared-focus workspace with the ability to collaborate or operate independently, whilst also demonstrating the problems faced in trying to provide the capability to transition between shared and private views. Their display management behaviours were heavily reliant on use of the touch surface table-top display. We would suggest that more generalised behaviours for managing full use of the display, and transitions between available views, are required if multi-view displays are to be usable in home contexts.

---

[2]Pixel persistence: the time it takes a pixel to transition from its current state to its next state

[3]Crosstalk: the extent to which one image is retained into the next image e.g. where one view is a car and the other a boat, crosstalk would be manifested as the boat being visible (from a faint outline to wholly superimposed) in the car view, and *vice versa*.

[4]lg.com/us/tv-audio-video/discoverlgtvs/dualplay

[5]samsung.com/us/video/tvs/KN55S9CAFXZA

Shared-Use TV: From Devices To The Display

The private "digital bubble" [8] of device usage offers a problematic barrier to socialization and interaction, with mobile phone use in particular having significant anti-social connotations [28]. Efforts have been made to penetrate this bubble, for example Lucero *et al* [11] proposed mobile collocated interactions, whereby users would "take an offline break together", pooling their device resources toward "shared-multiuser experiences". They aimed to create the capability for joint attention, whilst enforcing a break from online socialization, appropriating mobile device displays for passing photos around a table. This emphasis on shareability and joint attention is important as it underlines how co-located interactions are made to be more effective, through the ability to share awareness and activities. This link between awareness and our capability to collaborate has been a frequent topic of discussion within CSCW [6].

However, mobile devices are not necessarily the most shareable displays in the room. McGill *et al.* [14] demonstrated that physically sharing device views was inferior to utilizing the TV in terms of sharing activity with others and thus collaborating effectively, whilst Terrenghi *et al* [25] discussed the scale of displays relative to users' visual angle and distance, noting that the scale of the display must match the social interaction space.

There are a variety of ways in which TV displays can be shared, from proxemic approaches employed by Ballendat *et al* [2] where the display adapted to the angle and proximity of whomever was interacting with it, to approaches where the sharing was based on social behaviours [13]. However, in all cases, interfaces and interactions have likely been compromised by the fact that there is inevitably only one TV view to be shared, limiting the potential for independent activity.

Finally, there is the concept of engagement to consider. Pohl & Murray-Smith's focused–casual continuum describes interaction techniques according to the degree to which they allow users to determine how much attention and effort they choose to invest in an interaction i.e. the ability to adapt how engaged they are [22]. This concept has rarely been explored within the space of TV displays. Whilst it is beneficial to be able to give users the ability to dictate their level of awareness and engagement in others activity, there is an inherent difficulty in varying engagement when physically sharing a display. Multiple users could be attending to, and interacting with, the display without the ability to personally control their level of engagement with others' activity, e.g. employing split-screen approaches.

Summary

Multi-view capable TVs have the potential to facilitate multi-user collaborative use in home contexts, removing the reliance on less social and shareable second screen interactions. As such, this paper investigates how we can design generalised multi-view interfaces that can support transitions between independent and collaborative tasks, whilst providing the capability for awareness regarding on-going activity occurring across available views.

STUDY 1 - MULTI-USER MULTI-VIEW TV

Given the potential of multi-view displays, the aim of our first study was to design, develop and evaluate a fully functional Android-based multi-view TV. Throughout this paper we chose one important limitation: that we would be investigating only the visual component of such a system, and not the audio. Enabling per-user audio whilst retaining the ability to hear and converse with others is an area of active research, with solutions ranging from bone-conductance headphones, to directional sound-beams (e.g. BoomRoom [17]) and it is reasonable to expect these systems being incorporated into future multi-view displays. The study had the following aims:

- To allow users to gain awareness of each others' activity through a simple set of behaviours by which they could transition between virtual views without compromising in terms of distraction, aspect ratio and utilized screen area;

- To determine how multi-view TVs compared to single-view TVs in terms of perceived workload, usability, and ability to collaborate.

- To determine the extent to which users were aware of each others' activity and how close this was to their optimum level of awareness.

In order to accomplish this, we designed and built a two-view (meaning two interactive virtual views), two-user (meaning the system supported two independent physical views made up of whatever we wish to render of the virtual views) multi-view system with the capability to allow two users to transition between collaborative and independent activity. An overview of this design can be seen in Figure 1.

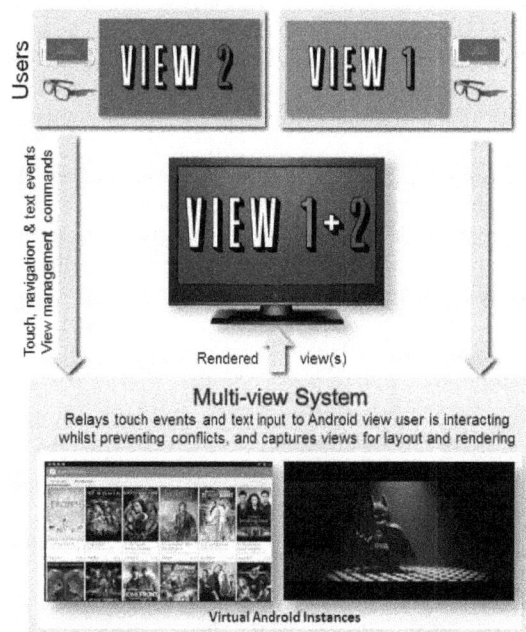

Figure 1. Overview of multi-view system in both studies. Here two users can have completely independent physical views (labeled View 1 and View 2) made up of however we wish to render our virtual Android views, with inputs routed appropriately.

We provided users with two touch gestures (enacted via a touchpad; see *Implementation*) to switch between the two available virtual views. The *transition* gesture switched the user between the two available virtual views, at which point they were free to interact with the current view. The *peek* gesture allowed the user to switch to the view they were not currently interacting with for so long as they performed the gesture, at which point they would return to their current interactive view. Through these behaviours, we hypothesized that users would be able to adequately determine their awareness of each others' activity, transitioning between independent and collaborative states, and gaining awareness of what activity their partner was performing, if they felt the need.

Implementation of Multi-view Display

To provide users with a fully-functioning multi-view TV we realised that the typical approach of implementing software capable of allowing users to only perform a given task (e.g. implementing a multi-view photo browsing application) would not be representative of smart TV usage. Thus, we built a generalised, ecologically valid multi-view system that would give users capabilities above and beyond current smart TV capability, allowing them to interact commonly used consumer applications. Given the adoption of Android into the smart TV area, we believed that building a system utilizing multiple emulated Android devices would best approximate this. As such, we used instances of Genymotion[6], a high-performance x86 Android emulator, running Android 4.x.

To present users with entirely separate views, which could be of the same virtual Android device, or different devices, depending on the users current display settings, we utilized nVidia 3D Vision, an active-shutter IR transmitter for the PC, coupled with an nVidia graphics card performing stereoscopic rendering at 120Hz, 60Hz worth of "left" eye frames, and 60Hz worth of "right" eye frames. To provide users with independent views, we needed to be able to present only the "left" eye frames to one user, and the "right" eye frames to another. This was achieved using Youniversal active-shutter glasses[7] which had the capability to be set into a "2D" mode where only one of the left or right frames of the 3D image was allowed through both eyes. Our emulator screen-capture software then rendered a stereoscopic image, such that the left image constituted of whatever view we wished to provide one user, and the right image whatever view we wished to provide the other user. This gave users the ability to view

6 genymotion.com/
7 xpand.me/products/youniversal-3d-glasses/

separate Android emulators (hereafter virtual views), or transition to the same virtual view, all without affecting their partner's physical view. To minimize crosstalk, we utilized a 24" BenQ XL2411T Display which supported nVidia LightBoost, resulting in little to no perceptible ghosting between views; this was important as it meant that awareness could only be gained through our multi-view behaviours and mechanisms, not through inadequacies in the technology.

To interact with the Android virtual views, we used Samsung S3 phones as touchpads, rendering coloured cursors which matched the colour of the user's touchpad on whichever view they were interacting with. Additionally, when occupying a view, a coloured eye would be rendered in the bottom right corner, to allow users to be aware of when they were both sharing the same view. These touchpads supported a simple set of gestures: dragging one finger moved the on-screen cursor, tapping one finger made a selection; dragging two fingers performed a scroll gesture; tapping four fingers caused a *transition* action, whilst pressing four fingers performed a *peek* action for so long as the fingers were on the touchpad. Additionally the physical back, home, and application switcher buttons were mapped to the same functions in the emulator. Text input was provided via the onscreen keyboard. These interaction events were sent to our software then routed to the appropriate Android virtual view via the Android Developer Bridge.

Experimental Design

The study design incorporated three Conditions: *(1) Single display* with one LCD display and one shared virtual Android view, as a comparative baseline for a standard smart TV; *(2) Two displays* with two LCD displays with a virtual Android view on each, allowing us to measure the default level of awareness of each others activity as users could transition between views by gaze; *(3) Multi-view display* with a single LCD display providing two independent physical views, each displaying either of two virtual Android views depending on the users usage of the system (see Figure 2).

For our task we chose movie browsing, a loosely coupled and ecologically valid collaborative task that commonly occurs on TVs e.g. collaborative searching for entertainment in [15]. Movie browsing can be performed independently or together, but the eventual outcome (having to select acceptable movies to the group) necessitates collaboration. Users were instructed to browse a given set of categories of movies in the Google Play store application, with the task of selecting movies to watch together with mutual friends for the du-

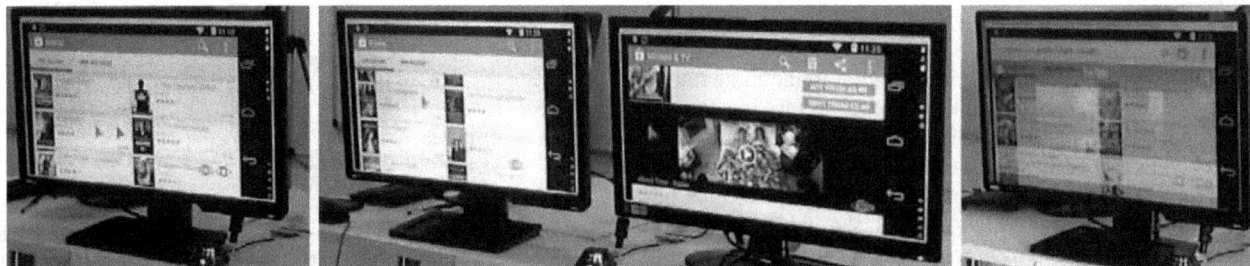

Figure 2. Left: Condition 1, single display with one virtual view. Middle: Condition 2, two displays, each with its own virtual view. Right: Condition 3, multi-view display when viewed without active-shutter glasses. This supports two independent physical views (and thus two users), constituting of whichever Android virtual view each user wishes to interact with.

ration of each Condition. Three categories were selected for each Condition, with users instructed they could browse them however they saw fit. Additionally, users had the capability to watch trailers (with the instruction to moderate trailer viewing time to under a minute per trailer) and use a selection of other applications if they so wished, namely the Chrome web browser and the IMDB app. Users were tested for 15 minutes per Condition in a within-subjects design, and there were 9 pairs, 18 users in all (mean age=23.6, SD=5.5, 16 male, 2 female) recruited from University mailing lists as pairs that knew each other (e.g., friends, family, etc.).

To determine the effects on users' abilities to collaborate effectively, we utilized post-condition questionnaires derived from a previous collaborative TV [14]. We also measured the effect our systems had on workload (NASA TLX) and usability (System Usability Scale (SUS) [3]). Additionally, users were asked to rank the Conditions in order of preference.

To establish the default / optimal level of awareness of each others' activity, for the *two displays* Condition we recorded and analysed video footage of each participant, coding timestamps regarding which display the participant was looking at, if any. These timestamps, along with logs of viewing in the multi-view display Condition, were parsed such that we could accurately compare the viewing behaviour across Conditions. Where applicable, Gini coefficients were calculated. These are a measure of inequality used for analysing viewing distribution in previous studies[30, 14]; 1 denotes maximum inequality i.e. $100-0$ or $0-100$, and 0 maximum equality i.e.

a 50-50 distribution when dealing with two items. As our use of Gini coefficients typically involves two comparison points, for both studies in this paper we also used directed Gini coefficients where applicable, whereby we encode the direction of the inequality such that 100-0 would resolve to 1, whilst $0 - 100$ would resolve to -1 (meaning the Gini coefficient resolved to a measure of distance between two points).

Results

Where appropriate a repeated-measures ANOVA (GLM) or Friedman test with *post-hoc* Wilcoxons was performed, green indicates $p < 0.05$. We found significant differences between the Condition 1 (single display) and Conditions 2 (two displays) and 3 (multi-view display). Conditions 2 and 3 were superior in terms of capability to collaborate (e.g. WS-1, MO-1), ability to work independently (WS-2), and workload/usability (see Table 1). However there were no significant differences between Conditions 2 and 3, with Condition 2 typically having only moderately higher mean scores.

User rankings (see Figure 3) again showed significant differences between Condition 1 and Conditions 2/3, with both conditions ranked better. There was no significant difference between the mean rankings of Conditions 2 and 3, however Condition 2 was ranked better than Condition 3. Given that the two display condition provided users with the ability to attain their optimal level of awareness with respect to their partners activity, this implies that our behaviours for managing awareness failed to match this standard.

Question	Condition 1: Single Display	Condition 2: Two Displays	Condition 3: Multi-view Display	Friedman Test	Wilcoxon *Post-hoc* ($p < 0.05$)
WS-1: We were able to collaborate effectively	3.11 (1.81)	4.94(1.21)	5.00 (0.77)	$\chi^2(2) = 16.0, p < 0.01$	1-2, 1-3
WS-2: We were able to work independently to complete the task	1.94(1.47)	5.67(0.49)	5.33(0.49)	$\chi^2(2) = 31.5, p < 0.01$	1-2, 1-3
WS-3: It was easy to discuss the information we found	4.39 (1.65)	5.50 (0.62)	5.39 (0.78)	$\chi^2(2) = 7.61, p < 0.05$	None
WS-4: We were able to work together to complete the task	3.94 (1.70)	5.28 (1.07)	4.78 (1.44)	$\chi^2(2) = 7.4, p < 0.05$	1-2
WS-5: I was able to actively participate in completing the task	3.83 (1.425)	5.61 (0.50)	5.33 (0.77)	$\chi^2(2) = 21.4, p < 0.01$	1-2, 1-3
MO-1: How well did the system support collaboration?	2.56 (1.72)	4.72 (1.18)	4.78 (0.88)	$\chi^2(2) = 17.2, p < 0.01$	1-2, 1-3
MO-2: How well did the system support you to share particular information with your partner?	3.94 (2.01)	4.61 (1.75)	5.17 (0.92)	$\chi^2(2) = 1.82, p = 0.4$	NA
MO-3: I was able to tell when my partner was looking at what I was browsing?	4.89 (1.60)	5.17 (0.92)	5.39 (0.61)	$\chi^2(2) = 0.383, p = 0.83$	NA
MO-4: How well did the system support you to see/review what your partner was talking about?	4.83 (1.25)	5.33 (0.69)	5.50 (0.62)	$\chi^2(2) = 5.57, p = 0.06$	NA
WE-1: The system was helpful in completing the given task	3.11 (1.68)	5.06 (0.94)	5.06 (0.87)	$\chi^2(2) = 20.8, p < 0.01$	1-2, 1-3
WE-2: I was aware of what my partner was doing	5.39 (0.85)	5.00 (1.33)	4.67 (0.97)	$\chi^2(2) = 9.48, p < 0.01$	None
PE-1: My partner was aware of what I was doing	5.28(0.96)	5.06 (1.06)	4.56 (1.10)	$\chi^2(2) = 9.49, p < 0.01$	None
TLX: Overall Workload	38.50 (24.70)	19.40 (16.00)	22.20 (15.40)	$\chi^2(2) = 10.6, p < 0.01$	1-2, 1-3
SUS: System Usability Scale	58.10 (22.20)	83.30 (14.30)	78.90 (13.80)	$\chi^2(2) = 13.2, p < 0.01$	1-2, 1-3

Table 1. Questions from [14]: (WS) WebSurface[27], (MO) Mobisurf[23], (WE) WeSearch[16], (PE) Permulin[10]. Questions were 7-point Likert scale (results range from 0-6, higher is better). TLX is from 0 (lowest) to 100 (highest), SUS is from 0 (worst) to 100 (best). Means with standard deviations are presented across Conditions. A Friedman test was conducted with *post hoc* Bonferroni corrected Wilcoxon tests.

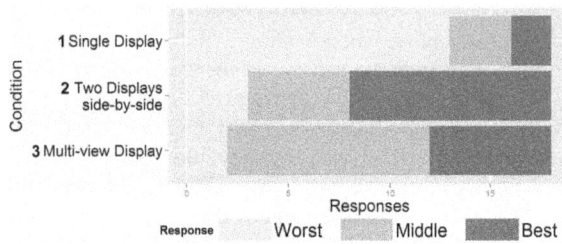

Figure 3. User ranking – Friedman test $\chi^2(2) = 10.3$ p < 0.01, *post hoc* Bonferroni corrected Wilcoxon test showed differences between 1-2 and 1-3

Viewing and Interaction

Examining the viewing patterns and behaviours exhibited in Conditions 2 and 3, we find significant differences in terms of viewing behaviour (see Table 2 and Figure 4). This difference is visualized in Figure 4, where we can see that in Condition 2 ~50% of overall viewing and ~90% of viewing instances were accounted for in viewing instances which lasted under 10 seconds; in comparison, Condition 3 demonstrates that users relied on much longer views, showing a clear difference in behaviour.

	Condition		
	2	3	RM-Anova
Mean Duration of Views (secs)	3.39 (3.51)	40.64 (37.40)	$\chi^2(1) = 16.6, p < 0.01$
Gini: Interaction	0.839 (0.27)	0.641 (0.34)	$\chi^2(1) = 3.75, p = 0.053$
Gini: Viewing	0.394 (0.233)	0.447 (0.306)	$\chi^2(1) = 0.356, p = 0.55$

Table 2. Mean (SD) viewing and Interaction comparison between Conditions 2 and 3. Gini coefficients show equality regarding how likely users were to view or interact with either Android view, 1 is maximum inequality, 0 is maximum equality.

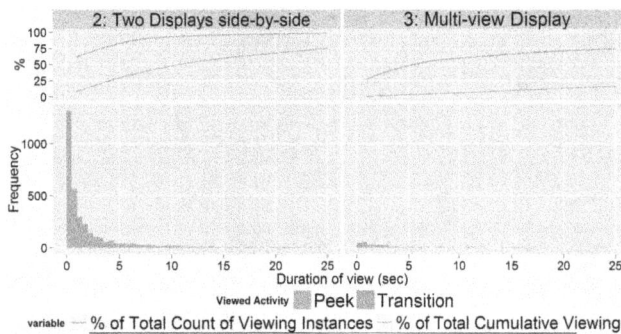

Figure 4. Individual viewing behaviour across participants. Bottom: Histogram (0.5 second bins) counting number of instances of viewing at a given duration. Top: Graph presenting percentage of overall cumulative viewing and percentage of overall number of viewing instances.

In terms of how this viewing was accomplished in our multi-view display, Table 3 demonstrates that our *transition* behaviour was utilized for the majority of this viewing, with the *peek* gesture accounting for only ~5% (~32 seconds) worth of viewing on average. Given that the peek gesture was intended to allow quick and casual viewing of a partners activity, the lack of usage evidenced in Figure 4 suggests that this gesture, whilst utilized, was not sufficient for providing casual awareness.

	Viewing Mechanism		
	Transition	Peek	RM-Anova
Mean Total Viewing (SD)	566.8 (36.4)	32.9 (36.4)	$\chi^2(1) = 146, p < 0.01$
Mean Duration of Views (SD)	45.98 (36.3)	8.22 (18.3)	$\chi^2(1) = 13.5, p < 0.01$

Table 3. Mean (SD) viewing for Condition 3 (multi-view display) broken down by whether a transition or peek resulted in said view.

With respect to how likely users were to view or interact with (i.e. perform touchpad or textual actions on) either virtual view (see Table 2) there were no significant differences between Conditions 2 and 3. There was a bias toward equality with respect to interaction with the multi-view display, however this was likely due to the fact that once a user performed a transition in Condition 3, they were free to interact with the view they had transitioned to. In Condition 2, these transitions were typically managed by gaze, thus users would have to explicitly perform the transition gesture to then interact with this view. This suggests an interesting benefit of multi-view displays when coupled with touchpad remote controls: inputs can always be routed to the view the user is attending to. For a MDG system to accomplish this would require gaze tracking, a different input modality or additional effort on behalf of the user to manage which display they were interacting with, effort which the results of Condition 2 suggest users were unlikely to undertake.

We also asked about the acceptability of using a shared audio space. We found that being able to hear audio coming from both displays was less acceptable in the multi-view Condition compared to the two displays (Condition 2 mean=3.50 sd=2.15; Condition 3=2.61, sd=1.85, 0=Unacceptable, 6=Acceptable; no statistically significant difference).

Discussion

Our results demonstrated that a multi-view TV is preferable to a single-view TV, which is not entirely surprising: as much as we can design an interface for multi-user use, the physical bottleneck of having to share the display inevitably negatively affects performance. The comparison between our multi-view display and the two physical displays did however demonstrate some marked differences not in how well users perceived their ability to collaborate or gain awareness of each others activity, but in how this awareness was accomplished. The two physical displays in Condition 2 were used to facilitate a casual and continual awareness of the activity of the other participant, through a multitude of shorter glances at each display. In contrast, the multi-view condition featured much longer views of each virtual view. Whilst we attempted to facilitate the ability to gain casual awareness through the *peek* gesture, this difference in viewing behaviour suggests that casual awareness is more readily accomplished by gaze, and not through system functionality. Whilst having two displays is marginally preferable to multi-view, it is unlikely that this would be an acceptable configuration in the home, thus these results suggest we must design to accommodate for casual awareness.

STUDY 2: CASUAL AWARENESS IN MULTI-VIEW TV

The results of our first study raised a significant question. If perceived awareness and ability to collaborate was not significantly different between the two-display and multi-view conditions, but the way in which this awareness was accomplished was (with much shorter glances between displays), should we attempt to enable this more casual, continual gaze based awareness, and how? Incorporating continual and casual awareness necessitates a compromise with respect to distraction due to other user's activity. Some aspect of the user's physical view must be used to provide this awareness. This goes against one of the primary aims of our initial study, which was to develop a set of behaviours that would allow for management of multiple views whilst not compromising the users current physical view in terms of distraction, aspect ratio and utilized screen. To study this, we designed a system that could answer the following questions:

- How much of their physical view are users willing to sacrifice to gain a casual awareness of other virtual views?

- Given the ability to transition between a casual awareness mode and a fullscreen mode, how would users appropriate such a system? Would they rely on only one mode, or use both, and if so to what degree would they use both modes?

We designed two additions to our previous multi-view TV system, applying the concept of the casual–focused continuum [22] to awareness. The first was to give users the ability to vary their engagement with others by directly controlling how much of their personal physical view was given up to awareness of what is happening in virtual views other than that which they are currently interacting with (see Figure 5). This was accomplished through the use of a slider on the touchpad (see Figure 6). At its extremes, it would devote the majority of the user's physical view to either to the virtual view the user was interacting with, or the other available virtual view; as the slider moves to the center of the touchpad, the user's physical view would begin to be split evenly between both virtual views.

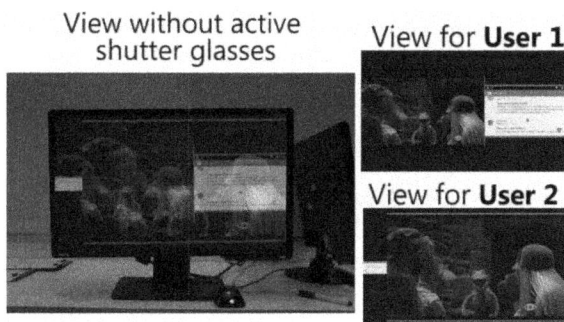

Figure 5. Example of two users in the dynamic split-screen mode, with different levels of engagement with each others activity. The user's currently interactive virtual view is always on the right of the physical view.

We anticipated that this mechanism could encompass a variety of behaviours, from selecting an appropriate ratio between the virtual views as a one-off, or repeatedly employing the slider to dynamically change the ratio between the virtual views as and when required, for example allowing users to be aware of a trailer their partner might be watching in the other virtual view. Through this, we hoped to establish if there were any norms with respect to how much of the physical view users were willing to give up for casual awareness. It is important to note that the aspect ratio of the content being viewed was preserved at all times, thus resulting in portions of the screen remaining unused, as can be seen in Figure 6.

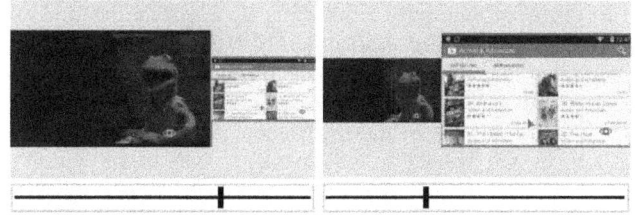

Figure 6. Example of the dynamic split-screen slider design. Here we see a user's physical view (shaded grey) being transformed Left: from a bias toward the currently non-interactive virtual view on the left; Right: to a new bias toward the interactive virtual view on the right.

The second addition was the ability to transition between this casual awareness mode and the fullscreen / fully-focused awareness mode that was the multi-view display in the previous study. As such, we incorporated a 3-finger tap gesture that would allow users to switch between the casual awareness mode, utilizing whatever screen ratio it was previously set at, and the fullscreen awareness mode. In both modes, the *transition* and *peek* behaviours functioned as before; in casual awareness mode, these actions resulted in the two virtual views swapping positions for that user.

Implementation And Experimental Design

The implementation was the same as the first study, aside from the two additional interactions. Transitions between modes, use of the slider and transitions between views were all animated, with changes to the slider affecting the rendering in real-time. Users could interact with only one virtual view at a time; this interactive view was always to the right of the user's screen, and signified with a grey border.

For this study, we had three Conditions. They were *(1) Multi-view display* which was the fullscreen multi-view display from the previous study, serving as a baseline for new iterations of our multi-view design; *(2) Dynamic Split-Screen Multi-view* which was a display that provided only the casual awareness mode; and *(3) Selective Multi-view* which provided users with the ability to switch between the modes from Conditions 1 and 2 using a 3-finger tap. As the aims of this study were primarily investigating how users would appropriate a system which supported both casual and fullscreen awareness behaviours, we chose not to counter-balance all Conditions. Instead, we counter-balanced with respect to Conditions 1 and 2, before moving on to Condition 3. This was done so that users received significant training with respect to using the fullscreen and casual awareness systems before using the dual-mode system in Condition 3. With respect to measures, all transitions between views and modes were logged in order to see both users default behaviour in each condition, and how they appropriated our selective multi-view system. The same task design and post-Condition questionnaires were utilized as from the previous study, with the addition of asking users how distracting they found their partner's activity and how in control they felt regarding awareness of their partner's activity. Users had access to the same set of applications as before. There were new 7 pairs of participants, 14 users in all (mean age=26.4, SD=3.3, 14 male) that again knew each other (friends, family etc.), recruited from University mailing lists.

Results

In terms of our questionnaire analysis from the previous study, we found that whilst the fullscreen Condition was often rated the poorest in terms of ability to collaborate, awareness, and distraction there were no significant differences between Conditions. Additionally, there were no significant differences with respect to workload or system usability.

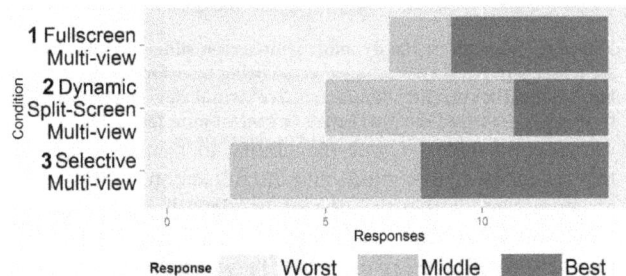

Figure 7. User ranking (lower is better) ordered by mean ranking - Friedman test $\chi^2(2) = 1.71$ p = 0.42.

There were no significant differences with respect to user rankings (see Figure 7), however, there was a somewhat dichotomous split between users preferring either the selective mode or the fullscreen mode. Similarly, with respect to the proportion of viewing and interaction between the virtual views, there were no significant differences (see Table 4).

	Condition			RM-Anova
	1	2	3	
Interaction	0.73 (0.29)	0.65 (0.29)	0.75 (0.35)	$\chi^2(2) = 1.39, p = 0.5$
Viewing	0.47 (0.25)	0.57 (0.29)	0.55 (0.32)	$\chi^2(1) = 1.39, p = 0.5$

Table 4. Mean (SD) Gini coefficients for viewing and interaction. Gini coefficients show how likely users were to view or interact with virtual view. 1 is maximum inequality, 0 is maximum equality.

Casual vs. Fullscreen Awareness

Figure 9 details how the usage of our selective multi-view system compared to our comparative baselines. Here we see a

surprisingly even split between behaviour usage in our selective multi-view system. Every capability, aside from the peek gesture, was utilized to a similar degree. Significantly, the most utilized function was our gesture for switching between fullscreen and dynamic modes. Transitions between virtual views occurred in both modes, however somewhat diminished in the dynamic mode, supplanted by use of the slider for enacting changes in screen ratio.

	Viewing Mechanism		RM-Anova
	Dynamic Mode	Fullscreen Mode	
Mean Total Viewing (SD)	206.0 (212.0)	274.0 (212.0)	$\chi^2(1) = 2.23, p = 0.136$
Mean Duration of Views (SD)	26.6 (33.3)	30.5 (34.2)	$\chi^2(1) = 0.291, p = 0.589$

Table 5. Viewing for Selective Multi-view display, broken down by whether the display was in Dynamic or Fullscreen mode.

Indeed users appeared to split their viewing between the Dynamic and Fullscreen modes relatively evenly, as evidenced in Table 5. In examining this split per user in Figure 8, we can see that the majority of users split their viewing time between modes equally. However, there were 3 users who somewhat favoured fullscreen mode and 3 who almost entirely favoured fullscreen mode.

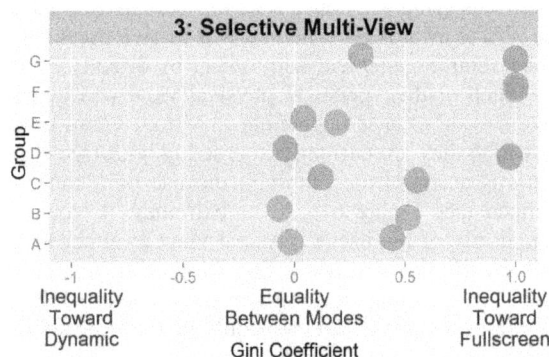

Figure 8. Directed Gini coefficient viewing in Dynamic and Fullscreen modes by group and participant (coloured) for Selective Multi-view. As an example, -1 indicates complete inequality toward the Dynamic mode, meaning users spent the entire duration in that mode. Jitter was added to Group axis in order to allow overlapping pairs to be differentiated.

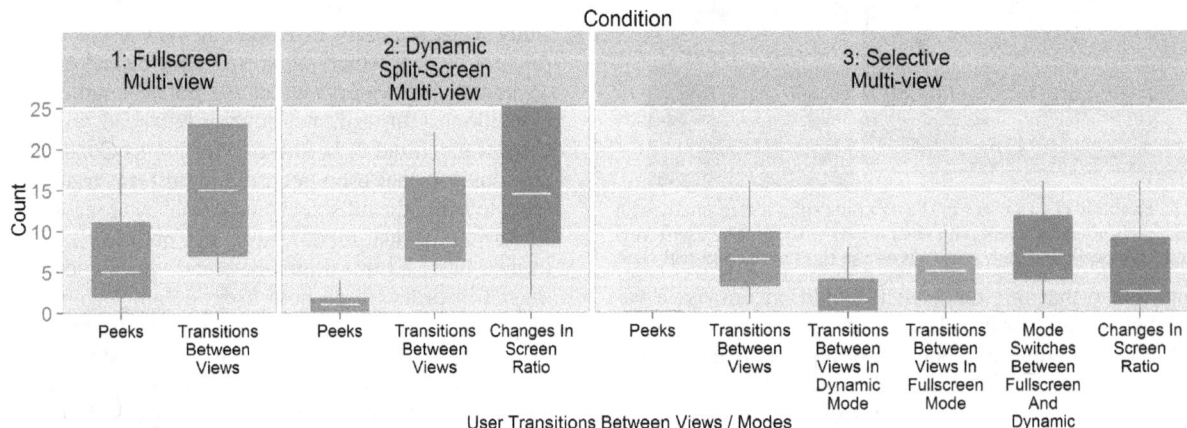

Figure 9. Boxplot of inter-quartile range of display management actions available to users: peeks (a non interactive look), transitions between views (moving between virtual views), changes in screen ratio (a slider manipulation), and mode switches between fullscreen and dynamic states.)

Usage of Casual Awareness Mode

Figure 10 visualizes the usage of the slider bar to show how much of the display the user was willing to dedicate to casual awareness. In Condition 2, we can see two clear peaks, meaning that users were typically moving between using ~8% and ~31% of the width of the display for casual awareness. In Condition 3, there was a much wider variety of usage, with peaks at 7%, 20%, 43%, 67% and 95%.

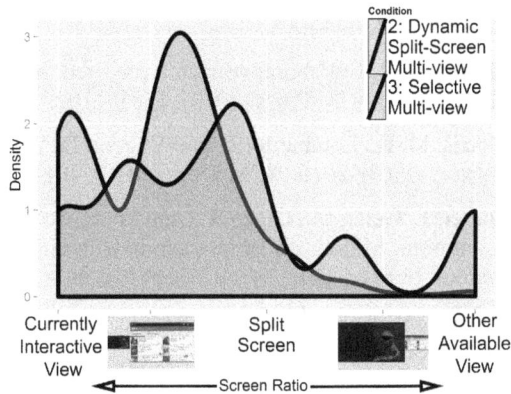

Figure 10. Kernel density plot of probability of distribution of slider values, determining the ratio by which the two virtual views are displayed. Left is biased toward the view the user is interacting with, right is biased toward the other available view, typically used by their partner. Condition 2 peaks at 8%, 31%; Condition 3 at 7%, 20%, 43%, 67%, 95%

Discussion

Our results indicate some interesting behaviours regarding how much of the display users were willing to allocate to awareness of others' activity. Users of the selective multi-view display dynamically varied awareness of their partners activity, the majority of the time dedicating between 7% and 43% of the display to this, but occasionally dedicating the majority of the display to awareness, whilst either retaining the ability to interact (the peak at 67%), or forfeiting interaction entirely by making the interactive view essentially non-visible (95%). We suggest that this approach could be used to determine empirically how much of a given display should be used for casual awareness (likely varying based on the physical properties of the display). However, given the dynamic usage exhibited it would be worthwhile to expose this functionality to users, if not in a continuous form then perhaps a discrete slider moving through derived ratios.

With respect to how users appropriated our selective multi-view system, our management behaviours were utilized in both casual and fullscreen / focused modes, with some users reporting that, in the fullscreen mode, having the ability to transition between views was conveniently like having a "previous channel" button. Notably, three users were entirely unwilling to use the dynamic mode, instead remaining in fullscreen mode for the duration of the Condition. This suggests that in a consumer multi-view system, the ability to transition between views without compromising the maximal rendering of content on the display is an important property. However, there is also significant value in incorporating the ability to be casually aware of the activity of other views, for example when performing independent activity but with some shared aspect such as video content.

GENERAL DISCUSSION & FUTURE WORK

Through our two studies we have demonstrated a viable design for a two-user, multi-view TV display. Our initial multi-view display was significantly better than the single shared display in terms of the ability to collaborate and operate independently, demonstrating a set of behaviours which allowed users to effectively share usage of the TV display whilst minimizing the impact on each others' physical view and capability to interact effectively. However, a viewing comparison between our multi-view display and an ideal awareness display using two TVs indicated significant differences in terms of how this awareness was accomplished, with much shorter casual glances occurring in the ideal case.

Given this, we iterated upon the design of our multi-view TV display, incorporating mechanisms to allow users to transition between casual and focused states, and dynamically determine their level of engagement when in a casual state. The usage of this "selective" multi-view system confirmed the importance of both modes, demonstrating that given the ability, users will transition between modes and vary their engagement with others' activity in both modes. In the fullscreen mode, engagement was varied through transition gestures, whilst in the casual awareness mode users dynamically varied their engagement through use of our view slider for controlling the amount of display given over to casual awareness.

With respect to future work, there are a number of interesting areas. Examining the usage and effect of multi-view displays across different collaborative tasks might have a significant impact on the results, and thus the contexts in which multi-view might prove most useful. There is also the issue of effectively using the physical display area when in casual awareness mode. Our approach involved scaling virtual views whilst preserving aspect ratio, resulting in parts of the screen being under-utilized. We would suggest that for certain types of content (e.g. video) it may be acceptable to truncate this content, presenting only a portion of the virtual view sufficient to provide awareness whilst maximizing usage of the screen. Similarly, there may be ways of communicating sufficient awareness in a more discrete and unobtrusive fashion e.g. textually.

There are additionally questions regarding scale and appropriation: in scaling the interactions up to support more than two views, and more than two users, how many views/users are manageable before the complexity undermines the benefits of such a TV? And what kind of social impact might such a display might have in the home. Would users transition from devices to the the more shareable TV for some subset of their activities? Answering this would require a longitudinal deployment and the availability of an HD, glasses-free multi-view display, however this paper does provide the foundations for such future work.

Finally, for multi-view to work across a breadth of media tasks, solutions will be required to either help users in managing a shared audio space (preventing potentially frustrating conflicts), or provide personal and private audio spaces in an acceptable manner (i.e. excluding previously used solutions such as in-ear headphones that impact socialization).

CONCLUSIONS

This paper has presented two studies iterating upon the design of an Android-based two-user multi-view TV. Through this process, we have established a set of functionality necessary for users to be able to operate independently and collaboratively using a multi-view TV. We suggest that given the findings of this paper, multi-view TVs should ideally support both transitions between views (and thus independent and shared activity), and transitions between focused fullscreen usage, and usage supporting casual awareness of other pertinent activity. Furthermore, there appears significant merit in giving users the ability to dynamically determine their requisite level of awareness based on their engagement with others' activities in this casual awareness state. This research demonstrates that multi-view TVs have the potential to supplement or supplant the secondary device usage that is now commonplace in the home, bringing interaction and activity back toward a shared-and-shareable focal point, the TV.

ACKNOWLEDGMENTS

This work was supported in part by Bang & Olufsen and the EPSRC. This publication only reflects the authors' views.

REFERENCES

1. Agrawala, M., et al. The two-user Responsive Workbench. In *Proc. SIGGRAPH '97*, ACM Press (Aug. 1997), 327–332.

2. Ballendat, T., Marquardt, N., and Greenberg, S. Proxemic interaction. In *Proc. ITS 2010*, ACM Press (2010), 121–130.

3. Brooke, J. SUS-A quick and dirty usability scale. *Usability evaluation in industry* (1996).

4. Dodgson, N. A. Multi-view autostereoscopic 3D display. In *Stanford Workshop on 3D Imaging*, Stanford University (2011).

5. Gross, T. Supporting Effortless Coordination: 25 Years of Awareness Research. vol. 22 (June 2013), 425–474.

6. Gross, T., et al. User-Centered Awareness in CSCW-Systems. *International Journal of Human-Computer Interaction 18*, 3 (2005), 323–360.

7. Kitamura, Y., et al. Interactive stereoscopic display for three or more users. In *Proc. SIGGRAPH '01*, ACM Press (Aug. 2001), 231–240.

8. Kreitmayer, S., Laney, R., Peake, S., and Rogers, Y. Sharing bubbles. In *Proc. UbiComp '13 Adjunct*, ACM Press (Sept. 2013), 1405–1408.

9. Kulik, A., et al. C1x6: A stereoscopic six-user display for co-located collaboration in shared virtual environments. In *Proc. SIGGRAPH Asia '11*, ACM (2011), 188:1–188:12.

10. Lissermann, R., et al. Permulin: mixed-focus collaboration on multi-view tabletops. In *Proc. CHI '14*, ACM Press (2014), 3191–3200.

11. Lucero, A., et al. Mobile collocated interactions: Taking an offline break together. *interactions 20*, 2 (Mar. 2013), 26–32.

12. Matusik, W., Forlines, C., and Pfister, H. Multiview user interfaces with an automultiscopic display. In *Proc. AVI '08*, ACM Press (May 2008), 363.

13. McGill, M., Williamson, J., and Brewster, S. A. How to lose friends & alienate people. In *Proc. TVX '14*, ACM Press (June 2014), 147–154.

14. McGill, M., Williamson, J., and Brewster, S. A. Mirror, mirror, on the wall. In *Proc.TVX '14*, ACM Press (June 2014), 87–94.

15. Morris, M. R. Collaborative search revisited. In *Proc. CSCW 2013*, ACM Press (2013), 1181–1192.

16. Morris, M. R., Lombardo, J., and Wigdor, D. WeSearch. In *Proc. CSCW 2010*, ACM Press (2010), 401–410.

17. Müller, J., Geier, M., Dicke, C., and Spors, S. The boomroom: Mid-air direct interaction with virtual sound sources. In *Proc. CHI '14*, ACM (2014), 247–256.

18. Nacenta, M. A., et al. The LunchTable. In *Proc. PerDis 2012*, ACM Press (2012), 1–6.

19. Newton, T. Digital Divorce: 24 per cent of couples watch on-demand TV in different rooms. recombu.com, 2013.

20. Ofcom. Communications Market Report, 2012.

21. Ofcom. Communications Market Report, 2013.

22. Pohl, H., and Murray-Smith, R. Focused and casual interactions: Allowing users to vary their level of engagement. In *Proc. CHI 2013*, ACM (2013), 2223–2232.

23. Seifert, J., et al. MobiSurf. In *Proc. ITS 2012*, ACM Press (2012), 51–60.

24. Shoemaker, G. B. D., and Inkpen, K. M. Single display privacyware. In *Proc. CHI '01*, ACM Press (2001), 522–529.

25. Terrenghi, L., et al. A taxonomy for and analysis of multi-person-display ecosystems. In *Personal and Ubiquitous Computing*, no. 8 (2009), 583–598.

26. Thinkbox. TV Together: a very social medium, 2013.

27. Tuddenham, P., et al. WebSurface. In *Proc. ITS 2009*, ACM Press (2009), 181–188.

28. Turkle, S. *Alone Together: Why We Expect More from Technology and Less from Each Other*. Basic Books, Inc., Jan. 2011.

29. Wallace, J. R., et al. Investigating teamwork and taskwork in single- and multi-display groupware systems. In *Personal and Ubiquitous Computing*, no. 8 (2009), 569–581.

30. Wallace, J. R., et al. Collaborative sensemaking on a digital tabletop and personal tablets. In *Proc. CHI 2013*, ACM Press (2013), 3345–3354.

31. You, W., et al. Studying vision-based multiple-user interaction with in-home large displays. In *Proc. HCC 2008*, ACM Press (2008), 19–26.

First Person Omnidirectional Video: System Design and Implications for Immersive Experience

Shunichi Kasahara
Sony CSL, The University of Tokyo
Tokyo, Japan
kasahara@csl.sony.co.jp

Shohei Nagai
The University of Tokyo
Tokyo, Japan
shohei.nagai14@gmail.com

Jun Rekimoto
Sony CSL, The University of Tokyo
Tokyo, Japan
rekimoto@acm.org

ABSTRACT

Fully recording and sharing an immersive experience is one of the ultimate goals of media technology. As extensive technical evolution, omnidirectional video is one of promising media to capture an immersive experience. First person omnidirectional video provides a unique experience of world through someone elses perspective. However, difficulties in wearable camera design and cybersickness induced by shaky video has been obstacle to explore applications of first person omnidirectional video. In this research, we introduce the design and implementation of "JackIn Head" a system including a wearable omnidirectional camera and image stabilization to alleviate cybersickness. Our evaluation revealed the alleviation of cybersickness. Then we report the series of workshops to explore user experience and applications in actual use cases such as virtual travel and virtual sports. We have compiled design implications about cybersickness and motion, immersive sensation, visualization and behavior data of spectators in experience with first person omnidirectional video.

Author Keywords

First person; Omnidirectional video; Wearable camera; Image processing; immersive experience;

ACM Classification Keywords

H.5.1 Information Interfaces and Presentation (I.7): Multimedia Information Systems- video; H.5.2 Information Interfaces and Presentation (I.7): User Interfaces - interaction styles, evaluation, User-centered design

INTRODUCTION

Recording and sharing own experience completely has been an ultimate goal of media technology. As envisioned by the SF movie Brainstorm [25], recording and sharing immersive sensations will allow us to virtually experience what we could not experience by our own. Small wearable wide-angle cameras such as the GoPro[1] enables to record a video of the ones

---

[1] GoPro http://gopro.com/

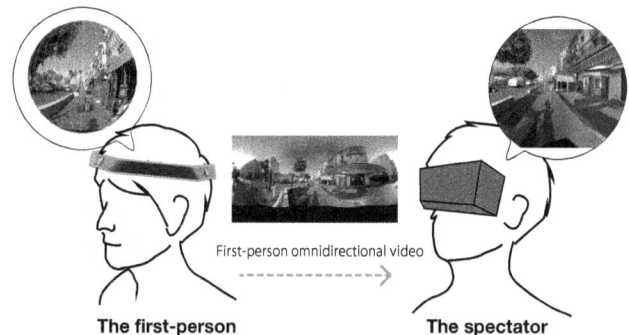

Figure 1. JackIn Head Overview, immersive experience record and playback architecture with a wearable omnidirectional camera.

perspective and then be shared with others. Whereas ordinary cameras capture only a limited field of view in front of them, omnidirectional video cameras are able to capture the entire space. Such a Omni-directional video (ODV) provides spectator experience with impressive and immersive sensations as if they were present in.

There have been active research efforts related to ODV ecosystem in several domains: capturing technology, displaying technology, interaction and control interface technology for ODV, and contents distribution systems for online video workflow. These series of research and development will make ODV more common and bring highly immersive user experience in the context of interactive television and online videos. Therefore, first person omnidirectional video (FODV) will bring a lot of opportunities for ODV applications. Bleumers et al. [6] recently presented a number of interesting findings regarding users expectations of ODV, especially FODV will play important role in various applications such as entertainment, sports viewing, education and simulation training, news casting and therapy.

Although design implications for FODV have been required, it has not been well explored due to two major difficulties. The first is design of capturing device for FODV. A wearable omnidirectional camera attached to the head is one of reasonable design to acquire video from one's perspective. However, there is still no existing solution to satisfy all of robustness, wearability and eye-level position. Another issue is quality of the first-person video from wearable cameras. Video from wearable cameras are often shaky due to the body movement during capturing. Viewers often feel dizzy when watching video from wearable cameras, and this gets worse when the visual experience is immersive on a large screen or HMD [11]. This is called as cybersickness. Then this should be investigated to make better user experience.

Our aims are to provide a solution for these existing problems, and to explore design implication of FODV with actual use cases. In this study, we proceed following research steps. We first describe "JackIn Head" system design including a wearable omnidirectional camera and image processing for stabilizing FODV (Fig 1). Then we evaluate how our system alleviates cybersickness and we collect findings from the investigation and interviews. After we understand the risk and prevention of cybersickness with FODV, we perform series of demos and workshops with three activities to prove actual benefit of FODV and collect insight from participants. The results of our inquiries and observations inform design implication and possible applications of FODV.

The main contributions of this paper are: (1) a system design including capturing device and image processing for stabilizing FODV, (2) an investigation of cybersickness and user experience of the system, and (3) design implications for FODV from series of demo and workshop with our proposed FODV system. Out system design and implication will contribute to make FODV a significant interactive video media in ODV eco system.

RELATED WORK

User experience in omnidirectional video
Omnidirectional video is expected as a novel medium that offers immersive and interactive experience. Bleumers et al. [5] reported various users expectations of ODV, and many of them are also supposed to use first person omnidirectional video. Zoric et al. [27] investigated viewing and interaction with panorama video in a TV screen, the result informs benefits of interacting with panoramic content and design challenges including the active - passive viewing and the social aspect. Barkhuus et al. [2] show the possibilities of omnidirectional video streaming for a live performance. FascinatE project developed comprehensive eco-system that enables capture, delivery and reproduction for immersive media including ODV[19]. Decock et al. reported about a case study of an interactive performance called C.A.P.E which uses first person omnidirectional video and HMD, and inform user experience drivers for effects of presence and identification on enjoyment [8].

A series of research and development for immersive displaying technologies provide various options for ODV, such as large screen TV, light weight HMD with mobile screen [2], CAVE like spherical environment [4], HMD with head tracking [3] and projection mapping for the room [12]. In term of researches for user interface, Neng et al. [17] explore about navigation and visualization mechanisms of ODV. Second screen interface [27, 2] and mid air gesture [28] has been studied as an interface for control ODV. Ruiz et al. [21] provide comprehensive interaction design for mid-air gestures to

control ODV from individual and collocated usage. These researches effort present many possible scenarios in terms of social viewing with collocated person as well as personal immersive environments and increase the expectation of ODV contents as an interactive media.

Omnidirectional camera
Previous researches of interactive panorama video or ODV has been performed with footages from fixed position. However, in view of various possibilities in ODV, first person omnidirectional video (FODV) should be studied to expand ODV-ecosystem. There have been many approaches that acquire omnidirectional video such as hyperboloid mirror from single camera, multiple cameras, multiple mirror projection.

Recent miniaturization of image capture module and lens technology enables more compact systems and several commercial companies offer omnidirectional cameras from on-vehicle equipment [4] to handheld omnidirectional camera [5]. Another solution could be a holder for multiple wearable camera[6].

However these solutions enable wearable shooting near the first person perspective, the cameras should be located above one's head. This causes the gap between the camera viewpoint and the eye-level position of a wearer. This will lead gaze mismatching [15] and feel of hovering rather than standing at the same position as first person [5]. Furthermore, attaching cameras on top of the head causes shift of the center of gravity toward higher than one's head. This is inappropriate especially for shooting physically dynamic activities such as sports. Kondo et al. [15] proposed the capture devices system that enable eye-level recording of omnidirectional panorama video with uniform resolution with the special designed mirror. They have shot the FODV footage of actual ball sports from the POV of non-player. However to capture the first person ODV form the actual player, the robustness of the head gear and wearability has been should be solved. By considering these advantage and disadvantages in several approaches, reasonable design is required.

Cybersickness
Wearable camera footages contain a lot of shaky scenes, then viewers often become dizzy or nauseous especially with immersive visual environment. Especially in virtual reality applications, it's called "cybersickness"[24]. One of the main theories as to what causes simulator sickness is based on sensory conflict. When the perception of self-motion from visual optical flow patterns is not corroborated by inertial forces transmitted through the vestibular system, humans will experience symptoms of sickness including dizziness, disorientation, and even vomiting[13]. Moreover, an immersive visual setup such as large screen, HMD or CAVE could intensify cybersickness [11]. Inconsistency between visual movement of FODV and physical motion of spectators will cause cybersickness. Then the investigation and prevention technology for cybersickness with FODV is required.

[2]cardboard google.com/get/cardboard/
[3]Oculus rift www.oculus.com
[4]Ladybug http://www.ptgrey.com
[5]THETA theta360.com
[6]360heros http://www.360heros.com

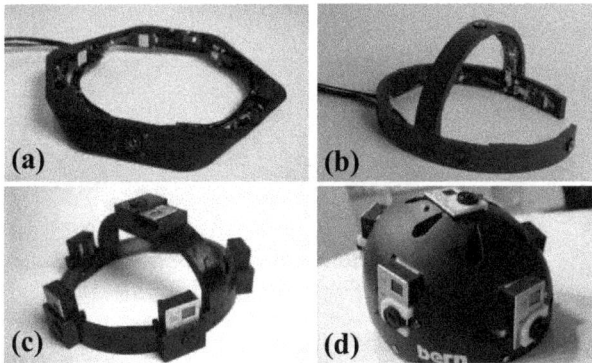

Figure 2. Variation of JackIn Head headgear. (a) and (b) are lighter version with usb cameras. (c) and (d) are HD version with six HD cameras.

Figure 3. Actual use of the headgear type-d in several situation. (a) playing the squash, (b) track, (c) giant swing on the high bar

Omnidirectional image processing and stabilization

Image stabilization is a fundamental technology to prevent cybersickness, as well as to improve quality of video. Johannes Kopf et al. proposed hyper-lapse generation, which converts first-person video into smooth time-lapse videos [16]. Omnidirectional video has been used in research relating to ego-motion estimation of the camera or self-localization[10, 1, 26], as well as omnidirectional visual immersive simulations[18]. There are various procedure to estimation rotational motion of camera, with only images [10, 26] or with the motion sensors [1]. Bazin et al. proposed a method which can estimation translational movement and rotation [3]. These technology were applied for robot navigation and vehicle control [3, 9]. The estimation of ego-motion from visual information, called as Visual Gyroscope[7], is can be applied for video stabilization. Then, to deploy these technologies for stabilization of omnidirectional video from wearable camera, special requirement of FODV such as intense rotational motion, generation of smoothed movement, and realtime feasibility for practical usage should be also considered.

SYSTEM DESIGN

In this sections, we first give a system design description of JackIn Head we developed: the system for immersive experience sharing with first person omnidirectional video. JackIn Head system includes a wearable headgear(Figure 2) with multiple camerasto capture omnidirectional video, image processing for FODV stabilization, the streaming video data and a playback system with screen or HMD. Video images from these cameras are stitched together into a spherical omnidi-

rectional video and image processing for stabilization is performed. The stabilized omnidirectional video and the head ego-motion information of video are streamed to the viewer device on the spectator side application (Fig. 1). In the spectator side, there are various options for viewing device, example setup is a HMD with head motion tracking (such as Oculus rift [7]) that the spectator uses to look around the first person visual environment.

In the following sections, the design of headgear and image processing are described in detail.

Headgear with omnidirectional camera

The headgear includes six wide-angle cameras with fix position in a rigid body. The head gear was designed with two design considerations. One is lower center of balance, which allows users to move their body and head dynamically. The high center of balance is dangerous for even usual activity. In our preliminary studies, attaching the omnidirectional camera on top of the head affects the physical movement, then weassess that it will be dangerous. Another is that the captured environment should be close to the first person viewpoint. This provides a realistic sensation of the first person perspective. This design of embedding cameras into headgear will produce gap of focal point of each cameras. However this result in noticeable gap between each cameras image especially near by objects are on image seam, we prioritize those design considerations.

We designed several versions of headgear prototype including the light weight version with USB camera (Fig 2 -(a,b)) and Figure 2 -(c,d) shows HD version with 6 HD cameras (Gopro Hero3). Although the light weight version is one of our design targets, existing USB camera module has limitation in terms of image quality and video frame rate. In this study, we employ HD version headgear to record FODV. Figure 3 shows actual use in sports context.

The range of capture is shown in Figure 4, which cover omnidirectional except for the bottom part. Each camera capture 960x1440 pixel, high frame rate (100 fps) with 122.6

---

[7]Oculus rift DK-2 : http://www.oculus.com/

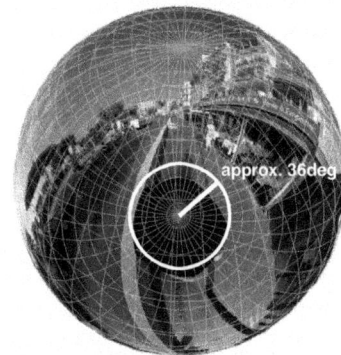

Figure 4. The range of capture area by omnidirectional camera. The headgear can capture spherical omnidirectional video except the bottom 2 x 36deg area.

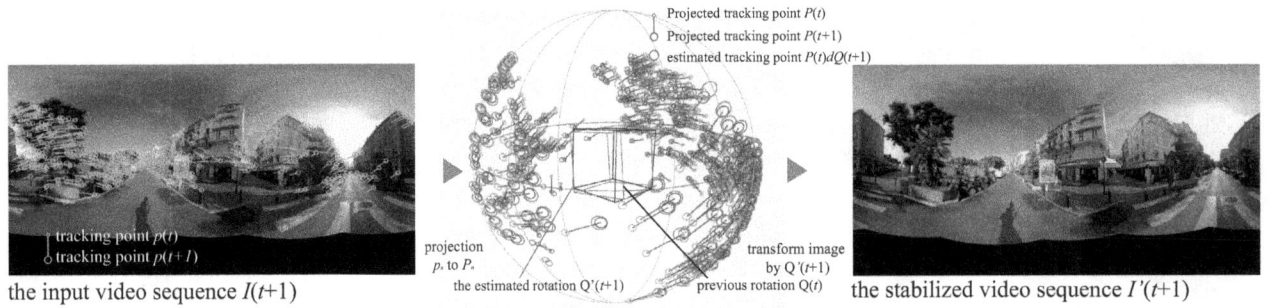

the input video sequence $I(t+1)$ the estimated rotation $Q'(t+1)$ the stabilized video sequence $I'(t+1)$

Figure 5. Image processing procedure for estimation of head rotation and stabilization.

deg horizontal and 94.4 deg vertical field of view. Camera calibration for six cameras is performed using the Omnidirectional Camera Calibration Toolbox [22]. In the computer, six video streams are stitched into an omnidirectional video as equirectangular video with a GLSL shader

Design parameter about FOV of each cameras and number of camera are trade off relationship. Wider FOV wearable camera will reduce number of camera, thus will reduce the visual gap in stitched omnidirectional video. However, there is also design trade-off in between FOV and the image quality. Through our initial exploration, longer shutter speed or lower frame rate produce image blur which cause error in stabilization. Another important technical detail is frame synchronization. Stitching multiple lower frame rate videos generates not only visual gap, but also unexpected jitter through the stabilization process. Through our initial exploration, multiple video with 100 fps (i.e. maximum temporal error is 5ms) did not cause this problem. From these conditions, we chose our current configuration for HD version head.

Image stabilization for first person ODV

In our preliminary exploration, we recorded and gather FODVs with our headgear in various activities. We assessed that image motion in FODV is mainly caused by rotation of the wearer. Then we implemented image processing for estimating of rotational motion in FODV, and image stabilization by eliminating rotational motion from FODV (Figure 5).

This stabilizing algorithm has two phases, it first calculates rotation then eliminate its rotation, then it re-produce smoothed rotation to follow the wears head direction with variable parameter as describe later. If this parameter is zero or quite small, the output footage will be **independent view** which are completely decoupled from the head motion of the wearer. By contrast, if the following parameter is larger value, the output will be noise reduced **smoothed view**, which gradually traces the head motion of the wearer.

An omnidirectional video from the headgear is treated as an equirectangular image, which is the standard format for spherical geometry such as global maps.

In each equirectangular video frame $I(t)$, image feature points $p_n(t)(n = 1000max.)$ are extracted by finding the visual corner in the equirectangular image[23]. High latitude and bottom areas are excluded from ROI for this process.

We use the pyramidal KLT method [6] to calculate the optical flow $f_n(t)$ for each $p_n(t)$. Tracked points in the next image sequence $I(t+1)$ are then estimated as $p_n(t+1) = p_n(t) + f_n(t)$.

Next, the 2-D image feature points $p_n(t+1)$ and $p_n(t)$ are converted into 3-D points $P_n(t+1)$ and $P_n(t)$ on spherical geometry with spherical polar coordinates. Here, the radius for conversion does not affect successive processes.

Then, the affine transform matrix $M(t+1)$ to describe the affine transform as $P_n(t+1) = P_n(t)M(t+1)$ is estimated using RANSAC and a differential rotation from $I(t)$ to $I(t+1)$ is acquired as quaternion $dQ(t+1)$. The rationale of using RANSAC is for handling a lot of outlier in the matching space.

Here, the estimation error is calculated. If the error $Err(t+1)$ is larger than a threshold, it is considered an estimation failure and the prediction is done using a Kalman filter instead.

$$Err(t+1) = Pn(t+1) - dQ(t+1)Pn(t)$$

By multiplying all differential rotation $dQ(i)(i = s, ...t)$ from the reference start time s to the current time t in every frame, the rotation from the reference start time can be calculated:

$$Q(t) = \prod_{i=s}^{t} dQ(i)$$

The rotation eliminated equirectangular image $I'(t)$ can then be generated by converting $I(t)$ by the inverted rotation $Q(t)^{-1}$:

$$I(t) = I(t)Q(t)^{-1}$$

Note that the sequence of $I'(t)$ is a stabilized video sequence and the sequence of quaternion $Q(t)$ represents the decoupled head ego-motion.

In practice, it often happens that the wearer is walking in a town and turns right and the spectator would like to follow in the same direction the wearer is headed. However, the process described above is just for the elimination of rotational motion, and it forces the spectator to keep heading to the right in order to follow the direction.

By observing the time sequence of quaternion $Q(t)$, in the playback application, the system evaluate whether the movement is noise or intentional motion. If the rotation movement is evaluated as intentional motion, the playback system gradually sift the viewing reference direction Q_{view} of ODV with spherical linear interpolation.

$$Q_{view}(t+1) = slerp(Q_{view}(t), Q(t), k)$$

The parameters value (k) for interpolation varies depends on the context of FODV. A smaller interpolation results **independent view** that suites for video with intense motion such as sports contexts. In contrast, A larger interpolation rate results noise reduced **smoothed view** that suites for human dairy activity.

EVALUATION OF CYBERSICKNESS

In this section we report the evaluation about how our system alleviates cybersickness and collected findings from the investigation and interviews. We conducted experiments to evaluate the cybersickness alleviation and to investigate how individual viewing experience can be achieved.

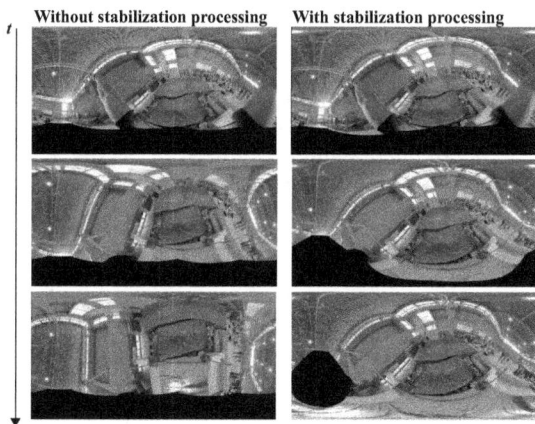

Figure 6. Example of stabilized omnidirectional video sequence.

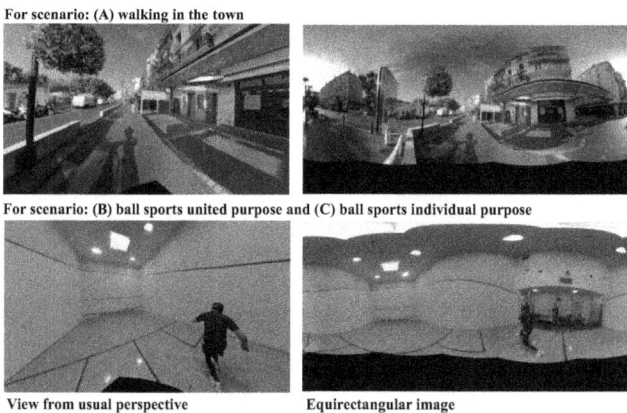

Figure 7. Sample frame from omnidirectional video for test scenario: (A) walking in the town, (B) ball sports, watching to trace the ball, and (C) ball sports, watching to trace another player. Experiment conditions are consists of these video sequences with and without Stabilization.

Experiment Procedure

JackIn Head aims for active viewing experience as well as passive viewing. Thus, to investigate the effect of activity, we designed an experiment with three scenarios: (A) virtually traveling, (B) experiencing a sport, and (C) experiencing a sport with different interest against wearer with intense motion.

Scenario (A): Walking in the town

In this scenario, we assume virtual travel in which the spectator observes an immersive scene of the walking around in an unknown town (Figure7-(A)). Omnidirectional video is captured from JackIn Head gear while walking a street in Cannes at 90 m/min. The estimated average rotational speeds in Euler angle are 12.0(pitch), 19.4(yaw), 13.5(roll) deg/sec. The maximum speeds are 185.5(pitch), 353.0(yaw), 137.5(roll) deg/sec. The participant is asked to find as many potential restaurants for lunch and dinner as possible. In this scenario, The FODV footage was stabilized as **smoothed view**.

Scenario (B): Ball sports, watching to trace the ball

In this scenario, we assume a sports experience in which the spectator observes an immersive scene of playing squash and tries to track the movement of the ball (Figure7-(B)). Omnidirectional video is captured from JackIn Head gear while the squash game in a 6.4 x 9.75 m court with another player also on the same side of the court. The estimated average rotational speeds in Euler angle are 15.7(pitch), 50.7(yaw), 20.3(roll) deg/sec, the maximum speeds are 531.2(pitch), 793.4(yaw), 63.5(roll) deg/sec. The participant is asked to track the ball as much as possible.

Scenario (C): Ball sports, watching to trace another player

In this scenario, we assume a remote assistance situation in which the spectator observes an immersive scene of the squash game and looks at the other player with difference interest. This scenario uses the same omnidirectional video (Figure7-(B)) as scenario (B) so as to compare the two scenarios. The participant acting is asked to track the other player as much as possible. In scenario (B) and (C), The FODV footage was stabilized as **independent view**.

It is assumed that scenario (A) contains a lot of unconscious movement while scenarios (B) and (C) contain intentional movement.For each scenario, the participants perform the tasks with stabilized omnidirectional video and conventional omnidirectional video. The participant uses Oculus DK2 as the HMD with a display refresh rate of 60 Hz; the movie fps is also 60 Hz.

Experiment setup

Participants perform six tasks in total, i.e. Non-stabilization or Stabilization in condition A, B, C, then we describe A-N, A-S, B-N, B-S, C-N, C-B respectively. Each task is two minutes with a recovery time of 30 minutes interval. The order of scenarios is counter-balanced, as is the order of stabilized and conventional vision.

Before and after each task, the participant filled out a simulator sickness questionnaire (SSQ) [14], which is a well-known

Average(SD)	A	B	C
No Stabilization	27.1(26.8)	12.2 (23.2)	30.5 (25.2)
Stabilization	11.8(15.2)	5.6(13.2)	0.6 (11.26)

Table 1. Overview of results for SSQ score change values, average and standard deviation. (A): walking in the town, (B): ball sports, watching to trace the ball, (C): ball sports, watching to trace another player

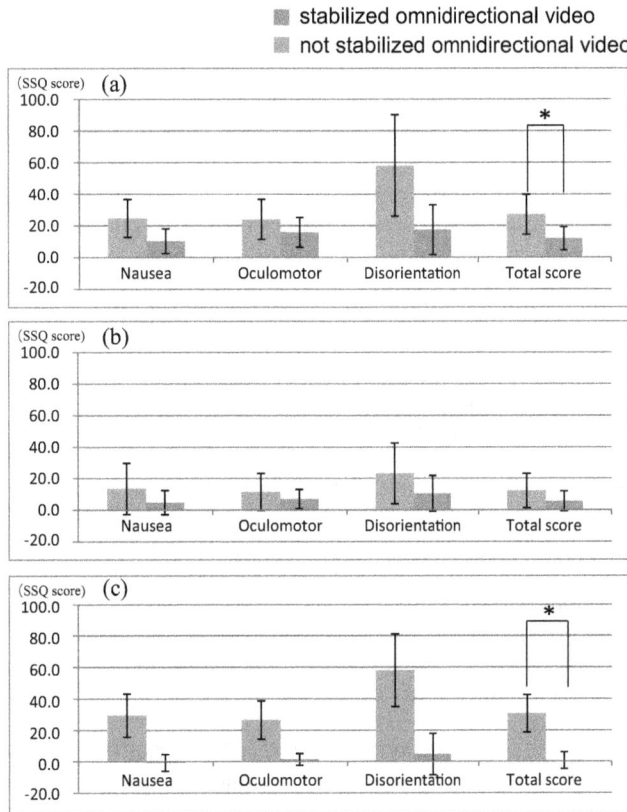

Figure 8.　Detail of results for SSQ score change values, about nausea, oculomotor discomfort, disorientation, and general cybersickness. Error bar represent 95 % confidence interval.

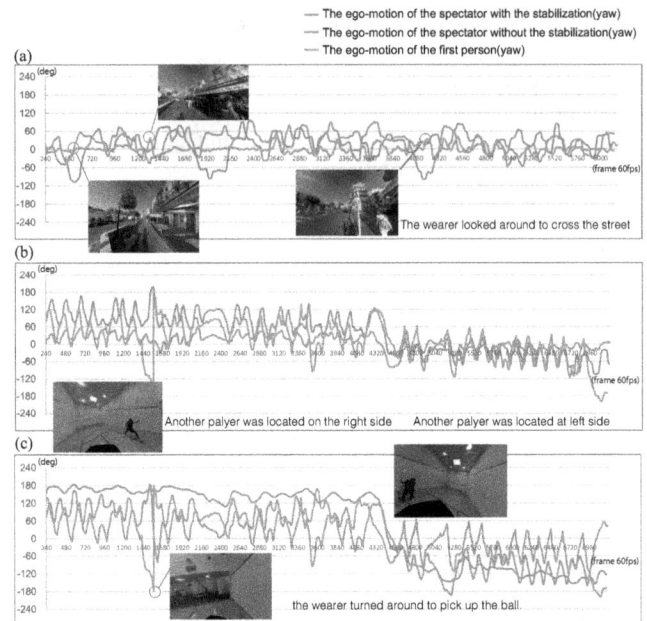

Figure 9.　The sequence of yaw rotation of the most representative sample to describe characteristics of the spectator ego-motion.

measurement tool to evaluate simulator sickness and cybersickness. The SSQ value derived from the questionnaire indicates the degree to which the participant felt nausea, oculomotor discomfort, disorientation, and general cybersickness. Here, the larger the SSQ value, the stronger the feeling of a particular symptom. Twelve volunteers aged 20-38 participated in our study after providing informed consent and were allowed to give up at any time, even in the middle of a task, although the questionnaires had to be filled out in any case. The head motion which can be acquired from the head tracking HMD was recorded during tasks.

Results of Experiment

In general, according to the averaged SSQ values, the stabilization lessened the instances of cybersickness in each scenario. In our analysis, we compare the SSQ score changes before and after each task. Table 1 shows the average and variance value of differential SSQ values for all symptoms and Figure 8 shows the detailed results from the SSQ values for both the total and detailed symptoms. There was a sig-

nificant difference ($p < 0.05$), between A-N and A-S, also between C-N and C-S. We observed that C-N was the worst condition because half of the participants gave up before task time (2 min) was completed. As for the detailed results, "Disorientation" in scenario (A) and all detailed symptoms in scenario (C) exhibited significant difference between with and without stabilization. Interestingly, in scenario (B), there was no significant difference.

Analysis and Observation

We also observed the ego-motion sequence of spectators and wearer. Fig 9 shows the sequence of yaw rotation of the most representative sample to describe characteristics. The head motion of spectators can be acquired from head tracking HMD, and the head motion of first-person was acquired from image processing. After completion of all tasks, we conducted interviews about how they felt during viewing FODV, what made them sick and what created good experience.

The analysis of time series data and interviews yields a set of findings that is variable insight and challenges to improve user experience.

Active viewing behavior or not

In scenario (A) without stabilization (A-N) , almost all participants reported that they felt strong disorientation when sudden motion in the direction opposite to their intention occurred. This phenomenon was also evident in C-N in Fig. 9. Interviews with participants who did not feel much disorientation in these conditions revealed that they were able to identify what made them feel disoriented during the task and then refrained from moving their heads as much as possible. Because an active viewing behavior is a significant interaction in ODV viewing experience. In this sense, the stabilization would be a beneficial feature in FODV application. Furthermore, the interview and time sequence data of condition (A)

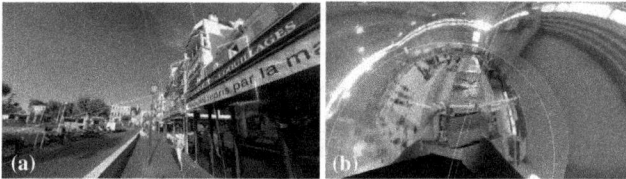

Figure 10. Overlay indication of wearer's head direction in omnidirectional video. (a) walking in the town, (b) giant swing on the high bar.

reveals that many head motion of spectators stem from the own motivation of spectators in A-S, on the other hands, the head motion in A-N was induced from the motion of FODV as noise.

Synchronization and Asynchronization
In condition (B) this is evident that the wearer was also tracing the ball as well, and the spectator didn't need to trace it actively, in contrast to in condition B-S, the spectator had to trace the ball by their own. This phenomena are also obvious with concurrently synchronized ego-motion sequence in Figure 9. Here note that the condition B-N also shown this synchronous behavior, even though both head motions do not have completely the same value, the direction of the motions was consistent.

Although there is no significant difference between B-N and B-S, seven of twelve participants made comments like "I had a realistic feeling in B-N conduction". Analysis of the head motion sequence (Figure 9) suggests that synchronization in motion of FODV and the spectator will lead lessen cybersickness, and also produce more realistic sensations.

Existence of first person
In interviews after all tasks, several participants reported that condition A-N was worse than C-N, even though both caused conflicted motion. The reason for this can possibly be summed up in the comment that "in the motion in condition A-N, I could not predict the motion of the video so, even the motion itself was small, I felt stronger sickness".

In addition, other participants commented that "in stabilized FODV condition, I felt it was difficult to understand what the wearer was doing, because I counld not find a cue for movement". This indicates the head direction is an important indication of awareness, and was eliminated by stabilization.

This feedback reveals that visualization of the wearer's head direction in the immersive view for the spectator will be key in addressing these problems. We therefore implemented an overlay indication of the wearer's head direction for the viewer based on the rotation information acquired from image processing (Figure 10). We also note that, to reproduce more precise first person video, dedicated eye tracking is required along with JackIn head gear. This should be addressed as technical challenge for future work

Cybersckness induced by translational movement
Some participants commented that even with stabilization, they felt cybersickness temporarily. In depth-interviews about the moment at which cybersickness occurred, it indicated there are two cases in the stabilization footage.

The first case is a sudden change of speed in translational motion, such as lunging forward to pick up the ball in the squash scenario (B) and (C), and suddenly stopping to look around when crossing the street in scenario (A). In general, situations in which the viewer expects to experience acceleration from the visual motion caused temporal cybersickness.

The second case is walking vibrational motion where, participants feel some oculomotor discomfort. This might be caused by the vertical translational motion, which cannot be eliminated by current stabilization process. From those feedbacks, compensating for the translational acceleration change and translational vibration noise should be addressed as technical challenge for future work.

EXPLORATION THROUGH WORKSHOPS
After we found the stabilization works for prevention of cybersickness with the FODV, we performed series of demo and workshop with three activities, a virtual travel, virtual gymnastics and virtual flying experience of paraglider. We selected two sport activities because we found these physical activity will produce a lot of insight and challenges for system and user experience. In series workshops and demos, over 50 people participated our activity. The first person omnidirectional video in each demo was viewed with HMD with head tracking[8] and 15 inch laptop screen. Participants of workshop were also allowed to explore the way of viewing FODV footages, we interactively tested the various viewing experience. The results of our inquiries and observations inform set of finding and possible applications of FODV.

Virtual travel
In the this demo material, FODV that captured walking in street, beach and historical place in Cannes. A part of this material was also used for evaluation of cybersickness. Although the task duration in out experiment for cybersickness was just 2 min, many of participants in the demo enjoyed to watch longer especially with HMD. This virtual travel with beautiful landscape is generally well received. The moment that the wearer was talked by a local person provide realistic feeling such as "I was a bit upset, because the person in the video talked to me" commented from a participant. This realistic feeling was provided from the eye-level position of the headgear. However some participant complained about visual gap when watching near object especially a someone's face. Another remarkable finding among them is a possibility of revisiting own experience. The collaborator who recorded this footage commented that "I felt like I revisited this place from my own perspective. I found an interesting scene behind me that I could not see at that time".

Virtual gymnastics
To investigate the possibilities of viewing intense sport activities. We recorded FODV during the giant swing on the high bar and trampoline of gymnastics. Participants both with and without experience of gymnastics watch FODV with our system. In this workshop, we also showed the overlay indication with FODV like Figure 10.

---

[8]Oculus rift www.oculus.com

Figure 11. (a) : Example view of first person omnidirectional video of the paraglider. (b) HMD playback with a harnessfor practice greatlyincrease realistic feeling and excitement.

In general those contents were well received with both screen and HMD. The person who shot the FODV of the giant swing commented that *"For me, non stabilized version of FODV is similar to own experience. Maybe because I usually focus on the bar during the swing."*. In the other hand, Participants who haven't experience gymnastics commented that *"I could not understand what is going on without the stabilization. The indication graphics helped me understand the movement"*. One of athlete player comments that *"I like to use it for own practice, if it's more light weight"*.

Virtual flying experience of the paraglider

As envisioned by many time from a lot of participants of workshop, we also performed a workshop to examine the virtual flying experience. Participants were persons who usually experience the paraglider as their hobby or as professional. One of participants in the workshop used our headgear to capture FODV during the flight Figure 11-(a). Then we discussed the benefit of FODV and explore the way how to reproduce the experience that they are usually feel.

Many of participants excited about that they can watch the right above and even behind themselves where they could not watch during the flight. One of participant who could not have a flight that day tried our demo and commented that *"This (partially) gave me the satisfaction, I would like to use it for my parents to give virtually experience of mine"*.

Participants found a lot of beneficial use cases in training, education and promoting scenario. One of professional player comments that *"This could be useful fora virtual tutorial, a novice player can understand what will be happened and how they will feel"*. An intermediate player in participants also suggested a possibility ofskill acquisition *"I would like to watch the FODV of the professional perspective, that would be very beneficial instructional material"*. The owner of the paraglider school also mentioned that *"I usually use the GoPro to capture the flight, I would like to capture with this headgear, and use that material for a promotion of the paraglider"*.

Several participant tried our HMD playback system with a harnessfor practice that is hung from the bar, and we found it greatlyincrease realistic feeling and excitement Fig 11-(b). This especially indicates that those kind of haptic equipment to produce an imitational physical sensation with our system will achieve higher immersion.

DISCUSSION AND IMPLICATION FOR DESIGN

Technical challenges

In our studies, one of our aims is to provide technical and design solution for existing problems. Through this exploration, we have also found further technical challenges. From series of workshops with actual sports athletes, we found the headgear should be less weighted and more suitable for wear, and even flexible form factor. The stabilization also should be improved in terms of compensating for the translational acceleration and vibration noise. Due to the form factor of our headgear design, visual gaps in the omnidirectional image also should be addressed. A prior research achieved visually adaptive multi camera image stitching with image feature extraction such as faces and objects [20]. These technology will improve the quality of the first person omnidirectional video. Throughout the series of workshops, we've also got expectation about a realtime version of our system, a realtime processing will be also future technical challenge.

Design Implication

Our JackIn Head systemallow to explore design implication of FODV with actual use cases as our second aim of this research. In what follows, we summarize our findings and insights into design implications.

Cybersickness and FODV

In our evaluation of cybersickness with first person omnidirectional video, we proved that the stabilization process is fundamental feature even for short footages. The findings showed the risk of cybersickness even with footage of walking activities. Especially a conflict between the motion of the ODV and the motion of the spectator will cause an intense sickness, then we need to assess what kind of motion are contained in the video and how the spectator will watch it. Then the stabilization greatly contribute the prevention of cybersickness in immersive viewing environment. Although our investigation is focusing on viewing experience with HMD, these findings can also be useful in other viewing environment for omnidirectional video.

Visualizing motions of the first person

We found that overlaying ego-motion of the wearer in omnidirectional video will help the spectator to understand what the wearer was watching and doing. This feature was especially well received in sports context in the workshop. This design implication is valuable in various applications with a large option of viewing devices. However the current implementation only supports the head ego-motion, adding the gazing information will also open the possibilities of application in the context of professional sports player. musical performance.

Design space for first person omnidirectional video viewing

Throughout our research, we defined design space for viewing application with two dimensions. The first dimension is the activity of wearer that varies from the one physical embodiment matters (ex. sports.) to the one doesnt (ex, sightseeing, travel and shopping). The second dimension is the spectators viewing activity which varies synchronizing, passive and independent. "synchronizing" and "independent" are

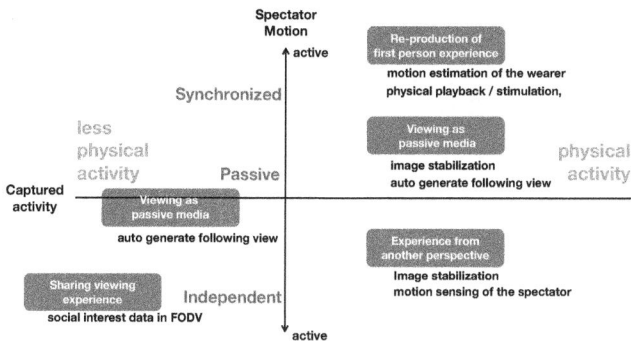

Figure 12. Design space for first person omnidirectional video. This consist of two design dimensions ; What kind of activity of the wearer was captured and how spectators will be expected to see the FODV.

responded to synchronization and asynchronization between the motion of FODV and the spectator respectively. It indicates what kind of user experience is expected, how stabilization should be applied and what other implementation matters. In our early study, the main application region was assumed to be providing another perspective in recorded FODV (Fig 12 - **re-experience from another perspective**), However, other application region has been also found alongside the design space. Other type of experience will be referred in following section.

Designing Synchronization and Asynchronization of motion
The results of our investigation of cybersickness also yield a interesting design possibility about synchronization and asynchronization between the motion of FODV (i.e. the motion of the wearer) and the motion the spectator. Synchronization of motion will lessen the induction of cybersickness, but also more interestingly, will produce an immersive realistic sensation. For instance, adaptive control of stabilization will be one of possible application to increase immersion.

The analysis of the rotational data sequence indicates that the motion synchronization will not need to be the same intensity, the smaller motion with the similar direction would be enough to induce a perceptual cues for virtual sensation. This indicates that we can augment physical sensation and allow users to feel another person's physical motion as their own (Fig 12 - **re-production of first person experience**). In other words, by fine design of FODV application, the spectator can feel the realistic sensation of a physical motion that we cannot perform in real life, such as a triple jump in figure skating.

Viewing angle information of spectators
From an interesting finding about the head motion of the spectator, the stabilization of omnidirectional video will produce meaningful behavior data of the spectator. This is because that the spectator would move their head for their interest in the stabilized ODV without distraction of the head motion of the wearer. The collected date of those information will generate meaningful information about social interest in ODV, and will be significant property in the eco-system of omnidirectional video (Fig 12 - **sharing viewing experience**). For instance, this kind of information will be an important ingre-

dient of automatic contents generation from ODV footage for the conventional passive viewing application (Fig 12 - **viewing as passive media**).

CONCLUSION
Extensive technical developments in recent years allow various immersive experience in the interactive media eco-system. Omnidirectional video is one of promising media and have capability to capture an immersive first person experience. However, difficulties in capturing device and cyber-sickness induced by the first-person video have been obstacle to explore applications of first person omnidirectional video.

In this paper we aimed to provide a solution for existing problems and to explore design implications. We first introduced the system design and implementation including capturing device and image stabilization to alleviate cybersickness. Our evaluation revealed the alleviation of cybersickness by our system. Based on our system, we performed the series of workshops to explore user experience and applications. Then we summarized our findings and insight into design implications. These design implications will contribute a further exploration of first person omnidirectional video, but also, more broadly, contribute to expand the eco-system of interactive experience of various media.

We're researching about human to human telepresence" whereby individuals can record and share their own immersive experiences and concurrently experience shared sensations and communicate with others. Toward "human telepresence , this paper presented one tangible topic that focuses recording and sharing ones immersive experience with omnidirectional video.

REFERENCES
1. Albrecht, T., Tan, T., West, G., and Ly, T. Omnidirectional video stabilisation on a virtual camera using sensor fusion. In *Control Automation Robotics Vision (ICARCV), 2010 11th International Conference on* (Dec 2010), 2067–2072.

2. Barkhuus, L., Engström, A., and Zoric, G. Watching the footwork: Second screen interaction at a dance and music performance. In *Proceedings of the 32Nd Annual ACM Conference on Human Factors in Computing Systems*, CHI '14, ACM (New York, NY, USA, 2014), 1305–1314.

3. Bazin, J.-C., Demonceaux, C., Vasseur, P., and Kweon, I. Rotation estimation and vanishing point extraction by omnidirectional vision in urban environment. *Int. J. Rob. Res. 31*, 1 (Jan. 2012), 63–81.

4. Benko, H., and Wilson, A. D. Multi-point interactions with immersive omnidirectional visualizations in a dome. In *ACM International Conference on Interactive Tabletops and Surfaces*, ITS '10, ACM (New York, NY, USA, 2010), 19–28.

5. Bleumers, L., Van den Broeck, W., Lievens, B., and Pierson, J. Seeing the bigger picture: A user perspective on 360° tv. In *Proceedings of the 10th European*

Conference on Interactive Tv and Video, EuroiTV '12, ACM (New York, NY, USA, 2012), 115–124.

6. Bouguet, J.-Y. Pyramidal implementation of the affine lucas kanade feature tracker description of the algorithm. *Intel Corporation 5* (2001).

7. Carlon, N., and Menegatti, E. Visual gyroscope for omnidirectional cameras. In *Intelligent Autonomous Systems 12*. Springer, 2013, 335–344.

8. Decock, J., Van Looy, J., Bleumers, L., and Bekaert, P. The pleasure of being (there?): an explorative study into the effects of presence and identification on the enjoyment of an interactive theatrical performance using omnidirectional video. *AI & SOCIETY* (2013), 1–11.

9. Gandhi, T., and Trivedi, M. Parametric ego-motion estimation for vehicle surround analysis using an omnidirectional camera. *Mach. Vision Appl. 16*, 2 (Feb. 2005), 85–95.

10. Gluckman, J., and Nayar, S. Ego-motion and omnidirectional cameras. In *Computer Vision, 1998. Sixth International Conference on* (Jan 1998), 999–1005.

11. Howarth, P., and Costello, P. The occurrence of virtual simulation sickness symptoms when an hmd was used as a personal viewing system. *Displays 18*, 2 (1997), 107–116.

12. Jones, B. R., Benko, H., Ofek, E., and Wilson, A. D. Illumiroom: Peripheral projected illusions for interactive experiences. In *Proceedings of the SIGCHI Conference on Human Factors in Computing Systems*, CHI '13, ACM (New York, NY, USA, 2013), 869–878.

13. Kennedy, R. S., Drexler, J., and Kennedy, R. C. Research in visually induced motion sickness. *Applied ergonomics 41*, 4 (2010), 494–503.

14. Kennedy, R. S., Lane, N. E., Berbaum, K. S., and Lilienthal, M. G. Simulator sickness questionnaire: An enhanced method for quantifying simulator sickness. *The international journal of aviation psychology 3*, 3 (1993), 203–220.

15. Kondo, K., Mukaigawa, Y., and Yagi, Y. Wearable imaging system for capturing omnidirectional movies from a first-person perspective. In *Proceedings of the 16th ACM Symposium on Virtual Reality Software and Technology*, VRST '09, ACM (New York, NY, USA, 2009), 11–18.

16. Kopf, J., Cohen, M. F., and Szeliski, R. First-person hyper-lapse videos. *ACM Trans. Graph. 33*, 4 (July 2014), 78:1–78:10.

17. Neng, L. A. R., and Chambel, T. Get around 360° hypervideo. In *Proceedings of the 14th International Academic MindTrek Conference: Envisioning Future Media Environments*, MindTrek '10, ACM (New York, NY, USA, 2010), 119–122.

18. Neumann, U., Pintaric, T., and Rizzo, A. Immersive panoramic video. In *Proceedings of the Eighth ACM International Conference on Multimedia*, MULTIMEDIA '00, ACM (New York, NY, USA, 2000), 493–494.

19. Niamut, O. A., Kochale, A., Hidalgo, J. R., Kaiser, R., Spille, J., Macq, J.-F., Kienast, G., Schreer, O., and Shirley, B. Towards a format-agnostic approach for production, delivery and rendering of immersive media. In *Proceedings of the 4th ACM Multimedia Systems Conference*, ACM (2013), 249–260.

20. Ozawa, T., Kitani, K. M., and Koike, H. Human-centric panoramic imaging stitching. In *Proceedings of the 3rd Augmented Human International Conference*, AH '12, ACM (New York, NY, USA, 2012), 20:1–20:6.

21. Rovelo Ruiz, G. A., Vanacken, D., Luyten, K., Abad, F., and Camahort, E. Multi-viewer gesture-based interaction for omni-directional video. In *Proceedings of the 32Nd Annual ACM Conference on Human Factors in Computing Systems*, CHI '14, ACM (New York, NY, USA, 2014), 4077–4086.

22. Scaramuzza, D., Martinelli, A., and Siegwart, R. A toolbox for easily calibrating omnidirectional cameras. In *Intelligent Robots and Systems, 2006 IEEE/RSJ International Conference on*, IEEE (2006), 5695–5701.

23. Shi, J., and Tomasi, C. Good features to track. In *Computer Vision and Pattern Recognition, 1994. Proceedings CVPR '94., 1994 IEEE Computer Society Conference on* (Jun 1994), 593–600.

24. Stanney, K. M., Kennedy, R. S., and Drexler, J. M. Cybersickness is not simulator sickness. In *Proceedings of the Human Factors and Ergonomics Society Annual Meeting*, vol. 41, SAGE Publications (1997), 1138–1142.

25. Trumbull, D. Brainstorm, 1983.

26. Vassallo, R. F., Santos-Victor, J., and Schneebeli, H. J. A general approach for egomotion estimation with omnidirectional images. In *Proceedings of the Third Workshop on Omnidirectional Vision*, OMNIVIS '02, IEEE Computer Society (Washington, DC, USA, 2002), 97–.

27. Zoric, G., Barkhuus, L., Engström, A., and Önnevall, E. Panoramic video: Design challenges and implications for content interaction. In *Proceedings of the 11th European Conference on Interactive TV and Video*, EuroITV '13, ACM (New York, NY, USA, 2013), 153–162.

28. Zoric, G., Engström, A., Barkhuus, L., Ruiz-Hidalgo, J., and Kochale, A. Gesture interaction with rich tv content in the social setting. In *Exploring and Enhancing the User Experience for Television, Workshop of ACM SIGCHI Conference on Human Factors in Computing Systems, CHI'13* (Paris, France, 04/2013 2013).

Interactive UHDTV at the Commonwealth Games - An Explorative Evaluation

Judith Redi
Delft University of Technology
Delft, The Netherlands
J.A.Redi@tudelft.nl

Lucia D'Acunto
TNO
The Hague, The Netherlands
lucia.dacunto@tno.nl

Omar Niamut
TNO
The Hague, The Netherlands
omar.niamut@tno.nl

ABSTRACT

In conjunction with BBC R&D experiments and demonstrations at the 2014 Commonwealth Games, an explorative field trial was conducted with a live zoomable UHD video system. The unique field trial featured the world's first live tiled streaming of 4K UHD video to end users. During the trial, we studied and evaluated the attractiveness and novelty of an interactive UHD application, and investigated system design aspects of a live UHD tiling system. In this paper, we evaluate the overall perceived quality of experience (QoE) of the application and to what extent the QoE depends on system factors and/or network conditions. We observe that interactive UHDTV is well received by users, but the delivered experience may decrease in presence of low bandwidth availability.

Author Keywords

Immersive media; ultra-high definition; quality of experience; tiled streaming; MPEG-DASH; field trial.

ACM Classification Keywords

H.5.1 Information Interfaces and Presentation: Multimedia Information Systems - evaluation/methodology

INTRODUCTION

Ultra High Definition (UHD) television plays a large role in establishing the future of the TV experience. With increased resolution (e.g. 4K), higher frame rates, larger colour space and increased dynamic range [16], viewers can expect an enriched media experience. Whereas online content providers such as Netflix are among the first to offer series and films in initial UHD formats such as 4K, live UHD broadcast of large-scale sport events are still some years away. In addition, although the added value of UHD to TV-display-based visual experiences is clear, for mobile devices such as smartphones and tablets, this is not the case. The benefit of a higher resolution is reduced with the increasing pixel density in small screens. To allow enjoying the benefits of UHD on constrained screen size of mobile devices, zoomable video systems have been recently proposed. These provision users of mobile devices for *spatial random access*, i.e. the ability to

only receive and decode specific regions of video. End users can then navigate through the video using pan/tilt/zoom commands; when zooming into a particular area, they can enjoy the full UHD resolution for that area. Several approaches exist to enable zoomable video on mobile devices, but most recent zoomable video systems are based on tiled video streaming. The advantage of tiled streaming lies in the fact that specific regions of UHD video content are made available on request, allowing a large number of users to simultaneously explore the video content at their preferred level of detail.

Although the effectiveness of tiled streaming has been validated in terms of quality of service, little is known about the quality of the user experience [2] with interactive UHDTV on mobile devices. Quality of Experience (QoE) is a multi-faceted quantity [15], that evaluates the "degree of delight or annoyance of a user with an application or system" [2]. As such, it quantifies the effectiveness of a system from a user-centered perspective. Interestingly enough, not many studies have evaluated QoE of systems based on spatial random access or on tiled video streaming, with some exceptions [18].

In this paper, we present the results of a QoE evaluation of an interactive UHD application based on tiled streaming, performed "in the wild". In conjunction with the BBC R&D demonstrations at the 2014 Commonwealth Games, we conducted an explorative field trial in households across the UK. This unique field trial featured the world's first live tiled streaming of 4K UHD video to end users, through a novel iOS application that was made available for iPads and iPhones via the Apple App Store. The trial took place in a challenging, uncontrolled setting, and required complex integration with state-of-the-art BBC R&D networks and systems. During the trial, we could study the attractiveness and novelty of the interactive UHD application, also investigating system design aspects. Specifically, we were interested in answering the following two research questions:

(i) *What is the overall perceived quality of experience of the interactive UHD application?* and (ii) *To what extent does the QoE depend on system factors and/or network conditions?*

For the first question, we were particularly interested in long-terms aspects of the experience such as app usability and endurability. Specifically for the second question, we studied the effect of the number of resolution layers on QoE - a system factor with significant impact on the computational complexity of our live tiling system - as well as objective parameters related to the network conditions.

TVX'15, June 03 - 05, 2015, Brussels, Belgium
Copyright © 2015 ACM. ISBN 978-1-4503-3526-3/15/06...$15.00
DOI: http://dx.doi.org/10.1145/2745197.2745203

The paper is structured as follows. In the following section we discuss related work. Afterwards, we revisit the basic concepts of tiled streaming and describe the system that was deployed during the field trial. Next, we elaborate on the setup of the experiments. We then present an evaluation of the experiments and finally we put forward our conclusions and possible directions for future work.

RELATED WORK

With recent capturing systems for UHD video, new types of media experiences are possible where end users have the possibility to choose their viewing direction and zooming level. Different examples of such interactive region-of-interest (ROI) video streaming have been demonstrated or deployed. For example, in the entertainment sector, web streaming and mobile app solutions are available that cover events with a 360-degree video camera. However, such solutions rely on streaming or downloading a complete spherical panorama to end user devices, where the final rendering of the interactive viewport takes place. In an alternative approach, [3] has shown a solution where rendering takes place on the server side. Here, a low-powered and low-resolution mobile phone sends a spatial request to the server, requiring the server to reframe and rescale the content accordingly before compression and streaming to the end user device. Such a solution has the drawback that the servers need to maintain a processing session and a delivery channel for each individual client. With ROI-based coding [10], a client decoder only needs to access a subset of a compressed video, i.e. the macroblocks containing the relevant pixels, and to track dependencies on other macroblocks/video regions created by the encoder. Unfortunately, this approach is not standard-compliant as it requires the decoder to have knowledge of a tree of macroblock dependencies. That is, in addition to the direct dependencies due to intra- and inter-frame prediction, this technique must also track all the coded elements that are required at the client side to avoid any drift in the entropy decoder. Such a drift would create an unrecoverable desynchronisation between the encoder and the decoder states.

Interactive ROI video streaming was further explored in-depth by [4, 5]. The authors developed various methods in the context of an interactive ROI streaming system, ClassX, for online lecture viewing, selecting tiled streaming as the best compromise between bandwidth, storage, processing and device requirements. Tiled streaming, explained in more detail in section "Tiled Streaming System Description", relies on a tiling of video into independent video streams. The ClassX system [8] allows for capture and interactive streaming of online lectures. To reduce tile switching delay, [9] studied a crowd-driven ROI prediction scheme to prefetch future selected regions. This scheme exploited user viewing statistics collected at the server to make ROI predictions. The experiments showed that crowd-driven prefetching can substantially reduce average ROI switching delays compared to a system without prefetching.

Some of the first comparisons between regular encoding and coding for tiled streaming were investigated by [10]. In particular, they compared regular monolithic streaming with tiled streaming. Their results indicated that a monolithic stream with proper choice of parameters achieves better bandwidth efficiency than tiled streams. The research was later extended with studies of user access patterns in [11]. A zoomable video system was further explored by [12]. There, the focus was on enabling low-delay interaction with high-resolution and high-quality video, with constraints on the available bandwidth and processing capabilities as encountered in current network technologies and devices. The authors studied bandwidth requirements for tiled streaming as well as the performance of media containers. The authors also noted that, since rapid seeking is required for tiled streaming, the choice for a particular media container has an impact on seeking performance. Several codec and container implementations only support seeking to the nearest I-frame only. This results in increased switching delays, as the client waits until all decoded tile frames can be synchronised.

More recently, [18] explored the perceptual effect of mixed-resolution tiles in a tiled video system, in which tiles within a video frame could come from streams with different resolutions, with the aim to trade off bandwidth and perceptual video quality. To understand how users perceive the video quality of mixed-resolution tiled video, the authors conducted a psychophysical study with 50 participants on tiled videos where the tile resolutions were randomly chosen from two resolution levels with equal probability. The experiment results showed that in many cases, a mix of tiles from HD (1920x1080p) stream and tiles from 1600x900p stream could be constructed, without being noticed by the viewers. Even when participants noticed quality degradation in videos combined with tiles from HD stream and tiles from an 960x540p stream, the majority of participants still accepted the degradation when viewing videos with low and medium motion; and more than 40% of participants accepted the quality degradation when viewing video with dense motion.

In this paper, we provide novel contributions by presenting the results of a full QoE evaluation of an interactive UHD application based on tiled streaming, performed "in the wild", and by investigating important system aspects and network usage of an operational live UHD tiling system. In particular, we study the effect of different resolution layers on the overall QoE. The scale and complexity of the field trial makes these contributions very relevant for assessing the business opportunities of the interactive UHD system and application.

TILED STREAMING SYSTEM DESCRIPTION

For our field trial, we leveraged the tiled adaptive streaming system and mechanisms as presented in [6, 17]. These have been previously demonstrated and validated during a live dance performance in Manchester, May 2013, and as a training tool for professional skiers in Schladming, host of the Alpine Skiing World Championship 2013 [7]. We revisit here the concepts behind this tiled streaming system and provide a description of the live tiling system that was employed during the field trial, and the related experiments.

Concepts of tiled streaming

Tiling refers to a spatial partitioning of a video where tiles correspond to independently decodable video streams. A tiled

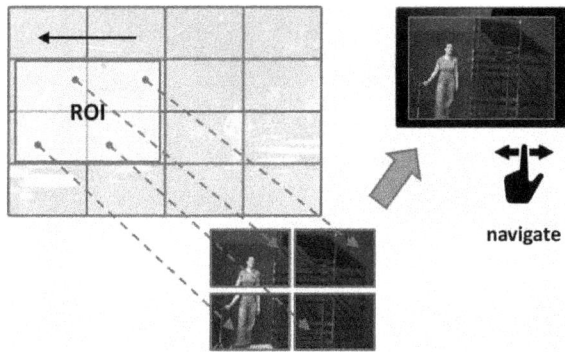

Figure 1. Tiling refers to a spatial partitioning of a video, and tiles correspond to independently decodable video streams. When navigating through a tiled video, individual tiles are requested and received by a client device, to construct a specific ROI.

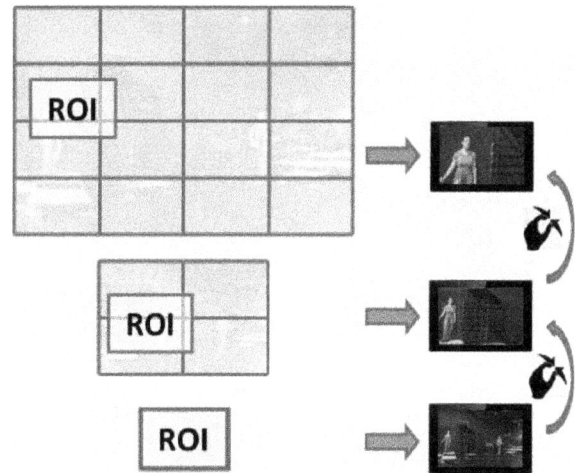

Figure 2. Multiple resolution layers are created from the original source video to increase the quality of user-defined zooming factors on tiles.

video can be obtained from a single video file or stream by partitioning each individual video frame into independently-encoded videos. Tiles are thus defined as a spatial segmentation of the video content into a regular or overlapping grid of independent videos. As depicted in Figure 1, tiling enables spatial navigation on client devices. That is, when a client device requests a specific ROI, the corresponding tiles are mapped onto the ROI and retrieved by the client device. For zoomable video, multiple resolution layers are created from the original source video. Each additional layer originates from a lower resolution version of the original video frame, tiled into a grid with fewer tiles. This multi-resolution tiling increases the quality of user-defined zooming on tiles. Once a user zooms into a ROI, the system provides the highest resolution tiles that are included in the requested region. Figure 2 depicts the use of multiple resolution layers.

Tiled adaptive streaming

Spatial segmentation can be complemented with temporal segmentation of HTTP Adaptive Streaming (HAS). This leads to a form of tiled adaptive streaming, where all tiles are temporally aligned such that segments from different tiles can be recombined to create the reassembled picture. An advantage of using HAS for the delivery of spatial tiles is that the inherent time-segmentation makes it relatively easy to resynchronise different spatial tiles when recombining tiles into a single picture or frame. The temporal segmentation can be performed according to any of the common HAS solutions (e.g. MPEG DASH or Apple HLS). Our system leverages Apple HLS, but we pursue in parallel the standardization of tiled streaming within MPEG. MPEG has recently initiated the publication process of the Spatial Relationship Description (SRD) feature, that allows an author of an MPEG-DASH media presentation description to describe how various tiles are spatially related to each other.

Live tiling system

For the trial, we designed and developed a live UHD tiling system. The system ingested a studio quality 4K video (3840x2160 pixels) at 25 fps, encoded in mezzanine MPEG-4 AVC-Intra format at 700 Mbps. This video was then transcoded to a lower bitrate of 200 Mbps. The system created 3 different resolution layers and 21 tiles; a primary layer

with the original 4K resolution with a tiling grid of 4x4 overlapping tiles of 1536x864 pixels, an intermediate layer with 2x2 tiles and a fallback layer. The transcoded stream was processed according to the following system pipeline: (i) decode the full 4K panorama as received from the ingest node, (ii) crop a tile region, (iii) encode this tile region at 4 Mbps in H.264 and (iv) segment each encoded tile stream in Apple HLS-compliant segments of 3 seconds.

The initial transcoding operation was performed due to hardware bottlenecks in the ingest node. No further transcoding was employed before segmentation, e.g. to create different bit-rates for adaptive streaming. In the application, initial playback would start when 3 segments where downloaded, giving rise to an initial startup buffer period of 9 seconds. The transcoding step at ingest was performed by an Intel Media SDK-based application, configured to exploit the encoding and decoding speed performance of the Intel Quick Sync Video feature. The machine running the transcoder was equipped with an Intel Core i5-3570K processor. The system pipeline was implemented with a number of tiling nodes that were able to provide enough processing power to sustain up to 17 parallel pipeline instances in real time, and consisted of two machines both equipped with an Intel Core i7 4770R processor. As the system had a limit on the number of tiles it could create in real time, and thus, on the number of resolution layers it could process, the addition of an intermediate resolution layer with a 2x2 tiling grid put a limit on the system usage to offline scenarios. As such, determining the perceived value of this intermediate layer was an interesting aspect of our study.

EXPERIMENTAL SETUP

BBC R&D pioneered IP-based production and delivery of UHD content during the 2014 Commonwealth Games in Glasgow[1]. For the duration of the games, they experimented with a second broadcast in parallel to their regular one supplying TV, radio and web content to UK households. They

---

[1]http://www.bbc.co.uk/rd/blog/2014/07/bbc-rd-at-the-commonwealth-games-2014

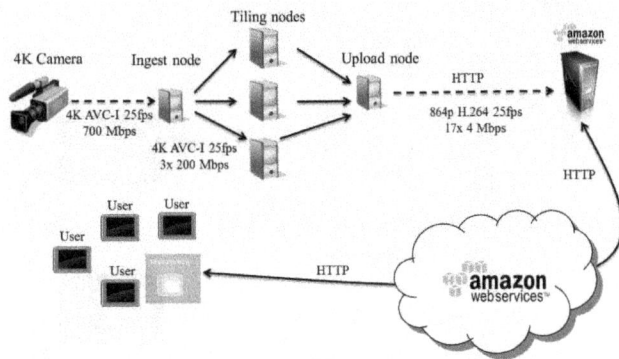

Figure 3. Live UHD tiling system as deployed on Amazon Web Services, with an S3 instance serving as a CDN origin node for a Cloudfront-based CDN.

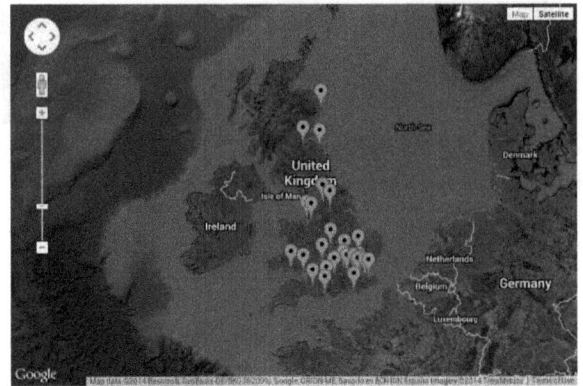

Figure 4. Location of users on the first day of the trial.

held a series of demonstrations at a public Commonwealth Games Showcase in the Glasgow Science Centre[2]. Within this context we have conducted a field trial with a number of experiments around our live UHD tiling system and related application. Using a static 4K camera in the Hampden Park stadium, several of the athletics games were captured and streamed live to mobile devices. This section reports on the system deployment and experimental setup for these experiments.

Deployment of UHD tiling system

The live UHD tiling system described in section "Live tiling system" was deployed at BBC R&D Centre House in London and integrated with the BBC experimental systems via JANET, UK's nationwide high-bandwidth research network. We sought to use Amazon Web Services as a content delivery network (CDN). An S3 instance functioned as a CDN origin node, whereas Cloudfront leveraged a set of delivery nodes. Figure 3 depicts the deployed system. In addition to the video, an audio feed accompanied the full panorama video to provide both the ambient sound of the event as well as the BBC Sports commentary.

iXperience app

For the purpose of the trial, we have developed the front-end of our UHD tiling system for mobile devices as an iOS app, called *iXperience*. iXperience is available for both iPhone and iPad on the Apple App Store (`https://itunes.apple.com/us/app/tno-ixperience/id895475926?mt=8`). After a login screen, the app presents to the user a menu with the videos that can be played at that time. Upon selection of the video, playback starts in full screen. At this point, it is possible to navigate within the video using pan-tilt-zoom movements and to use trickplay functionalities, e.g. play, pause, seek. During the experiments, the app also contained a link to an evaluation questionnaire, to be filled in by participants after each usage.

Participants recruitment

To take part in the trial, interested individuals from the UK had to register via email. To incentivise user participation,

[2]http://www.bbc.co.uk/rd/blog/2014/07/how-the-commonwealth-games-is-helping-define-the-future-of-broadcasting

we have offered gift vouchers. Participants throughout the UK were recruited via a BBC website which reported a description of the experiment and the conditions for participation, as well as via our direct contacts in the UK. Figure 4 shows a snapshot of the location of users on the first day of the trial. A total of 78 people registered for the trial and 44 actually participated.

Experiment description

The experiment ran for 5 days, from July, 30, until August, 3. It consisted of a smoke test and two experimental periods. The smoke test had the purpose of ensuring that our system as a whole worked correctly. The two subsequent experimental periods were aimed at answering the research questions mentioned in the Introduction. In particular, the second experimental period was designed as a 'formal experiment', in which different resolution-layer setups have been tested. The goal here was to understand whether and to what extent QoE was influenced by system factors (second research question) and specifically the number of resolution layers, being this system factor critical for the computational complexity of our live tiling system. The third experimental period was designed to cater for the first research question (*what is the overall perceived quality of experience (QoE) of the interactive UHD application?*). In particular, we wanted to verify the system endurability [?], i.e. whether trial participants liked to use our system and decided to return and use it again. Furthermore, questionnaires were used to further investigate the different aspects of this research question (as mentioned in the Introduction). A detailed description of each experimental period is reported below.

Smoke test

The first experimental session took place on the evening of July, 30, and was used to check that the UHD tiling system worked correctly. In particular, we had to verify that the streams were successfully captured and processed; that the participants could login, stream the video and use the app; and that the evaluation questionnaires were accessible by the participants. All participants were provided a single live stream consisting of 2 resolution layers, as showed in Table 1. For this experiment, participants were instructed to use the app for 5 minutes, trigger all relevant app functionalities (zoom in/out, pan, play/pause/seek) and then answer the

Table 1. Resolution layers settings

Test group	Smoke test	Formal experiment	Free Use experiment
#1	2 resolution layers, (1 / 16) tiles	3 resolution layers, (1 / 4 / 16) tiles	3 resolution layers, (1 /4 / 16) tiles
#2	2 resolution layers, (1 / 16) tiles	2 resolution layers, (1 / 16) tiles	3 resolution layers, (1 / 4 / 16) tiles
#3	2 resolution layers, (1 / 16) tiles	1 resolution layer, 1 tile	3 resolution layers, (1 / 4 / 16) tiles

questionnaire. Given the short timespan given to users to interact with the system and the quite 'mechanical' actions that they were asked to perform, we believe the smoke test did not bias the user perception of the system, as they wouldn't have the opportunity to fully grasp the system functioning and potential. This would rather become clear with prolonged usage, and during the following experimental sessions. The smoke test also marked the world's first live tiled streaming of 4K UHD video to end users.

Formal experiment
The second experiment (afternoon and evening of 31st of July) had the purpose to evaluate the general perceived QoE delivered by the system and the impact of different resolution layers settings on it. To this end, we have divided participants into 3 test groups, each of them being served video streams with a different number of resolution layers, as reported in Table 1. In particular, we aimed at verifying whether (i) an additional intermediate resolution layer would improve QoE and (ii) what the QoE of users only receiving the base resolution layer was. The first aspect is important for the design of our live UHD tiling system, while the second aspect gives insights into the QoE perceived by users whose Internet connection is low and can only transport the base resolution layer. For this experiment, 2 pre-recorded video streams were made available and participants were instructed to use the app for 15 minutes before answering the questionnaire. Also in this case, participants were asked to trigger all relevant app functionalities (zoom in/out, pan, play/pause/seek).

Free Use experiment
Our third and last experiment ran for 3 days from August, 1, until August, 3. With this experiment we wanted to verify the endurability of our system, therefore participants were given the freedom to use the app for as long and as many times they liked, with no requirement on testing specific or all functionalities. They had, however, been instructed to answer a questionnaire after their usage. All participants were provided 2 pre-recorded video streams consisting of all 3 resolution layers (Table 1).

Collected data
To evaluate our trial and experiments, we have collected both objective data (by logging parameters measured by the iXperience app), and subjective data (through questionnaires).

Subjective evaluations
To be able to evaluate the QoE of the application, we asked participants to fill in a questionnaire after each usage experiment. As QoE is a multifaceted quantity, related to multiple perceptual, cognitive and affective characteristics of the experience [15, 2], the questionnaire touched upon different aspects. The questionnaire presented during the first experimental period had the purpose to collect general demographics about the users (gender, age, nationality), their degree of interest in the Commonwealth games, as well as to check that they could use all the app's functionalities and receive the video stream correctly. During the second experimental period, users had to evaluate their enjoyment and satisfaction [?] with the app and the UHD tiling concept, and the quality of the video streaming. Likert and ACR scales [14] were used for this purpose, as indicated in table 2. The third experimental period included the same questions already investigated in the second experimental period, to verify whether the improvement in tiling scheme would have an effect on the users' evaluations of QoE. In addition, we included six extra questions, investigating long-terms aspects of the experience such as app usability and endurability [13] (i.e., willingness to reuse and recommend the system, considered to be a strong indicator of high quality of experience [?]). A comprehensive list of questions for each experiment can be found in Table 2.

Objective measures
Throughout the experiments, the iXperience app logged a number of usage and network metrics from participants. Every minute, the app would send the data collected in the last minute to one of our servers. The metrics being logged are reported in Table 3 and are described more in details here:

- *currentBitrate*: the current download rate of the video stream.

- *totalDataUsage*: a cumulative sum of all data, relative to the video stream, downloaded by the app.

- *startupTime*: the initial time that the user needs to wait before playback will start.

- *bufferTime*: a time during which playback was blocked due to lack of data in the playout buffer.

- *completedSwitchTime*: the time it takes to switch to a new tile (either for zoom or pan).

- *cancelledSwitchTime*: the time it takes to cancel a switch.

- *currentVideoArea*: the area in the screen currently selected by the user, gives an indication of where and how much the user zoomed in, and where she is navigating to.

The cancelledSwitchTime parameter was introduced to indicate that a tile switch, although triggered, has not occured. We distinguish two cases: (i) the user is moving with her fingers on the device and continues to pan or zoom. Every time the zoom or panning action causes the ROI to change to another tile before the tile in the previously selected ROI gets displayed, the switch is cancelled. In this case we observe a sequence of one or more cancelledSwitchTime followed by one completedSwitchTime. The completedSwitchTime in

Table 2. Overview of the items included in the questionnaires adopted in the three experiments. Experiment 1 indicates the Smoke Test, Experiment 2 is the Formal experiment and Experiment 3 indicates the Free Use experiment (see table 1).

Question	Experiment	Scale	Variable	Abbreviation
Very interested in the Commonwealth Games	1	Agreement	Interest in CWG	Interest
You enjoyed using the iXperience app	2 and 3	Agreement	Enjoyment of the app	Enjoyment(2/3)
The iXperience app met your expectations	2 and 3	Agreement	Expectations with respect to the app	Expectations(2/3)
You are satisfied with the startup delay of the iXperience app	2 and 3	Agreement	Satisfaction with Startup delay	Startup Satisfaction (2/3)
You were able to smoothly navigate within the video area	2 and 3	Agreement	Quality of navigation	Navigation (2/3)
Continuity of the video stream when zooming in/out	2 and 3	ACR	Continuity of the video stream	Zoom continuity (2/3)
Continuity of the video stream when navigating around the video area	2 and 3	ACR	Continuity of the video stream	Nav continuity (2/3)
Overall continuity of the video stream (in relation to presence/absence of interruptions)	2 and 3	ACR	Continuity of the video stream	Overall continuity (2/3)
Overall quality of the video stream	2 and 3	ACR	Overall quality	Overall quality (2/3)
The iXperience app was easy to use	3	Agreement	Usability of the app	Usability
You liked the functionalities of the iXperience app (navigate/zoom, play/pause, seek, ""live"" button)	3	Agreement	Appreciation of the functionalities	Functionalities
The quality of the iXperience app improved as compared to the second experiment	3	Agreement	Quality increase with respect to exp2	QImprovement
The Commonwealth Games content was interesting to watch	3	Agreement	Interestingness of the content	Content Interest
You would like to use the iXperience app again	3	Agreement	Endurability	Endurability
You would recommend the iXperience app to others	3	Agreement	Endurability	Recommendation

this case refers to the time needed to switch to the tile corresponding to the latest ROI selected by the user, starting from the previously selected ROI; (ii) the user zoomed in, but there is not enough bandwidth to download the tile from a higher resolution layer. The user then remains in the lowest resolution layer and such a cancelledSwitchTime is not followed by a completedSwitchTime.

EVALUATION OF EXPERIMENTS

Data preparation

Subjective evaluations. In total, we obtained 171 responses to our questionnaires, across the three experiments. It should be noted, though, that many users repeated the experiments multiple times, sometimes only partially filling in the questionnaire. In the following analysis, all data relative to incomplete questionnaires were discarded. Furthermore, because we were interested to capture participants' first impressions with the system, for each participant we retained only the data corresponding to the first usage session in a specific experiment. Table 4 presents an overview of the responses recorded and retained per experiment. To enable a numerical analysis, for all our valid entries corresponding to unique participants, we re-encoded the responses to questions evaluated on categorical and Likert scales into numerical ordinal values. To do so, we adopted the following scheme: ratings on the agreement scale were assigned a growing value from 1 = "fully disagree" to 5 = "fully agree"; similarly ratings on the ACR scale were assigned a value from 1 = "bad" to

5 = "excellent", as per [14]. The questions included in the three questionnaires, along with their evaluation scales and the abbreviations used to refer to the corresponding subjective measures in the following can be found in Table 2.

Objective measures. Objective measures of network functioning and app usage were recorded throughout the three experiments. In the following, we will analyse only data relative to the Formal and the Free Use experiment, for which we collected the bulk of the subjective evaluations. As for subjective evaluations, we collected a large quantity of data (relative to 114 sessions in Experiment 2 and to 129 sessions in experiment 3); nevertheless, of those only 21 for the formal and 24 for the Free Use experiment corresponded to a session for which we had the subjective evaluations available. Thus, the following analysis is based on the 45 sessions for which the pairs objective − subjective measures were available.

As mentioned in section "Objective measures", some objective measures were recorded on occurrence (e.g. bufferTime, completedSwitchTime, cancelledSwitchTime), others were sampled regularly (e.g. currentBitrate and totalDataUsage), yet at a different frequency. Thus, these measurements had different granularity and sparsity over time. To simplify the analysis, we extracted specific features of the recorded data to describe both network conditions and application usage. For each user and session separately, we computed the following objective features:

Table 3. Objective Data

Metric	Unit	Sample rate
currentBitrate	bps	1 second
totalDataUsage	Bytes	60 seconds
startupTime	milliseconds	at startup
bufferTime	milliseconds	at occurrence (playout buffer empty)
completedSwitchTime	milliseconds	everytime user zooms or pannes
cancelledSwitchTime	milliseconds	everytime user zooms or pannes
currentVideoArea	string	1 second

- *Mean bitrate*, calculated as the mean of the *currentBitrate* measure, and indicating the average bitrate recorded for a given user in a given session;

- *Startup time*, corresponding to the *Startup* measure, and as such representing the waiting time experience by the user for the session to start;

- *Mean buffer length*, computed as the average of all entries in *bufferTime* and indicating the average length of the buffering episodes had during a specific session;

- *Mean switch length*, computed as the average of all entries in *completedSwitchTime* and indicating the average length of the switch events had during a specific session;

- *Mean cancelled switch length*, computed as the average of all entries in *cancelledSwitchTime* and indicating the average length of the cancelled switch events had during a specific session;

- *Mean data*, calculated as the mean of *totalDataUsage* and representing the average amount of data used per minute by a given user during a given session;

- *No. buffering episodes*, computed as the number of entries recorded for the measure *bufferTime*, indicating the number of distinct buffering episodes during a specific session;

- *No. switches*, computed as the number of entries recorded for the measure *completedSwitchTime*, indicating the number of distinct switches episodes during a specific session;

- *No. cancelled switches*, computed as the number of entries recorded for the measure *cancelledSwitchTime* and indicating the number of distinct switches episodes had during a specific session.

The first five features monitor network conditions: besides bitrate, startup length and length of buffering and switch events all depend on bandwidth availability. The remaining features depend instead on both network conditions and app usage. Buffering as well as switches depend on user requests for different functionalities (e.g. a zoom or a seeking action); data usage also increases as a consequence of a more intensive use of the app functionalities. In addition to these features, we also defined two parameters describing app usage only: (1) *No. Feature calls*, representing the number of different

Table 4. Overview of the responses to the questionnaires across the three experiments.

Experiment	Smoke Test	Formal	Free Use	Total
No. Responses	66	46	59	171
No. Valid Entries	33	31	38	102
No. Unique Participants	30	30	32	44
No. Sessions with both objective and subjective data	–	21	24	45

calls to functionalities that a user did during a specific session, and computed as the number of entries for the feature-Call measure; and (2) *No. changes video area*, representing the number of distinct video areas explored by a user during the session and computed as the number of unique entries in the currentVideoArea measure. These two features describe specifically the level of user interaction with the app; thus, they will be considered as dependent variables for the following analysis (as the interaction modalities may depend on the network/application measurements). The network and application features will instead be studied as dependent variables.

System QoE
Our first research question revolved around the quality of the user experience with the iXperience app and with interactive UHD video streaming. To answer this question, we analysed the scores provided by users in the questionnaires for the Formal experiment and the Free Use experiment. Figure 5.a depicts the mean ratings given to each subjective measure across both the experiments. Figure 5.b reports the mean scores obtained for the additional subjective measures investigated during the Free Use experiment only. Figure 5 shows clearly that, in general, the app is well received. All subjective measures obtain a mean rating above three, with *Startup satisfaction*, *Navigation*, *Usability*, and, quite importantly, *endurability* (i.e., the willingness to use the app again) and *recommendation* scoring on average above 4. Points for improvement relate instead to matching of user expectations and overall quality. In both cases, the achievement of a relatively lower evaluation may depend on the fact that the mean values shown in Figure 5 aggregate scores collected from both the Formal experiment and the Free Use experiment, the first of which included sub-optimal tiling schemes. In addition, network conditions may have also been suboptimal, inducing longer buffering and switching times, in turn lowering the quality of the overall experience [1]. As a result, in the following we verify (1) whether the number of resolution layers affects QoE, within the Formal experiment and between the Formal and Free Use experiment, and (2) whether subjective evaluations do depend on objective measurements of the app and network functioning.

Effect of the number of resolution layers on QoE
As mentioned in section "Experiment description", participants in the Formal experiment were split in three groups, each exposed to tiling schemes including a different number of resolution layers. In the Free Use experiment, instead, all

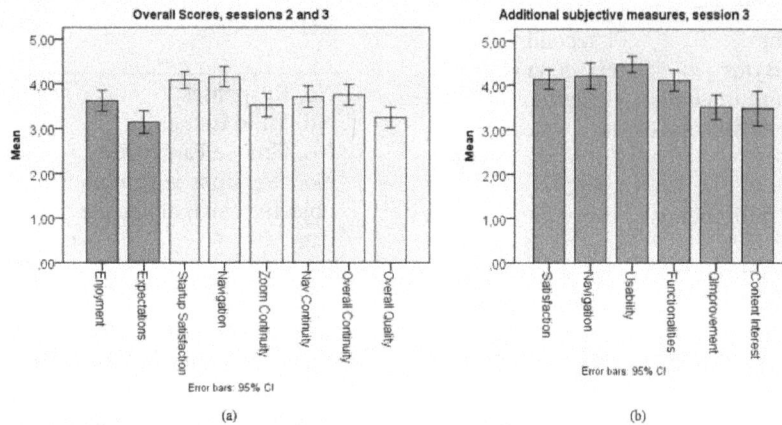

Figure 5. Mean ratings for (a) the subjective evaluations in experiment 2 and 3, and (b) the additional subjective measures evaluated in experiment 3 only.

users experienced only the scheme with the highest number of resolution layers, which we expected to provide the better experience. Because of this, we hypothesized that the mean scores collected for our subjective evaluations would increase from the second to the third experiment; furthermore, we expected to see differences in the ratings collected for the three groups of users within the Formal experiment.

We checked first the within-subjects effect of changing the number of resolution layers between the formal and the Free Use experiment. To do so, we had to limit our data points to those corresponding to the users which participated in both experiments (N = 22; as mentioned earlier, some users did not commit to participate in all parts of our experiment). A Wilcoxon test revealed that, although an increasing trend could be spotted (see figure 6), there were no significant differences in the subjective ratings across the two experiments, for any of the variables of interest (in all cases, $p < 0.05$).

We then checked the between-subjects effect of using a different number of resolution layers on the experienced quality of the app. To do so, we compared the medians of the subjective ratings provided by the three different groups of users (each experiencing a different number of resolution layers) during the Formal test. A Kruskal-Wallis test revealed that, also in this case, no significant differences between the evaluations of three groups of subjects existed.

Relation between network conditions, app usage and QoE
From the analysis above, we may conclude that the number of resolution layers adopted for the tiling scheme does not significantly influence the Quality of Experience. Nevertheless, this effect may be hidden by that of other, more prominent factors, such as disturbances due to poor network conditions. To verify this, we investigated the relationship between the objective features describing both network and app-usage conditions and the corresponding subjective measure.

As a first step, we checked whether network conditions were homogeneous across the two experiments. To do so we ran

a set of non-parametric Mann-Whitney U-tests between the objective feature values recorded for the usage sessions during the Formal experiment and those recorded for the Free Use experiment. No significant difference was found, indicating a similarity of conditions across the two experiments. We found instead a significant decrease, from the second to the third experiment, in the number of Buffering events (U=143.00, p = 0.016), along with a decrease in the number of features called (U=123.00, p = 0.003) and video areas switched (U=161.50, p = 0.039). This decrease can be easily explained, especially for the number of features called (medians: 15 during the Formal experiment, 5.5 during the Free Use experiment). During the Formal experiment, users were requested to try a number of different functionalities, whereas they did not have such obligation during the Free Use experiment. As a consequence, they may have interacted less. Furthermore, we may see this decrease as a consequence of learning in the app usage: whereas in earlier experiments users would need to explore the app capabilities more, this was not necessary during the last experiment, when users were already familiar with its functioning.

To verify relationships between objective parameters and subjective evaluations, we computed pairwise non-parametric Spearman correlations for all objective and subjective measures. Figure 7 reports the Spearman correlations between objective measures (columns) and subjective measures (rows) for both experiments. Significant correlations are highlighted with a (*). Interestingly, we found a rather different situation, for the two experiments.

In the Formal experiment, we found subjective scores to be not significantly correlated with network features, but to be positively correlated with app usage features, such as *Mean Data Usage* and *Number of Switches*, as well as number of features called and changes in the video area. Thus, the more interaction with the app, the more data usage, the higher the satisfaction with the app, and in particular with the navigation. These relationships seem to be lost in the Free Use

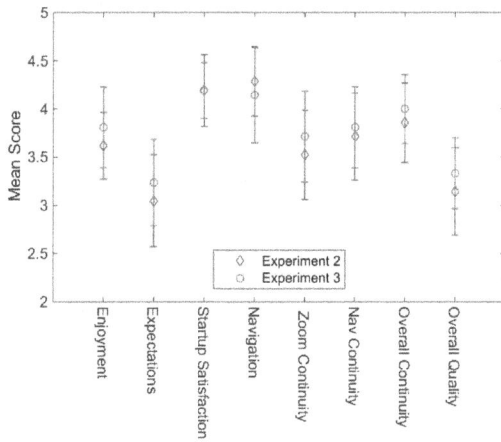

Figure 6. Mean scores for subjective measurements during both the Formal (blue diamonds) and the Free Use (red circles) experiments.

Formal Trial	Network Features					Network and Interaction Features				Interaction Feat.	
	Mean Bitrate	Startup time	Buffer Length	Switch Length	Canc Switch Lenght	Mean Data Usage	No. Buffer	No. Switch	No. Canc Switch	Change s video area	No Feature calls
Enjoyment	0,25	,077	-,078	,187	,248	,520*	,219	,416	,284	,345	,217
Expectations	0,06	-,201	-,058	-,021	,021	0,23	,161	,037	,020	,126	,268
Startup Satisf.	0,32	,135	-,021	,029	,147	,592*	,436*	,591*	,347	,565*	,572*
Navigation	0,17	,237	,139	,201	,348	,740*	,404	,664*	,495*	,784*	,542*
Zoom Cont.	0,33	-,128	-,049	-,003	,115	,590*	,423	,402	,136	,561*	,564*
Nav Cont.	0,23	-,050	,103	,039	,158	,472*	,230	,403	,160	,590*	,360
Overall Cont.	0,36	,021	-,053	,037	,107	,446*	,423	,383	,078	,419	,444*
Overall Quality	0,15	,207	,026	,360	,208	0,43	,328	,462*	,289	,394	

Free UseTrial	Mean Bitrate	Startup time	Buffer Length	Switch Length	Canc Switch Lenght	Mean Data Usage	No. Buffer	No. Switch	No. Canc Switch	Change s video area	No Feature calls
Enjoyment	,126	-,048	-,345	,068	,163	,193	,056	,253	,364	,330	,098
Expectations	,023	,205	-,334	-,262	,309	,032	-,217	-,052	-,024	-,060	-,175
Startup Satisf.	-,079	-,052	-,392	-,215	-,088	-,060	-,110	-,128	-,248	-,167	-,074
Navigation	-,053	-,043	-,345	-,073	-,067	,013	,014	-,087	,020	-,021	-,058
Zoom Cont.	,043	,040	-,279	,042	,132	,011	,014	,032	,001	,129	-,114
Nav Cont.	,138	-,138	-,430*	-,012	-,126	-,018	,101	-,013	,045	,016	-,001
Overall Cont.	,118	,030	-,293	,055	-,018	,022	,020	-,089	-,055	-,019	-,111
Overall Quality	,099	-,008	-,073	,068	,016	,029	-,034	,073	,084	,082	-,034

Figure 7. Correlations between objective (columns) and subjective (rows) measures of our experiment, for the Formal (top) and the Free Use (bottom) experiments. Correlations significant at the 0.05 level are marked with an asterisk (*).

experiment. Correlation between app usage features and subjective measures are mostly non significant. We found instead an interesting negative correlation between the scores in continuity (both zoom and navigation) and network features such as buffer length. That is, the longer the buffering, the lower the satisfaction of the user with the continuity of the stream, as we would expect.

Summarizing, it seems that in the last experiment, network conditions may have played a more dominant role than in the previous one. A possible reason for this may be that, initially, users were still not familiar with the app, and had a number of features to try out and evaluate. Their focus may have been therefore on evaluating the opportunities for interaction with the app, rather than the smoothness of the video stream. Once acquainted with the app functionalities, though, in the Free Use experiment they may have switched from evaluating the opportunities for interaction to evaluating the quality of the visual experience, penalizing more those streams delivered in poor network conditions. The latter observation may also partially explain the lack of significant improvement from the Formal experiment to the Free Use one (with more resolution layers): users, now acquainted with the application functioning and novelty, started weighing more the disruptions in video delivery in their overall experience, thereby minimizing the benefit coming from an increased number of resolution layers available.

DISCUSSION AND CONCLUSIONS

In this paper, we presented the implementation and results of a field trial of an interactive UHD streaming system for mobile devices. The system was accessible via an app available for iOS systems, which allowed video content exploration at multiple resolution levels. In our experiments, we were able to reach out to 44 UK households, having users interacting with our app and system in a real usage settings, and in three different experiments at least. During each experiment, we logged (i) the user interaction with the system, (ii) the app usage and network conditions, as well as (iii) subjective eval-

uations related to user QoE of the system. This allowed us to perform, a posteriori, a quantitative evaluation of the QoE our interactive UHD system and application. Our data showed that the system was in general well received by the users, with evaluations in some cases well above 4 (i.e., good) on a 5-point scale, for a number of QoE aspects that we considered in our experiments. In particular, the system was rated high in endurability, as also demonstrated by the fact that users returned multiple times for a Free Use experiment, although they were not explicitly requested to do so. A more in-depth analysis showed that the number of resolution layers adopted for the tiling scheme had a negligible effect on QoE within the Formal experiment and between Formal and Free Use experiments. Nevertheless, a trend of increasing QoE from the Formal experiment (including suboptimal number of resolution layers) to the Free Use experiment (presenting only the optimal number of resolution layers) was recorded. This increase was again found to be not significant; nevertheless, we cannot exclude that, with a larger number of observation, the increase may achieve significance. Because of the uncontrolled, live setting of the experiment, indeed, many observations had to be discarded as incomplete: in some cases users did not participate in the three experiments, or did not fill in the questionnaires, or objective data were recorded in an incomplete way. This reduced the number of valid observations for the quantitative analysis, lowering the chance of detecting small and medium-size effects. On the other hand, our analysis captures QoE in a real-life usage situation, thus our findings reflect the actual user QoE, which may instead be mediated by other factors should the measurements have been performed in a controlled, laboratory setting. Finally, we found that, depending on the experiment, app usage rather than network measurements were predictive for QoE. In our Formal experiment, where users were asked to perform a predefined set of actions on the app, the amount of used data, correlated with the number of feature calls and changes in the viewed video area, was found to be predictive for the quality of navigation. In the following, Free Use experiment, this relationship was not found, whereas (1) a decrease in the amount of interaction as well as (2) a negative correlation of QoE with buffering events length was found. The reasons for this discrepancy may be diverse, and possibly touch upon problems related to long-term usage of applications and services [19]. The relevance of network conditions as well as system factors in the overall QoE evaluation may indeed change over time, being limited in a first moment, where app capabilities are more striking for the user, and increasing with the level of the acquaintance of the user with the application. Future work will focus on investigating further these long-term usage and QoE aspects, as well as on verifying in controlled conditions the findings obtained for this first, "in the wild", trial.

ACKNOWLEDGMENTS
The authors would like to thank BBC R&D for their support and cooperation during the field trial. Figures 1 and 2 contain images from a live demonstration based around the performance of 'Deeper than all roses', a composition from Stephen Davismoon, featuring rockband Bears?Bears! and live performance artists Joseph Lau and Shona Roberts. This work has also been also partially supported by the NWO Veni grant 639.021.230.

REFERENCES
1. Hoßfeld, T., Seufert, M., Hirth, M., Zinner, T., Tran-Gia, P., and Schatz, R. Quantification of youtube qoe via crowdsourcing. In *Multimedia (ISM), 2011 IEEE International Symposium on*, IEEE (2011), 494–499.

2. Le Callet, P., Möller, S., Perkis, A., et al. Qualinet white paper on definitions of quality of experience. *European Network on Quality of Experience in Multimedia Systems and Services (COST Action IC 1003)* (2012).

3. Macq, J.-F., Verzijp, N., Aerts, M., Vandeputte, F., and Six, E. Demo: Omnidirectional video navigation on a tablet pc using a camera-based orientation tracker. In *Distributed Smart Cameras (ICDSC), Fifth ACM/IEEE International Conference on*, ACM/IEEE (2011).

4. Mavlankar, A., Agrawal, P., Pang, D., Halawa, S., Cheung, N.-M., and Girod, B. An interactive region-of-interest video streaming system for online lecture viewing. In *Packet Video Workshop (PV), 2010 18th International*, IEEE (2010), 64–71.

5. Mavlankar, A., and Girod, B. Spatial-random-access-enabled video coding for interactive virtual pan/tilt/zoom functionality. *Circuits and Systems for Video Technology, IEEE Transactions on 21*, 5 (2011), 577–588.

6. Niamut, O., Prins, M., van Brandenburg, R., and Havekes, A. Spatial tiling and streaming in an immersive media delivery network. *Adjunct Proceedings of EuroITV* (2011).

7. Niamut, O., Thomas, G., Thomas, E., van Brandenburg, R., D'Acunto, L., and Gregory-Clarke, R. Live event experiences-interactive uhdtv on mobile devices. *The Best of IET and IBC 2014 6* (2014).

8. Pang, D., Halawa, S., Cheung, N.-M., and Girod, B. Classx mobile: region-of-interest video streaming to mobile devices with multi-touch interaction. In *Proceedings of the 19th ACM international conference on Multimedia*, ACM (2011), 787–788.

9. Pang, D., Halawa, S., Cheung, N.-M., and Girod, B. Mobile interactive region-of-interest video streaming with crowd-driven prefetching. In *Proceedings of the international ACM workshop on Interactive multimedia on mobile and portable devices*, ACM (2011).

10. Quang Minh Khiem, N., Ravindra, G., Carlier, A., and Ooi, W. T. Supporting zoomable video streams with dynamic region-of-interest cropping. In *Proceedings of the first annual ACM SIGMM conference on Multimedia systems*, ACM (2010), 259–270.

11. Quang Minh Khiem, N., Ravindra, G., and Ooi, W. T. Adaptive encoding of zoomable video streams based on user access pattern. *Signal Processing: Image Communication 27*, 4 (2012), 360–377.

12. Quax, P., Issaris, P., Vanmontfort, W., and Lamotte, W. Evaluation of distribution of panoramic video sequences in the explorative television project. In *Proceedings of the 22nd international workshop on Network and Operating System Support for Digital Audio and Video*, ACM (2012), 45–50.

13. Read, J., MacFarlane, S., and Casey, C. Endurability, engagement and expectations: Measuring children's fun. In *Interaction design and children*, vol. 2, Shaker Publishing Eindhoven (2002), 1–23.

14. Recommendation, I. 500-11, methodology for the subjective assessment of the quality of television pictures. *International Telecommunication Union, Geneva, Switzerland 4* (2002).

15. Redi, J. A., Zhu, Y., de Ridder, H., and Heynderickx, I. How passive image viewers became active multimedia users. In *Visual Signal Quality Assessment*. Springer International Publishing, 2015, 31–72.

16. Sugawara, M., Masaoka, K., Emoto, M., Matsuo, Y., and Nojiri, Y. Research on human factors in ultrahigh-definition television (uhdtv) to determine its specifications. *SMPTE Motion Imaging Journal 117*, 3 (2008), 23–29.

17. van Brandenburg, R., Niamut, O., Prins, M., and Stokking, H. Spatial segmentation for immersive media delivery. In *Intelligence in Next Generation Networks (ICIN), 15th International Conference on*, IEEE (2011).

18. Wang, H., Nguyen, V.-T., Ooi, W. T., and Chan, M. C. Mixing tile resolutions in tiled video: A perceptual quality assessment. In *Proceedings of Network and Operating System Support on Digital Audio and Video Workshop*, ACM (2014), 25.

19. Weiss, B., Guse, D., Möller, S., Raake, A., Borowiak, A., and Reiter, U. Temporal development of quality of experience. In *Quality of Experience*. Springer International Publishing, 2014, 133–147.

Towards an Extended Festival Viewing Experience

Raphaël Velt[1,2], Steve Benford[1], Stuart Reeves[1], Michael Evans[2], Maxine Glancy[2], Phil Stenton[2]

[1] Mixed Reality Lab
The University of Nottingham
Nottingham, NG8 1BB, United Kingdom
{raphael.velt, steve.benford}@nottingham.ac.uk,
stuart@tropic.org.uk

[2] BBC Research & Development
MediaCityUK, Greater Manchester
M50 2LH, United Kingdom
{michael.evans, maxine.glancy,
phil.stenton}@bbc.co.uk

ABSTRACT
Media coverage of large-scale live events is becoming increasingly complex, with technologies enabling the delivery of a broader range of content as well as complex viewing patterns across devices and services. This paper presents a study aimed at understanding the experience of people who have followed the broadcast coverage of a music festival. Our findings show that the experience takes a diversity of forms and bears a complex relationship with the actual experience of being at the festival. We conclude this analysis by proposing that novel services for coverage of this type of events should connect and interleave the diverse threads of experiences around large-scale live events and consider involving more diverse elements of the experience of "being there".

Author Keywords
Television; Festival; Multi-screen interaction;
User Experience.

ACM Classification Keywords
H.5.m. Information interfaces and presentation (e.g., HCI): Miscellaneous.

INTRODUCTION
Broadcasting large-scale live events, such as music festivals and sports competitions like the Olympic Games and Football World Cup, is very complex and usually involves simultaneous coverage of multiple venues, producing live commentaries, recording interviews from a wide range of participants and may involve multiple points of view over the same event. Further coverage of such events is also often available as part of highlights and magazine shows and increasingly online. Social media updates offer another source of coverage, and include content generated by a wide range of users, including broadcasters themselves,

TVX'15, June 03 - 05, 2015, Brussels, Belgium
Copyright 2015 ACM 978-1-4503-3526-3/15/06...$15.00
http://dx.doi.org/10.1145/2745197.2745206

performing participants, spectators present at the venues as well as remote spectators.

On the television viewer side, new technologies such as video recorders [6] and mobile devices [14] are driving a change in viewing patterns, with time-shifted viewing as well as multiple screen interactions becoming more prevalent [30]. These new behaviors provide opportunities for broadcasters to customize the delivery of content but they also add a layer of complexity to the experience of viewing these events. This raises challenges such as how to navigate across content, services and devices.

Finally, an important challenge when covering these events lies in the gap between the experience of spectators on location and those at home. Given how limited and expensive access to some of these festivals has become, broadcasters may be interested in giving their viewers an experience that can compare as much as possible to what they could have had on location. One way of addressing this gap would be to harness emerging immersive forms of television [8, 29] to provide a stronger sense of 'being there' in the audience or even onstage. Another might be to involve physical spectators in the global coverage experience, which may be driven by the widespread use of camera-phones as well as improvements in wireless networking on location. Catch-up television services also add opportunities for onsite spectators to make the recorded version part of their whole experience.

Given this range of possibilities, it is important to properly understand the ways in which viewers experience television coverage of large events and to gain a sense of how they may wish to do this in the future. In this article, we therefore unpack the experience of watching large-scale live events on TV and propose a series of dimensions to describe of the richness and diversity of viewing patterns that can inform the design of future services.

In the following sections, after looking at previous work addressing these issues, we will take the example of a music festival in England, present a two-part study in which we have tried to understand the experience of TV viewers who have watched this festival, discuss the findings of this study and present our implications for design.

RELATED WORK
We start by describing how several of these challenges have been addressed first in the entertainment industry and then

in the academic literature in Human-Computer Interaction (HCI) and Interactive Television (iTV) research.

Industrial state of the art
International sports events such as the Olympic Games and the Football Association World Cup, being broadcast around the world with considerable budgets, are often used to introduce new technologies, for example ultra-high definition (UHD) or three-dimensional video. Broadcasters have also relied on the prevalence of digital television and broadband internet to distribute more footage. For example, during the 2012 London Olympic Games, the British Broadcasting Corporation (BBC) provided viewers across the UK access to 24 simultaneous high-definition (HD) video streams.

The BBC also took into account multiple-device viewing patterns to extend coverage with mobile and tablet applications and a specific website. Metadata about events was used to organize navigation through content: webpages were created for individual sports, venues and athletes, giving access to relevant video footage and related information about each, including incentives for viewers to try these sports for themselves. Social media were also taken into account, as a complementary source of coverage (Twitter feeds created for the event) or embedded in the viewing experience, with a specific Facebook application that allowed users to comment on specific broadcasts and report their viewing activity.

Prototypes of novel interfaces created by broadcasters for accessing coverage of live events include the *Venue Explorer*, which allows users to zoom in from a UHD master video showing a whole track-and-field stadium to a single zone, the soundtrack being adapted to fit the video content. This was showcased, along with the *Augmented Video Player*, which adds customized dynamic overlays to videos, by the BBC during the Commonwealth Games in Glasgow in 2014. [10]

Augmenting broadcasts by pushing additional content on interactive devices (often described as "second screens", the TV set being the primary screen) has also been seized as an opportunity for third-party players that operate independently of broadcasters, for example *L'Équipe Connect*[1], developed by a daily sports newspaper in France for football games, or *Beamly*[2], a service for all genres of TV displaying show-specific feeds mixing user-generated content (UGC), social media and official content.

Broadcasting innovations also impact the experience on location as sports and concert venues are now deploying network infrastructures and mobile applications used together (for which commercial integrated solutions exist

---

[1] http://www.lequipe.fr/connect/
[2] http://www.beamly.com/

[9]) to offer video feeds showing different angles and action replays during live shows.

Participative media in large-scale events
One significant trend in academic research has been to integrate UGC within coverage of live events. Prototypes involving the sharing of media created by local spectators in live events have sought to improve the experience of both other spectators [12, 26], extend coverage and/or make it more personalized [17, 27, 21] as well as to establish a bridge between venues and homes [13].

One source of UGC that has often been associated with large coverage of events is social media. Conversations around events, often gathered around an event-specific keyword (named "hashtag" on Twitter), have been described as "backchannels" commenting on events. It has been argued that these feeds bring audiences *"an augmented live viewing experience"* [16]. In the case of large scale events, visual representations of social media activity have been proposed as a way of giving a thematic overview and as a tool for exploring conversations [15]. This kind of visualization may be synchronized with the live or recorded viewing experience [25].

Addressing the complex structure of events
Another trend in academic research is to address the complex structures of events, for example by offering fine-grained navigation based on the structure of sports games [28], or adapting tools for authoring interactive video narratives [32] for personalizing coverage of events [18].

Works that address the complexity of navigating a diverse content include giving users multiple search strategies by encouraging both targeted search and serendipity [31].

Understanding multiple-screen ecologies
Relevant work also includes understanding how viewers interact with technologies, for example by studying the impact of multiple-screen ecologies [14], video recorders and downloads [6] in households or by handing groups multiple devices to access footage of a complex event [1].

Our review has revealed how a very diverse range of emerging technologies and practices might be harnessed to extend to coverage of major events. The key question then becomes how can broadcasters – and indeed viewers – navigate this landscape, making appropriate choices to shape more powerful future viewing experiences? In short, given a bewildering array of technical possibilities, what is it that viewers might actually want from such coverage? In response, we now present a study to uncover current and future possibilities for broadcasting major public events.

THE GLASTONBURY FESTIVAL AND ITS COVERAGE
Our study focuses on one major event, The Glastonbury Festival of Contemporary Performing Arts, a music and arts festival taking place almost every year in the south-west of

England in late June for five days. In 2014, 135,000 paying spectators attended. The festival extended on nine "main stages" and 78 smaller venues.

Glastonbury has also emerged as being something of a national TV phenomenon in the UK. Radio and television coverage, limited to the last three days of the festival was provided by the BBC, in the form of full concerts as well as edited "highlights". Footage was made available through a wide range of services: 30 hours of video broadcast on TV channels, 50 hours of audio broadcast on four radio stations, live online video from six stages, digital TV interactive services (Red Button) and iPlayer, the BBC's multi-device catch-up service, on which many musical performances were available for 30 days instead of the normal 7-day policy. On iPlayer, individual concerts were available separately and were indexed by performer name.

The BBC had created a specific web site for the festival (http://www.bbc.co.uk/glastonbury/), in which it gave access to all video content, as well as extras such as weather forecasts, a TV and radio program guide, static webcams showing stages and areas. Despite this very broad coverage, some acts were not made available due to artists not allowing the broadcast of their performance (often when they included songs from newly released albums), non-compliance to the corporation's taste and decency guidelines, or technical issues.

The Glastonbury festival in 2014 was broadcast in a context where other live events were scheduled, including the Football World Cup. Audience ratings showed a peak of 2.08 million live TV viewers for Dolly Parton's live performance [2].

There were two parts to our study of the television experience of Glastonbury. First, we undertook an online survey of over 1000 participants designed to elicit data on how they engaged with the current television coverage and their views on how it might be extended in the future. Second, we undertook a structured qualitative study with 17 participants to reveal further finer detail of how people engaged with the coverage on a day-to-day basis.

THE SURVEY

The first part of our study was a survey designed to yield a quantitative overview of how people were following the festival and what their attitudes towards the coverage were. It was delivered online on the week following the festival using an existing service that is routinely used to gather feedback from large numbers of viewers across the United Kingdom, aged 16 and over, on a weekly basis. 1301 participants responded to our survey. Results are summarized in the following table.

Q1. Did you watch or listen to the Glastonbury festival on TV, radio, etc. this year?		1301
Yes – go to Q2	28.4%	370
No – jump to Q7	71.6%	931

Q2. Who did you follow the festival with?		370
Alone	51.1%	189
With friends	12.4%	46
With partner or relatives	46.5%	172
Q3. Where did you follow the festival from?		**370**
At home	94.9%	351
In transportation	4.1%	15
Other, specify…	3.5%	13
Q4. Why did you follow the festival?		**370**
To listen to live music in general	51.1%	189
For headline artists	37.8%	140
I watch Glastonbury every year	20.0%	50
To discover new artists	13.5%	34
To feel like you are at the festival	9.2%	13
For the presenters	3.5%	74
Other, specify…	17.8%	66
Including: For a specific performer	7.3%	27
Stumbled upon it	4.3%	16
Q5. Did you do anything special to make your watching of the festival a special experience?		**370**
I arranged the room in a particular way	1.9%	7
Invited people or was invited	1.9%	7
I consumed specific food/drinks	4.9%	18
Organized my weekend around specific performers or sessions	6.5%	24
I didn't do anything special	87.6%	324
Q6. Are there parts of the festival that you would like to have seen/heard of more?		**370**
No/Dont know	62.2%	230
Behind the scenes	18.1%	67
Non-concert entertainment	14.6%	54
The life of festival-goers	11.9%	44
After hours atmosphere	11.6%	43
Accommodation and facilities	8.9%	33
Other, specify (All responses asked for more or more diverse music coverage)	3.0%	11
Q7. Which do you think is/would be better?		**1301**
Being at the festival	36.5%	475
Listening on radio	3.3%	43
Watching on television	30.9%	402
Don't know	29.3%	381
Q8. Have you ever been, or would you like to go, to the Glastonbury Festival?		**1301**
I have been there before	6.8%	89
Haven't been, but will try and go one year	10.5%	136
Haven't been and would like to go there in the future, but probably won't be able	16.4%	213
Haven't been and not interested in going	63.1%	821
Don't know	3.2%	42

Table 1. Summary of survey responses

For question 7, participants were asked to justify their answers. Common reasons for preferring being there were "the atmosphere" (over half of non-blank responses) and "the experience", followed by social interactions. Many of those who preferred the TV experience (70.9% of non-blank responses) described it as better in terms of comfort and/or weather conditions; other reasons were the sound and image quality (17.7%), the ease of selecting performances (8.6%) and the price of tickets (7.4%).

Results were provided broken down by gender, age group, social class and the part of the UK respondents lived in. The strongest difference in patterns this data shows is between age groups. Viewership is fairly constant across age groups, except for the 65 and older, who were 31% less likely to have followed the festival than average. Younger age groups (16-44) have a broader variety of viewing patterns and (especially for the 25-34) are more likely to have followed the festival with friends and/or outside their home. They are also more likely to have multiple motivations to watch it, to be interested in feeling like they're there (twice more than the 45+), to ask for broader coverage, and to be interested in going to the festival in the future. The survey doesn't show significant differences between social classes, apart from more watching in upper and middle classes.

THE QUALITATIVE STUDY

The purpose of the qualitative part of the study was to establish a richer picture of how individuals experienced the festival from home and to elicit a wider variety of facets of this experience. We chose to explore this through self-reporting, participant-driven methods that have commonly been used in HCI to elicit requirements and inform designs in domestic contexts, including for television services [5, 23]: Participants were asked to capture their experience in a multimedia diary [7] and to perform a series of creative activities that acted like cultural probes [20] designed to provoke and elicit further reflections.

Recruitment

17 participants were recruited through ads and mailing lists in two universities in the UK. All participants were students, university employees (academic, technical and administrative), or partners of a student or employee that was also part of the study. 10 of them were female, 7 male and their ages ranged from 19 to 48. 6 were non-British, non-native English speakers. A comparison of the sample (a high proportion of younger participants who are in or have had higher education degrees) with demographic data above leads us to believe that the viewing patterns encountered in the study are more diverse and less home-centric than the average. Targeting this demographic may allow us to support experiences that are less well catered for than a single-screen, living-room based one.

At the time of recruitment, one participant mentioned they would be at the festival during the study before catching up with it on iPlayer upon returning home. Participants were compensated with £40 (~$60) in shopping vouchers.

Description

The qualitative study took place in four stages:

1. A first questionnaire was sent via email to participants to capture their previous experience of the festival and their plans for this year's coverage.

2. During the festival, participants were asked to document their experience by keeping a multimedia diary in which they were encouraged to take photographs and screen captures from activity on their computers and mobile devices. At the same time, they were given a series of creative activities. These could be returned either via email or through an upload platform that was set up before the study. Briefs for activities were sometimes deliberately ambiguous to provoke deeper reflection [19]. Activities will be detailed along with findings.

3. After the end of the festival, participants had to complete a short online questionnaire about how, how much and what type of coverage they had watched or listened to and their attitudes towards it.

4. Finally, exit interviews were scheduled and conducted either face-to-face or by phone. All participants were interviewed, one couple being interviewed jointly. These were semi-structured interviews, aimed at enriching and explaining the results of the previous phases: general questions were asked about how participants did their planning, how their experience was interwoven with other activities and what they enjoyed about the festival. Then, a selection of their submissions from diaries and creative activities were recalled to understand the context in which they were produced as well as spark conversations about various aspects of the festival.

Findings

In this section, we will present findings from each phase of the qualitative study.

First questionnaire

The first questionnaire, taken by 16 out of 17 participants has shown a broad range of previous experience of the festival: a majority of them (11) had never been physically to the festival, and one had been there "13 or 14 times" before; only three (all originating from outside the UK) had never watched or listened to any coverage of it.

When asked how they planned to follow the festival, participants responded with a broad range of services and devices: live television and radio, online videos, BBC iPlayer, Sky+ (a video recording service and set-top box provided by a satellite operator), newspapers and social media (mostly Facebook and Twitter).

Questions about how viewing would be focused showed that, though a majority of participants were planning to focus on artists they already liked (with one who was mostly interested in a single band), some would focus on the headliners, others would look for smaller stages, including locations where friends may be watching live and other were envisioning a more spontaneous way of navigating content. One participant was specifically interested in looking at what *"most people talk about the next day"* to *"be part of the conversation"*.

Participants who had been to the festival were also interested in following entertainment outside the main concert stages that isn't well covered by the BBC, such as the "dance area" (P11) or *"anything about other [non-concert] stuff going on that the festival [whose] addition is what makes the festival for [P13]"*.

Attitudes towards watching it versus being there were also explored and the results were consistent with the survey: by not being there, participants felt they would miss the atmosphere, an "experience", the sociality of the event and the ability to see performers live. P14, who had been there in previous years, thought that *"coverage no matter how good [can't] compensate"* for missing this.

On the other hand, being at home means better comfort, is less costly and easier due to the low availability of tickets. Even though being there gives access to more artists (only a fraction being filmed), the home experience allows switching between performers without having to walk and seeing acts that happen simultaneously on different stages.

The multimedia diary
13 participants sent diaries, 12 of which included images. Common types of images included updates from social media (for 6 participants), screen captures or photographs of screens showing BBC video coverage as it was being watched (8 participants), screen captures of the BBC's Glastonbury website (6), of the festival's official website (2) and of articles talking of the festival on news websites and apps (6).

Images showing the festival being watched confirmed that it was mostly a home-based experience (e.g. when showing a TV screen in a living room) and that a variety of devices were used to watch video (tablets, computers and TV sets). P8 sent a full screen capture of his computer screen including several process windows to show how he was working at the same time as he was watching. P11 sent a link to a video she *"thought was incredible"*.

Creative activities
Assiduity in performing the creative tasks was very variable: 11 participants did at least one creative activity, 6 did at least five, and none did all. Activity uptake ranged from 10 participants for the most popular task to only 2. The interview showed that participants who skipped the activities or the diary did it because they were not expecting that level of commitment from the study, had external unexpected commitments or didn't feel creative enough. Activities were:

a. *Annotating the festival's official program*, which had a strong impact on participants' experience as it exposed them to the variety of available performances and led them to do more planning than they would have done

otherwise if at all. Most participants made a list of performances they wanted to see, with strategies ranging from looking for one's favorite bands to more exploratory and "broad-minded" ones, including choosing performers because their name sounded interesting. Several participants mentioned they would probably favor exploratory patterns on location and sticking to artists they know at home.

b. *Imagining "covert reporting"* technologies to get extra coverage, which elicited types of coverage that participants found interesting, e.g. capturing the *"festival goer's perspective"* (P14), *"interviews with bands live on stage"* or *"what goes on [...] when the final acts have finished"* (P3), as well as technical issues (e.g. going quickly from stage to stage, battery life, sound levels). One participant devised a system that tried to balance giving extra information to a covert reporter with letting them enjoy the festival. One participant also used this activity to call for more interactivity between festival goers and the stage (by sending text messages to a big screen).

c. *An "iSpy guide"*, in which participants could list sights to spot at the festival. Participants mostly filled it with features of the festival-going experience, including the appearance and behavior of spectators. A recurring item was the presence of celebrities, who are seen as an expected but seldom seen feature of the festival for British viewers. P14, who was the only participant who had both attended the festival in previous years and taken this activity, included specific items, such as iconic people or behaviors as well as performances, locations or moments not covered by the BBC.

d. *Recording oneself (audio or video) as a reporter*. Most participants who took this activity described the bands that they particularly enjoyed, one insisted on the specific atmosphere of a stage and another one used this activity to relate how upset he was that a performance had not been made available on iPlayer.

e. *Creating a list of awards:* Most of these were given to bands, though a few were also awarded to spectators that were spotted in the coverage. They were used to point out performers that were particularly entertaining, had interesting gimmicks, were better or worse than expected or didn't correspond to the usual musical styles found in this festival.

f. *Creating a newspaper cover.* Four participants undertook this activity, including two who wrote a short article commenting on the line-up of the festival.

g. *Crafting a festival-themed* frame to put around their mobile device. Two frames were made and mixed visuals and text.

h. *Summarizing their experience* by creating a playlist or a story using photographs: seven participants made a playlist and three used photographs.

Overview questionnaire

The questionnaire was taken by 16 out of 17 participants. Their experience was mostly home-based, with all participants reporting watching it or part of it from home. 11 participants also followed it from the place they work or study and 5 while commuting. The social viewing patterns were varied, with 3 participants reporting following coverage of the festival exclusively alone, 4 participants exclusively with others and the remaining 9 partly alone and partly with others. Co-viewers were part of the household for 9 participants, and 5 participants watched it with friends or colleagues. One participant also mentioned hearing the festival being played on the radio in a store.

Participants used a varied ecology of devices to consume festival coverage, with 11 using their TV set, 6 a video recorder, 7 tablets (all of which used it at least to watch videos and 6 for accessing other content), 11 smartphones (of which only 2 participants used it for video or audio coverage). Computers were the only type of device used by all 16 participants, including 3 who did not use any other type of device. Radios were only used by 6 participants.

Participants' Glastonbury experience was strongly video-based, with all participants reporting watching over one hour of video coverage and 9 out of 16 over five hours. Both live video (13 participants) and time-shift (12) were common modes. 8 participants also mentioned watching videos that were not part of the official coverage, e.g. non-festival clips of bands performing at the festival on Youtube. A couple of participants mentioned Soundcloud, an online music service, as they were interested in types of music not well covered by the BBC and were looking for dance music sets that were recorded by DJs themselves, directly from the mixer output.

On the other hand, 4 reported following no audio-only coverage at all and none five hours or more. 8 listened to the live BBC radio channels, 2 caught up later with radio coverage and 6 listened to non-festival recordings of artists present in Glastonbury. Interviews showed that some participants who listened to the festival on the radio did it as part of their usual radio-listening routines and not specifically to access festival coverage.

Websites accessed in relationship with the festival included the festival's website (reported by 13 participants), the BBC's website (12), Facebook (11). In the questionnaire Wikipedia was reportedly used by 3 participants, but 3 more mentioned it in the interviews. General news websites and newspapers were reported by 4 participants in the questionnaire but 4 more included captures of news websites in their diaries. Newspapers quoted included, for most participants, dailies, and one also mentioned specialized magazines about music.

Other questions about viewing patterns showed that most participants (10) had planned to watch specific artists, most (11) knew which artists would be playing before starting to watch, most (11) chose what to listen by jumping between channels and most (11) discovered new artists.

The questionnaire also looked at attitudes towards the coverage: a large majority of participants enjoyed the festival (all but one agreeing or strongly agreeing with that statement), enjoyed the selection of artists (15), enjoyed how the shows were and thought the technical quality of the coverage was good (14).

Finally, attitudes towards the study were explored: in general, participants found it time-consuming, but they didn't find that it distracted them from watching the festival. For half of them, it even had a positive impact on their enjoyment of the experience.

Final Interviews

Participants had generally very positive attitudes towards the breadth of coverage of the event, except for P7 who was frustrated by the fact that some performances had not been made available on iPlayer. One feature that was seen as particularly enjoyable was the possibility to switch between performances, though participants did it in very different ways: fast-forwarding on a video recorder, using the red button in a TV-based experience, using the Glastonbury website on a computer or the iPlayer app on a tablet. Attitudes towards the Highlights TV program were more ambivalent, with some participants happy to see a broad diversity of both concerts and other parts of the festival, but other frustrated by not seeing more than a few songs of each set or not knowing in advance what the program would contain. One participant noted that some segments covering the general atmosphere of the festival and non-concert entertainment venues, being included only in the highlights and therefore part of longer video clips, were hard to search for when catching up.

BBC presenters were a disputed feature of the coverage: some participants described them as talking too much in general or too much about their own experience of the festival rather than about the festival itself or the artists. On the other hand, some participants enjoyed the work of presenters, though different personalities appealed to different viewers: some preferred the older, more familiar ones and others liked younger, more dynamic ones or those who *"seem[ed] to be enjoying themselves"*.

Participants were questioned on how they used online media to complement their coverage and asked to comment relevant diary contributions. For news websites and social media, two different patterns were visible: either participants were actively looking for updates about the festival, or this was part of a news-checking or social media-checking routine. Another example of how Glastonbury fits into a daily routine was given by a participant who took a picture showing the weather forecast on her TV, on which she commented by saying that the presenter would specifically mention the weather at the festival location.

Social media could be used to obtain "official" coverage, either through feeds from news outlets or the official festival accounts, as well as personal points of views. Though in most cases, these "unofficial" personal experiences came from friends and acquaintances of participants, some turned to the personal social media accounts of band members, BBC journalists or the organizing team.

Facebook statuses posted by two participants who had been to the festival before but couldn't go that year included sharing very specific "insider" knowledge, as they mentioned locations outside the main stages and foods served at the festival in posts targeting friends who were or had been to the festival. One of them, P14, also noted that she and a group of friends who normally go to Glastonbury changed their profile pictures on Facebook to images of the festival and posted about what they would have done if they had been there.

A couple of participants also noted that social media updates were not expected to be live, and that they would normally have to wait until the next morning. P15, who was at the festival during the study, left her smartphone at home due to its battery life and only posted pictures and updates on social media after the festival.

Patterns of attention were also investigated and showed a broad range of levels of engagement, from the festival being played as a background sound to a focused attention on the video. Participants reported watching or listening to Glastonbury while commuting, working or doing household tasks. Focus on the festival was often driven by the pattern of other activities, with participants' attention increasing during pauses in activities, or by the general pattern of the day, in which evenings are dedicated to sitting in front of the television.

The interview also covered group dynamics and strategies participants used to select content as part of a group. Recording and queuing, as well as using catch-up services, was seen as very useful in making sure each household member gets to see what they want to, even when conflicting concerts happen simultaneously. In some cases, some members of the household took more control, for social reasons (such as P9, who chose to watch what others were choosing as she *"didn't want to isolate [her]self from [her] family"*) or when one acts as a recommender (*"[she] has wider music tastes than me, and she'll give me recommendations [...] so I was probably letting her decide"*, P8). Social dynamics may also distract participants away from the festival, as two participants reported having friends or relatives staying at home during the festival.

How participants discover and get recommendations of artists that match their tastes, be it during the festival or as part of their general music consumption, emerged as a theme during the interviews. Recommendations for music may come from friends or algorithms (one participant used

an online recommending service to select acts), as well as serendipitous discovery and following radio stations, magazines and specialized websites. For some, the festival was not only used to discover new artists, but also to update their knowledge of bands they already like: several participants reported that they only knew a few songs of a given artist and that watching a full set would expose them to a broader repertoire. Participants were also familiar with tunes without being able to name the song or band is and hearing these during the festival help them learn them. Two important pieces of information about artists were often searched for on YouTube and Wikipedia: what their greatest hits are and where they're from.

Whether the event was watched at the same time as it was happening was not an issue for most participants, and the convenience of watching it at any time was more valued than it being live. Participants who watched the World Cup the same weekend prioritized it over Glastonbury, which was justified by the fact that knowing the scores in advance is seen as spoiling the experience of watching sports and that such spoilers are hard to avoid. P14 mentioned that knowing the event is live was important as it added to her feeling of presence.

Most participants who had been to the festival combined this experience with watching it on TV, the motivations being catching up with missed performances, remembering one's experience and sharing it with others, e.g. after the festival, P15 watched it with a relative to make him understand what it was to be there. Participants have also tried to locate themselves on videos and still images, and P15 also complemented her souvenirs of the festival by looking for pictures her friends posted on social media.

Having been there also creates a tension due to expectations of missing out. P8 decided to limit his viewing to the main stage concerts as he expected that broader coverage would him *"feel like [he] was not there even more"* and P14, though she started with similar negative expectations, *"enjoyed it much more than [she] thought [she] would"*.

Participants may also wish to make sure the two experiences are kept separate. This was the justification for P8's decision not to catch up after coming back from the festival the previous year and he also feared that his memories of a performance he had *"really enjoyed"* would be affected by watching an excerpt on TV that viewers had rated poorly. P15 was glad that coverage misrepresented the festival as *"quite a commercial thing"*, as this gap between media and reality made her *"enjoy it more"*.

Communications by spectators at the festival were not only limited by network coverage (which some participants described as good) and battery life, but also by the fact that festival goers enjoy being "cut off" from what they call the "outside world". Another reason for not sharing was linked to who communications would be targeted at: P8 didn't publish any updates as *"the people that [he] mostly communicate[s] with were there anyway"*. On the other hand, P2, who had been to another festival, would post more updates than usual on social media as she wanted to share the fact that she was *"doing something exciting"*.

Though few participants directly said they felt they were there, various levels of immersion were reported. The quality of filming made P16 *"feel like you're on the stage or in the front row"*. P19 reported similar feelings when using headphones at a loud volume and P14 thought that quality *"makes up for not being there"*. Having lived the experience by oneself also added to the feeling of presence, with P15 declaring *"watching it again was exactly like being there"* and P14 thinking she wouldn't have felt connected to the festival if she hadn't been there.

DISCUSSION

Here we initially describe how our findings show that there is no single obvious trend of how participants engage with the event, but rather a multiplicity of routes through which participants experience this event. This is why, rather than offering a single way for broadcasters to address our results, our conclusion is that this multiplicity should be respected. We also conclude that these multiple routes should be interleaved to take advantage of the complementarity between specific personal experiences, and between the festival site and home, which we might treat as being a distinctive, complementary setting for festival experiences rather than as a competitor to "being there".

A diverse experience

Our findings have shown a diversity of viewing patterns when following the Glastonbury festival. These tend to revolve around a typical experience that happens at home, is consumed alone or shared with members of the same household, focuses on videos of familiar headline acts while occasionally jumping channels to try out new music, is motivated by the music itself, often incorporates information about the festival from newspapers and social media, and is accessed as part of viewers' regular media routines. This experience typically involves a familiar technological repertoire [11] including both live and time-shifted videos. This said, our findings also revealed other patterns that complement or disrupt this "canonical" experience, making it more personal, including:

- The festival as a support for a sociable experience (within a wider group that may be at the festival, away from it, or even split between locations).

- Television complementing, recalling or sharing one's experience of having been at the festival.

- Following friends around while they are at the festival.

- Collecting performances of one's favorite band.

- Listening to the festival as background music.

- Searching for specific content not covered by TV.

- Discovering what a live music festival is and understanding its wider cultural context.

- Discovering (and helping others discover) new music.

This diversity of viewing experience reveals that there is no "one size fits all" approach to broadcasting such events. Instead, it is important to develop services that improve the personalization of coverage, for example by scheduling playlists or sharing recommendations. This mirrors the findings of previous research on viewing patterns for complex events [1] which stressed the importance of supporting scheduling and queuing, as well as giving users awareness of the structure of their viewing and its relation to liveness, and an overview of available content [12].

Our study also suggests that coverage might usefully be extended to smaller stages and non-concert entertainment. This could be addressed by increasing the discoverability of existing content as well as providing raw footage used in highlight programs. This footage may be proposed as part of automated compilations generated on the basis of viewers' preferences, as proposed by Frantzis et al. [18]. However, it will become increasingly difficult for broadcasters to muster the resources to cover all aspects of large-scale events, suggesting the adoption of crowd-sourced videos to cover gaps in coverage as explored in previous research [13, 17].

Trajectories through viewing experiences

While it is necessary to consider more personalized viewing journeys, our study also points to the potential benefits of interleaving these journeys in various ways. This might involve connecting people who assume different roles, for example those present at the festival (spectators, organizers, reporters, performers) with remote viewers: the former might then guide the latter through available coverage or, conversely, the TV viewer may help a festival goer navigate the location.

This idea of connecting remote viewers with participants "on the ground" is reminiscent of previous attempts to create mixed reality performances and games that bring together so-called "street players" with "online players" to create new participatory media experiences. Studies of such experiences led to the idea that they can be designed in terms of various kinds of "interactional trajectories", extended journeys that integrate the physical and digital aspects of media experiences and that become interleaved to create rich social experiences [4]. We propose that this approach of designing interleaved trajectories might also inspire the design of future broadcast services for cultural events. We might identify "canonical" trajectories for different classes of participants, for example those who are going to the festival, those who have been before but cannot go this time, those who have never been but may go in the future, and those who only enjoy viewing from home. We might then interleave these to create new social viewing experiences as noted above.

Trajectories also encourage exploration of how experiences extend over time as well as how they are reflected on and recounted afterwards. Thus, a festival-goer may bookmark performances or locations on site to inform her subsequent catch-up experience; musical selections done when viewers are strongly engaged with content may be used to inform what will play when they listen to it in the background. Festivals may also be interleaved with other experiences in people's lives, and coverage may connect with long-term engagement in music or with media related routines. Finally, we should recognize that people often engage with cultural events over much longer time periods, potentially over a lifetime. This line of thinking encourages us to realize the potential of relating the current viewing experience to those of previous years. For example, a viewer may wish to reach back into their personal archive to recall performances from previous festivals that they have watched or attended.

Towards a socially immersive experience
Our study revealed mixed feelings about the importance of "being there" when watching large-scale live events from home, as this depends on sound and image quality, previous knowledge of the event, personal expectations and connections with people on location. This is consistent with previous literature [22] that has described presence as a subjective phenomenon depending on three dimensions: realism of stimuli (or "media richness"), realism of social interactions and the fact that one's interactions have an impact on the remote or simulated environment. One valid response to this observation would be to seek to improve these dimensions of the experience in order to increase the sense of "being there" for the remote viewer.

However, we also encountered viewers for whom an increased sense of being there was not desirable, for example participants who have been to the festival and wished to maintain this as unique and distinct from home viewing, or participants who simply would much prefer to be there for real. This invites us to treat the broadcast experience of Glastonbury not as a mere reproduction of a festival viewer's experience but as a distinct cultural experience in its own right. As Hollan and Stornetta have argued, improving the experience of remote communication may have more to do with embracing technological affordances than reproducing elements of presence [24]. The fact that around half of viewers watch coverage with others, and evidence that a minority are even willing to rearrange their setting or engage in special festival activities while watching, such as eating special foods, point to opportunities for extending the experience of viewing large-scale live events to a more socially immersive experience *at home*. How then might broadcasters enable viewers to create more powerful local shared festival experiences at home?

We end our paper by suggesting some possibilities for achieving this. Families might embrace the multiplicity of screens and other devices within the household to create a "festival at home" experience. The living room might become the main stage, devices in other rooms might be tuned into smaller stages, and radios in the kitchen and other communal areas might play ambient audio feeds from the festival site. People might even fall asleep to noises from the campsite. Community events might be encouraged, with stages distributed across a neighborhood or within a public place. An extended festival experience might also mean connecting TV viewers with live music, arguably the heart of the festival experience, and inviting them to watch or perform live music at the time of the festival, or sing-along to broadcast performances.

Whatever their form – the above ideas are only initial speculations intended to inspire further research – such ideas invite broadcasters to also reconsider how they engage views with events and the kinds of material that they should broadcast. In addition to capturing and showing high-quality footage from the major stages, it may also be beneficial to transmit ambient media and other data streams (e.g. unmixed or ambient audio, karaoke-like feeds of lyrics, schedules and news events) that enable viewers to create a more atmospheric sense of the event at home, perhaps even combining these with "maker kits" containing suggestions and tools for creating their own extended family and community viewing experiences.

Future work will involve designing the prototype of a service that supports such experiences, and deploying it around a festival. The evaluation of this prototype in a real world, "in the wild" setting, will offer the opportunity to conduct a second iteration of user studies, whose results will complement the findings described above and enrich our knowledge of the festival viewing experience.

CONCLUSION
We have described a study aimed at unpacking the experience of watching a broadcast large-scale live event. The results show that this is a complex and diverse experience that is interwoven in multiple ways with the lives of viewers. We recommended designing novel services for the coverage of this type of event that would embrace this diversity by offering an experience that would be more personalized and social, and include user-generated content. We proposed to design the festival viewing in terms of multiple interleaved trajectories and as a socially immersive experience.

ACKNOWLEDGMENTS
The first author's work is supported by the UK EPSRC through the iCASE grant EP/K504506/1.

REFERENCES
1. Anstead, E., Benford, S., and Houghton, R.J. Many-Screen Viewing: Evaluating an Olympics Companion Application. *Proc. TVX'14*, ACM (2014), 103–110.

2. BARB, Top 10 Programmes. Accessed on July 31st 2014. http://www.barb.co.uk/whats-new/weekly-top-10

3. BBC, Glastonbury 2014 Coverage FAQ. http://www.bbc.co.uk/programmes/articles/4pxRZh6dm9Y256CKwW8yBqQ/

4. Benford, S., Giannachi, G., Koleva, B., and Rodden, T. From interaction to trajectories: designing coherent journeys through user experiences. *Proc. CHI'09*, ACM.

5. Bernhaupt, R., Obrist, M., Weiss, A., Beck, E., and Tscheligi, M. Trends in the Living Room and Beyond: Results from Ethnographic Studies Using Creative and Playful Probing. *Comput. Entertain. 6*, 1 (2008).

6. Brown, B. and Barkhuus, L. The Television Will Be Revolutionized: Effects of PVRs and Filesharing on Television Watching. *Proc. CHI'06*, ACM (2006).

7. Carter, S. and Mankoff, J. When Participants Do the Capturing: The Role of Media in Diary Studies. *Proc. CHI'05*, ACM (2005), 899–908.

8. Chambel, T., Chhaganlal, M.N., and Neng, L.A.R. Towards Immersive Interactive Video Through 360° Hypervideo. *Proc. ACE'11*, ACM (2011), 78:1–78:2.

9. Cisco. StadiumVision. http://www.cisco.com/web/strategy/sports/StadiumVision.html.

10. Crowther, B. BBC R&D at the Commonwealth Games 2014, *BBC R&D Blog.* http://www.bbc.co.uk/rd/blog/2014/07/bbc-rd-at-the-commonwealth-games-2014.

11. Courtois, C. The Composition and Role of Convergent Technology Repertoires in Audiovisual Media Consumption. *Proc. EuroITV'12*, ACM (2012), 97–104.

12. Dezfuli, N., Huber, J., Churchill, E.F., and Mühlhäuser, M. CoStream: Co-construction of shared experiences through mobile live video sharing. *Proc. BCS-HCI'13.* BCS (2013).

13. Dezfuli, N., Günther, S., Khalilbeigi, M., Mühlhäuser, M., and Huber, J. CoStream@Home: Connected Live Event Experiences. *Proc. SAM'13*, ACM (2013), 33–36.

14. D'heer, E., Courtois, C., and Paulussen, S. Everyday Life in (Front of) the Screen: The Consumption of Multiple Screen Technologies in the Living Room Context. *Proc. EuroITV'12*, ACM (2012), 195–198.

15. Dork, M., Gruen, D., Williamson, C., and Carpendale, S. A Visual Backchannel for Large-Scale Events. *IEEE Transactions on Visualization and Computer Graphics 16*, 6 (2010), 1129–1138.

16. Doughty, M., Rowland, D., and Lawson, S. Co-viewing Live TV with Digital Backchannel Streams. *Proc. EuroITV'11*, ACM (2011), 141–144.

17. Flintham M., Velt R., Wilson M., Anstead E., Benford S., Brown A., Pearce T., Price D., and Sprinks J. Run Spot Run: Capturing and Tagging Footage of a Race by Crowds of Spectators. *Proc. CHI'15*, ACM (2015).

18. Frantzis, M., Zsombori, V., Ursu, M., Guimaraes, R.L., Kegel, I., and Craigie, R. Interactive Video Stories from User Generated Content: A School Concert Use Case. *In Interactive Storytelling.* Springer (2012), 183–195.

19. Gaver, W.W., Beaver, J., and Benford, S. Ambiguity As a Resource for Design. *Proc. CHI'03*, ACM (2003).

20. Gaver, B., Dunne, T., and Pacenti, E. Design: Cultural Probes. *Interactions 6*, 1 (1999), 21–29.

21. Guimarães, R.L., Cesar, P., Bulterman, D.C.A., Zsombori, V., and Kegel, I. Creating Personalized Memories from Social Events: Community-based Support for Multi-camera Recordings of School Concerts. *Proc ACMMM'15* ACM (2011), 303–312.

22. Heeter, C. Being There: The Subjective Experience of Presence. *Presence: Teleoperators Virtual Environments 1*, 2 (1992), 262–271.

23. Hess, J., Ley, B., Ogonowski, C., Wan, L., and Wulf, V. Jumping Between Devices and Services: Towards an Integrated Concept for Social Tv. *Proc. EuroITV'11*, ACM (2011), 11–20.

24. Hollan, J. and Stornetta, S. Beyond Being There. *Proc. CHI'92*, ACM (1992), 119–125.

25. Huron, S., Isenberg, P., and Fekete, J.D. PolemicTweet: Video Annotation and Analysis through Tagged Tweets. *Proc. INTERACT 2013.* Springer (2013), 135–152.

26. Jacucci, G., Oulasvirta, A., Ilmonen, T., Evans, J., and Salovaara, A. Comedia: Mobile Group Media for Active Spectatorship. *Proc. CHI 2007*, ACM (2007).

27. Kennedy, L. and Naaman, M. Less Talk, More Rock: Automated Organization of Community-contributed Collections of Concert Videos. *Proc. WWW'09.* ACM.

28. Lynn, S.G., Olsen, D.R., Jr., and Partridge, B.G. Time Warp Football. *Proc. EuroITV'09*, ACM (2009), 77–86.

29. Miller, A. Surround Video! *R&D Blog.* BBC (2010). http://www.bbc.co.uk/blogs/legacy/researchanddevelopment/2010/02/surround-video-yes-surround-vi.shtml.

30. Ofcom. Communication Market Report. 2013.

31. Simeoni, R., Geymonat, M., Guercio, E., et al. Where Have You Ended Up Today? Dynamic TV and the Intertainment Paradigm. *Changing Television Environments.* Springer (2008), 238–247.

32. Ursu, M.F., Kegel, I.C., Williams, D., et al. ShapeShifting TV: interactive screen media narratives. *Multimedia Systems 14*, 2 (2008), 11

Experimental Enquiry into Automatically Orchestrated Live Video Communication in Social Settings

Marian F Ursu
University of York
United Kingdom
marian.ursu@york.ac.uk

Manolis Falelakis
Goldsmiths University London
United Kingdom
m.falelakis@gold.ac.uk

Martin Groen
University of Utrecht
Netherlands
m.g.m.groen@uu.nl

Rene Kaiser
JOANNEUM RESEARCH
Austria
rene.kaiser@joanneum.at

Michael Frantzis
Goldsmiths University London
United Kingdom
m.frantzis@gold.ac.uk

ABSTRACT

'Orchestration' refers to the ability of a live video communication system to adapt in real-time to the communication context with a view to enhance the quality of mediation and subsequently the quality of interaction between participants. For example, this can be done by reframing the cameras and changing the way in which the video content is mixed on each screen. To be a feasible solution, orchestration has to be an automatic process. This paper reports a study of orchestration carried out in the social setting of a group of friends playing social games from two separate living rooms. The quality of the communication was assessed via two measures: one objective, in the form of task efficiency, and one subjective, in the form of a questionnaire. The objective measure indicated that mediated communication can be improved through orchestration, but the subjective measure was inconclusive. The paper also uncovers some of the complexities of the experimental space associated with orchestrated mediated communication and aims to provide motivation for further research into this new communication paradigm.

Author Keywords

Videoconferencing; Telepresence; Mediated communication; Group communication; Orchestration; Virtual Director; Video; Live; Communication; Group; Interaction; Television.

ACM Classification Keywords

H.5.m. Information Interfaces and Presentation (e.g. HCI): Miscellaneous

INTRODUCTION

The use of live video mediation in social communication is growing at a fast pace. Products such as Microsoft Skype and Google+ Hangouts are increasingly becoming part of our daily lives. Group communication is being addressed, but the current systems do not go beyond 'talking heads' [14]. The communication setups currently dealt with by live video communication systems are still quite restrictive.

Imagine, for example, a conversation across a live video link among a group of friends located in two separate living rooms, carried out over the rooms' TV screens. One fixed camera per location providing one fixed shot could suffice to mediate the conversation, particularly as people are able to adapt their behaviour [22] and find artful ways to overcome the limitations of the communication system [10]. However, there are also many reasons why it may not suffice [10, 22]. For example, the one shot may lack the necessary levels of detail to appropriately convey particular actions, facial expressions and messages expressed through body language, and so it may lead to 'unnatural behaviour', for example by constraining people to be aware of the camera and ensure that they are always in the frame. An alternative would be to employ more than one shot per location, through multiple cameras, with the corresponding communication system able to 'follow the communication as it progresses', choosing the right shots and mixing them in a manner similar to film and TV [21]. Figure 1 illustrates sample shots that could be captured from one of the locations and mixed on the TV screen of the other.

Figure 1. Example of shots that could be used in a multi-camera live video communication system.

Such an approach appears to allow people to have more natural interactions with each other, potentially increasing their sense of empathy [16], connectedness and presence, as well as counteracting spatial distortion [12], perceptual invariance [15] and increasing the 'transparency' of the communication medium itself. Furthermore, such an approach appears to be necessarily required in more comprehensive communication setups intended to be mediated through live audio and video, such as connecting more than two locations and providing for larger groups, involved in more complex social activities.

The ability of a communication system to dynamically reframe the cameras, control the microphones and mix the available live audio-video content on the available screens and speakers, to ensure, for each participant, an optimum in the perspectives and levels of detail perceived from the other spaces, has been denoted *communication orchestration* or, simply, *orchestration* [21]. Orchestration is similar to the compilation of live TV programmes, but it is fundamentally different, as its underlying principle is *communication*, not storytelling. Furthermore, in live orchestrated communication, the way in which the cameras and microphones are controlled and audio video content is mixed has a direct effect upon the conversation itself, whereas in TV, events are being merely depicted, the lens being a mere observer with no agency. Lastly, TV considers one viewpoint, namely that of the aggregated audience, whereas orchestration must take into account the perspective of each of the participating members. The success of such adaptable context-aware communication systems depends upon the 'recipes' according to which they perform orchestration – i.e., their orchestration *logics*, *grammars* or *knowledge*. Any body of orchestration knowledge subsumes two main reasoning processes:

• *understanding* the continuously changing context of the communication taking place, and

• *adapting* the communication system to appropriately provide for the identified communication context

The former process takes input from sensors and feature extraction procedures (e.g., voice activity extraction and face detection) and 'lifts' such primitive information into aspects of the communication context (e.g., the person holding the conversation turn). The latter process applies screen-language conventions to determine how to control the cameras and how to mix the available live content in order to best mediate the identified communication context (through the former process) among all the participants.

Orchestrated communication is a rather new area of work and, consequently, there is very little orchestration knowledge available. There is significant work regarding the understanding of the context of communication (see the related work section), but this has not been linked, yet, to directing cameras and screen 'vision mixing' for live video-mediated communication. Conversely, there is significant expertise and knowledge regarding directing cameras and mixing content, but this is geared towards film and TV, not to adaptive, context-aware communication systems. Orchestration logic represents the *grammar of the language of live video communication*. Orchestration could (and should) take video-mediated communication to where film and TV are today. Orchestration grammars should be refined incrementally, through experimental enquiry and ought to be possible to be automated.

Refining and validating orchestration knowledge is not straightforward. On one hand, orchestration knowledge is made of a combination of rules with potentially strong interdependencies. Its study, therefore, is radically different from that of the effect of a single variable (such as the size of the head) upon the mediated communication. On the other hand, orchestration is not a *general* recipe to any video-mediated communication setup. Each particular setup requires its own specific orchestration logic. Yet, more generic bodies of orchestration knowledge, applicable to wider communication setups, need to be identified, if the whole approach of orchestrated communication is to be feasible and effective. There is tight coupling between choosing the communication setup and refining the corresponding orchestration knowledge, each influencing the other. These aspects create a highly non-deterministic space, very dynamic and quite challenging for experimental enquiry.

This paper presents an experimental investigation into *automatically orchestrated* video-mediated communication within a particular setting of social group interaction: friends playing social games, chatting and having fun, from two separate living rooms, using the TV as the communication conduit to the other room. It is motivated by [21], which showed, by carrying out orchestration *entirely by human operators*, that orchestration can have a positive impact in such communication setups. The study presented here addresses the questions of whether a *completely automatic* system could have a similar impact. In the process of answering this question, the study also uncovered aspects regarding the complexity of the experimental enquiry into this novel communication paradigm.

RELATED WORK

As already mentioned, there is a significant body of research related to the automatic understanding of communication contexts. The conceptual underpinning is provided by 'conversation analysis' [20], with 'turn-taking' [19] being probably the most investigated concept. More recently, this line of research has been extended to 'social signal processing' [6, 23]. Its ultimate aim is the development of procedures for the automatic extraction of features of social interaction, taking verbal as well as non-verbal behaviour (such as prosody, posture, gaze, gestures, etc.) as the object of analysis. Various conceptual models have been designed and validated. The review provided in [6] groups them into four categories, namely those pertaining to *interaction management* (e.g., addressing and turn-taking), *internal states* (e.g., interest and emotional engagement), *personality traits* (e.g., dominance and extroversion), and *social relationships* (e.g., formal roles, such as interviewee, and social roles, for example determined by the social status). The more recent review provided in [24] uses a similar taxonomy, namely *social actions* and *interactions*, *social emotions*, *social attitudes*, and *social relations*. The state of the art is impressive when it comes to implementations able to automatically extract such features of social interaction. They are directly relevant to orchestration. However, orchestration places two very demanding requirements on such implementations: they need to work in real-time and operate in uncontrolled, complex and 'noisy' environments. Many of the existing implementations do not meet these requirements. Nevertheless, they can certainly inform of what is possible and might become available in the (near) future. It is also rewarding to notice that some of these implementations are made available as open source, such as OpenSMILE [2], which provides a rich set of low level features that can be extracted from audio (e.g., waveform properties, signal energy, loudness) [3] and from video (e.g., face detection) [2]. They can be processed jointly in a single framework allowing for time synchronization of parameters, on-line incremental processing as well as off-line and batch processing, and the extraction of statistical data. In conclusion, there already are insightful research results with regards to the understanding of communication contexts, and the momentum behind this work is increasing. However, when it comes to orchestration, this is only half of the picture: the part that maps such identified traits into camera and mixing decisions still needs to be developed.

The other half of the orchestration reasoning process – i.e., controlling cameras and vision mixers – is also the subject of related research, but most of this work is carried out in the context of games, film and TV production. The main problem dealt with by games research is the selection, at each point in the game interaction, of the most appropriate viewpoint – referring to position, orientation, focal distance, etc. of the virtual camera – to represent the 3D world. The selection is constrained by editing principles, adapted from film and TV, related to concepts such as 2D/3D continuity, rhythm, story and emotion. Such editing principles, together with the techniques employed in their computational expression, are surveyed in [18]. The description is made from the viewpoint of the approach taken for knowledge modelling: procedural, declarative and optimization. Narrative techniques from film and TV have already made their way into game screen language to provide for more dramatic and engaging interactions. This is strong motivation for orchestration research, which is also hypothesizing that film and TV techniques could be used to enhance the means of social interaction. However, orchestration addresses communication within social groups which is mediated by video, whereas games are about interaction within virtual worlds.

On a parallel track, in the area of film and TV, the most relevant research to orchestration concerns the formalization of shot description, directing, and other aspects of the film production workflow, with a view to providing for more rigorous descriptions and to automate parts thereof. [25], for example, presents a symbolic language to express the content of film, which is accompanied by a number of software tools intended for use during film planning and visualization of ideas. This is relevant to orchestration, as such work, too, is concerned with deciding upon the right shots for a specific situation, according to some embedded logic. However, this is about narrating events to a passive audience, not about live communication, as orchestration is.

Related work that connects the two main reasoning components of orchestration – context understanding and directing video expression – is scarce. [1] investigated the identification of 'floor control' in group meetings, using a multi-modal approach that combines patterns of speech (e.g., the use of discourse markers) with visual cues (e.g., gaze exchanges). Identifying who has control of the floor provides an important focus for information retrieval and summarization from audio-video recordings. This work focuses on the definition of a model, using manual annotations of audio and video recordings, and not on its implementation. Also, its application is summarization and retrieval, not communication. [17] reports a study that employed principles from television production to capture meetings of small groups. Events such as 'speaker change', 'posture change' and 'head orientation' are mapped, according to an internal logic, onto different types of shots, such as 'close-up', 'two-person' and 'overview'. Automatically compiled representations are compared with representations compiled by a film crew. This work is closely related to orchestration, but its overall aim is to better recount meetings (to passive viewers), not to provide for real-time communication between participants. [1] and [17] consider face-to-face communication and aim to develop better ways for their recording and recounting, whereas orchestration considers mediated communication. Also, [1] and [17] are set in the more structured space of meetings, whereas orchestration, here, is studied within the less structured space of social interaction.

The work reported in [7] is about 'orchestration' (our terminology). Two groups of people have a meeting across a video link. One direction of communication was orchestrated, employing one mobile camera, whereas the other one was 'conventional', using a static wide shot. The orchestration logic was refined by analysing TV debate programmes. Eight types of shots were refined, including 'speaker', 'listener' and 'speaker and listener'. The duration of each shot was clocked and so a frequency distribution was compiled from the TV content. The orchestration logic was subsequently expressed as two-shot transition tables, each specifying the probability of transition from any shot to any other shot. One table was used when the speaker changed, the other was used in conjunction with the frequency distribution. The 'change in speaker' cue was inserted manually, by a human operator. This is inspiring work, but the setup was limited: context understanding was not automatic, only one direction of communication was orchestrated and the interaction context was that of a structured meeting. Benefits of the orchestrated communication have been observed, such as better conveyance of the feelings and intentions of the active speaker, but also benefits of the conventional link have been noticed, such as making the situation easier to grasp. The conclusion was that orchestration can be a way of improving the quality of communication in structured meetings. However, interestingly, the study hypothesized that this paradigm is not portable to the less structured conversations of the social space, as speaker identification is not portable to situations when people take short turns or speak over each other.

The work reported in [21] attempts to invalidate this hypothesis and takes orchestration into a social setting. A group of friends play social games and have idle chats from two separate living rooms. Both communication directions are orchestrated, the system employing a number of fixed cameras per location, each able to provide a particular functional shot. The orchestration logic is expressed as a set of rules, but the corresponding reasoning process is being entirely carried out by human operators. The logic is based not only on 'conversation turns' (similar to active speaker in the previously cited work), but also on other features of conversation analysis, such as 'crosstalk' and 'quick turn taking'. The study concluded that orchestration can improve the quality of the communication and interaction experiences in a social setting, and motivated enquiries into automatically performed orchestration. Our paper reports on such an enquiry, in a setting similar to [21] and using a similar orchestration logic, but automatically executed.

In conclusion, there are various bodies of research related to the two main reasoning processes subsumed by orchestration, but there is no study yet of an automatically orchestrated video communication system employed in a social setting – i.e. a system *aware* of the communication context and able to *dynamically configure* itself in real-time to best address the communication needs. Such a study is presented in this paper.

EXPERIMENT DESCRIPTION

Communication setup
As stated in the introduction, orchestration is not a general recipe to any communication setup. Rather, particular setups require particular bodies of orchestration logic. However, such 'particular setups' ought to have a level of generality to ensure reuse of the orchestration logic to the extent that the proposition is feasible and cost effective.

The general setup chosen for this study is that of friends playing social games, chatting and having fun, from two separate living rooms (see Figure 2).

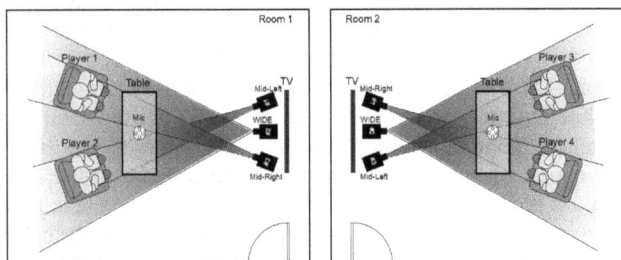

Figure 2. Communication setup.

Each room had two armchairs, a coffee table, a lamp shade hanging over it, and a TV table. Each room used one HD 50 inch TV screen and 3 HD cameras (Sony EVI-HD1), positioned next to each other on the same table as the TV. Each camera provided a specific functional shot which was framed at the beginning of each interaction session, but not dynamically reframed afterwards – orchestration was carried out through dynamic mixing only. There was stereo

sound with echo cancellation between the two rooms. A star-4 microphone array was concealed in the lampshade, some 1.5m equidistant from the two people, and the speakers were aligned with the TV. Each group consisted of 4 people, 2 per room. They played a variant of the game of Articulate, where players have to describe words to their team as quickly as possible, in a window of 30 seconds. If the word is not guessed, the other team can join and the description continues for another 30 seconds.

Orchestration logic
Any corpus of orchestration knowledge should be founded on a combination of key interaction principles, such as: following the most active speaker(s); providing a balanced view of all the people involved in the conversation; following the conversation flow by focusing on the active speakers as well as the listeners who actively react to what is being said (e.g., by interjecting or nodding); or others. The principle behind the orchestration logic used here was that of following and giving visual prominence to the active speakers, but ensuring that the visual continuity of the representation is preserved.

The former requirement was based on the concepts of *turn shift* and *short turn taking*, which were automatically inferred from a more primitive cue, namely 'start voice activity by person P'. The definition of the concepts is given below:

Only one person can have the turn at any one time.

Person P takes the turn if there is voice activity detected from P and P is not currently holding the turn and P is not cross talking over someone else.

Person Q is cross talking over person P if P has the turn and there is voice activity detected from Q.

There is a pattern of short turn taking if 3 or more turn shifts occur within 5 seconds.

For the dynamic construction of the visual representation, a small set of types of shots was considered to be sufficient: a *wide shot*, framed to include both people in the room, allowing them also a bit of space for movement, and two tighter shots, *mid-shots*, one for each person in the room (Figure 3). Orchestration was done solely through their mixing (i.e., there was no camera reframing), using only clean cut transitions.

The mixing logic, expressed as rules in natural language, is described below (the rules are stated from the point of view of the room/screen *for* which the mixing is taking place, therefore, the persons referred to in the rules are from the other room):

1. *If person P starts a conversation turn (i.e., a turn-shift to P occurs), show the medium shot of P.*

2. *If there is a pattern of short turn-takings, then show the wide.*

3. *If there is no turn-shift for 5 seconds, then show the wide.*

4. *No change of shot is allowed within 2 seconds of the previous cut (highest priority, when there are conflicts).*

Figure 3. The shots for orchestration: a wide and 2 mid-shots.

The last rule, inspired by TV production, aimed to avoid too often cuts, which would break the visual continuity.

Conditions

Four experimental conditions were found necessary for this investigation, which were all mediated through the same communication infrastructure and differed only with regards to orchestration: *context aware automatic orchestration (CA-A)*, *context aware manual orchestration (CA-M)*, *static* and *context unaware mixing (CU)*. All the conditions were of equal length (15 minutes) and their order was counterbalanced as follows: CA-A was experienced by the participants 2 times as first condition, 2 as second, 3 as third and 2 as fourth; CA-M was 3 times the first one to take place first, 2 times second, 1 time third and 3 times fourth; the static condition was 2 times first, 3 second, 2 third and 2 fourth; while the CU condition was experienced 2 times as first, 2 as second, 3 as third and 2 as fourth.

In the CA-A condition, the whole reasoning process was entirely automatic, from the extraction of primitive cues to the issuing of mixing decisions. In the CA-M condition, the entire reasoning process was performed by two human operators (one per screen/room). They were instructed to follow rigorously the rule-set aforementioned and rely as little as possible on their mixing experience and knowledge (tacit or explicit). As orchestrated communication experiences are determined by the bodies of rules on which they are based, any rule change could have a significant impact upon the group communication experience. This was the reason why the operators were instructed to follow rigorously the given set of rules. Otherwise, there would have not been any comparable behaviour between manual and automatic orchestration, nor continuity across experiments (if the operators are not constrained by a given set of rules, in each experiment they would have applied their tacit knowledge differently). However, the experience of the manual operators was somewhat reflected in their interpretation of the rules, which were expressed in natural language.

In the static condition there is no reasoning process involved at all, a wide shot of the room being always shown in the other room. The CU condition was included as a reference for measuring the effect of context-awareness (both of the CA conditions). In the CU condition, a simple time-based algorithm was used to drive the mixing process: a change of shot, from the available three, was continuously made at a random interval of time varying between 2 and 5 seconds (uniform distribution). This simulated the pace with which human op-erators cut between shots for this communication setup (inferred through prior experimentation) and was aligned with the thresholds used in the orchestration rules.

A number of criteria informed the choice of these conditions. To make manual orchestration possible, the size and expression of the logic had to be sufficiently small and clear to allow the human operators to digest it and apply it rigorously. To ensure that the static condition was not disadvantaged by design, the setup was chosen such that the wide shot captured all the necessary information from the other room. In order to not distract the participants on reverse engineering the system or 'playing' with its capabilities, they were not briefed beforehand on the conditions they were going to experience. Although the CU condition involves random choices, it is still an informed way of mixing, as: (i) it mixes the available shots with, more or less, the same pace as the CA conditions; and (ii) out of the 3 shots available for mixing, 2 are always relevant, as they always capture the active speaker.

Sessions and participants

A total of 9 interaction sessions were carried out with a total of 36 participants – a session being defined by a group of 4 people undertaking all 4 conditions. There were 2 teams of 2 participants in each session who experienced the 4 different conditions in succession, giving a 4 factorial within-participants design. The participants were chosen such that all the team members knew each other from before, but they did not necessarily know the members of the opposite team. Out of the 36 participants, 13 were male and 23 female, they were aged between 18 and 51 (mean 23.1, variance 4.8) and 28 of them were native English speakers. 21 of them knew their teammate for longer than 6 months.

There were 2 orchestration operators for the manual condition, both with prior film editing experience and they were in charge of all 9 experimental sessions.

Communication system

The architecture of the bespoke communication system used in the experiment is depicted in Figure 4. Video and audio were processed on parallel channels. The round-trip video delay was about 600ms and audio was slowed down to ensure synchronicity. The audio chain was supported by the audio communication engine clients (ACEs) and the server component, the ACE Multipoint Control Unit (MCU) (described in [5]). They provided for a high quality stereo connection between the two rooms with very good echo cancellation. The video chain was supported by the video acquisition clients (VACQs), the video router (VR) and the video composition engines (VCEs). Of key importance here are the VCEs [8], which were able to execute the commands of the orchestration engine. The VCEs decoded in parallel all the streams received from the other room, to ensure that they could cut instantaneously between them.

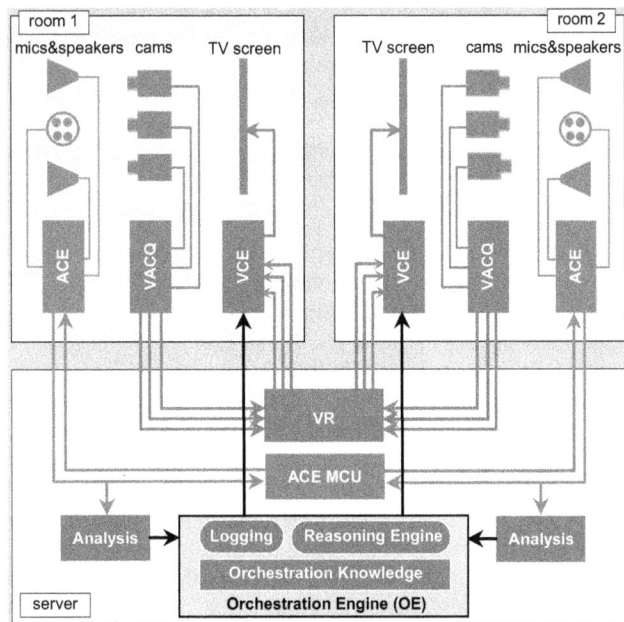

Figure 4. Orchestrated communication system for 2 rooms.

The network connectivity was chosen such as to impose no constraints on the system described above, i.e. there was sufficient bandwidth for each room to upload 3 HD streams and download 3 HD streams.

The output of the Orchestration Engine (OE) consisted of cut commands sent to the VCE. The input into the OE consisted of the primitive cues received from the Analysis components [13]. Two types of primitive cues – 'directional audio activity' and 'face detection' – extracted by the Analysis engines were further fused by it into the 'start/stop voice activity by face X' cue, which was the primitive cue used by the OE to infer the required conversation cues – turn-shift and short-turn-taking.

The Orchestration Engine (OE) was built in a declarative model, with the knowledge base separated from the reasoning engine [4]. The logic was implemented using rules in an event-based framework [9], using the JBoss Drools inference engine[1]. The main issues that needed to be considered in the implementation included: (i) conflict resolution (ii) processing of asynchronous events, (iii) management of imprecision in measurements and definitions, (iv) real-time event processing (v) ability for temporal reasoning.

All the inferences of the OE were time-stamped logged, including detection of conversation turn-shifts, short turn taking, and decisions to cut.

---

[1]http://www.jboss.org/drools

In the manually orchestrated condition, the OE was replaced by two human operators, one per room, each operating via a live-mixing interface, in-house implemented, plugged into the communication framework. Each operator had a view of the room *from* which they were mixing and the screen of the room *for* which they were mixing. Three buttons, corresponding to the three possible shots, were mapped onto three adjacent keys for shot selection. In order to assist them with the application of the rules, rule 4 was enforced in the live-mixing interface by disabling the keys and buttons for 2 seconds from the previous action.

For the context-unaware mixing condition, the OE was replaced by a simple piece of code implementing the time-based mixing algorithm.

RESULTS
The objective measure used was that of 'task efficiency', defined as the average game points won per condition (Figure 5). Significant differences were found here, as participants performed considerably poorer in the context unaware mixing condition (CU), achieving their best results in the automatically orchestrated one (CA-A). More specifically, the results show that different conditions affected the gameplay of the participants, $F(3, 30) = 4.34$, $p = .01$, $\eta\,p^2 = .30$. The mean number of game points won in the automatic condition (CA-A) was 25.91 (SD = 8.07), in the manual condition (CA-M) was 24.00 (SD = 9.74), in the static condition was 23.09 (SD = 11.42) and in the context-unaware condition (CU) was 17.27 (SD = 9.03). Planned pairwise comparisons, Bonferroni corrected, showed that only the automatic orchestration condition contributed to the observed difference in effect of orchestration, $p < .05$.

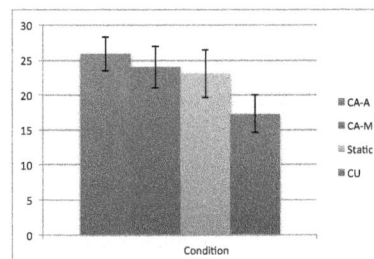

Figure 5. Objective evaluation: Average game points won per condition: Context Aware Automatic (CA-A) orchestration, Context Aware Manual (CA-M) orchestration, Static and Context Unaware (CU) mixing. The corresponding standard error is represented as error bars.

The questionnaire proposed in [11] was used for the subjective evaluation of the mediated communication across the four selected conditions. It targeted four factors describing mediated interaction: *naturalness*, *immersiveness*, *presence* and *social presence*. The average assessment for each factor is shown in Figure 6 by experimental condition. There were no significant differences measured in these four factors (p >.05), which means that all the four conditions were more or less equivalent with regards to the specific subjective evaluation.

The average number and duration of 'turn shifts' was also measured for each condition (see Figure 7), with a view to

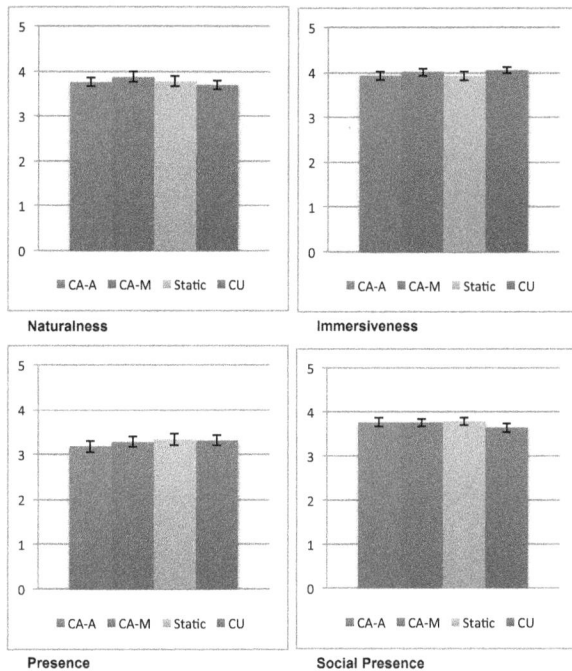

Figure 6. Average participant experience per condition.

providing further data for the evaluation of the quality of the communication experience. The two are related, but not inferable from each other, as the state where no participant holds the turn is possible. These results were log-transformed and entered in a repeated analysis of variance. There were no differences in turn shifts across conditions ($p > .05$), see Figure 7a. Figure 7b shows that turn durations were also not affected by the different conditions ($p > .05$); no significant pairwise differences were observed in the duration of turns.

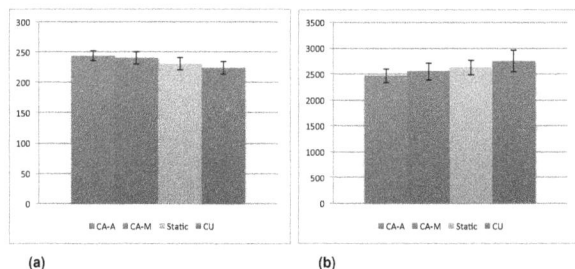

Figure 7. (a) Average number of turn shifts per condition. (b) Average duration of turns per condition.

DISCUSSION

Recall that the aim of the current experiment was to investigate the effect of *context-awareness and dynamic configurability*, defined as *orchestration*, on the quality of video-mediated communication, using an objective measure of task performance and a subjective assessment of the experience. The hypothesis was that orchestration can improve the ability of participants to communicate and collaborate effectively and that this would be reflected through both measures, objective and subjective.

The results did confirm, albeit marginally, the expectations with regards to the objective measure, as participants were indeed more efficient when collaborating in the two context-aware conditions. This can probably be attributed to the availability of more relevant information for each side of the group from the other, as provided through orchestrated mediation. The results overall, however, are more suggestive than conclusive. Yet a conclusive result which indicates the potential of automatic orchestration to improve live mediated communication did emerge from the fact that *statistically significant* ($p < .05$) differences were observed *only* between the automatically orchestrated condition (highest in terms of points won) and the context unaware mixing (CU) condition (lowest in terms of points won); neither the static condition nor, surprisingly, the manually orchestrated condition showed statistically significant differences with respect to the CU condition.

In order to further investigate the positive effect of automatic orchestration on task efficiency and to attribute this effect or correlate it with other factors, two other objective measures were considered: the average number of conversation turns and their average duration per condition. As shown in Figure 7, there is a decrease in number of turn shifts from automatic, through manual, static and down to context unaware and a converse increase in the average duration of the turns. They could be interpreted as indicating a decrease in the degree of how 'animated' the conversation was. Given the chosen communication setup – guessing within a short interval of time – there is a reasonable case to make that the best communication experience, from this point of view, is the most animated one, namely that had in the automatically orchestrated condition. Yet, this, too, is suggestive, not conclusive, but it backs up the same pattern observed with regards to game points won (Figure 5).

There is also an indication of automatic orchestration outperforming manual orchestration. When compared with each other, there are no significant differences between them, neither with regards to task efficiency nor to number of turns. However, the better experience in the automatic condition is suggested by the fact that the manual orchestration condition did not show statistically significant differences when compared with the CU condition ($p > .05$), whereas the automatic one did. On a first look, this appears counterintuitive, as manual operation in such a setup could be expected to establish some sort of 'ground truth' hard to reach through automatic operation; humans are expected to have a much better understanding of the context of communication than what could be implemented in automatic procedures. Yet, the opposite conclusion is suggested here. To further explore this aspect, we measured the average number of mixing decisions applied by the two manual operators, per communication session (Figure 8).

There are very significant differences in the numbers of decisions per operator, $t(8) = 9.60$, $p < .001$: in room 1 on average 93 decisions were applied (SD = 10.08), whereas in room 2 on average 147 decisions were applied (SD = 16.76). The results also show that one operator (for room 1) is more constant in

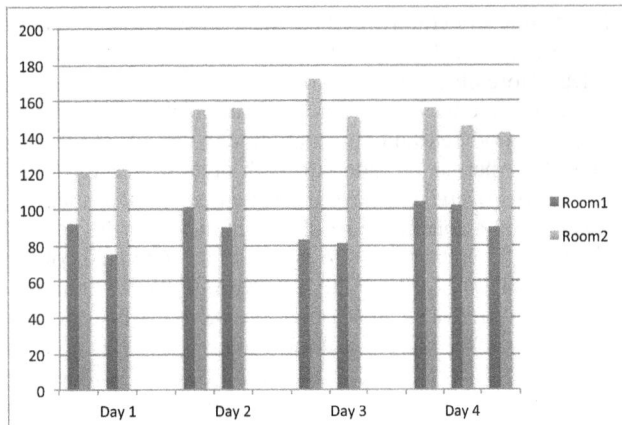

Figure 8. Number of mixing decisions per human editor per session grouped by experiment day.

number of decisions made across the four days, whereas the other one fluctuates quite considerably. Also, the number of decisions, per operator per day, decreases from one session to the other for all 4 days, for one of the operator, and for the last 2 days, for the other. This reduction in responsiveness may be attributed to fatigue.

These aspects clearly indicate that different human operators, and even the same operator at different moments in time, will interpret the same body of rules expressed in natural language differently, even when it is as simple as the one used here. Most probably, such differences would increase with the increase in complexity of the rule set. Any experimental evaluation of orchestration knowledge through manual operation must account for this aspect (e.g., train the operators in the rule set, average manual operation across a representative sample of operators, etc.) and cannot assume that manual operation provides the 'ground truth' of the experience. The implications are even more significant, as the whole process of orchestration knowledge elicitation and implementation is affected, giving rise to questions such as: *whose or which interpretation of a rule set expressed in natural language is being implemented*? and *how is a particular implementation validated*? This uncovers an added degree of complexity of an already rather complex experimental space.

The subjective evaluation of the communication experience was inconclusive (Figure 6).

The discrepancy between the objective evaluation and the subjective one provokes the thought that the questionnaire, despite being validated in a related application area [11], could somehow 'hide' more subtle but meaningful differences, possibly due to the aggregation of scores in different questions or participants going into narrative mode reflecting on their performance instead of actually recounting their experience. Trying to unpick this aspect, we considered each individual question separately. Four of the ones that showed significant differences between conditions are presented in Figure 9.

For q10 – 'I felt equally aware of people in the other room as of people in my own room' – the static condition was eval-

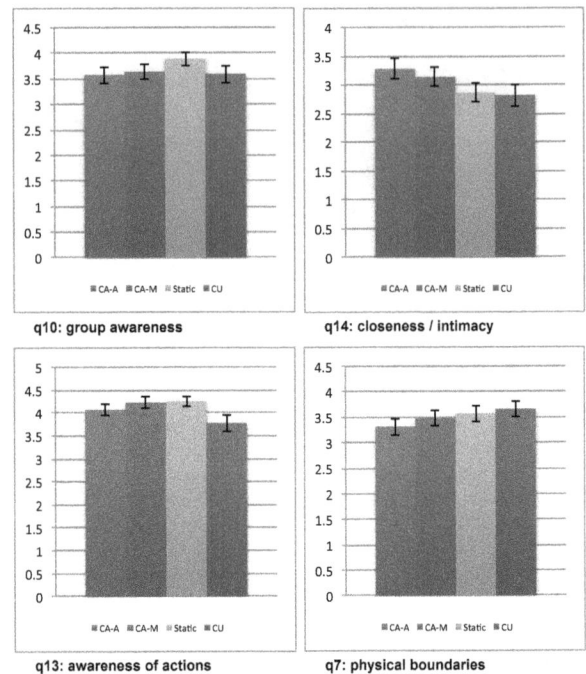

Figure 9. Responses to indicative questions.

uated higher than the other conditions. This can potentially indicate its appropriateness for better conveying *group awareness*.

For q14 – 'People in the other room felt more distant than people in my own room (transposed)' – automatic orchestration was evaluated higher than static and context unaware mixing, with manual orchestration closely following. This can potentially indicate its appropriateness for better conveying *closeness* and *intimacy*.

For q13 – 'I was aware of what the other participants were doing' – context unaware mixing performed worse than the other three (static and manual being top). This can potentially indicate that the *ability to keep track of a task* requires context awareness or an appropriate static condition.

For q7 – 'I felt like the boundaries between my and the other room disappeared' – automatic orchestration performed worse than the other three conditions. It is hard to find an explanation as to why *spatial awareness* was affected in this way.

These interpretations, save q7, are aligned with some of the conclusions presented in [7] and represent hypotheses for further research. They also indicate that other questionnaires than [11] might work better for the evaluation of orchestrated video mediated communication.

With regards to *manual* orchestration, the results of this study are not as strong as those reported in [21], as, here, manual orchestration does not show any statistically significant differences compared to the static and context unaware mixing conditions. There is no disagreement. This shows how relevant the details of the communication setup can be to mediated communication experiences. In all the three experiments (two reported in [21] and one here), the generic setting was that of a group of four friends, two in each living room, playing social games across a live video connection through the room's TV screens. However, in [21] the social game was Pictionary, and so the overall interaction had stronger visual requirements than that around Articulate, which was the game of the study here. The number of shots available for orchestration in the experiments reported in [21] was greater than those employed in this study and the orchestration logics employed in [21] were more complex that the logic used here. This illustrates the complexity of the orchestrated experience space, which presents various co-ordinates such as: (social) activity undertaken between people, number and type of cameras, their placement, the shots available for orchestration, the orchestration logic, the number of people and locations, and others. Any variation along these co-ordinates generates a new setup that needs to be investigated. Finding ways to evaluate orchestration in larger, more generic setups is an extra challenge.

In the communication setup considered here, the differences between the four experimental conditions were not substantial. One view may be that the measures employed were insufficiently sensitive to pick up existing differences. Another view may be that the communication setup itself (2 rooms, 2 people per room in fixed positions, relatively short communication session, high quality audio and video, wide shot in static condition captures all the necessary details, simple orchestration logic, etc.) was simple enough to be served well by all the four methods of mediation. In more complex setups, for example involving more locations, more people, and possibly different activities, it can be hypothesised that more sizeable differences might arise. The automatically orchestrated condition, conceptually, appears to scale better than both the static and the context-unaware orchestrated conditions. For a three room setup, for example, the level of detail provided by the static condition is halved compared to the two room setup – each room has to place two static shots, as opposed to one, on its screen. For the same setup, considering that each room provides three shots, similarly to the experiment reported here, the probability of showing a meaningful shot in the context unaware condition is more or less half of the same probability in the two room setup – a simplistic calculation indicates that 2 out of 6 shots will always include the active speaker in the three room setup, whereas 2 out of only 3 shots will include the active speaker in the two room setup. However, the *informed* choice of 1 shot out of a possible 6, in the three room setup, is hypothesized to work more or less similarly to the informed choice of 1 shot out of a possible 3, as in the two room setup, as 'following' the active speaker within a group of 4 is similar to 'following' the active speaker within a group of 6. Context awareness is thus hypothesized to provide more significant improvements to the communication experience in more complex setups compared to the two context unaware possibilities.

CONCLUSIONS

Live video mediation is penetrating the social sphere at a fast pace. Currently, all there is available for group social communication is offered within the paradigm of 'talking heads', which serves very well simple communication setups. This paper was motivated by richer, more complex setups of social communication, which were assumed to require multiple cameras to capture all the necessary details and, consequently, dynamic mixing of the available live content. The decision making process that directs the cameras and controls the mixing process was denoted as orchestration.

The paper presented an experimental enquiry into a completely automatic orchestrated live video communication system. The evaluation was carried out within a generic setup, namely that of a group of friends (4), located in 2 living rooms and playing social games (Articulate). The overall principle underlying the specific orchestration logic employed was to follow the conversation flow and to keep the focus of the representation on the person most actively involved in the conversation. This was implemented via a relatively simple rule set.

Automatic orchestration was found to enhance task efficiency and to better facilitate the communication style required by the social activity undertaken: animated conversation with short turns and quick exchanges of turns. This was attributed to the provision of more relevant information through automatically orchestrated mediation than through the other methods of mediation.

In an attempt to attribute the observed difference to and correlate it with other factors, additional objective and subjective instruments were employed. However, they led to no conclusive results. Further differences and trends were observed, but they lacked statistical significance. The objective measures of number of conversation turns and their average duration backed up the trend observed with regards to task efficiency, but not with statistical significance. The questionnaire used for the subjective evaluation of the communication experience through four factors (naturalness, immersiveness, presence and social presence) [11] did not lead to any significant differences either between the four experimental conditions. However, by considering individual questions, it showed that differences did exist, with orchestration appearing better at conveying closeness and intimacy, and the static condition appearing better at maintaining group awareness.

On one hand, these results could suggest that the measures employed were insufficiently sensitive to pick up existing differences in the communication experiences. On the other hand, they could also suggest that the investigated communication setup was rather simple and therefore well served by all the four methods of mediation and not conducive to more significant differences. More complex setups, it can therefore be hypothesised, could impose stronger requirements for context-aware mediation, i.e. orchestration. This hypothesis is backed up by the observation that, conceptually, context-unaware mediation (e.g. static and context unaware mixing) does not scale up for more complex setups as well as orchestrated mediation. We suggest both perspectives as avenues for further research required in the ever-growing landscape of social live video-mediated communication.

ACKNOWLEDGMENTS

The research leading to these results has received funding from the European Community's Seventh Framework Programme (FP7/2007-2013) under grant agreements no. ICT-2011-287760 and ICT-2007-214793.

REFERENCES

1. Chen, L., Harper, M., Franklin, A., Rose, T. R., Kimbara, I., Huang, Z., and Quek, F. A multimodal analysis of floor control in meetings. In *Proceedings of MLMI'06*, Springer (2006), 36–49.

2. Eyben, F., Weninger, F., Gross, F., and Schuller, B. Recent developments in opensmile, the munich open-source multimedia feature extractor. In *Proceedings of ACM MM '13*, ACM (2013), 835–838.

3. Eyben, F., Wöllmer, M., and Schuller, B. Opensmile: The munich versatile and fast open-source audio feature extractor. In *Proceedings of ACM MM '10*, ACM (2010), 1459–1462.

4. Falelakis, M., Kaiser, R., Weiss, W., and Ursu, M. Reasoning for video-mediated group communication. In *Proceedings of IEEE ICME'11* (2011), 1–4.

5. Fraunhofer. Fraunhofer IIS audio communication engine raising the bar in communication quality. In *White Paper* (2012).

6. Gatica-Perez, D. Automatic nonverbal analysis of social interaction in small groups: A review. *Image Vision Comput. 27*, 12 (2009), 1775–1787.

7. Inoue, T., Okada, K.-i., and Matsushita, Y. Learning from tv programs: Application of tv presentation to a videoconferencing system. In *Proceedings of the 8th Annual ACM Symposium on User Interface and Software Technology*, UIST '95, ACM (1995), 147–154.

8. Jansen, J., Cesar, P., Bulterman, D. C. A., Stevens, T., Kegel, I., and Issing, J. Enabling composition-based video-conferencing for the home. *Multimedia IEEE Transactions 13*, 5 (2011).

9. Kaiser, R., Weiss, W., Falelakis, M., Michalakopoulos, S., and Ursu, M. A rule-based virtual director enhancing group communication. In *Proceedings of IEEE ICME'12 Workshops* (2012), 187–192.

10. Kirk, D. S., Sellen, A., and Cao, X. Home video communication: Mediating 'closeness'. In *Proceedings of CSCW'10*, ACM (2010), 135–144.

11. Lessiter, J., Freeman, J., Keogh, E., and Davidoff, J. A cross-media presence questionnaire: The itc-sense of presence inventory. *Presence: Teleoper. Virtual Environ. 10*, 3 (2001), 282–297.

12. Liu, Z., Cohen, M., Bhatnagar, D., Cutler, R., and Zhang, Z. Head-size equalization for improved visual perception in video conferencing. *Multimedia, IEEE Transactions on 9*, 7 (2007), 1520–1527.

13. Motlicek, P., Duffner, S., Korchagin, D., Bourlard, H., Scheffler, C., Odobez, J.-M., Galdo, G. D., Kallinger, M., and Thiergart, O. Real-time audio-visual analysis for multiperson videoconferencing. *Adv. MultiMedia* (2013), 4:4–4:4.

14. Neustaedter, C., Oduor, E., Venolia, G., and Judge, T. K. Moving beyond talking heads to shared experiences: The future of personal video communication (workshop). In *Proceedings of ACM GROUP'12*, ACM (2012), 327–330.

15. Nguyen, D. T., and Canny, J. Multiview: Improving trust in group video conferencing through spatial faithfulness. In *Proceedings of CHI'07*, ACM (2007), 1465–1474.

16. Nguyen, D. T., and Canny, J. More than face-to-face: Empathy effects of video framing. In *Proceedings of CHI'09*, ACM (2009), 423–432.

17. Ranjan, A., Birnholtz, J., and Balakrishnan, R. Improving meeting capture by applying television production principles with audio and motion detection. In *Proceedings of CHI'08*, CHI'08, ACM (2008), 227–236.

18. Ronfard, R. A Review of Film Editing Techniques for Digital Games. In *Workshop on Intelligent Cinematography and Editing*, R. M. Y. Arnav Jhala, Ed., ACM (Raleigh, United States, 2012).

19. Sacks, H., Schegloff, E., and Jefferson, G. A simplest systematics for the organization of turn-taking for conversation. *Language 50*, 4, Part 1 (1974), 696–735.

20. Sidnell, J. *Conversation Analysis: An Introduction.* Language in Society. Wiley, 2009.

21. Ursu, M. F., Groen, M., Falelakis, M., Frantzis, M., Zsombori, V., and Kaiser, R. Orchestration: Tv-like mixing grammars applied to video-communication for social groups. In *Proceedings of ACM MM'13*, ACM (2013), 333–342.

22. van der Kleij, R., Schraagen, J. M., Werkhoven, P., and De Dreu, C. K. W. How conversations change over time in face-to-face and video-mediated communication. *Small Group Research 40*, 4 (2009), 355–381.

23. Vinciarelli, A., and further authors. Open challenges in modelling, analysis and synthesis of human behaviour in human-human and humanmachine interactions. *Cognitive Computation* (2015), 1–17.

24. Vinciarelli, A., Pantic, M., Heylen, D., Pelachaud, C., Poggi, I., D'Errico, F., and Schroeder, M. Bridging the gap between social animal and unsocial machine: A survey of social signal processing. *Affective Computing, IEEE Transactions on 3*, 1 (2012), 69–87.

25. Yannopoulos, A. Directornotation: Artistic and technological system for professional film directing. *J. Comput. Cult. Herit. 6*, 1 (2013), 2:1–2:34.

Broadcast, Video-on-Demand, and Other Ways to Watch Television Content: a Household Perspective

Jeroen Vanattenhoven
Centre for User Experience Research
KU Leuven – iMinds
Parkstraat 45 bus 3605
3000 Leuven, Belgium
jeroen.vanattenhoven@soc.kuleuven.be

David Geerts
Centre for User Experience Research
KU Leuven – iMinds
Parkstraat 45 bus 3605
3000 Leuven, Belgium
david.geerts@soc.kuleuven.be

ABSTRACT

This paper presents an explorative investigation into households' uses of traditional broadcast television (TV) and more recently introduced video-on-demand (VoD) services. More specifically, we explain how each way of viewing TV and video content relates to different viewing situations in the home. We conducted in-home interviews with seven households in The Netherlands in order to obtain rich data that are required for understanding these phenomena. Our results elaborate on the uses of watching broadcast TV, catch-up services, and video-on-demand streaming services, the recording of content, and the downloading of content. While the traditional broadcast model is on the decline to some extent, our data still revealed essential uses of broadcast concerning certain types of content and specific viewing situations. Based on the results, a number of implications for the design of recommender systems and interfaces, service providers and broadcasters, and TV manufacturers are presented.

Author Keywords

Television; Context; Viewing Situations; Video-on-Demand; User Experience.

ACM Classification Keywords

H.1.2 [**Models and Principles**]: User/Machine Systems – *Human factors*; H.5.1 [**Information Interfaces and presentation**]: Multimedia information systems – *Evaluation/methodology*; H.5.3 [**Information Interfaces and presentation**]: Group and Organization Interfaces – *Evaluation/methodology*

INTRODUCTION

In a seminal article, Barkhuus and Brown described how the changes in television technologies influenced the

TVX'15, June 03 - 05, 2015, Brussels, Belgium
Copyright is held by the owner/author(s). Publication rights licensed to ACM.
ACM 978-1-4503-3526-3/15/06...$15.00
http://dx.doi.org/10.1145/2745197.2745208

respective viewing practices [3]. They focused on how personal video recording (PVR) systems such as TiVo allowed people's viewing to be less dependent from the broadcast schedules. The functionality offered by PVRs empowered viewers to engage in more active viewing of television programs compared to traditional television. Since 2009, the TV landscape has evolved significantly along: next to PVR systems, several streaming options are available and have attracted many customers. Meanwhile, people still download illegal content; certain technologies such as network attached storage (NAS) has made handling such activities somewhat easier. Given these quite important evolutions in the media landscape, we believe it is important to revisit these insights for the current situation.

One of the most important evolution regarding television services nowadays are streaming VoD services such as Netflix, YouTube (which can be viewed on TV via certain apps), and broadcasters' VoD initiatives in the form of program libraries and catch-up TV applications. In some countries this evolution has lead to the phenomenon of "cord-cutting", where people are cancelling traditional cable subscriptions, and rely entirely on streaming services [4]. In contrast to [3], where the participants were described as early adopters, we believe current products are more widely available to a much larger audience. The advent and adoption of streaming services caused traditional broadcasters and content producers to rethink their business. As a consequence of the increased competition from streaming services, many broadcasters started offering their content via on-demand platforms. At the same time, video streaming services are also available via TV. YouTube, for example, started as web platform mainly used on computers, but is now trying to look and feel more as television [5]. The result of all this is that traditional TV content is now increasingly available on computing platforms (PC, laptop, mobile devices), and that streaming solutions originally more associated with computing platforms offer their content increasingly on TV platforms. The evolution towards more on-demand services has made media consumption more complex for the user: they might have a traditional cable subscription, a SmartTV app for

Netflix or their broadcaster, downloaded content, and a set of DVDs. Switching from on to the other [10], and making sense of the content offering for each option, can seem quite overwhelming.

Therefore, we conducted an exploratory study to investigate how households use different ways of watching TV, such as broadcast, catch-up and video-on-demand, recording and downloading. Furthermore, we describe how these practices relate to their everyday household routines. This contribution, providing an updated view on viewing practices in the home, allows us to formulate specific recommendations for the design of recommender systems and interfaces, service providers and broadcasters, and TV manufacturers.

RELATED WORK
The first study we will discuss in this section is [3]. Barkhuus and Brown conducted an in-depth interview study into the changing practices of households that are using PVRs or download content in the UK. They described the significant impact the introduction of Sky+ had on the way participants watched TV. Sky+ is largely similar to TiVo and offers a pre-recording service. The participants using this service were very unlikely to watch live TV anymore. They buffered many content items, usually different episodes of a certain series, and watch this as needed. Therefore, their viewing habits became more detached from the broadcast schedule. It also allowed them to organize the television viewing better around the households' routines. At the time, participants also downloaded content because show that were launched in the US were not yet available in the UK. These downloading activities were described as "a lot of work". The authors further reported that TV remained a social activity as participants talked about the programs with friends and families. The watching of broadcast content resembled "ambient watching": a form of viewing where people are easily engaged in other activities. In contrast, watching PVR or downloaded content required people's attention and focus – also called "focused watching". This happened later on in the evening when there were no significant other obligations such as watching over the children or making dinner. We will compare our results mainly to this seminal study. In that regard we note that since the publication of [3] in 2009, significant evolutions have taken place in the media landscape, as described in the introduction. In 2009, these technologies were rather new and the authors described their participants as "early adopters". Currently, several streaming options are available and are used on a larger scale. Therefore, our contribution will be able to provide an updated view on TV and video viewing uses in the household.

Another study investigating the role media services and television in the home was [17]. Tsekleves et al. (2011) created a home media device and evaluated how 27 families used this device in their home environment. They found that people want support for media presentation and

consumption through the TV, and that they like to engage in social activities by sharing photos and video through the device. Concerning television participants enjoyed the very simple interaction model, and they preferred to have instant access to content. At the time – the results were obtained in 2007-2008 – participants still viewed TV as lean-back medium. The latter is the main reason why a new study is required to investigate the influence of novel technologies and services on household viewing practices.

Important to know is how people watch TV in the home: which constellations of viewers exist, and what do we know about the time people spend watching TV. Saxbe et al. [16] therefore studied families' everyday television viewing patterns. By recording in-home activities of 30 families at 10-minute intervals they obtained an accurate account of how often they were watching, who was watching, in what rooms, and which other activities coincided with television watching. They determined that in 61% of the time participants were watching TV with at least one other person: the whole family together, the children, and several parent-child constellations each amount to approximately the same proportion of this 61%. Activities conducted together with TV viewing were talking, eating and other leisure activities. These insights present a detailed image on the part of the families and the activities, but do not unveil what is watched and how.

A more recent study by Abreu et al. [2] investigated viewing behaviours and practices via a survey that received 550 valid responses. One interesting topic to consider is the way people choose what to watch. According to the survey the program genre, state of mind, being alone or accompanied, and available time determine what people want to watch, in that order. The results identify which contextual elements play a role in viewing behaviour.. Chaney et al. [6] conducted another quantitative inquiry into viewing patterns by employing a data mining technique on a very large dataset containing more than 4 million logged household views. They were able to determine how the viewing patterns shift by viewer and content type. Their results show how these viewing patterns shift significantly with age, and illustrate differences between male and female viewing behaviour per genre. Furthermore, the results include insights in how different compositions of group – for example, an individual adult vs. an all child group – impacts the observed viewing behaviour per genre. The above quantitative studies offer valuable information but are not able to provide a rich understanding of these contextual aspects of viewing behaviour.

We will now discuss the results of two studies that employed qualitative methods to provide a richer insight into the viewing behaviour in the home. Mercer et al. [14] investigated how the viewing activities are understood or perceived by people as viewing situations comprised of several contextual factors; their results include different archetypical viewing situations and descriptions of the role that the contextual elements solitary vs. shared experience, public vs. private spaces, and temporal characteristics play. Furthermore, they indicated that streaming options were more often used in the evening, and were related to more engaged viewing. In [18], we expanded on these viewing situations by taking into account more contextual aspects of viewing behaviour. Seven different viewing situations were derived; for each of these situations we determined the manifestations of six contextual aspects: mood, viewers, content, time, content delivery type, and viewing mode. In this paper our contribution consists of relating these viewing situations to the different forms of TV watching. These contextual aspects informed the interviews conducted in this article.

METHODOLOGY

This section clarifies the methodology by discussing the sampling, the participating households' characteristics, the data gathering, and the analysis procedure.

Sampling

For this study we conducted in-home interviews with seven households from a user panel in The Netherlands. The user panel is taking part in a field trial in which several HbbTV applications are evaluated for the European research project TV-RING (http://www.tvring.eu). For the recruitment of the households to form such a user panel a call was spread via television pop-ups on HbbTV-capable television sets with DRM support (the total number of people that use SmartTV apps by NPO was approximately 350.000), email and Twitter by the Dutch public broadcaster. In addition, the call was promoted via two websites http://www.npo.nl and http://www.totaaltv.nl. 40 households have signed up for participation in user panel of the research project, for which they receive a six-month subscription to "NLZiet", a novel HD on-demand service created by several Dutch commercial and public broadcasting companies.

For the interview study in this paper, a separate, specific call was launched toward the households in the user panel. When this first call did not result in any participant applications, we offered an additional incentive in the form of a voucher worth 30 Euros. Subsequently, eight households applied for participation. One of those households lost track of the interview appointment, resulting in seven households participating in the interview sessions conducted at their homes.

Participants

Our sample includes a young couple, two young couples with a young child, a retired single man, a working single man, a younger working single man, and one retired elderly couple who occasionally - and at the time of the interview - were having their grandchildren over. An overview of the participating households is given in Table 1, which presents details regarding age, composition, technical proficiency, and some of the equipment in each household.

House-holds	Description
H1	37-year-old single man with a job in IT; high technical proficiency; higher education; mobile devices and SmartTV linked to a Network Attached Storage (NAS)
H2	A single man in his fifties working in the hotel business abroad with three SmartTVs, a laptop and tablet; higher education; relative technical proficiency.
H3	62-year-old single man (retired); higher education; high technical proficiency; owns mobile devices and SmartTV linked to a NAS
H4	40-year-old parents with a seven-year-old son; the father is an IT consultant, the mother a professional musician; higher education; one SmartTV and one normal TV.
H5	A younger couple; higher education; high technical proficiency; two SmartTVs, three laptops and a tablet; both employed.
H6	30-year-old father, 27-year-old, and a one-year-old toddler; high technical proficiency; higher education; father employed; mother self-employed; one SmartTV.
H7	Senior couple, 70-year-old man and 68-year-old-man; higher education; high technical proficiency; three TVs; frequently having their grandchildren over for several days.

Table 1. Overview and description of the participating households.

Data gathering

An interview guide was composed taking into account the contextual aspects that comprise different viewing situations in [18]. All household members were interviewed together in their own homes. The interviews were held during one weekend in November and one weekend in December, 2014. The semi-structured interview included questions about the following topics:

- What do you watch, when, with whom, and on what device?

- Can you tell me more about this moment? Are you really focused on the TV or are you performing other activities as well?

- How do you find interesting programs?

- Which TV and video products do you currently use? For which of those do you pay? Do you find this price acceptable? What aspects are important for you in such products?

- Do you watch content you have already seen again sometime?

The interview proceeded as follows: the participants were given a blank sheet of paper in which they were asked to write down what they usually watch each week: when, what, with whom etc. Based on this sheet the semi-structured interview was conducted by going through the interview guide, and using the sheet as a means of elicitation. Throughout the interview participants usually added more items onto the sheet as they recalled more programs they watched. In total 264 minutes of interview were audio recorded and then transcribed. The interviews lasted between 18 and 51 minutes. Generally, the interviews with singles were shorter than the ones with the families.

Analysis

For analysis, qualitative analysis software (NVivo) was used to code the transcripts and to find meaningful topics arising from the data. However, not all nodes in the coding scheme arose from the data: the contextual elements from [18] served as an additional lens for analysis. To clarify, we did not follow a complete Grounded Theory approach. The relevant themes emerged from the data and helped us to interpret our data. The used NVivo software facilitated this process to a great extent.

RESULTS

In the first part we will elaborate on the viewing behaviours surrounding broadcast TV, video-on-demand, catch-up services and downloading mechanisms, followed by the genres that are still important for broadcast TV. Then, we illustrate how people also like to watch content they have already seen again, and present the findings about the many difficulties viewers currently experience. Finally, we illustrate how people find interesting content, and present the results that relate broadcast, video-on-demand, catch-up services to the different viewing situations.

Different Ways of Watching TV

When we talk about different ways of watching TV, we mean video-on-demand, recorded TV, downloaded programs, live TV, and catch-up TV.

In The Netherlands, the site of our study, the public broadcaster offers a free catch-up service ("Uitzending Gemist") in which viewers can watch content they missed up to a week back in time, in normal quality. Broadcast TV sometimes functions as a catch-up service, in that participants watch repeats of shows occurring shortly after the original broadcast. The difference with a real catch-up service is not that clear. Participants indicate that they do not search for these programs – as is the case in catch-up TV; the programs just happen to be repeated at a time they can or would like to watch it.

Interviewer: *"So this Sunday morning is rather easy-going?"*

Boyfriend: *"Yes, that is the way I feel about it. It is broadcasted on Saturdays, 'Eigen Huis en Tuin' [My Home and Garden], usually around 18.00h; at 9.30h on Sunday*

morning you can watch the relay, so we always watch this. This [practice] has grown over time."

There is important relation between the genre of the content, and the way TV or video is watched [6]: news, talk shows, comedy, musical programs and soaps are still watched mostly on broadcast TV, whereas movies and TV series were watched most via on-demand services. The latter includes downloaded content, recorded content, DVDs and video-on-demand services such as Netflix.

Mother: *"Today, there is a new episode of this; there is a new episode of that. So, we go and have a look. Mad Men, Girls... those kinds of series. American series, which I usually watch the day after they have been broadcasted in the US."*

We found very little instances of households recording content. Instead, we found a lot of instances for video-on-demand services such as Netflix.

Father: *"No, we watch when it is on TV, or via the Internet, but we have no hard disk recorder. Well, the functionality is available on my TV, but I barely use it. On occasion, when I have tuned in on a program and I'm watching it, I press the record button [to finish watching it when it suits me better]. But other than that, I don't use it."*

Grandfather: *"I sometimes record it. I did not mention this, but we can record everything on a hard disk upstairs."*

Interviewer: *"So do you use it frequently?"*

Grandfather: *"Well, less and less, because I'm very chaotic. I have recorded hundreds of hours, but at a certain moment you think: 'I'm not doing that anymore'."*

We also inquired about the possibility of using the catch-up TV repository as a kind of video-on-demand service. Catch-up TV usually entails that you have something in mind – the program you missed – and want to look for that. But it is technically possible to use it as a video-on-demand library, which contains the content from the past week in this case. But the participants were adamant: catch-up services are used as catch-up services.

The video-on-demand services do not always suffice. Several participants downloaded content for two reasons: because that specific program they would like to see was not available via their own channels, or the program was not yet available. As soon as something is broadcasted somewhere, usually the US, they want to have that same content. The content they are referring to are series and movies.

Interviewer: *"So, you do not watch this via the TV? Do you record it?"*

Mother: *"Hmm... yes, let us put it like that [laughter]."*

Another participant is more explicit:

Single man: "*Yes, I have a NAS, a networked-attached-storage by Synology. So I have channels, so many channels.*"

Important genres for Live TV

As broadcast TV is on the decline, it is useful to capture in which situations it still is valuable to viewers, or perhaps even irreplaceable.

A first genre relevant for broadcast TV are the live events such as the world championship of football, which in The Netherlands is watched in, and just outside of pubs. These events are quite huge, and present a unique atmosphere.

Grandfather: "*And when there is something very special such as the World Cup football for example... we don't like football at all. But we liked it; we saw it in a number of cafés in Volendam. That is an experience, in a pub tucked together with about 500 fans.*"

There are also other types of content that most likely are most valuable via broadcast TV. Although the news can be watched in an on demand fashion, we noticed that all participants still watch the news via traditional live TV.

Father: "*Yes, the news, we watch that every day. News and current events. It depends on what day it is. What day is 'Twee Vandaag' or 'Nova', or what is it called today? 'Nieuwsuur' and those kinds of programs. It is the public broadcaster. The news is around 20.00h; current events is broadcasted somewhere around 22.00h.*"

We did not find any instances where the news is watched on-demand, but the repeat broadcasts are watched on several occasions. One single man watches news broadcasts in the morning when having breakfast and preparing to get to work:

"*They actually make the news repeat. They start at eight and then it is fresh. At 8.15h it repeats itself, and at 8.30h it is updated again. [...] I'm usually sitting in front of the TV with a cup of coffee and a cigarette. The one at 8.00h I usually see entirely. Then, there is a commercial break, the perfect time to grab my bag and collect my things. Around 8.30h I can get out the door.*"

A mother, a freelance musician, frequently arrives home late after a concert, and then needs to watch some TV to wind down before going to bed:

"*I sometimes have a performance late at night, and when I come home I cannot sleep. So I watch some TV first, and then fall asleep. [...] When I arrive late, because these things continuously repeat.*"

There are also a number of TV shows that generate quite a lot of buzz among friends, family or colleagues. These are shows such as "Wie is de Mol?". They run for a limited period of time. Each week an episode is broadcasted and the tension is built up resulting in a grand finale at the end. As these shows are talked about so much, it is very impractical to watch these shows on demand.

Mother: "'*Wie is de mol?', that is something we always discuss right after the broadcast.*"

Father: "*Yes, even with the whole family.*"

Mother: "*Then, we discuss it with our family, and with whom we are watching it; whether we are watching over there, or they are watching over here.*" "*These are still moments that we are watching live TV and that we plan our entire evening around it. So everything has to move a little bit.*"

Watching the same content again

People are not only looking for new content on TV; in some instances they just watch content that they have already seen. Some of these instances occur via relays of series; other instances happen via on-demand services or downloaded content. When it happens on broadcast TV, it is not something that one is looking for; rather, it just happens. This involves comedy shows in many cases.

Father: "*No, TV programs? No. He does [referring to his son]. He watches a lot of things anew. He can watch an episode of [Fireman Sam] four times. Sometimes, there is a movie on that you have seen earlier. Then, you say, well let's watch it again.*"

Mother: "*A show such as 'Little Britain', which I watch, is sometimes repeated on TV. Or 'Keeping Up Appearances'*"

Father: "*Yes, but then you are not looking for it. You just encounter a show that is repeated for the nth time.*"

Another participant explains that comedy is really suited for watching content over and over again:

"*Certainly for cartoons this is the case. Family Guy for example, American Dad, those kinds of programs. Those things are endlessly repeatable for me. You can easily see this 10 or 20 times. It also means that you are not really watching it. It is just 'filling the time'.*"

Another reason why people watch content again is to get up to speed again with the story line of the past season, in order to prepare for the coming season. There are drama series that are broadcasted in the US, one episode every week. After that, it takes a whole year before the next season starts. One participant explains:

"*You have the cliff-hanger right before you enter the new season of a series. Then I always watch the two latest episodes as preparation of the new season. There are these series of which 12 episodes per year are broadcasted. There are three quarters of a year between the seasons, so then you have lost it a little bit.*"

Another couple illustrates the fact that comedy is very suitable for watching content again. Furthermore, it implies that they are not really watching it:

Father: "*The Big Bang Theory for example. We do watch some older episodes again, when we don't have anything else to do: 'Let's turn on season two'. The same goes for 'Friends'; the same for 'Family Guy'."*

Mother: *"Yes, usually those comedy things. They are playing on the background while you are doing something on your laptop. A moving picture is nice to watch. For a drama series for example you are really focusing on what is happening."*

Finally, nostalgia is another reason why people like to watch specific content again. They really enjoyed watching a specific kind of content or a specific program a long time ago and would enjoy watching it again. A grandfather explains this phenomenon:

"I find the offering too limited. I know this from America, because we have a daughter over there; we have lived there for years. And there, on Netflix, I found several older movies, famous older movies. But they don't have those here [on Netflix in The Netherlands]."

Important features for TV and video services
The fact that several different services are available for watching TV – cable subscriptions, special catch-up services, and video-on-demand services – makes the market a complex place for the consumer. There are differences in image quality, content offerings, the speed of the content offerings after broadcast in the US, the amount of money to be paid, and the different ways to access these services. Most of our participants are willing to pay for such products, but then the formerly mentioned factors need to be addressed. The main issue here is that these products are usually thought of from a broadcaster or company perspective; not from a user perspective. For the user, all these products exist next to each other, and in their homes these products have to make sense, and together they have to be usable.

Father: *"I use it, but when I'm watching 'Uitzending Gemist' [public broadcaster's normal quality free catch-up service] then I view it via 'NL Ziet' [public broadcaster's higher quality, subscription catch-up service]. The quality is better. What I find regrettable, is that it is yet another separate service. I just took a trial subscription; the first month was free. The problem is that I also have 'Netflix', with a lot of series, and then also 'NL Ziet', which is another nine euros. Then, I just think: 'Why can't they just put it in 'Netflix'?'."*

Another participant explains how a catch-up service is not an alternative for a video-on-demand service, especially in the case of watching series:

Father: *"Suppose, you could take a kind of 'Uitzending Gemist' subscription, then it's interesting that you can go back in time for weeks or even months for content, so that it is more like an archive. Now, you can only go back a week."*

Mother: *"What you can do with Netflix off course is accessing complete seasons."*

Image quality and sound quality also play an important role; though not for every type of content. One more demanding participant explains this:

"When I see what I can download, a 24-bit colour version, which corresponds to a 12 Mbit stream with them [Netflix], then you lose a lot of pixels to colour. I can just notice the difference."

The image quality participants prefer however depends on the kind of content they are watching. For movies and series, it has to be high quality. For news or other specific items, it is of lesser importance.

Grandfather: *"I find image quality very important. Well, if there is a jazz program on TV with music from the fifties, it's really about the music."*

There are also very clear demands with regard to the offering. Participants want to have access to anything they like; moreover, they want to see it as soon as it is available anywhere in the world.

Father: *"Immediately when it is broadcasted in America, we also have it [via downloads]". Netflix is just a little slower. We would like a paid service, but it just hasn't worked out yet. [...] Well yes, we wanted to watch via Netflix, but it is running behind and it doesn't have all the shows."*

Finding interesting content
Before watching compelling television content, people first have to know what they can watch, and which programs would be interesting to watch. We found that participants use many different sources, and that there is no clear pattern in this. The sources include: paper TV guide, trailers on TV or radio, social media, recommendations, newspaper, friends, flicking channels, EPG, and dedicated sites such as IMDb.

The paper TV guide is still used, but only by one senior participant. The newspaper is used a little bit more often; some have a subscription to a national newspaper. Others refer to a free newspaper ('Metro') that can be found on the train in The Netherlands. In this free newspaper they consult the TV guide for that day and certain highlighted programs, usually while commuting. Trailers on traditional broadcast channels are also still very relevant for picking up programs to watch; this includes both radio and TV.

Mother: *"Then, in between programs sometimes there are promos for movies or a series, and then we think: 'This could be fun to watch. How good would the pilot be?' Usually we take a look at Wikipedia to see if the series has already ended. Suppose a series does not continue after its first season, then there is no point really in watching it, because just when it starts to become interesting, it does not continue."*

Interesting ideas for what programs to watch travel in both directions: people receive recommendations from friends; they can also make recommendations to their friends:

"The first sources off course are the people around you. I have a number of friends and acquaintances. You do notice that you tend to have friends with a similar taste. [...] In general, I'm also someone who puts others onto interesting programs."

Sources that are used more often are dedicated platforms for television content such as IMDb or TV.com. Though, usually these dedicated platforms are not consulted directly; participants reported going there when they were already watching something in order to look up an actor or other details about the movie. Then, they browsed further, looking into the actor, or they noticed the recommended shows – shows similar to the one being watched.

Interviewer: *"So how about the actors? Do you really look for information about the show?"*

Mother: *"Yes, the one we are already watching; then we look up a number of categories. Moreover, at the shows you also watch: 'you like Game of Thrones, perhaps you like this one and this one too'. And then you try to find out whether it sounds interesting, or receives a good score from IMDb."*

Finally, social media, such as Facebook and Twitter, were also reported by a number of participants to be a source of interesting content. They do not look for interesting content on these social networks. Instead, they sometimes watch certain programs being discussed or recommended on their feeds.

Mother: *"For me it is social media I think. There are things on Facebook you see passing by, of which you think... if it's some kind of hype. It's in this way you get curious."*

Viewing situations

In this section we aim to illustrate how different ways of watching television content relates to contextual factors that determine specific viewing situations.

A first situation involves the moment that the children have gone to bed, allowing the parents, or a parent, to decide what they would like to watch. In this situation the participants mostly watch video-on-demand content; that is, series. They have a number of shows they follow; and this is the moment to watch this.

Mother: *"At 19.30h she goes to bed, or sometimes a little bit earlier, it depends on how tired she is. So from 19.30h on she is lying in bed; from that moment on we start watching series together."*

Couples without children also view a lot of series in similar situations; only, they don't have to wait for their children to go to bed. It might lead us to think that they would start earlier with watching series, but one viewing situation precedes the watching of TV series:

Father: *"'De Wereld Draait Door' [a very popular Dutch talkshow] is also such a show. It's about something but it is not too difficult, so you don't really have to think hard*

about it. And the subject is interesting at one time, the next time it is not, but you are able to continue watching. That's indeed a moment of arriving home from work and pff..."

The above situations illustrate that it is mostly broadcast TV at this time, and that the kind of content does not require, or the participants do not engage in, focused viewing. People are winding down from a day's work, and conducting household chores such as starting to prepare supper. This type of content allows them to engage in other activities while the TV is playing.

Children experience similar situations as parents who are coming home from work. When children arrive home from school, they also turn on the TV to relax.

Father: *"I come home between six and seven, and then we have supper. Then, there are also some children's programs between approximately 15.00h and 18.00h. What do you watch when you come home from school?"*

Son: *"Sometimes I watch Telekids [broadcast TV]; and sometimes Netflix."*

Mother: *"Yes, [her son] also experiences this [relaxing after school]. They do have a lot of activities at school such as theatre."*

Another viewing situations occurs later at night, after the watching of series, namely at the time participants are about to turn in. Then, they also tend to watch something easy going such as talk shows. This usually concerns broadcast TV. In contrast to the previous viewing situation during the evening, some of these late night instances occur in the bedroom where a second TV has been installed, or where an iPad is used for viewing.

Other instances in our data concerning children watching TV are related to weekend mornings and bank holidays.

Mother: *"Well, early in the morning, he can by lying in bed and watch [TV] on his tablet."*

Father: *"Because on Saturdays and Sundays you can view a lot of this between 8.00h and 11.00h."*

The grandparents in our study had other reasons for letting children watch TV early in the morning:

Grandfather: *"We make them watch TV from 7.00h to 8.00h sometimes, because we don't like to get up at 7.00h in the morning. So we turn on a channel such as 'Jimjam' or example. [...] I usually stay for a while, because it is cozy. But furthermore, it is that quarter of an hour that I join them just to see what happens."*

The final viewing situation we will discuss here is called 'lazy afternoons'. These can occur on weekends or on bank holidays. In these moments people have a lot of time, which means that they can watch long-form content such as movies. The content here is usually consumed via on-demand services or downloads.

Mother: "*Sometimes we watch movies for children, movies for families.*"

Father: "*Yes, we watch those in the weekend when I'm home. And bank holidays; the first of January for example. Then, [my son] gets to pick something.*"

This also goes for singles:

"*If I consider a weekend day, I often watch a movie to relax.*"

DISCUSSION

Related work
When we review our results we notice that many of the findings by Barkhuus and Brown (2009) still hold [3]. The fact for example that on-demand content is usually associated with focused viewing and that broadcast content often implies that people are engaged in other activities. Our participants also reported doing household chores during this kind of content, or using it to entertain the children. An important shift is that the time-shifting function of PVRs now seems to be taken over by downloaded content, video-on-demand and catch-up services. Another similar finding is that people tend to download programs because they want to view them immediately; with the regular channels there is usually a significant delay between the launch in the US and in Europe. The only difference we can see here, is that our sample, which is not that large, did not appear to be recording a lot of content. One important finding in this article seems to suggest that the PVR of five years ago is currently replaced by on-demand services and catch-up services.

Concerning downloads, people were already downloading content five years ago. In [3] participants found this process to be difficult. Our study also involved many participants getting illegal content from the Internet. The difference is that certain technologies such as NAS devices made this process somewhat easier. Parts of finding specific content on the Internet to watch are automated, and the fact that participants attached these devices to their SmartTV made the whole process of downloading content easier.

We also confirm the social organization of television [3][17]. Television is watched around the everyday activities in the household, and the content that is watched depends on who is watching at a certain time. Participants also follow a number of programs; the same programs on broadcast TV (talk shows, news) and the same programs via on-demand services (series). Another social aspect of television that we also find in our data is the fact that people like to talk about TV, and share their thoughts and experiences.

Implications for recommender systems
The insights of our study relating to the viewing situations can help build better recommender systems. We described different viewing situations that occur in different households, and linked these to specific contextual elements. Taking this into account allows recommenders to better judge what people might watch at a certain time, with whom and in what way. Our goal in the TV-RING research project is to use these insights to come to better recommendations, recommendations that are not solely based on taste, but on viewing situations: a viewer might really like "Breaking Bad" but that does not mean he/she will want to watch it on a Sunday morning. Existing recommender systems mostly take into account personal taste. But as we have noticed it does not always make sense to offer all kinds of content all the time. Depending on the viewing situation, certain types of content can be brought to the fore.

Part of such a solution can be written into recommender algorithms; part can be via novel user interface concepts such as in [1]. An interesting consideration in this regard was made by Churchill [7]. Most of the research has focused on *outcome personalization*; the way algorithms can generate a better set of options. However, there is also *process personalization*, which focuses on the quality of the interaction. In certain situations we would like to have a high quality service, a great deal of interaction. In other instances however, such as paying a bill, we would like a minimal interaction. Transferring this idea to our viewing situations, it is our goal to not only improve the suggested items for each situation, but also to explore what kind of interaction is wanted or preferred in each situation. When the children have gone to bed for example, it would be interesting to present an interface with mainly the latest episode of the series parents are following at this time. Improving novel systems for TV viewing entails more than just recommendations; the entire TV lifecycle should be supported. Another idea that can be explored is when it is appropriate to show what kind or recommendations. Perhaps it is not useful to show recommendations between two episodes of a series; perhaps it is better to show a couple of suggestions after finishing the last episode. Using our insights into the different viewing situations, we aim to explore this further in the TV-RING project.

Implications for service providers and broadcasters
Service providers and broadcasters can benefit from knowing when people like which kind of content. Although they already have certain information available to them, qualitative studies offer more contextual insights. They can now better align the offering on their own video-on-demand services with the offering on their broadcast channels. Concerning content, news, sports, and certain popular weekly TV entertainment shows still remain very important to broadcast TV, while drama series, movies and programs for children seem to be more valuable for on-demand platforms. Concerning time of day, the evening, when the parents are alone, or free moments during the weekends or holidays are more tied to on-demand ways of watching. Finally, new episodes of certain drama series are broadcasted during a part of the year. As there is a lot of

time between seasons, relays or summary content could be offered via broadcast or via the recommender interface of an on-demand platform before the new season is about to start.

Implications for SmartTV manufacturers

Our results also show how the current media landscape is making things quite difficult for the viewer. Even as more (legal) services become available, and are used by an increasing number of people, it does not seem provide an adequate solution. Certainly when we compare today's options with the very simple interaction model of traditional TV [17]. The viewing of series for example is possible, but not immediately after the first broadcast in the US. Similarly, when paying for a service as Netflix, one might still miss out on very good TV content from other sources. Adding a catch-up service from the public broadcaster might solve the problem entirely. Furthermore, setting up all the accounts, switching between these services, trying to get hold of new and interesting television content on all of these viewing options can become quite staggering.

We argue that novel applications should look at all viewing options for people from their perspective, thereby taking into account the different activities: finding interesting, new content; being able to access and view this content when it suits the viewer; being able to easily manage the program that are being followed, sharing and talking about television content with friends, family or colleagues. We have seen that people use many different sources for finding interesting new content. It should be easy for the viewer to get any of these sources, finding relevant supporting information such as reviews, ratings and user comments, and add it to their queue of interesting programs to watch. Because people are using many different applications and content providers, TV manufacturers might explore applications and interfaces that make every service and content a user has access to more transparent for the user. Furthermore, over time SmartTV sets can inquire greater insights into the broadcast TV patterns of the household. One could then explore personalized broadcast TV. Although it seems to be somewhat contradictory, the TV could establish at what time people switch to certain broadcast channels. A novel system could then automatically start broadcasting the right channel, for example when people arrive home from work. Currently, as far as we know, TVs start up at channel number one, or on the channel that was chosen when the TV was turned off.

LIMITATIONS

There are some limitations to our study. First of all, there is the relatively low number of households. Given that this is an explorative and qualitative study, we believe that this does not pose a significant disadvantage. Although we do not believe saturation has been reached, and consequently our results are explorative and indicative, we are still providing relevant insights. The second point concerns the sampling. As the user panel was asked to participate in a

project in which they would test novel applications, it is possible that there is some self-selection bias. When looking at the different products they owned, the many different devices and screens they had in their homes, and the sometimes advanced downloading mechanisms set up, might point to a user group that is more technically proficient than average. However, many people use the public broadcaster's applications, and Netflix had approximately 940.000 subscribers in The Netherlands at the time [15]. Likewise, many on-demand and catch-up services have known significant adoption in recent years [8]. Finally, we did not make use of diaries in this study. participants were asked to recall what programs they typically watch, and what they watched the week before the interview. Consequently, participants relied more on recall than would have been the case with diaries. However, we believe participants are able to recall the programs they watch most often and programs they watched over the past week to a great extent. Furthermore, as stated in earlier in the methodology section, many participants continued to add programs to the sheet throughout the interviews, sometimes asking for, or being corrected by other household members. Regarding the viewing situations, the use of retrospective user experience methods is not uncommon when asking participants to make sense of past experiences [11].

CONCLUSION

This article reported on the current uses of broadcast and on-demand content in household. Besides the traditional broadcast model and on-demand video services, this also includes recorded TV, catch-up services and downloaded content. In sketching the uses of these viewing mechanisms, we specified how these are related to contextual aspects of specific viewing situations. We found that most viewing behaviour is very much organized around the daily household activities and routines. Video-on-demand services are mainly used to watch series during the evening, when the kids have gone to bed, or on free moments in the weekend when the situation allows for longer form content such as movies. The video-on-demand services usually imply that people's attention is really focused on the content, whereas with broadband content it is more likely that people are engaged in other activities. In the latter case, the content mainly entails news and current event shows, talk shows and other lighter television genres. We have illustrated that people do not only like to view new shows, but that on occasion they can enjoy watching content again that they have seen before. Finally, we also illustrated how the current situation of several fragmented services, each with their own image qualities, price, and technological set-ups, can make it quite hard for the end users to watch TV the way they would like.

We formulated a number of implications for the design of better solutions for television products: recommender systems and interfaces that better incorporate contextual aspects of current viewing practices, a better alignment between broadcasted and on-demand content, and perhaps SmartTV applications that make it easier for the viewers to oversee and use all of their content and services.

ACKNOWLEDGMENTS
The research leading to these results was carried out in the TV-Ring project (EC grant agreement ICT PSP-325209).

REFERENCES

1. Abreu, J., Almeida, P., and Teles, B. TV Discovery & Enjoy: A New Approach to Help Users Finding the Right TV Program to Watch. *Proceedings of the 2014 ACM International Conference on Interactive Experiences for TV and Online Video*, ACM (2014), 63–70.

2. Abreu, J., Almeida, P., Teles, B., and Reis, M. Viewer Behaviors and Practices in the (New) Television Environment. *Proceedings of the 11th European Conference on Interactive TV and Video*, ACM (2013), 5–12.

3. Barkhuus, L. and Brown, B. Unpacking the television: User practices around a changing technology. *ACM Transactions on Computer-Human Interaction (TOCHI) 16*, 3 (2009), 15.

4. Brodesser-Akner, T. Life Without Cable TV? Not Such a Tragedy. *The New York Times*, 2012. http://www.nytimes.com/2012/11/25/arts/television/life-without-cable-tv-not-such-a-tragedy.html.

5. Cain Miller, C. YouTube Tries to Become More Like TV. *Bits Blog*, 2012. http://bits.blogs.nytimes.com/2012/12/06/YouTube-tries-to-become-more-like-tv/.

6. Chaney, A. J. B., Gartrell, M., Hofman, J. M., Guiver, J., Koenigstein, N., Kohli, P., & Paquet, U. (2014). A Large-scale Exploration of Group Viewing Patterns. In *Proceedings of the 2014 ACM International Conference on Interactive Experiences for TV and Online Video* (pp. 31–38). New York, NY, USA: ACM. doi:10.1145/2602299.2602309

7. Churchill, E. Putting the person back into personalization. *Interactions 20*, 5 (2013), 12–15. New York, NY, USA: ACM. doi:10.1145/2504847

8. Clover, J. Counting Netflix by country. *Broadband TV News*. http://www.broadbandtvnews.com/2014/07/24/counting-netflix-by-country/.

9. Geerts, D., Cesar, P., and Bulterman, D. The implications of program genres for the design of social television systems. *Proceedings of the 1st international conference on Designing interactive user experiences for TV and video*, ACM (2008), 71–80.

10. Honan, M. No One Uses Smart TV Internet Because It Sucks | Gadget Lab | Wired.com. *Gadget Lab*. http://www.wired.com/gadgetlab/2012/12/internet-tv-sucks/.

11. Kujala, S., Vogel, M., Pohlmeyer, A.E., and Obrist, M. Lost in Time: The Meaning of Temporal Aspects in User Experience. *CHI '13 Extended Abstracts on Human Factors in Computing Systems*, ACM (2013), 559–564.

12. Knijnenburg, B.P., Willemsen, M.C., Gantner, Z., Soncu, H., and Newell, C. Explaining the user experience of recommender systems. *User Modeling and User-Adapted Interaction 22*, 4-5 (2012), 441–504.

13. Masthoff, J. Group Modeling: Selecting a Sequence of Television Items to Suit a Group of Viewers. *User Modeling and User-Adapted Interaction 14*, 1 (2004), 37–85.

14. Mercer, K., May, A., and Mitchel, V. Designing for video: investigating the contextual cues within viewing situations. *Personal and Ubiquitous Computing 18*, 3 (2014), 723–735.

15. Netflix near 1 mln subscribers in Netherlands. *telecompaper*. 15 February, 2015. http://www.telecompaper.com/news/netflix-near-1-mln-subscribers-in-netherlands--1065387.

16. Saxbe, D., Graesch, A., and Alvik, M. Television as a Social or Solo Activity: Understanding Families' Everyday Television Viewing Patterns. *Communication Research Reports 28*, 2 (2011), 180–189.

17. Tsekleves, E., Whitham, R., Kondo, K., and Hill, A. Investigating media use and the television user experience in the home. *Entertainment Computing 2*, 3 (2011), 151–161.

18. Vanattenhoven, J. and Geerts, D. Contextual aspects of typical viewing situations - a new perspective for recommending television and video content. Conditionally accepted for *Personal and Ubiquitous Computing*, Special Issue: Interactive Experiences for Television and Online Video (2015).

Who's The Fairest Of Them All:
Device Mirroring For The Connected Home

Mark McGill†
m.mcgill.1@research.gla.ac.uk

John Williamson‡
jhw@dcs.gla.ac.uk

Stephen A. Brewster†
stephen.brewster@glasgow.ac.uk

† Glasgow Interactive Systems Group ‡ Inference, Dynamics and Interaction Group
School of Computing Science, University of Glasgow, Glasgow, G12 8QQ, Scotland, UK

ABSTRACT

In the UK alone smartphone adoption has reached 61% in 2014. In home and living-room contexts, this adoption has led to "multi-screening", meaning the concurrent use of devices such as smartphones and tablets alongside the TV. The resultant private "digital bubble" [12] of this device usage has been discussed as raising a problematic barrier to socialization and interaction, with mobile phone use in particular having significant anti-social connotations [24]. However mobile devices have evolved new capabilities for sharing their activity, most notably through screen mirroring. This paper explores how we can utilize the TV to view screen-mirrored device activity, decreasing the digital isolation of device usage. We examine the extent to which users can attend to multiple devices on one TV, the effect this and prior systems have had on existing TV viewing, and propose ways in which we can aid users to manage their viewing of device activity on the TV. Moreover, we examine new approaches toward the accessibility of device activity, investigating systems which allow users to attend to whichever device activity they wish using multi-view displays, and discuss the social and privacy implications of having "always-on" screen-mirrored devices.

Author Keywords

Screen Mirroring; Screen Casting; Screen Annexing; Multi-User; TV; Multi-Device

ACM Classification Keywords

H.5.m. Information Interfaces and Presentation (e.g. HCI): Miscellaneous

INTRODUCTION

In recent years smartphones and tablets have seen significant adoption; in the UK alone smartphone usage has reached 61% in 2014 (up 10% since 2013), whilst tablet adoption almost doubled (to 44%) in the past year [19]. These devices have impacted our lives for the better in many cases, however there are some contexts where their influence has potentially been negative. In the home this adoption has led to what is termed "multi-screening", meaning the concurrent use of devices such as smartphones and tablets alongside the TV. The

resultant private "digital bubble" [12] of this device usage has long been discussed as raising a problematic barrier to socialization and interaction, with mobile phone use in particular having significant anti-social connotations [24].

However, as devices have evolved, they have gained new capabilities for sharing their activity, most notably through screen mirroring. Consumer screen mirroring is now a reality in many homes, in part thanks to low-cost consumer receivers such as Chromecast and Apple TV, combined with devices capable of mirroring their displays in real-time at high resolution through standards such as Airplay and Miracast [9].

Given this, efforts have been made to diminish the isolating effects of device usage through the utilization of screen-mirroring, using the TV as a shared display/receiver upon which device activity could be mirrored. Notably McGill *et al.* [16] demonstrated a shared screen-mirroring system where mirrored use of the display could be managed within a group, allowing for users to selectively mirror their device content and activity for others to attend to, significantly improving a groups ability to collaborate effectively.

Existing research and commercial screen-mirroring systems often treat the display as being capable of viewing only one-device-at-a-time [16], however thanks to technological developments this limitation is now arbitrary. Given the advances in home networking and the processing capabilities of existing smart TVs and smart TV dongles such as Chromecast the broadcast and reception of multiple device streams is now feasible. This development means there is significant scope for investigating new designs both in terms of how this mirrored activity is viewed on the TV, and how/when it is made available to others to view.

This paper builds upon existing literature and consumer screen-mirroring technology, exploring how we can utilize the TV to view screen-mirrored device activity. We examine the extent to which users can attend to multiple devices on one TV display, the effect this and prior systems have had on existing TV viewing, and propose ways in which we can aid users to manage their viewing of device activity on the TV. Moreover, we examine the potential for new approaches toward the accessibility of screen-mirrored activity, investigating systems which allow users to attend, personally and privately, to whichever device activity they wish using multi-view displays, and examine the social and privacy implications of having passively shared, "always-on" screen-mirrored devices.

RELATED WORK

Multi-Screening And Shareability

Devices such as phones or tablets have seen widespread adoption and usage in the home. They circumvent many of the problems TVs have in multi-user contexts, by guaranteeing the user full use of a display that remains private through social conventions but physically shareable if they so choose. Because these devices are personal, they are additionally invariably connected to personal social media and messaging accounts, and offer a semi-private space for conducting activity to suit the spatial context the user inhabits [11]. These are devices that are widely available, and have had a significant impact on the TV viewing experience, through their use alongside the TV in what is known as "multi-screening". This refers to usage of a wireless, mobile internet device at the same time as television viewing. A report by Google [6] found that:

> "TV no longer commands our undivided attention, with 77% of viewers watching TV with another device in hand. In many cases people search on their devices, inspired by what they see on TV."

Of particular note within the context of the TV is simultaneous usage [6] - that is, usage of more than one screen at the same time. Whilst estimates vary regarding the extent of simultaneous usage currently (e.g. a report by Millward Brown [17] suggesting this constitutes 35% of the time, whilst an Ericsson Consumerlab study [3] suggested that 75% of users polled had at some point engaged in multi-screen multi-tasking), this is nonetheless a highly prevalent behaviour in the home. For example, a Nielsen study of Australian multi-screen usage [10] suggested that 74% of online Australians dual-screened, whilst 26% had triple-screened (meaning they typically utilized a combination of TV, phone, and tablet/laptop). This simultaneous behaviour typically relied on a combination of smartphone and TV displays, with 81% of users polled using this combination every day. One user remarked that:

> "My phone... I consider it my personal device, my go-to device. It's close to me, if I need that quick, precise feedback" [6]

Given the adoption and usage of multi-screen devices, it is reasonable to assume that multi-screening fulfils the majority of user needs: the living room TV remains a shared social focal point with one common media experience, whilst independent and collaborative activity is offloaded to personal devices of varying capabilities and sizes. However, supposing that everyone in the room has access to alternate displays to the TV, this usage presents two problems: namely that users are together, but alone, ensconced in their own private media experiences, and that users are having to resort to relying on smaller, less immersive displays whose content is not readily accessible or attainable to others in the room; whilst there is a capacity for explicitly sharing content, shared-use interactive content and casual awareness of non-private activity are impeded. The result of this is that users are potentially cut off from a significant portion of the experiences and activities of those around them.

This private "digital bubble" [12] of device usage has long been discussed as raising a problematic barrier to interaction. However efforts have been made to penetrate this bubble, for example Lucero et al. [14] proposed mobile collocated interactions, whereby users would "take an offline break together". They aimed to facilitate joint attention, whilst enforcing a break from online socialization, appropriating mobile device displays in order to pass photos around a table. This emphasis on shareability and joint attention is important as it underlines how co-located interactions are made to be more effective through the ability to share awareness and take part in shared activities. However mobile devices are not the most shareable displays in the room. McGill et al. [16] demonstrated that physically sharing device views was inferior to utilizing the TV in terms of sharing activity with others and thus collaborating effectively. In using multi-screen devices, we erect barriers to socialization: our ability to be casually aware of, and perhaps join in with, the activity of others is thus impeded. We must thus find new ways to share our activity in the home.

Screen Mirroring

Screen mirroring (also screen {sharing, casting, annexing}) was first demonstrated by Doug Englebart in 1968 [5] as a tool for remote collaboration. This is a recurring theme of this technology e.g. Greenberg et al. [22] utilized distributed screen-sharing to facilitate artifact awareness (awareness of documents and tools others are using). Commercially, screen mirroring technology has seen widespread deployment, if not yet uptake, in the home. With respect to sharing device content, support for wireless video streaming and mirroring standards such as Miracast (in Android 4.0+, Windows 8.1+ and Chromecast tab casting) and Airplay (in Apple iOS) is now commonplace [9], meaning that new phones, tablets, and laptops all have the capability to mirror their displays, or mirror virtual displays, to an available receiver.

With respect to receiving this content, a variety of Smart TVs and Smart TV dongles now support screen mirroring e.g. Chromecast, Roku, Amazon Fire, Microsoft wireless display, Apple TV etc. To what extent this capability is being used we cannot yet say, however we predicate this research on the fact that this technology is now available in a variety of consumer devices. An NPD survey conducted in 2013, prior to many of these receivers supporting screen mirroring, found that 40% of smartphone users had an awareness of the existence of screen-mirroring capabilities, with only 7% having ever used such features. Of these individuals, 75% had used this capability for mirroring videos, whilst approximately 50% had mirrored photos. This study suggested that to accelerate uptake and usage of such technologies would require "simplifying hardware requirements [and] amplifying the value of being able to share content across screens". Whilst the hardware requirements have been effectively dealt with, the usability and utility of screen mirroring remains an open question.

Whilst screen-mirroring is a relatively low-cost way of sharing content between multiple users, it also has some notable limitations. In mirroring screen content, artifacts that are not relevant, or not being attended to, may also be shared. Additionally, screen-mirroring as it has been used thus far restricts the ability for multiple users to concurrently engage in use, being at best essentially multi-screen single-interface groupware. Recent research has examined how screen mirroring systems can be designed to better fit the shared, multi-user multi-device contexts they reside. McGill *et al.* [16] built and evaluated a shared screen mirroring system, whereby users could selectively pass mirrored use of the display between devices, or take mirrored use of the TV display from whomever was currently using it. They demonstrated that physically sharing device views was inferior to utilizing the TV to selectively mirror device content as required, in terms of sharing activity with others and thus collaborating effectively. Moreover, they demonstrated that providing some basic management behaviours for controlling which device was mirrored to the display, and when, was sufficient to significantly expand the usefulness of screen mirroring in a collaborative context. However, this system failed to take into account existing usage of the TV, with mirrored use of the display requiring that the whole of the display be dedicated to viewing the mirrored device, precluding users from, for example, attending to both TV content and device content based on need, or attending to multiple devices.

Overcoming Barriers to Shared Use of the TV

The work by McGill *et al.* emphasized the utility of having a shared-and-shareable TV display to which anyone in the room could attend, however such a display poses two problems. Firstly, there is the issue of existing usage; it is likely to be unacceptable to take mirrored use of the display while others might be attending to other content e.g. a TV programme. Secondly, there is the issue of being unable to choose which content you use the shared display to attend to, independent of others' usage. Fundamentally this is due to a physical limitation of TV displays: they support only one physical view. However this limitation will not necessarily hold in the future.

Multi-view displays are singular displays that are capable of providing two or more independent views to one or more users, providing the capability to allow for both independent operation and collaboration [21]. There are a number of technologies that are capable of achieving this aim [4] e.g. Lenticular displays, parallax-barrier/masked displays etc. Today's state of the art multi-view technology currently is that of Active-shutter displays combined with "Active Shutter" glasses which can selectively reveal or mask frames as they are displayed. These displays offer platforms for developing and evaluating gaze-angle agnostic multi-view interfaces. Multi-view displays already exist in COTS TVs in a limited fashion: consumer 3DTVs rely on active-shutter techniques in order to convey stereoscopic left and right images to users, and typically also have options for two-view content consumption and gaming e.g. LG "dual-play" displays supporting two-view usage.

Multi-view displays can be used by solitary users or groups, and have a number of advantages over comparable smart TVs in each case, however more-so in multi-user usage. For example, in single-user scenarios they have been used to present different aspects of an interface based on view position, allowing users to move their head in order to peek at a menu

[15]. In multi-user contexts, they have been used to for example support independent and collaborative activity on tabletops e.g. Permulin[13] which supported two users sharing a 120Hz two-view display, or Permulin's precursor[1].

The Connected Home

The "Connected Home" [7] refers to the idea that the devices in our homes will eventually be interconnected through our local networks, in a local "Internet of Things". With respect to screen mirroring, the connected home is becoming a reality, with a variety of devices providing the capability to view their activity on-demand from any display. For example Sony Remote Play and PS Vita TV, Wii U Off-TV Play, and nVidia Shield game streaming all allow the ability to remotely view and in some cases control activity on other devices via phones, tablets, or TVs. This potential "always-on" approach to screen-mirroring could be applied to the awareness of activity on devices such as phones or tablets, allowing users to "dip in" to content and activity occurring around the household, but raises questions regarding privacy, acceptability, and scope of use.

STUDY

Given the prior work by McGill *et al.* regarding shared screen mirroring, our aim was to examine unanswered research questions regarding how screen mirroring might be used in the home, namely:

RQ 1 - Fragmentation of viewing To what extent does taking use of the display fragment and disrupt existing usage e.g. viewing TV content, and can this fragmentation be reduced through screen division approaches

RQ 2 - Screen division Do the potential benefits of screen division approaches (e.g. viewing multiple content streams simultaneously) outweigh the potential negative effects (e.g. distraction, increased complexity of the system used to manage the display).

RQ 3 - Inferred focus Can we reduce the complexity of a screen division-based mirroring system through inferring focus on activities, and would this be acceptable?

RQ 4 - Active versus passive screen-mirroring Previous systems have relied on actively and explicitly mirroring the personal device, however given the potential for devices that are always available to be viewed, what effect would turning control of viewing over to the viewer have on the mirroring experience, in terms of acceptability, awareness, and privacy considerations.

In order to investigate these questions, we designed, built, and evaluated a screen-mirroring system capable of displaying up to three content views simultaneously, in the form of a TV content view, and the mirrored displays of two Nexus 4 Android 4.X phones. Our design required 4 conditions, these were:

1 - Shared screen mirroring This was our baseline, analogous to the screen mirroring system from McGill *et al.* [16], providing users with the capability to take the display (at which point their device was mirrored fullscreen)

or stop mirroring (at which point the TV would revert to playing previously viewed TV content).

2 - Split-screen mirroring Here each user was able to selectively choose to show/hide both their own device and the TV content, with the screen layout changing as appropriate to accommodate the content being viewed. If both TV and device content was visible on the display, users would have the option to select which they wished to listen to.

3 - Inferred split-screen mirroring This condition builds upon Condition 2 (split-screen mirroring) by inferring focus on content dynamically. If a device was visible on the TV and audio was detected, that device would be made fullscreen and listened to, inferring focus based on device activity. When the device stopped producing audio, the system would revert back to its previous state. The intention here is that if the participant was viewing a movie trailer, that the system would pause the TV and focus on the trailer.

4 - Multi-view passive screen mirroring In order to allow users to independently determine which mirrored device content they attended to, this condition would utilize a multi-view display giving users completely independent views upon which they could selectively mirror whichever content they wished. Management of audio was shared between users as with split-screen mirroring.

In all conditions the TV content would pause if not visible, and resume playing when visible. All user functions were made accessible via an on-screen UI that was rendered on-top of phone activity, as seen in Figure 1. The visibility of these buttons could be toggled, and the buttons could be moved via long press if necessary.

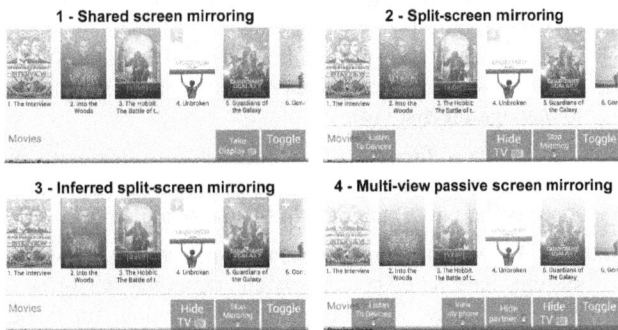

Figure 1. Mirroring UI: buttons controlling the mirroring functions were rendered on-top of all phone functionality, with the ability to toggle their visibility and move the buttons via long-press.

The Android devices were locked to landscape and wirelessly mirrored (both video / audio, H264 encoded to 520p resolution) to a PC where they, along with TV content were captured and dynamically rendered on a 24 inch 120Hz display. Our software could dynamically render any combination of the mirrored devices and TV content, allowing for anywhere from one to three content views (TV and two devices) to be shown on a users given view (see Figure 2).

For Conditions 1-3 the TV operated as a single-view display. In Condition 4 it was used as a multi-view display presenting users with entirely separate physical views. To do this,

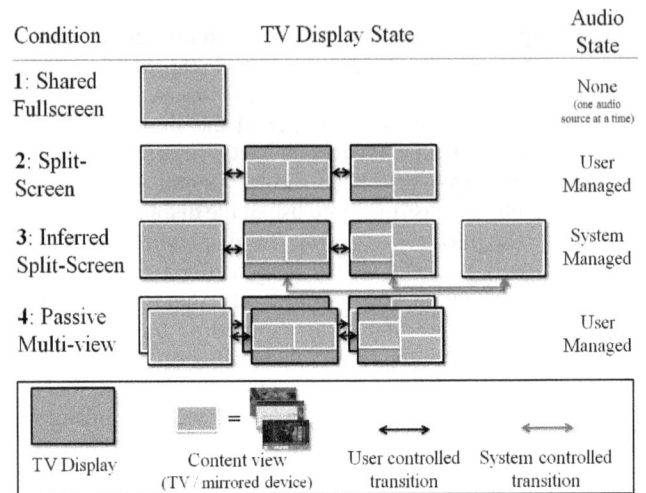

Figure 2. Overview of display and audio management across conditions. In Conditions 2, 3, and 4 the system could dynamically layout up to 3 content views out of the available device views and TV content view, based on what the user(s) wished to monitor. In Conditions 1, 2, and 3 (utilizing a standard single-view TV) there was one shared user view. In Condition 4 (using a multi-view TV) there were two independent views.

we utilized nVidia 3D Vision, an active-shutter IR transmitter, coupled with an nVidia graphics card performing stereoscopic rendering at 120Hz, 60Hz of "left" eye frames, and 60Hz of "right" eye frames. To provide users with independent views, we needed to be able to present only the "left" eye frames to one user, and the "right" eye frames to another. This was achieved using active-shutter glasses which had the capability to be set into a "2D" mode where only one of the left or right frames of the 3D image was allowed through both eyes. Our software rendered a stereoscopic image, such that the left image constituted of whatever view we wished to provide one user, and the right image whatever view we wished to provide the other user.

For Condition 3 (inferred mode) a sliding 1 second window calculated the average audio volume devices being mirrored; if this exceeded a set threshold the device was considered to be playing audio-visual content. When a device was visible on the display, an eye icon was rendered in the top-left corner of the device in order to inform the participant their activity was being viewed on the TV.

Experimental Design

For our task we utilized an ecologically valid collaborative media browsing and TV viewing task. Users were instructed to browse a given set of categories of movies in the Android IMDB app whilst watching TV content together, with the task of selecting movies to watch together later, for the duration of each Condition. Whilst browsing for movies they would also be watching a nature documentary in place of TV content, providing a motivation to use the TV as standard. Four movie categories were selected for each Condition, with users instructed they could browse them however they saw fit. Additionally, users had the capability to watch trailers (with the instruction to moderate trailer viewing time to 30 seconds per trailer). Users were tested for 10 minutes per Condition in a within-subjects design. Users were evaluated in a mock living-room setting. We made this space as living-room like as possible, however we would not claim that it had equivalence to real world living rooms due to the unfamiliar surroundings. Whilst we considered other approaches such as a real-world deployment, the prototype nature of our system prevented this e.g. only supporting two physical views (and thus two users). There were 12 pairs (24 users, mean age=21.9, SD=4.3, 21 male, 3 female) recruited from University mailing lists as pairs that knew each other (intimacy groups e.g. friends, family) so that they would be able to collaborate realistically. Given that our system involved the mirroring of smartphone activity and thus required a level of familiarity with smartphone interaction, we recruited regular smartphone users. Conditions were counter-balanced. In terms of dependent variables, we measured users' ability to collaborate effectively, and garner awareness of their partners activity, through a questionnaire derived from [16], as well as workload (NASA TLX) [8] and usability (System Usability Scale (SUS) [2]). Viewing of TV/devices was logged, allowing us to examine durations of viewing, whilst UI actions were logged, allowing us to examine how frequently the features we provided were used.

Results

Display Viewing

As would likely be expected, the shared screen mirroring Condition (1) featured both the lowest total TV and device viewing, with the screen-division conditions allowing for simultaneous viewing of both TV and device activity (see Figure 3). Notably, the multi-view condition featured less device viewing than the other screen-division approaches, as well as the most TV viewing, indicative of benefits of this condition in terms of allowing users to attend only to the content they wished.

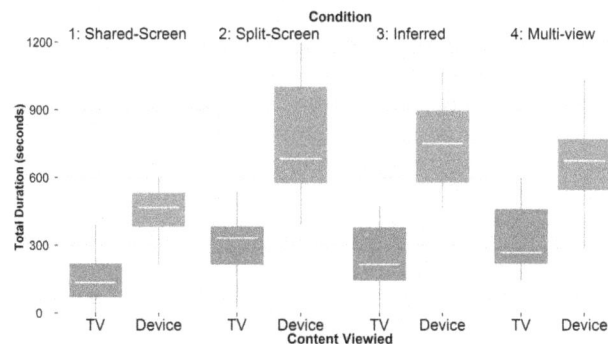

Figure 3. Total duration of viewing of TV and Device content by Condition. For Condition 4 viewing was divided by 2 to adjust for independent user views of the display. RM ANOVA for TV viewing: $\chi^2(3) = 22.88, p < 0.01$, *post hoc* Tukey's Test: 1-2, 1-4, and 3-4. RM ANOVA for Device viewing: $\chi^2(3) = 21.87, p < 0.01$, *post hoc* Tukey's Test: 1-2, 1-3. and 1-4.

The shared screen mirroring condition also featured the most fragmented TV and device viewing (see Figure 4), with the lowest duration viewing instances of all conditions. The screen-division conditions were used to view only 1 content view at a time for approximately half of the total viewing (see Figure 5), with users less reliant on 2 and three views, however screen-division was still used for approximately half the viewing time across conditions.

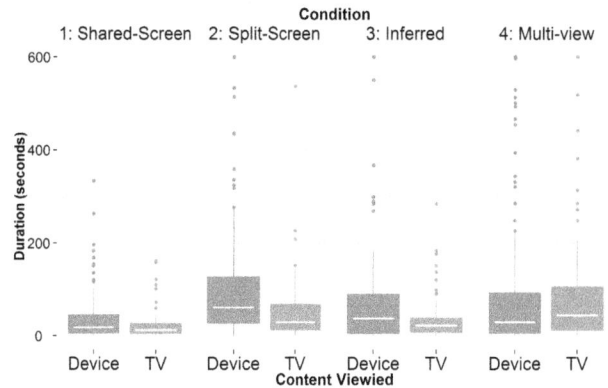

Figure 4. Duration of viewing instances by content (TV and Device) and Condition. RM ANOVA for TV viewing: $\chi^2(3) = 14.56, p < 0.01$, *post hoc* Tukey's Test: 1-4, 3-4. RM ANOVA for Device viewing: $\chi^2(3) = 11.69, p < 0.01$, *post hoc* Tukey's Test: 1-2.

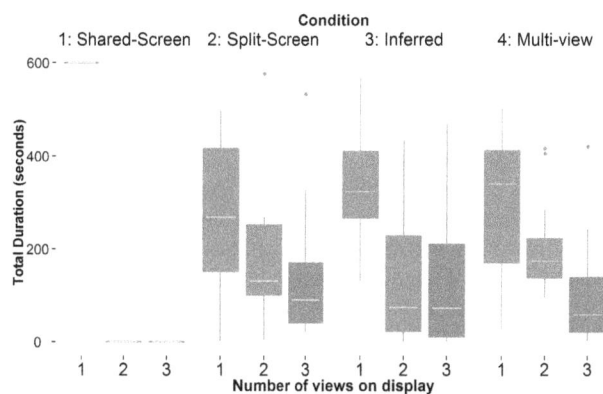

Figure 5. Total Duration of viewing content by number of content views on display (1 to 3 views selected from TV and the two participant's devices). Condition 1 was omitted from statistics tests as it supported showing only 1 view at a time. RM ANOVA for 1 view: $\chi^2(2) = 1.79, p = 0.41$. RM ANOVA for 2 views: $\chi^2(2) = 2.01, p = 0.37$. RM ANOVA for 3 views: $\chi^2(2) = 1.34, p = 0.51$.

In Condition 4 (Multi-view) there was a tendency toward having 2 views displayed as opposed to three, indicative that in multi-view users would often choose to attend to the TV and their partners device, with device viewing was biased toward their partners device (mean=384 seconds, std. dev.=167 seconds) rather than their own device (mean=290 seconds, std. dev.=187 seconds). In Condition 3 the inferred mode functionality resulted in focused mirroring of audio-visual device content on average for 248.83 seconds (std. dev.= 129.13 seconds), indicating inferred mode was active a significant proportion of the time.

Usage of System

Action counts reflected the number of functions available (see Table 2), with the exception of the inferred system (Condition 3), which featured similar mean total actions to the shared-screen system (Condition 1) and significantly lower total actions compared to Condition 2, suggesting the automatic management of viewing helped to lower workload. Condition 4 featured the most user actions of the conditions.

Viewing Action	Condition			
	1: Shared-Screen (1 button)	2: Split-Screen (3 buttons)	3: Inferred (2 buttons)	4: Multi-view (4 buttons)
Own Device	9.32 (5.93)	6.41 (3.22)	5.95 (6.45)	5.91 (3.71)
Partners Device	NA	NA	NA	9.77 (7.99)
TV	NA	5.86 (4.09)	3.50 (3.46)	6.05 (5.95)
Toggle Audio	NA	3.50 (2.82)	NA	3.45 (2.32)
Total Viewing	9.32 (5.93)	12.27 (5.77)	9.45 (7.82)	21.73 (13.47)
Total All Actions	9.32 (5.93)	15.77 (7.29)	9.45 (7.82)	25.18 (13.72)

Table 2. Mean (Std. Dev.) total mirroring UI actions by condition and by function. NA indicates function was not applicable for the given condition. Viewing actions refer to any action which toggled the mirroring of the specified content view to the display. RM ANOVA for Total Viewing Actions: $\chi^2(3) = 37.20, p < 0.01$, *post hoc* Tukey's Test: 1-4, 2-4, 3-4. RM ANOVA for Total All Actions: $\chi^2(3) = 49.78, p < 0.01$, *post hoc* Tukey's Test: 1-2, 1-4, 2-3, 2-4, 3-4.

Workload and Usability

User workload measured both how effectively they performed the overall task of viewing TV whilst browsing movies (TLX Task) and how effectively they managed to watch the TV content (TLX TV). Condition 4 featured the highest workload (see Figure 6 and Table 1) across conditions, reflecting the previous usage demonstrated in the action counts. This was most evident in the effort subscale, with significantly increased effort. The inferred mode of Condition 3 did decrease workload compared to Condition 2, however not significantly so. Condition 1 featured the lowest workload of all the conditions. In terms of usability, the SUS scores indicate that the increased complexity of Conditions 2 and 4 impacted perceived usability, with Condition 1 featuring the highest rating.

Table 3 details questions from prior collaborative studies. WS-4 suggests that the passive screen-mirroring multi-view display impacted participants ability to work together compared to the single-view displays, suggesting that active

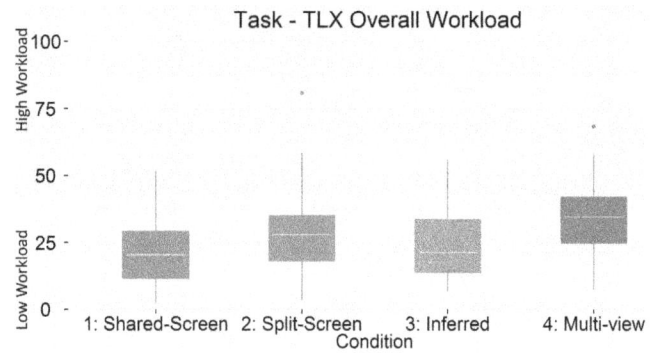

Figure 6. Overall workload for task - Friedman test $\chi^2(3) = 16.28, p < 0.01$, *post hoc*: 1-4, 3-4

screen-mirroring may be beneficial in some respects, but also reduced distraction (DIST-1) and allowed for finer control of their awareness of their partners activity (DIST-2).

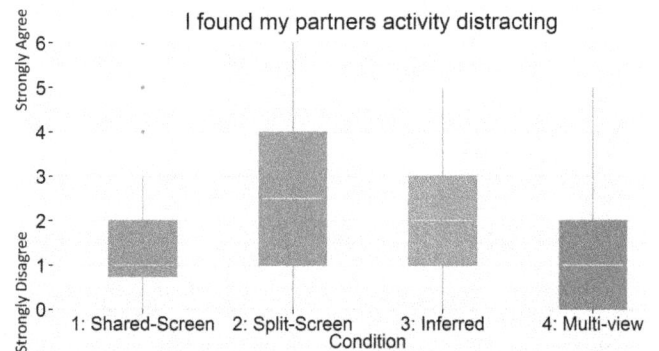

Figure 7. Responses to "I found my partners activity distracting" (lower is better) - Friedman test $\chi^2(3) = 12.63, p < 0.01$, *post hoc* Bonferroni corrected Wilcoxon test showed no significant differences.

In examining DIST-1 in more detail (see Figure 7) it is evident that the shared screen-division approaches led to increased distraction due to unnecessary or unwanted attention being paid to the partners activity, distraction minimized in the multi-view passive screen mirroring condition and the shared-screen mirroring condition, where there could only be one view at a time competing for attention.

Question	Condition				Friedman Test	Wilcoxon *Post-hoc* ($p < 0.05$)
	1	2	3	4		
TLX Task: Effort	5.50 (3.89)	6.92 (4.67)	5.38 (4.14)	9.50 (4.05)	$\chi^2(3) = 24.66, p < 0.01$	1-4, 2-4, 3-4
TLX Task: Frustration	3.08 (4.41)	3.92 (4.18)	2.71 (2.99)	3.96 (4.27)	$\chi^2(3) = 5.46, p = 0.14$	NA
TLX Task: Mental Demand	4.17 (3.45)	7.63 (4.89)	6.46 (3.91)	8.75 (4.76)	$\chi^2(3) = 17.68, p < 0.01$	1-2, 1-3, 1-4
TLX Task: Physical Demand	3.21 (2.55)	4.67 (4.56)	3.96 (3.70)	5.67 (3.71)	$\chi^2(3) = 9.07, p < 0.05$	1-4
TLX Task: Performance	14.75 (3.29)	13.42 (3.06)	13.83 (3.54)	14.46 (2.36)	$\chi^2(3) = 3.22, p = 0.36$	NA
TLX Task: Temporal Demand	4.63 (4.02)	5.75 (4.56)	5.71 (4.12)	7.75 (4.53)	$\chi^2(3) = 8.97, p < 0.05$	1-4
TLX: TV Overall Workload	25.62 (19.28)	31.39 (17.33)	25.24 (14.71)	34.24 (15.65)	$\chi^2(3) = 15.55, p < 0.01$	3-4
TLX: Task Overall Workload	20.69 (12.13)	28.72 (16.60)	24.48 (12.67)	33.47 (14.55)	$\chi^2(3) = 16.28, p < 0.01$	1-4, 3-4
SUS: System Usability Scale	83.75 (13.95)	73.02 (15.32)	82.60 (15.47)	73.85 (17.91)	$\chi^2(3) = 8.50, p < 0.05$	None

Table 1. Workload and usability. NASA TLX [8] is from 0 (lowest) to 100 (highest), SUS [2] is from 0 (worst) to 100 (best). Means with standard deviations are presented across Conditions. A Friedman test was conducted with *post hoc* Bonferroni corrected Wilcoxon tests.

Question	Condition				Friedman Test	Wilcoxon *Post-hoc* ($p < 0.05$)
	1	2	3	4		
WS-1: We were able to collaborate effectively	4.92 (1.41)	4.67 (1.20)	5.04 (0.86)	4.46 (1.41)	$\chi^2(3) = 6.31, p = 0.09$	NA
WS-2: We were able to work independently to complete the task	4.88 (1.39)	4.67 (1.24)	4.92 (1.21)	5.29 (1.16)	$\chi^2(3) = 7.35, p = 0.06$	NA
WS-3: It was easy to discuss the information we found	5.17 (1.34)	5.17 (0.96)	5.38 (0.65)	4.92 (1.18)	$\chi^2(3) = 4.66, p = 0.19$	NA
WS-4: We were able to work together to complete the task	4.88 (1.33)	5.04 (0.91)	5.29 (0.75)	4.50 (1.53)	$\chi^2(3) = 10.7, p < 0.05$	3-4
WS-5: I was able to actively participate in completing the task	5.00 (1.06)	5.09 (0.83)	5.38 (0.65)	5.08 (0.93)	$\chi^2(3) = 3.77, p = 0.29$	NA
MO-1: How well did the system support collaboration?	4.88 (1.19)	4.71 (1.37)	5.08 (0.97)	4.79 (1.67)	$\chi^2(3) = 0.37, p = 0.95$	NA
MO-2: How well did the system support you to share particular information with your partner?	5.00 (1.22)	5.25 (0.79)	5.42 (0.78)	5.13 (1.15)	$\chi^2(3) = 1.27, p = 0.73$	NA
MO-3: I was able to tell when my partner was looking at what I was browsing	4.04 (2.27)	4.46 (1.67)	4.54 (1.31)	3.83 (2.26)	$\chi^2(3) = 0.61, p = 0.89$	NA
MO-4: How well did the system support you to see/review what your partner was talking about?	4.71 (1.63)	5.08 (0.83)	5.08 (1.06)	5.08 (1.14)	$\chi^2(3) = 0.16, p = 0.98$	NA
WE-2: I was aware of what my partner was doing	3.88 (2.09)	4.67 (1.20)	4.79 (1.29)	4.79 (1.53)	$\chi^2(3) = 4.25, p = 0.24$	NA
PE-1: My partner was aware of what I was doing	3.71 (1.99)	4.79 (1.18)	4.54 (1.35)	4.67 (1.34)	$\chi^2(3) = 4.35, p = 0.23$	NA
DIST-1: I found my partners activity distracting	1.71 (1.83)	2.67 (1.71)	1.88 (1.45)	1.29 (1.30)	$\chi^2(3) = 12.63, p < 0.01$	None
DIST-2: I felt I could control how aware I was of my partners activity	2.54 (1.77)	3.54 (1.82)	4.08 (1.50)	4.58 (1.53)	$\chi^2(3) = 15.52, p < 0.01$	1-3, 1-4

Table 3. Questions derived from previous studies. WS: WebSurface[23], MO: Mobisurf[20], WE: WeSearch[18], PE: Permulin[13]. Questions were 7-point Likert scale (results range from 0-6, higher is better). Means with standard deviations are presented across Conditions. A Friedman test was conducted with *post hoc* Bonferroni corrected Wilcoxon tests.

Figure 8 suggests that whilst Conditions 1 and 4 shared similar levels of distraction, they had very different capabilities regarding how well users could control their awareness; the downside to Condition 1 was the lack of control over gaining awareness of their partners activity.

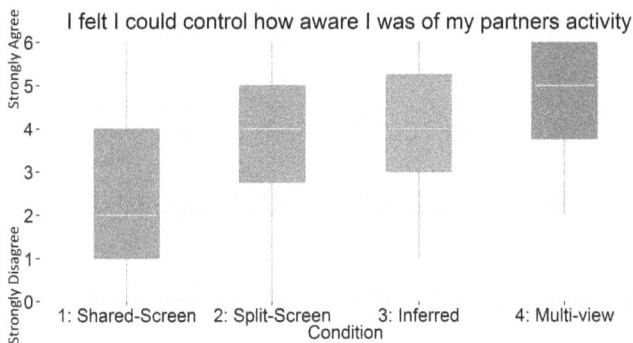

Figure 8. Responses to "I felt I could control how aware I was of my partners activity" (higher is better) - Friedman test $\chi^2(3) = 15.52, p < 0.01$, *post hoc* Bonferroni corrected Wilcoxon test showed differences between 3-4.

For user rankings (see Figure 9) all conditions were somewhat dichotomous, with no significant differences, albeit the multi-view passive screen mirroring condition featured the best mean ranking, followed by the inferred condition.

Acceptability and Privacy

As part of our debrief we asked groups whether there were any aspects of the systems they used that they liked or disliked, probing for detail where appropriate. Table 4 lists the most frequently mentioned common themes during these interviews. For quotes, G# indicates Group number.

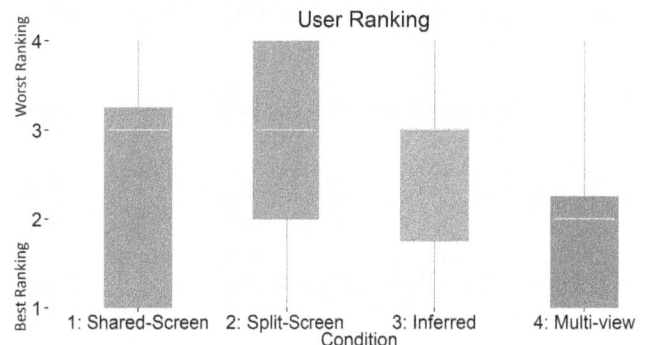

Figure 9. User ranking (lower is better) - Friedman test $\chi^2(3) = 5.55, p = 0.14$.

Being able to choose to view their partners content or the TV independently was a frequently cited benefit of Condition 4 (passive multi-view):

"I liked the last one, it was the best one. I could do whatever I want, I was independent." *G2*

"I liked the one with the glasses the most too because I wasn't distracted by those videos he was watching and I was independent to choose my screen." *G3*

Comment	No. Of Participants
Liked Condition 4 (multi-view)	11
Liked inferred focus function	7
Disliked Condition 1 (fullscreen)	5
Liked simplicity of Condition 1 (fullscreen)	4
Disliked Condition 4 (multi-view)	3
Found 3 views complex	2

Table 4. Most mentioned aspects of system usage.

Participants also appreciated the ability of Condition 3 to automatically infer usage of the display:

"I liked the fact that when you start a trailer it comes up on the big screen, that's handy." *G4*
"I liked the (Condition 3) where it senses the video is played and it pauses the TV, because then I don't have to explicitly say play the sound for this." *G5*

However user preferences were divisive, as the previous rankings illustrated. For example some preferred the simplicity and speed of Condition 1:

"I preferred the third one where it was fullscreen on the one press of a button, because it was the fastest to share with the other person and the sound also was changed automatically." *G6*
"I kind of liked the simplicity of just the normal pushing things to the screen and taking them back." *G10*

Whilst others believed it might lead to conflict:

"On the last one I feel like it was me and my sister doing it we would get in a lot of fights." *G7*
"The second one was just not helpful because you could just steal the screen, I was fighting trying to watch TV and he takes the TV." *G8*

Users raised privacy concerns regarding personal device usage, specifically regarding privacy filtering of screen content, when to make the screen available to be viewed, and awareness regarding whether someone is viewing the screen:

"The only thing is that you can control what they see on their screen, I think you'd have to be able to control what you can see and what you can't see.. you could be like, texting your girlfriend you know?" *G8*
"I liked having the option to show my device but I wouldn't mind having it be automatic in some cases... If I'm viewing a video or a trailer... I want it to be available automatically. It would be a bit cumbersome if I was to explicitly say this app can be shared" *G5*

"I quite liked being able to dip in and out of viewing, so if you were talking about a film I could see what you were viewing then close it again" *Partner interrupts*: "I didn't know that was happening, and I feel kind of weird about that..." *G10*

The issue of spatial/social context affecting shareability was also raised:

"If I'm in the living-room with other people and IMDB or Youtube are white-listed then fine, share it with others. If I'm in bed watching stuff then I don't want people in the other room to see what I'm doing because that's happening without my knowledge." *G5*
"I would have privacy concerns if I'm not using this at home among people that I don't know for a long time... with friends and family wouldn't be a problem" *G2*

As the final part of the debrief we also asked participants to rate the social acceptability of different screen mirroring behaviours, namely:

User control of mirroring "The user of the device chooses when, and for how long, to mirror the device to a TV"

Selective sharing for on-demand viewing "The user of the device chooses to make the device available and accessible to others in the home to view on-demand on the TV for a period of time"

Always-on sharing "Others in the home can view the device on-demand at any time"

For this set of mirroring behaviours, we attempted to elicit the acceptability of usage of these behaviours within two additional factors: privacy, and device ownership. For device ownership we examined personal devices (e.g. their phone) against shared devices (e.g. family tablet), whilst for privacy we examined no privacy filtering against a capability to automatically filter device content where privacy was likely to be violated (with the examples given of hiding notifications or only sharing certain application activity). The aim of this

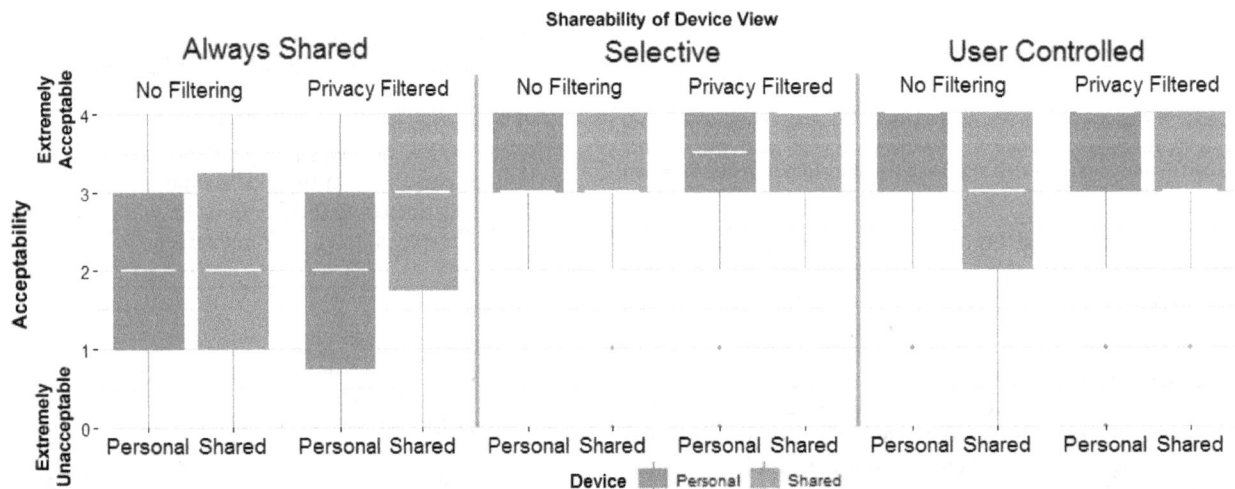

Figure 10. A factorial RM ANOVA found a significant effect on the type of sharing questioned $\chi^2(4) = 43.6$, $p < 0.01$, *post hoc* Tukey's on sharing found significant differences between Selective - Always Shared, and User Controlled - Always Shared. There were no interaction effects.

was to establish both which sharing behaviours were most acceptable, as well as the extent to which immediate privacy concerns regarding shared activity might impact adoption, and usage of personal devices might influence willingness to share their device activity, as shown in Figure 10. A factorial three-way repeated-measures ANOVA showed a significant effect on the type of screen sharing only, with no significant effects on privacy filtering or personal versus shared device. This suggests that the biggest concern regarding the acceptability of sharing device activity through screen mirroring is regarding the possibility of "always-on" sharing, with users preferring that the device be made available to be viewed selectively, regardless of device ownership or our suggested real-time privacy filtering measures.

DISCUSSION

The results of this study provide a number of insights into the usage of screen-mirroring behaviours on a shared-use TV. With respect to RQ 1 (fragmentation of viewing) we have found that in attempting to utilize screen-mirroring whilst consuming TV content there is significant fragmentation regarding the TV viewing experience, as evidenced by viewing instance durations. Whilst this is rather obvious, it does at least underline the necessity for having the ability to pause TV in screen-mirroring contexts, in order to preserve some semblance of a TV viewing experience. Fragmentation is naturally reduced using screen-division.

Screen-division infact allows for greater awareness of the activity of others whilst preserving TV viewing, as evidenced by our questionnaire (addressing RQ 2 - screen division), but at the expense of an increase in distraction; with multiple content streams on the TV at once, and each user having no control over whether other user's content was mirrored, this forced attention is unavoidable. Additionally, the workload (measured by TLX) of managing multiple content streams on the display is significant. Our inferred focus condition (RQ 3 - inferred focus) addressed this issue, evidenced by decreased TLX effort subscale scores, improved SUS (usability) scores, decreasing distraction (questionnaire), and improving user ranking. This suggests that, for screen-division approaches to be feasible, the TV needs to be able to help users adaptively manage what is on the display / what they listen to.

Finally, with respect to active versus passive screen mirroring (RQ 4), distraction, control over awareness, independence, and user rankings were rated best for this condition. The multi-view display allowed us to evaluate passive screen-mirroring in a context where users could personally dictate what they attended to, without interrupting their partner. However this had some negative effects, namely with respect to workload and awareness as to what their partner was attending to. Moreover, the prospect of shifting control of the viewing of a device from the owner/user of the device to other inhabitants of the household brings with it significant social issues. Our post-study questionnaire demonstrated that, for such a system to be deemed acceptable to users, controls over when the device was to be made available to be viewed would have to be implemented, regardless of any further developments in screen-mirroring technology such as automatic pri-

vacy filtering, and regardless of whether the device is personal or shared-use with others in the household.

IMPLICATIONS FOR SCREEN MIRRORING SYSTEMS

Our findings have both short and long-term implications for how we interact with, and view, other devices in the home.

Extensions To Active Screen Mirroring

Currently, single-view displays are the *de facto* standard in the home, with multi-view displays reliant on technology such as active-shutter glasses which limit their uptake and adoption. As such, we must first consider implications for how screen-mirroring can be better facilitated on single-view displays. Whilst our findings indicate that passive screen-mirroring shows promise, and whilst such an approach could be designed for single-view displays, it is likely that without the ability to personally dictate what content is on the TV display, the benefits of such an approach might well be cancelled out in a single-view display.

As such, we would suggest that for the short term, screen-mirroring in single-view displays further develop active screen-mirroring systems. We have demonstrated the utility of screen-division for both preserving existing TV content viewing, and allowing for attending to multiple content streams, however we have also demonstrated that for such solutions to be viable we must have TVs that are capable of aiding the user in the management of the display e.g. selecting which content stream to listen to and inferring focus on a given content stream based on its current activity, essentially managing audio/visual conflicts for users. With such functionality, we can build screen-mirroring systems whose capabilities go beyond that previously researched and currently available to consumers, taking advantage of large displays to share the activity ongoing in the room, if the user so chooses.

Viability Of Passive Screen Mirroring

On a longer term basis, we would suggest that there is potential for a shift in how the viewing of device activity is managed. Passive screen mirroring, allowing users to selectively and personally choose to attend to activity going on within other devices in the household, shows significant promise, however there are significant acceptability issues that would need to be dealt with before such a system can become viable to consumers. Beyond filtering what is on the display for privacy, there needs to be a contract between user and device that dictates when the device should make its activity available, and to whom. Additionally, this functionality needs to be simple to manage, so as not to introduce new and esoteric barriers toward shareability.

We would suggest that a combination of geo-fencing [25] and management based on spatial context (that is, ensuring that such activity is only made available on the home network, and then that its scope is limited only to the room the user is currently residing, and then only if the room is used socially) and inferred acceptability based on device context such as what application is running, or what activity is being undertaken (e.g. watching a movie trailer being acceptable, whilst browsing personal email being unacceptable) would likely provide a simple and powerful means of managing the accessibility of device activity, but this would require future research to adequately determine. There is also the issue of awareness regarding viewing - to what extent do users want to be aware of the attention of others? In our study, one user remarked at the disconcerting nature of being unaware of the attention of their partner, suggesting that for such a system to be viable we must enhance the social communication aspect.

Applicability To Other Content Types

We would suggest that the techniques we have demonstrated for managing the TV could equally be applied to other forms of sharing content aside from screen mirroring. For example the casting paradigm of throwing content onto the TV (e.g. a picture or video) could be supported by our system, allowing multiple content streams to be casted, with inferred management of focus preventing audio conflicts.

Future Work

We also envision the potential for screen-mirroring applications outside of the TV, for example enabling device-to-device mirroring, and the application of some of the concepts we have discussed regarding TVs being applied to, say, larger tablets. There is also the unaddressed problem of reciprocal control; thus far, we have treated devices as read-only portals into the activity of others, but there is no technological barrier to there being input provided back to the device from others, however there may be significant social barriers to doing so. Finally, there is the idea of inferring what to present on the TV, what activity to focus on, and when. We would suggest that, given the plethora of devices and activities available, that TVs operating in conjunction with devices might be able to significantly expand interaction with, and awareness of, others in the household. This work has demonstrated how we can significantly enhance this awareness, but at a cost of increased user workload for example, and thus our TVs must become smarter and more able to assist us in making us aware of what is happening around us.

CONCLUSIONS

This paper has presented extensions to existing research regarding shared screen-mirroring, demonstrating ways in which we can enhance our capability to view and attend to mirrored device activity through screen-division, inferring focus, and empowering users to control their own viewing experience. Through such extensions to screen-mirroring, we have been able to improve user activity awareness, capability to collaborate, and aid existing TV content consumption, thus providing the capability to decrease the digital isolation that has become prevalent in our multi-screen homes.

ACKNOWLEDGMENTS

This work was supported in part by Bang & Olufsen and the EPSRC. This publication only reflects the authors' views.

REFERENCES

1. Agrawala, M., et al. The two-user Responsive Workbench. In *Proc. SIGGRAPH '97*, ACM Press (1997), 327–332.

2. Brooke, J. SUS-A quick and dirty usability scale. *Usability evaluation in industry* (1996).

3. Consumerlab. TV and Media: Identifying the needs of tomorrow's video consumers, 2013.

4. Dodgson, N. A. Multi-view autostereoscopic 3D display. In *Stanford Workshop on 3D Imaging*, Stanford University (2011).

5. Engelbart, D., and English, W. A research center for augmenting human intellect. *FJCC* (1968).

6. Google. The New Multi-Screen World. *Google Think Insights* (2012).

7. Harper, R. *The Connected Home: The Future of Domestic Life*. Springer Publishing Company, Incorporated, Dec. 2011.

8. Hart, S., and Staveland, L. Development of NASA-TLX (Task Load Index). In *Human mental workload* (1988).

9. Hsu, C.-F., et al. Screencast in the Wild. In *Proc. MM '14*, ACM Press (2014), 813–816.

10. Ingrey, M. Triple-Screening: A New Phenomenon, 2014.

11. Kawsar, F., and Brush, A. B. Home computing unplugged. In *Proc. UbiComp '13*, ACM Press (2013), 627.

12. Kreitmayer, S., Laney, R., Peake, S., and Rogers, Y. Sharing bubbles. In *Proc. UbiComp '13 Adjunct*, ACM Press (2013), 1405–1408.

13. Lissermann, R., et al. Permulin: mixed-focus collaboration on multi-view tabletops. In *Proc. CHI '14*, ACM Press (2014), 3191–3200.

14. Lucero, A., Jones, M., Jokela, T., and Robinson, S. Mobile collocated interactions. *interactions 20*, 2 (Mar. 2013), 26.

15. Matusik, W., Forlines, C., and Pfister, H. Multiview user interfaces with an automultiscopic display. In *Proc. AVI '08*, ACM Press (May 2008), 363.

16. McGill, M., Williamson, J., and Brewster, S. A. Mirror, mirror, on the wall. In *Proc. TVX '14*, ACM Press (2014), 87–94.

17. MillwardBrown. Marketing in a multiscreen world. Tech. rep., 2014.

18. Morris, M. R., Lombardo, J., and Wigdor, D. WeSearch. In *Proc. CSCW '10*, ACM Press (2010), 401.

19. Ofcom. Communications Market Report, 2014.

20. Seifert, J., et al. MobiSurf. In *Proc. ITS '12*, ACM Press (2012), 51.

21. Shoemaker, G. B. D., and Inkpen, K. M. Single display privacyware. In *Proc. CHI '01*, ACM Press (2001), 522–529.

22. Tee, K., et al. Artifact awareness through screen sharing for distributed groups. *International Journal of Human-Computer Studies 67*, 9 (Sept. 2009), 677–702.

23. Tuddenham, P., et al. WebSurface. In *Proc. ITS 2009*, ACM Press (2009), 181–188.

24. Turkle, S. *Alone Together: Why We Expect More from Technology and Less from Each Other*. Basic Books, Inc., Jan. 2011.

"I'm just on my phone and they're watching TV": Quantifying mobile device use while watching television

Christian Holz, Frank Bentley, Karen Church, Mitesh Patel

Yahoo Labs, Sunnyvale, CA

{christianh, fbentley, kchurch, miteshp} @ yahoo-inc.com

ABSTRACT

In recent years, mobile devices have become a part of our daily lives—much like television sets had over the second half of the 20th century. Increasingly, people are using mobile devices while watching television. We set out to understand this behavior on a minute-by-minute quantified level as well as users' motivations and purposes of device use while watching television. We conducted a novel mixed-methods study inside seven households with fourteen instrumented phone and tablet devices, capturing all app launches and app use durations, correlated with the moment in the television program when they occurred. Surprisingly, we found little difference between the volume of device use during programs and commercials. Our two main findings are that 1) participants often joined family members in the TV room to physically be *together*; when they lack interest in the program, they spend the majority of the show on a secondary device and watch TV only during key moments. 2) Virtually none of participants' app and web use during TV consumption was directly related to the running show. With our study, we set the stage for larger-scale investigations into the details of mobile interactions while watching television. Our novel method will aid future work of the community as a means of fully understanding multi-device use alongside television consumption.

Author Keywords

Television; mobile devices; app usage; smartphone; tablet; indoor tracking; commercials.

ACM Classification Keywords

H.5.m. Information interfaces and presentation (e.g., HCI): Miscellaneous.

INTRODUCTION

For many years, researchers (e.g., [1, 4]) and the press (e.g., [5, 12, 19, 20]) have been discussing "dual-screen" television viewers—people who watch television while simultaneously using another device, such as a smartphone or a tablet. While researchers have found that this is a common phenomenon via self-report surveys, to-date there has been no in-depth study on precisely how people are using their devices in conjunction with television viewing.

Many questions remain and no method that has been explored in the existing literature can fully answer them. For example, what percentage of mobile app use happens during commercials compared to during TV programs? And how does this compare to general app use throughout the day? Is application use different for different genres of shows? Does use increase or decrease during a program? Are the apps that people use while watching television different from those they use when they are not watching television? And which websites do they visit on their mobile devices while watching different types of television shows?

We designed a novel method to gather the data that is necessary to answer these types of questions, and ran a 14-day field study in 7 diverse homes to validate the capability of our method to capture complete data. To detect when a show is playing on participants' TV sets and which show it is, we placed a logging device by their TVs that is capable of sound printing television audio. We also developed an app logger that records the time and duration of app use, and installed it on participants' phones and tablets. Our app logger also records the web pages visited from the stock browser on the phone or tablet, including search queries.

Finally, we placed Bluetooth Low Energy (BLE) beacons throughout participants' homes, such that our app logger could determine whether devices were in the same room as the television while the television was on. In addition, we complemented this quantitative data collection with in-depth qualitative interviews and voicemail diaries to capture an understanding of why devices were being used and what the social context of their use was.

With this deployment, we begin to answer the complex quantitative questions about app use during television viewing that to-date have not been fully explored. In this paper, we describe our method and discuss the findings that we derived from our field study. We believe that our method can be critical to actually understanding the nuances of device use during television viewing, which cannot be ascertained through interviews, surveys, or other self-reported means.

RELATED WORK

Despite the great amount of public press around the phenomena of second-device use during television viewing

TVX '15, June 03 – 05, 2015, Brussels, Belgium
Copyright is held by the owner/author(s). Publication rights licensed to ACM.
ACM 978-1-4503-3526-3/15/06...$15.00
http://dx.doi.org/10.1145/2745197.2745210

[17], surprisingly little has been studied in-depth about its use. Research in this area tends to fall in one of several areas: self-report studies of use, studying online artifacts of second-screen use, or building new applications to engage users on second screens. In addition, unrelated to television viewing, other researchers have explored ways to log application use on mobile phones.

Several organizations have studied second-screen device use during television viewing. The PEW Research Center in the United States has conducted a large self-report study asking about people's everyday practices around phone and tablet use with television viewing [17]. They found that 38% of cell phone owners used their device during commercial breaks and that 22% used their mobile phones to check the validity of something presented in a television program. Of smartphone users, 20% looked online to see what others were saying about a program that they were watching (e.g., on Twitter or Facebook). Google also conducted a study and found that 22% of all simultaneous use of phones and tablets with television programming was complementary [8], meaning that the device use was in some way related to the content presented on the television screen. These studies show the prevalence of the phenomena, but they do not explore the details of these interactions beyond stating that they occur.

Cesar et al. explored early uses of second screens to interact with television content [4]. They found four main usage categories for these devices: Controlling, Enriching, Sharing, and Transferring content. However, this research was more exploratory and occurred before second screen devices were in regular use in the world. In 2011, Cesar and Geerts reviewed existing social television systems, many of which required the use of a second screen device [3]. However, again this was before these devices were in broad use, so little can be inferred about current everyday practices with a different variety of services.

Other researchers have studied the online traces of second-screen usage. Shamma et al. studied tweets that were posted during the 2008 American Presidential Debates [16]. They explored tweet volume over the course of the broadcast and found that the key moments of the debate could be identified from the online traces. PEW found that in the 2012 presidential debates, 11% of television viewers were also "dual screeners" and followed content related to the debates on their computer or mobile device [13].

Schirra et al. studied Twitter use during the British period drama "Downton Abbey" and explored the tension between paying attention to the show and viewing online content about the show [15]. They also found that social interactions on second screens provided an experience of being "together" with others while watching television, even if they were alone at home.

Through a diary study, Hess et al. explored second screen interactions while watching television [9]. Similar to the PEW studies discussed above, they enumerated many of the activities that occur on mobile devices while watching television, many of which were completely unrelated to the content of the programming. However, they were not able to look in more detail at what participants did on a minute-by-minute level as TV shows progressed.

A final area of research has been in creating novel applications for second-screen interactions and studying their use. Nandakumar and Murray created an application for the TV series "Justified" that provided additional context about the characters and plot [11]. Basapur et al. created the Parallel Feeds system to provide related content to the currently playing TV program on a second-screen device [1]. The studies of these systems in everyday use showed the demand for systems that extend the content presented on the screen, an activity presumed to be one of the tasks that people frequently perform on their devices while watching TV.

While showing that dual screen usage is becoming a widespread phenomenon, none of these studies has tried to quantify exactly what people are doing on their secondary devices using today's applications. For example, which apps are participants using? How long are they interacting with their devices? How does interaction change during commercials compared to regular programs or vary for different genres? And how does interaction differ based on the type of second screen device, i.e. tablet or phone?

Finally, in studying application use, several researchers have created loggers that keep track of the apps that people use on their device. Böhmer studied app usage patterns in a large-scale field study, explicitly looking at apps that are used at certain times of day and at specific points in the day, such as before going to bed [2]. We see these technologies as an exciting opportunity to learn about fine-grained device use, but in the context of television viewing, a topic that previous app logging studies have not approached.

Overall, this literature shows that second-screen device use is prevalent, but not very well understood. With the exciting technologies of app loggers, there is a large potential to quantitatively study exactly what people are doing on their phones and tablets while watching television.

METHODS

We conducted a two-week mixed-method field study in the homes of seven diverse participants in order to understand mobile device use during and away from television viewing. The study contained both quantitative data collection procedures over the 14 days as well as several instances of deep qualitative data collection to help explain the quantitative data and the circumstances around mobile device use.

Participants

To collect representative data, we enlisted a recruiting agency to sign up seven diverse households in the greater San Francisco Bay Area. Six households were family homes with two or more persons and a couple lived in the seventh household. Our set of participants consisted of three males and four females. Participants ranged in age between 22–57 (35.5 on average), and had a diverse set of occupations including nurse, analyst, office manager, and student. All participants owned Android smartphones as their main communication device and all also used an Android tablet. We captured data solely on each participant's mobile device as well as on their main tablet using our app logger, but not on other devices in the household. All participants were compensated for their time.

App logger and indoor tracking on participants' devices

We developed an app logger to inspect Android's running applications, obtain their app and package name, and observe their launches and run times. Additionally, the logger recorded participants' use of devices' stock browsers to log time-stamped web histories as well as search queries. Any time the screen on the device was lit, our app logger captured this data. The app logger ran as a passive background process and became active only when the screen was lit. It thus did not impact app use or battery life of the device.

Each log entry was appended with the room in the house that the user was in (or nothing if outside the home). We implemented room-based tracking of devices using Bluetooth low energy (BLE), as is increasingly used for this application in commercial systems (e.g., Apple iBeacon). BLE beacons are short-range wireless devices that emit a unique address, which our app logger used as the signature to match a beacon from the known placement [18]. Our logger estimated locations using the known placement of BLE beacons around the participant's house by interpolating between the signal strengths of all BLE beacons [6], which reveals the rough proximity to all beacon and enables the logger to estimate the location inside the home [14].

Our app logger triggered BLE scanning whenever the user accessed an app on the phone or tablet. The scanning continued for 30 seconds and the logger recorded the average value of the measured signal strength values for each of the beacons. The logger repeated the scanning every minute while a device was in use, but stopped scanning as soon as the phone screen was turned off.

Procedure

We conducted the study in December 2014 in three stages:

1) For the initial interview, we visited participants' homes and conducted short, semi-structured interviews. The interviews covered their daily mobile device habits across both, smartphones and tablets, their general mobile search use and concrete examples of their most recent mobile search, details of their app usage habits across their smartphone and tablet, and finally their TV viewing habits.

At the end of the initial interview, we installed our app logger on participants' phones and tablets and showed them samples of the app use data the logger would collect.

For the indoor tracking part of our study, we placed four BLE beacons around participants' homes, primarily in the

living area, kitchen, and bedroom. We placed the final BLE beacon in a location to maximize our ability to discern the room with the main television from other rooms. While we could not verify absolute tracking accuracy, all participants' homes were small and open-plan. All kitchens were connected to the living rooms, typically with a dining area or room as part of the living room. Hence, when our app logger detected the BLE beacon by the TV to be in medium range of the mobile device, the participant could hear and likely see the TV, which we considered TV consumption.

Finally, we placed a dedicated mobile phone that ran our sound-printing tool using IntoNow by participants' main television sets. Our tool captured a 15 second audio clip every minute, generated a "sound print" on the recorded segment, and uploaded the features of this print to the IntoNow server for classification. No raw audio was ever stored or transmitted off of the device. The IntoNow server compared the uploaded features with its back catalog database of television programs that have aired in the United States since 2011 (including reruns) and returned a match upon successful detection. Matches identified the program with associated metadata (e.g., title, episode, genre) as well as the timecode in the show that corresponded to the audio clip. IntoNow also identified commercials.

Logging TV consumption with a dedicated mobile phone allowed us to know what participants played on the main TV in the home regardless of the source; our tool also identified content played through services, such as Netflix and Hulu, as long as the TV show or commercial had aired on US television in the past few years.

We only analyzed television sessions when the main participant's device was in use and was close to the main television set. While the device we placed by participants' TV sets continuously collected television logs, we discarded those that occurred when the participant was outside or used no apps on either mobile device at all.

2) For the 14 days of the study, we asked participants to leave a voicemail message once per day summarizing how they used their smartphone and tablet that day. During this same 14-day period our application logger ran in the background on their devices and pushed data about their daily app usage to our servers. Likewise, the television logger ran and pushed data about their TV consumption to our servers. All data was sent over a secure HTTPS connection and did not contain any personally identifying information.

We analyzed the quantitative data as follows. For each app event we logged in the app logger, we cross-referenced the TV logs to determine the running TV show or commercial and estimated the location of the participant's devices using the BLE data. If no TV show was running or the BLE signals were out of range, representing the participant being outside their house, we discarded the respective app logs. Otherwise, we counted each app log either towards 'TV program' or 'commercial'. When a commercial came on and the participant decided to switch channels, for example, app use counted towards 'TV programs', since no commercial was actively watched. The app use we report for 'commercials' below thus exclusively represents times when a commercial was running.

3) At the end of the two-week logging period, we conducted a final in-home interview. Prior to the interview, we reviewed participants application use log data, their voicemail entries and their television viewing habits to list topics that we wanted to follow up on or get more details for. For example, we frequently asked about activity from their application logs that was not reported in their voice diary entries. Likewise, we probed about specific details of their app usage that occurred in parallel to watching specific programs and also asked if they had watched specific programs when they were logged as being in adjacent rooms to the television. This confirmed our assumption to count TV consumption during moments when participants were in the dining area of their house. Finally, at the end of the interview, we uninstalled the logging software from the participants' smartphone and tablet. All in-person interviews were audio recorded and transcribed and all voicemail dairy logs were transcribed to prepare for data analysis.

We analyzed the qualitative data using grounded theory and thematic analysis. We looked for repeating themes in participants' responses during our semi-structured interviews at the beginning and end of the study as well as in the voicemail data that participants provided throughout the study. The items of analysis were quotes from participants, which we combined to form the themes.

Results

Overall, the seven households in the study watched 415 hours of TV during the two-week study period. In total, they launched 1,447 apps on their phones and 485 apps on tablets, using their phones for a total of 867 hours and their tablets for a total of 497 hours. Half of all device usage occurred when participants were at home. On average, 2.8% of all app use occurred simultaneously on both devices. In their mobile browsers, participants visited a total of 1,343 web pages, 770 web pages from their phones and 573 web pages from their tablets. They performed 153 search queries through web search engines, such as Yahoo and Google, with 129 searches submitted from their mobile phone and the remaining 24 from their tablets.

During the time participants watched TV, they interacted with their phones for a total of 77.8 hours (17.9% of all phone use while at home) and tablets for 37.2 hours total (7.5% of all tablet use while at home). Participants accessed 136 web pages while watching TV (133 unique web pages, 43 unique domains) and conducted 28 web searches (15 unique queries) across both tablets and mobile phones. Most of these web pages were accessed via tablets (120 of the 136 webpages, 88.2%).

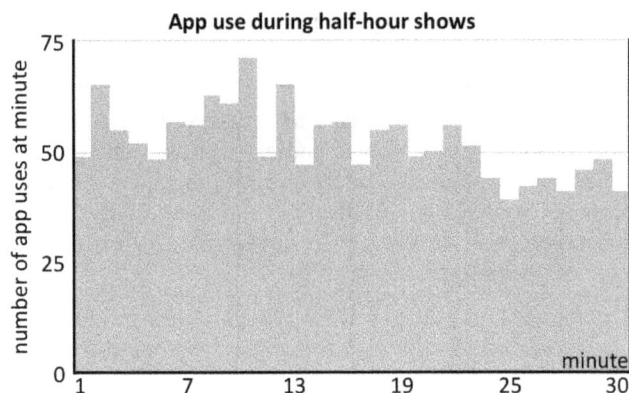

Figure 1: The number of times any app was used at each minute of all 30-minute shows. Note the fairly consistent use over the course of the program.

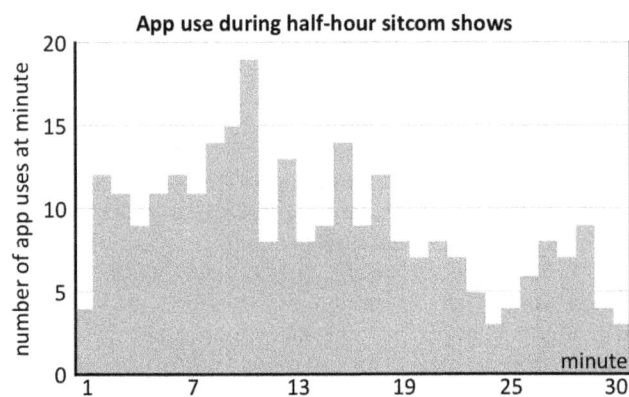

Figure 2: Histogram of app use during half-hour sitcoms. Note the sharp decline towards the end of the program.

App use during TV programs for different program genres
During the study, 21.2% of all of the shows that participants watched were a half-hour in length and 34.5% were one-hour shows. These were the two most-frequently watched show durations during the study and there were smaller numbers of 1.5, two, and three-hour programs. We present our analysis of app use separately for the most frequent show durations below.

Figures 1–3 illustrate the times during a TV show when participants interacted with apps on their devices. Figure 1 shows a histogram over all half-hour shows. Figure 2 shows this distribution for half-hour sitcom shows. App use generally declined after the typical point of the first commercial and waned even more towards the end of the program.

Figure 3 illustrates the histogram of app use for one-hour shows. We see an increase in app use during the middle part of the show, which tapers off again towards the end of the show. The large drop in app use around the 54-minute mark is likely attributed to the final twist of a show just before the last commercial upon which app use shows a final peak.

App use during one-hour show

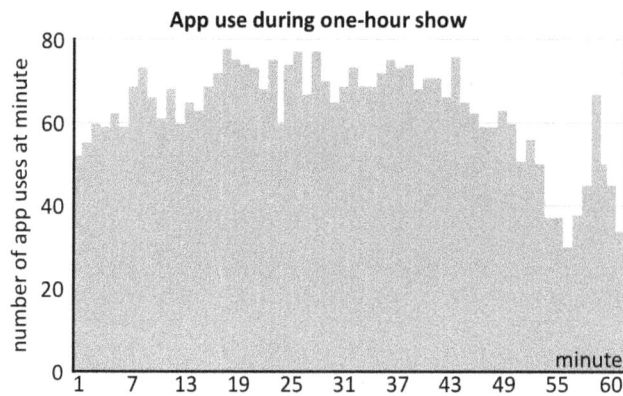

Figure 3: Here we show the number of times an app was used at each minute of a 60-minute show. Note the higher use throughout the show compared to 30-minute shows in the previous figure, and a spike at the end of the program.

App use during one-hour reality show

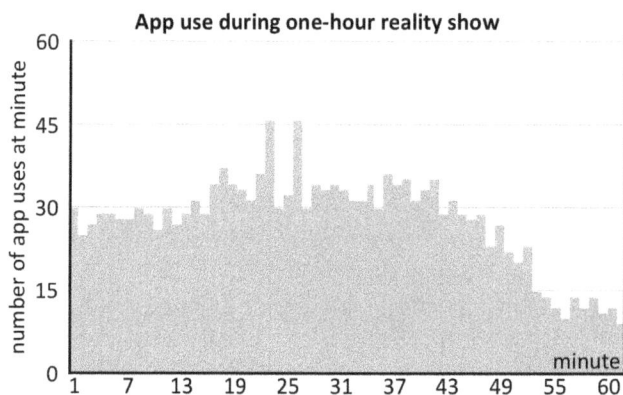

Figure 4: App use is fairly steady throughout one-hour reality shows, except for a large drop towards the end, typically when a candidate is selected to leave the show.

App use during one-hour crime drama

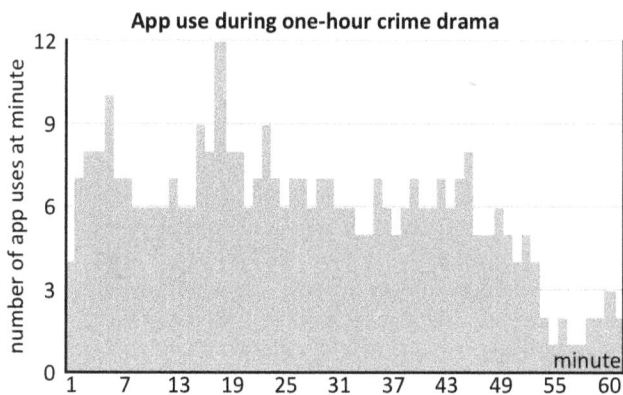

Figure 5: The app use pattern for one-hour crime dramas shows many fluctuations, which correspond to the times of commercials. Participants' lowest app use throughout crime dramas was at the end when the show's mystery is resolved.

Turning to exploring a particular genre for one-hour shows, Figure 4 displays the subset of app use for reality shows. During such shows, participants' use of apps was mostly steady (and higher than during other genres) with a peak in

app use around the 25-minute mark, a point that typically begins the longer mid-show commercial break. Otherwise, app use was fairly steady throughout the show, which is likely due to the rather steady level of suspense in such shows. The end of the episode marks a clear exception, where we can see a substantial drop in app use. This is often the moment when a particular candidate is selected to leave the show that week in a typical reality show, such as *Survivor* or *The Bachelor*.

Figure 5 shows the app use for one-hour crime dramas. The histogram shows a spike at the typical point of the first commercial break around the 15th minute. Similar to the histogram for reality shows, the final drop in app use is likely due to the resolution of the show's arc of suspense.

Times of watching shows

Figure 6 shows the times during a half-hour or one-hour show when participants were actively watching a show in a particular genre. Especially apparent in the 60-minute programs, there was a dip in program viewing in locations typically associated with commercial breaks, around the 25th minute and the 45th minute. In the data, we also saw channel surfing at these times in many viewing logs.

We explored the average time a user continuously watched a program. For example, if a participant watched a show for seven minutes, then tuned away for three minutes, and finally tuned back to the first show for the remaining 20 minutes, this would consist of three sessions (3 minutes, 7 minutes, and 20 minutes). Durations had local maxima around five and ten minutes, as well as just before the half hour mark. This, along with the previous figure, indicates that during the majority of time participants switched to different television channels once commercials came on.

Commercials compared to programs

Of the 415 total hours of TV watched, participants watched 14.9 hours of commercials (3.6%). While participants used a device 35.2% of the time during programs, they used it 30.2% of the time during commercials. Interestingly, while the overall smartphone usage went down during commercials, tablet usage went up: We found that on average participants used their mobile phones during 25.3% of the time of programs and 19.9% of commercials, while they used their tablets during 12.8% of programs and 12.4% of commercials. Simultaneous use of participants' smartphone and tablet devices dropped from 2.9% during TV programs to 2.2% during commercials.

During programs, participants on average launched 0.06 apps per minute on their phones and 0.02 apps per minute on tablets. During commercials, they launched only 0.04 apps per minute on their phones and maintained an average rate of 0.015 apps per minute on tablets. We saw a decrease of app launches for phones during commercials as well as an overall decrease in commercial viewing as shown in Figure 6, which indicates that participants either quickly

Tuning in during half-hour shows

Tuning in during one-hour shows

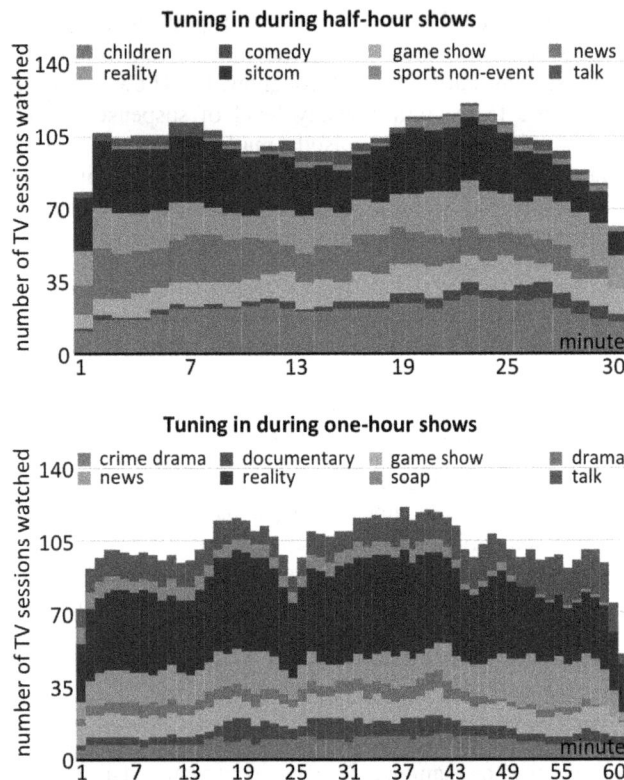

Figure 6: Times in program when participants were watching regardless of app use. Drops occurred at typical commercial breaks, such as at 25 and 45 minutes during one-hour shows.

flipped channels or used commercials for other activities, such as going to the bathroom or a different room.

The median duration of app usage on phones was 22 seconds on average for apps launched during programs and 19 seconds during commercials. Tablets showed the same trend with an average duration of 17 seconds during programs and 89.5 seconds during commercials. To obtain these numbers, we counted an app launch once for the type of TV show that was running (e.g., program or commercial), but split app runtimes when TV shows changed, such that the respective part of app runtime is always allocated to the running TV show or commercial.

Duration of app use
Comparing phone with tablet use, participants used their smartphones for shorter interactions while they interacted continuously with tablet applications. Interestingly, participants used apps on tablets longest during sports talk shows (3.1 minutes on average), sports non-events (3 minutes), sports events (2.7 minutes) and news (2.2 minutes). On phones, participants used apps longest during children shows (1.6 minutes on average), action and adventure shows (1.5 minutes), and talk shows (1.4 minutes).

Three large spikes appear when looking at app durations. The first peak during five-second interactions indicates a quick interaction with an application (e.g., viewing a text message) after which participants exited the app. This is

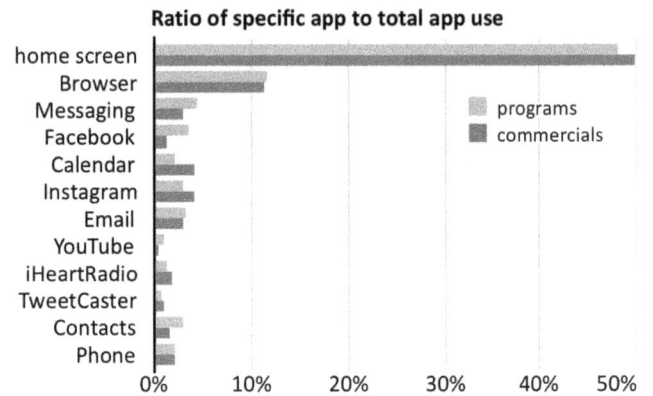

Ratio of specific app to total app use

Figure 7: Percentage of use for an app during television viewing compared to all apps used. While Facebook and YouTube were popular apps during TV shows, both saw substantially less engagement during commercial breaks.

quite different from app use outside the home, where after a typically short session the screen will be immediately turned off as the phone is put away. For example, Ferreira et al found that 40% of all app usage throughout the day is 15 seconds or less [7]. The wide spread of the last peak in the diagram between seconds 70 and 130 shows longer durations of interacting with an application such as browsing a Facebook feed or writing a reply to a message.

Types of applications used
We will now investigate the specific applications that were used while watching television. The browser, messaging and social network applications were most popular during TV consumption as shown in Figure 7. Most applications experienced a decrease in use during commercials. For example, Facebook dropped from 3.7% to 1.4% of its usage during programs, a difference of 38% (Figure 8). Equally interesting is that participants spent more time in the Calendar *during* commercials (rising from 2.2% to 4.2%).

Differences in app use by TV genre
Splitting app use by TV genres, we can see that certain TV genres provoke substantially more app use than others as shown in Figure 9. While TV genres such as comedy, sports, and romance prompted participants to use apps on their devices in more than two thirds of the time of a program, documentary-style genre such as nature, animals, history or science saw very little app use. These types of shows are providing more information per minute of program and often build on the data presented earlier in the show as the program continues which might be causes of the decreased application use.

Web and search use
Moving from app use to the specific URLs visited in the browser, we examined the websites participant surfed while watching TV along with the web searches they conducted during that time. Figure 10 lists the top 10 most accessed domains from the mobile browser while watching TV. Our goal was to get a sense of the type of websites participants visited and to determine if the topics or scope of the sites

program				commercial		
1	home screen	48.1%		1	home screen	54.1%
2	Browser	11.6%		2	Browser	11.4%
3	Messaging	4.4%	↓	3	Instagram	4.2%
4	Facebook	3.7%	↓	4	Calendar	4.2%
5	Email	3.4%		5	Email	3.1%
6	Instagram	3.1%	↑	6	Messaging	3.0%
7	Contacts	2.9%		7	Phone	2.1%
8	Phone	2.3%		8	VpnDialogs	2.0%
9	Calendar	2.2%	↑	9	iHeartRadio	1.8%
10	iHeartRadio	1.3%		10	Contacts	1.7%
11	YouTube	1.2%	↓	11	Facebook	1.4%
12	TweetCaster	0.8%		12	Xfinity TV Go	1.1%

Figure 8: Ranking of apps by proportional use during TV programs and commercials. During commercials, apps with quick interactions (e.g., Facebook, Messaging, Instagram) saw less engagement than those apps that require longer interaction, such as Email and Phone.

Top apps				Bottom apps		
genre	usage	#		genre	usage	#
comedy-drama	68.5%	13		action	16.2%	20
sports non-event	68.5%	41		horror	14.2%	18
sports event	61.5%	296		documentary	11.8%	53
romance-comedy	53.2%	14		soap	7.6%	6
music	47.8%	29		science	6.7%	6
sports talk	42.2%	17		entertainment	6.6%	10
crime drama	41.9%	96		newsmagazine	5.0%	24
bus./financial	40.0%	11		history	3.8%	17
reality	39.7%	272		animals	<.1%	5
news	37.1%	79		nature	<.1%	4

Figure 9: Top 10 and Bottom 10 TV genres during which participants interacted with apps for a fraction of the time.

Domain	Percentage of all domains
www.google.com	20.6%
www.amazon.com	9.6%
www.facebook.com	7.4%
m.yelp.com	5.9%
m.facebook.com	4.4%
truselforganics.com	4.4%
m.espn.go.com	2.9%
www.ehow.com	2.9%
www.surveymonkey.com	2.9%
smcl.bibliocommons.com	2.2%
www.urbanoutfitters.com	2.2%

Figure 10: Top 10 domains accessed during TV watching.

was related to the genre of the TV show in question, as suggested by previous work (e.g., [8]). In participants' logs, five of the top domains relate to top-trafficked websites, including Google and Facebook. We also found some sites that are knowledge bases, such as eHow, and sports-related sites like ESPN. The remaining URLs relate to shopping websites, such as Amazon and Urban Outfitters.

Surprisingly, on closer inspection, we found that none of the web pages or domains participants visited while watching TV related to the content of the programs being watched. This insight stands in sharp contrast to previous findings that show higher levels of complementary use (e.g., Google's report [8] and Pew's study [17]).

Next, we analyzed web searches that participants made from their phone or tablet during television viewing. Of the seven participants, we found that only three executed a search query while a television program was on. Of the 15 unique mobile search queries entered while watching TV, none of the queries appeared to be related to the topic or genre of the currently playing television program and none of the queries were issued during a commercial. Some of the example queries issued during TV use include "*spurs*

female coach", "*urban outfitters*", "*hair salon in san mateo*", "*yahoo mail*" and "*kim kardashian*".

Finally, we analyzed whether any of the search queries across all participants over the two-week period were entertainment or TV related. We examined all queries submitted through Google, Yahoo and Bing and verified whether or not the participant was watching TV at the time the query was issued. We found a total of 153 mobile search queries submitted over the study period, 80 of which were unique. The following queries were TV related: "*money in the bank wwe*" ("Money in the Bank" is a professional wrestling pay-per-view event), "*tablet tv*" (while not related to any TV show per se, it is related to watching TV on tablets), "*bridesmaids*" (P2, who later watched the reality show "NeNe's bridesmaids") and "*victoria's secret show 2014*", which is a fashion show that can be watched online. Three other queries pertained to personalities in television shows: "*kim kardashian*" "*spurs female coach,*" and "*kylie jenner plastic surgery tumblr.*" Compared to self-reported findings in the literature (e.g., [8, 17]), we again saw only little activity related to the current TV show or commercial.

What people were doing
Turning from the quantitative logs, we now explore some of the motivations for participants to use a second screen device during television programs. As mentioned in our methodology section, the themes we list below result from participants' quotes during our interviews at the beginning and end of our study as well as participants' voicemails. Each theme was supported by multiple users and will be discussed in the subsections below.

I want to be with my family
Participants frequently discussed times when their partners or children wanted to watch programs that they themselves were not very interested in watching. In many of these instances, our participants still wanted to be physically with their family members, but reported spending large chunks of the show using a device instead of paying attention to the show. This still allowed the family to be together, even if everyone wasn't focused on the television.

We asked P2 about app use while watching TV and she told us that "*It's usually because I just want to be in the same* room as them and I'm doing my own thing." P3 also talked about the desire to be with her family while watching television: "*The kids always take over the TV and I can never watch what I want to watch unless I go upstairs, but then I'm not going to be with everybody, so I just stay on my phone down here.*" During these times, she often does not pay attention to the television: "*I think I was doing my own thing, but I was relaxing at the same time, and I was playing with the baby, so I guess [looking] half and half.*"

P7 discussed several instances of device use while his wife was watching television. He went on Twitter "*probably just more out of boredom. I don't think that it's necessarily related to the television show or whatever I was watching. It was just, it may have been something my wife wanted to watch and I just couldn't get into it.*"

This can be confirmed as a more general pattern with the quantitative log data. For example, device use stayed high during most shows as shown in Figures 1 and 3. The qualitative data was able to add the interpretation to this data indicating that the participant often was not interested in the programming at all, and just wanted to be with their family.

In these cases, device use is almost always unrelated to the program being watched. It is the desire to be with family that drew participants to the same room as the television, and since they were not interested in the show, they did their own thing on their devices. We discuss some of these activities in the subsections below.

I get things (household chores) done
Often, participants discussed using time in front of the television to catch up on household chores using their mobile phones and tablets. P5 was using an app for her bank to review her recent spending: "*I was just adding all my transactions. ... I was always on my Citibank app. I don't manage my account like, I don't know, other people do, one by one. I just pay attention to how much I have and I was like, 'Okay.'*" P2 used television time while watching the news to catch up with friends and household tasks: "*I will send texts when, so when they're watching something I will be sending texts to get some things done and out of the way.*"

These participants were not always paying attention to the television, and the activities that they performed while watching television were related to household tasks and non-show related communications. As much existing literature has shown [9], in these cases the television was more background noise rather than the focus of attention.

The quantitative data also helps to support this use case, with 415 total hours of television watched across households (an average of 5 hours a day). It is unlikely that all of this time was spent actively watching TV programs.

TV in the background while consuming unrelated content
Beyond the functional tasks of household chores or communication mentioned above, app use was frequently unrelated to the television show. In some cases, it even involved

seeking another entertainment purpose. Returning to the log data, Figure 8 highlights the wide variety of apps used during programs, including other sources, such as YouTube. For example, P5 searched for YouTube videos and watched them with her kids while watching a pseudo-science show: "*We watched a lot of YouTube videos like old songs while watching TV ... We were all here watching TV. I think I was watching my reruns and my Ancient Aliens while I was on the tablet looking for ... I like to go to YouTube to look at ... I'm into 80s music, so I search a lot 80s music, and then I was searching a lot of just R&B, old songs from when I was young. ... I like to share with my kids.*" In this case, a repeat episode was on television, so instead of paying much attention to it, the family browsed videos on a tablet.

P2 discussed web browsing during sports event: "*I know that I will browse a lot when I am watching basketball. I can hear and I don't necessarily have to watch, so I can be doing something else with my phone and hearing the score.*" For him, it was not necessary to watch every basket. Instead he kept the game on to hear the ambient noise of the game and would glance up to see the score or major plays.

P7 discussed not being engaged in the TV show and checking email and browsing Twitter. "*It's probably why I was checking emails. It's maybe one of those evenings where I wasn't particularly engaged in whatever we're watching.*" P6 discussed using commercial breaks to catch up on other activities on his phone: "*I think I totally just disconnect with commercials. I pay attention and I don't. I could be doing multiple things, but yeah, I guess maybe that is a time that I use a break to do other stuff. Especially if it's a program I really like and I don't want to be disturbed.*"

For many participants, device use became an everyday part of watching television. P6 spoke about how there are no tensions when family members use devices while together watching television: "*No, we're all on devices. We don't get offended about it, and my daughter has her own little device that she plays stuff on. We actually like technology.*" P3 talked about how natural it has become to use a device while watching a program: "*I probably do it all the time ... I don't keep track of it, because I guess it's a natural thing. When everyone is here I'm just on my phone and they're watching TV, or Sunday, the games, that's a good example ... My mom's family comes here every Sunday, and that day is meant for football, all day watching football.*"

However, P5 spoke about how sometimes there is a tension around watching TV together as a family: "*It's very hard to watch a movie with all of us here ... my husband always says that, 'Gosh, we can't even watch the movie because you're always on the phone,' ... I think it's just a habit of ours to put something on TV, I guess to see it for a little bit, but not really pay attention.*" However, she said that this did not stop her, or her children from continuing to use devices while the television was on.

Overall, participants used devices for many activities that were unrelated to the TV show they watched. In many cases, the show itself was just background noise or visual distraction while participants watched online videos, communicated with friends or family, or browsed social networks.

I look for things related to the current show or commercial
Device use often went hand in hand with watching sports. For example, looking up scores, information about related teams or details about fantasy football teams. P7 uses the CBS sports app to look up player stats while watching a basketball game *"I use this one app because I was watching a basketball game ... I'm watching the Razorbacks and they're telling stats but they don't have the stat that I want to see, so I can look on the CBS sports app and I can see all the players and what their stats are, in the middle of the game, regardless of what they're telling me."*

P4 discussed checking scores for his fantasy team while the Sunday game is on in his household with friends, which at times cause some tensions, *"I like to check scores a lot cause I have a fantasy team so I'll have my phone out just checking scores. More often than not, others in the room might also be on a fantasy team. It kind of alienates a few other people when they'll bring out their phone and check out the real time stats ... You get looks from others who don't play and they're like, 'Hey, you're in a social situation, put that thing away.'"*

P3 talked about using her phone to look for things related to sports only if she misses something, e.g., *"Unless I miss something and I come later in the day, or I'm out all day and I come back and I want to know the score, then I would do that, but when I'm watching the game I don't search about the game on my phone, it's about other stuff."*

Aside from sports there were other examples of searching for things related to what was being watched on TV. As shown from the log data in Figure 8, browsers (and search in browsers) were often used during commercials. P6 talked about a commercial leading to her purchasing a toy car for her daughter, *"If we're watching a show and I see something I like, and to figure out the brand, we may go on and try to find it. ... we watch the show, and the commercials showed that car, and we bought that for my daughter."*

Television content, especially sports and commercials, led to a small amount of related application use. Here, the app use complemented the programs, in line with previous "complementary use" reports, yet at a much reduced level compared to previous findings (e.g., [8]).

Limitations
While the TV and app use dataset we collected during the study is very comprehensive, it is not perfect. The device that kept track of television viewing ran sound printing only over a period of 15 seconds each minute, which may have caused misclassifications or alignment issues with the beginning of commercial breaks, even when we broke down analysis by minute. Mislabelings in the soundprint data may

have also occurred also because some shows feature flashbacks of previous episodes, previews of future episodes, or because of commercials that advertise other shows. To help combat this, we leveraged the longest duration matches (15 seconds) that IntoNow supports to limit misclassifications. Finally, the IntoNow catalog does not comprise TV shows that have not aired on US satellite television, such as Netflix-only shows (e.g., *House of Cards*) or an Argentinean news program that one participant watched and would thus not be included in our numbers.

Another limitation is BLE-based tracking of *accurate* indoor locations. Older hardware in commodity devices and low battery levels may have impacted measurement accuracies. Such misclassifications could include participants that were located in a different story of their building but directly above the TV. However, tests of our setup in each of the authors' homes showed a tracking accuracy of 87%.

Finally, a sample of seven households, while still collecting hundreds of hours of television viewing and many thousands of application launches is not representative of the American population as a whole. We conducted this study in part to test our novel method of exploring device use, and to uncover initial trends that can be validated by larger-scale studies in the future, which is the natural next step.

Discussion and Implications
While previous work in the area of multi-device use in the home has sourced data primarily from surveys, in this work we provide a quantitative investigation of simultaneous TV consumption and app use on phone and tablet devices in addition to a qualitative analysis. Logging app use on such devices on a minute-by-minute basis during the study allowed us to precisely analyze device interactions and correlate them with events in each show, such as commercial breaks or identify trends over the course of a TV show. This analysis allowed us to produce a number of key findings, which we will now discuss in more detail.

During a large amount of TV consumption, the focus of the participant was frequently on their mobile devices. While this often occurred when participants desired to be in the same room as their other family members, but were not interested in the particular show that they were watching, we also observed a large amount of television watching in the background. This is particularly true of shows that require only little attention during the longest part of a show, such as sport events, comedy, reality, or romance shows. Here, TV served the function of background entertainment, sometimes used only for background sound exposure, while participants spent a large amount of time in apps on their mobile devices. But in the case of reality shows and crime dramas, the reduction in app use at the "reveal" moment at the end of the show illustrates viewers often re-engaged in the program at the key moment.

In contrast, TV programs that inform and educate their audience received much larger amounts of focus from participants, who engaged with applications only in a very small fraction of the time during shows in genres such as news, science, and history documentaries. Our data shows that during these shows, the program often serves a larger role of an active focus. Another potential explanation is that social conventions may prevent people from chatting with others during active shows that may be interesting to other members of the family, whereas it is generally okay to talk during sports or reality programming.

Our minute-by-minute analysis also uncovered interesting insights into participants' behavior during commercials, during which the average percent of time that participants interacted with devices changed only by a very small amount. Interestingly, during commercials participants spent more time in applications that seemingly take longer to interact with, but certainly require more focus, such as phone and email, compared to messaging and social networking during shows. The numbers, however, indicate that participants spent an even shorter average amount of time per app interacting during commercials.

Our study also opens up further questions for follow-up studies. In particular, we believe that our method can be used to answer a wide variety of other research questions. By analyzing a larger number of households across different regions and countries, statistically meaningful results can be found comparing cultures and genres of television programs. This information can be used by broadcasters, advertisers, and app creators in order to develop more engaging experiences for viewers.

CONCLUSIONS

We have described a study that investigates television consumption and simultaneous app and web use on phone and tablet devices. In this study, we collected data from the televisions of seven households and 14 phone and tablet devices with over 415 hours of consumed TV shows, 1,364 hours of phone and tablet use, 1,447 launched apps with room-level location, in addition to detailed qualitative interviews and voicemail diaries. We have shown how mobile devices are used at a minute-by-minute level during TV programming, the role of televisions (and importantly the act of being in the television room) in the context of the broader family at home, and how participants divide their attention in different television genres.

ACKNOWLEDGMENTS

We thank the IntoNow team at Yahoo for support with the soundprinting. We also thank our participants for their time and for allowing us into their homes.

REFERENCES
1. Basapur, S., Harboe, G., Mandalia, H., Novak, A., Vuong, V. and Metcalf, C. Field trial of a dual device user experience for iTV. *Proc. EuroITV '11*.

2. Böhmer, M., Hecht, B., Schöning, J., Krüger, A., and Bauer, G. Falling asleep with Angry Birds, Facebook and Kindle: a large scale study on mobile application usage. *Proc. MobileHCI '11*.

3. Cesar, P. and Geerts, D. Past, present, and future of social TV: a categorization. *Proc. CCNC '11*.

4. Cesar, P., Bulterman, D. C. and Jansen, A. J. Usages of the secondary screen in an interactive television environment: Control, enrich, share, and transfer television content. *Changing Television Environments*, Springer.

5. Dredge, S. Social TV and second-screen viewing: the stats in 2012. *The Guardian*, Oct. 29, 2012.

6. Fernandez, T.M., Rodas, J., Escudero, C.J. and Iglesia, D.I. Bluetooth Sensor Network Positioning System with Dynamic Calibration. *Proc. ISWCS'07*.

7. Ferreira, D., Gonçalves, J., Kostakos, V., Barkhuus, L., and Dey, A. Contextual Experience Sampling of Mobile Application Micro-Usage. *Proc. MobileHCI '14*.

8. Google. The New Multi-screen World: Understanding Cross-platform Consumer Behavior, Aug. 2012.

9. Hess, J., Ley, B., Ogonowski, C., Wan, L. and Wulf, V. Jumping between devices and services: towards an integrated concept for social tv. *Proc. EuroITV '11*.

10. Lapierre, M. A., Piotrowski, J. T. and Linebarger, D. L. Background television in the homes of US children. *Pediatrics*, 130(5).

11. Nandakumar, A. and Murray, J. Companion apps for long arc TV series: supporting new viewers in complex storyworlds with tightly synchronized context-sensitive annotations. *Proc. TVX '14*.

12. Perez, S. Nielsen: 85 Percent Of Tablet And Smartphone Owners Use Devices As "Second Screen" Monthly, 40 Percent Do So Daily. *TechCrunch*, Dec. 5, 2012.

13. PEW Research Center. One-in-Ten 'Dual-Screened' the Presidential Debate. *Pew Internet*, Oct. 11, 2012.

14. Pu, C.-C., Pu, C.-H. Lee, H.-J. Indoor Location Tracking Using Received Signal Strength Indicator, Emerging Communications for Wireless Sensor Networks. *Emerging Comm. for Wireless Sensor Networks*, 2011.

15. Schirra, S., Sun, H., Bentley, F. Together alone: motivations for live-tweeting a television series. *Proc. CHI '14*.

16. Shamma, D., Kennedy, L., and Churchill, E. Tweet the debates: understanding community annotation of uncollected sources. *Proc. WSM '09*.

17. Smith, A. The Rise of the "Connected Viewer". *Pew Internet*, July 17, 2012.

18. Specification of the Bluetooth System, Version 2.0 + EDR, Bluetooth SIG, 2004.

19. Stross, R. The Second Screen, Trying to Complement the First. *New York Times*, Mar. 3, 2012.

20. Titlow, J.P. Who's Actually Using Second Screen TV Apps? *ReadWrite*, Apr. 19, 2012.

Dynamic Subtitles: the User Experience

Andy Brown
BBC R&D
MediaCity, Salford. UK
andy.brown01@bbc.co.uk

Rhia Jones
BBC R&D
MediaCity, Salford. UK
rhia.jones@bbc.co.uk

Mike Crabb
School of Computing
University of Dundee, UK
michaelcrabb@acm.org

ABSTRACT

Subtitles (closed captions) on television are typically placed at the bottom-centre of the screen. However, placing subtitles in varying positions, according to the underlying video content ('dynamic subtitles'), has the potential to make the overall viewing experience less disjointed and more immersive. This paper describes the testing of such subtitles with hearing-impaired users, and a new analysis of previously collected eye-tracking data. The qualitative data demonstrates that dynamic subtitles can lead to an improved User Experience, although not for all types of subtitle user. The eye-tracking data was analysed to compare the gaze patterns of subtitle users with a baseline of those for people viewing without subtitles. It was found that gaze patterns of people watching dynamic subtitles were closer to the baseline than those of people watching with traditional subtitles. Finally, some of the factors that need to be considered when authoring dynamic subtitles are discussed.

Author Keywords

TV; Subtitles; User Experience; Accessibility; HCI; Eye-tracking; Attention Approximation

ACM Classification Keywords

H.5.1 Information interfaces and presentation (e.g., HCI): Multimedia Information Systems; K.4.2 Social Issues: Assistive technologies for persons with disabilities; H.5.2 Information interfaces and presentation (e.g., HCI): User Interfaces

INTRODUCTION

Traditionally, subtitles are positioned so they are centred at the bottom of the television screen. Guidelines for subtitles (e.g., [1]) have long recommended that 'viewers generally prefer the conventional bottom of the screen position', while noting that different placement (e.g., top-screen) might be necessary to avoid obscuring important information, and that 'it is most important to avoid obscuring any part of a speaker's mouth'. These guidelines also recommend 'horizontal displacement of

subtitles in the direction of the appropriate speaker', although this seems not to be widely implemented. In recent years, however, there has been an increase in research experimenting with non-traditional placement of subtitles [6, 17, 7, 15, 16, 8]. There are multiple drivers for this, including creativity [6], but the most common is a desire to help viewers associate subtitles with the correct speaker (e.g., [17, 8]). Jenesema [10] noted that the addition of subtitles 'results in a major change in eye-movement patterns', and eye-tracking studies have estimated the amount of time viewers spend fixating on subtitles as between 10–31.8% [4] and 84% [9]. An argument can be made for authoring subtitles in a way that minimises this disruption, so more time can be spent watching the action. From a User Experience (UX) standpoint there is a desire to deliver subtitle content in a more immersive, engaging, emotive [13], aesthetically pleasing and 'contemporary' [6] way.

One approach is to change the position of subtitles on the screen, placing each subtitle block so that it takes into account the underlying images [7, 8, 3]. These are known as 'dynamic captioning' [7] or 'dynamically positioned subtitles' [3]; in this paper we use the briefer term 'dynamic subtitles'. Hong *et al.* [7] presented a system that automatically recognised the speaker and used visual analysis of the scene to identify a placement for a subtitle; Hu *et al.* [8] extended this with more sophisticated algorithms. Both performed user studies to capture people's views on the placement, although these were not rich, collecting ratings on a scale of 1–10: Hong *et al.* asked participants to rate 'naturalness' and 'enjoyment', while Hu *et al.* asked their participants to rate 'eyestrain level' and 'overall satisfaction'. Both reported that their systems returned better scores than traditional subtitles, although it should be noted that participants in [8] were not habitual subtitle users, a factor which has been found to influence peripheral vision skills [2] and how attention is allocated [5]. Brooks and Armstrong's initial work [3] found that people spent less time reading dynamic subtitles, and more time looking at the drama, but did not explore the UX.

We wish to understand the user experience of dynamic subtitles in more detail, and hypothesise that they could provide an improved experience, making it easier to follow both the subtitles and the video content. This work seeks to explore that hypothesis, by extending the initial study of Brooks and Armstrong [3] in three ways:

- Additional eye-tracking data is collected, and the combined data analysed to discover how much gaze patterns differed between subtitled and non-subtitled content.

- Habitual subtitle users were asked to view an example of content with dynamic subtitles, and qualitative data was captured about their attitudes towards it.

- The question of what factors determine whether a subtitle is well or poorly placed was investigated.

PREVIOUS EXPERIMENT

This research uses data from Brooks and Armstrong [3], which is combined with new data and analysed in a novel way. This section summarises their study.

4 clips were taken from 3 episodes of the BBC drama 'Sherlock'. The clips lasted between 1:50 and 2:00 minutes, and 5 versions were created from each: French audio, traditional subtitles; French audio, dynamic subtitles; English audio, traditional subtitles; English audio, dynamic subtitles, and; English audio, no subtitles (baseline case).

24 participants (native English speakers, who did not understand French; participants were not habitual subtitle users) watched the clips, in the same order, on a television in a 'living room' lab. The clips were first presented in one of the 4 subtitle/language combinations, counterbalanced so that 5-6 different participants watched each version. 21 of the participants then viewed one of the clips (chosen at random) in the baseline condition: clips A, B and C were viewed by 6 people, and clip D by 3 people. The gaze of each participant was recorded using a Tobii X-120 eye-tracker. An initial analysis of the data, in which an area of interest was defined for each subtitle (420 across 4 clips, under 2 conditions), indicated that people spent less time reading subtitles, and more time looking at the drama when using dynamic subtitles than traditional subtitles.

METHOD

The second experiment was designed to collect additional baseline data to combine with that collected in experiment 1, and to capture qualitative data on the User Experience of dynamic subtitles from people who habitually used subtitles as an access service.

Participants

26 participants were recruited for inclusion in this study. Recruitment was performed by an external agency, and participants were recruited who: regularly use the internet to consume news and current affairs information; use subtitles at home to watch TV with the sound on, and; use subtitles on a daily basis. Participants were aged between 22–67 ($\bar{x} = 47.2, \sigma = 13.6$). A mix of gender (7 male, 19 female) and socio-cultural/economic backgrounds was used. In addition, 8 people were recruited (convenience sample; 5 male, 3 female, aged between 21 and 55) to watch the clip without subtitles. As in experiment 1, these people did not normally use subtitles.

Figure 1: The text used to present the subtitles.

Stimulus

Participants were shown a 1 minute 50 second clip from the TV drama "Sherlock" (Series 1, Episode 1). This segment included 3 main characters, plus a fourth who appeared briefly, and contained 34 subtitle blocks. Two characters, Mike, and John Watson, enter a chemistry laboratory, where Sherlock is performing an experiment. Mike introduces Watson to Sherlock; Sherlock deduces that Watson has just left the army and is, like himself, looking for a flatmate.

Dynamic subtitles were authored for the original experiment: each subtitle was assigned a position based on a number of factors: the character speaking the line; the background, and; the position of the previous and subsequent subtitles. All subtitles were displayed as white text (Helvetica Neue, 32 pixels high) with a slim black outline (Figure 1). In order to allow fair comparison, timing remained identical to that authored for the original (traditional) subtitles.

In order to explore the important factors for subtitle placement, alternative positions were authored for 4 of the dynamic subtitles (numbers 3, 19, 24 and 33 from the sequence of 34 in this clip). Re-authoring of these led to 2 further subtitles being re-positioned (numbers 23 and 25) so that the reader's gaze did not have to jump too far between consecutive subtitles. The original and revised positions of the four subtitles can be seen in Figure 2.

A Framework for Qualitative Data Capture

User experience is a highly subjective field, focusing on the potential benefits that a user may derive from a product [11]. To be of use to the scientific community, however, the measurement of UX needs to be meaningful and reliable [12]. A standard way of ensuring reliability is to develop a framework that identifies the important components of the UX so that each can be measured. A review of the literature failed to identify such a framework for subtitles, so a new framework is proposed here[1].

The structure of the framework was inspired by [14], while the components were developed from an analysis of the existing literature on the UX of subtitles. These components are described below.

Attention is awareness of what is going on in relation to the subtitled video content. Users with high levels

---

[1]The primary purpose of this framework is to provide an overall measure of the user experience when viewing different methods of subtitle display. This framework does not deal with reading rates or comprehension levels.

of attention would be focused heavily on the video content, while users with low levels would not.

Aesthetics is a measure of the visual appeal of the subtitled content. High levels indicate users believe that the content is visually pleasing, while low levels indicate that the content is not visually appealing.

Involvement measures how engaged users are with the subtitled content. Whereas attention is about focus on the content, involvement is about the depth of engagement with the subtitled content. Users with high levels of involvement would be 'drawn into' the subtitled content and would find this to be a engaging and enjoyable experience. Users with low levels of involvement would feel less involved in the subtitled content.

Familiarity measures how much users feel the current subtitle display matches their expectations. High levels of familiarity indicate a coherence in the relationship between the subtitles and the video content. Low levels of familiarity will indicate a disconnect in what is perceived as routine subtitle practice

Perceived usefulness measures how useful the display of the subtitled content is. Users who perceive high levels of usefulness will see a high levels of value in the subtitle display; users with low levels of perceived usefulness will see low levels of value.

Perceived usability measures the challenge that is faced while engaging with the subtitled video content. Users that report high levels of perceived usability are likely to have found the subtitled content easy to understand, while users with low levels of perceived usability are likely to have found viewing the subtitled content more demanding.

Endurability is defined as a user's willingness to view subtitled content using a similar method of subtitle display in the future. Users with high levels of endurability are likely to wish to use this method again, while users with low levels would be less likely to want to use this method again in the future

Design and Procedure

The session was run in the BBC R&D usability lab in Dock House, Salford which is set up as a living room, and has an adjacent control and viewing room. Sessions were recorded and transcribed. Participants watched the clip on a 47 inch television. A Tobii X-120 eye-tracker was used to record the gaze of participants as they viewed the clip; this was placed on a coffee table 1.8m in front of the television. To facilitate the process of positioning the participants correctly relative to the eye-tracker, participants were seated on an adjustable office chair approximately 0.7m in front of the eye-tracker.

The experiment was started by informing participants that the purpose was to capture their opinions on some subtitles they would see in a short clip. They were seated

in front of the eye-tracker and allowed to adjust the television volume to a comfortable level. Participants adjusted the position of their chair to within the range of the eye-tracker. Once comfortable, the eye tracker was calibrated, then recording started and the clip shown. The videos were counterbalanced so that half of the participants saw the video with the re-authored subtitles in their original positions, half with the revised positions.

After viewing the clip, participants were asked for their first reactions. In order to explore what makes a well-positioned subtitle, they were then asked to give their thoughts on the alternative positions for each of the 4 re-authored subtitles. Participants were shown the pairs as still images (using the first frame for which the subtitle was present) on the television screen. They were asked to comment on what they liked and/or disliked about each, and to give a preference.

The final part of the experiment was a semi-structured interview, designed to explore how people felt about viewing content with dynamic subtitles. The questions were aligned to the framework, above, and are detailed in the results, below.

Supplementing baseline data

To supplement baseline data from [3], participants were introduced to the study and seated in front of the eye-tracker (in the same configuration as above). The eye tracker was calibrated, and participants were asked to watch the clip as they would normally watch television.

EYE-TRACKING DATA ANALYSIS

The hypothesis being tested is that dynamic subtitles allow gaze patterns that are closer to those of viewers watching without subtitles, but it is not known, a-priori, where those viewers will fixate. Consequently, while it is possible to define areas of interest for the subtitles, it is not for the underlying video content. In order to explore the data, therefore, the scene is evenly divided into chunks, both spatially — as a grid — and temporally — into time slices. Having applied this approximation, it is possible, for each slice of time, to identify which regions of the scene were viewed by participants in each condition. Crucially, the application of regular approximation allows direct quantitative comparison of gaze patterns. In this case it is possible to measure how much the gaze pattern of a subtitled scene differs from that of the same segment without subtitles. Making this calculation twice, for traditional and dynamic subtitles, shows which condition resulted in the smaller change of gaze pattern. A smaller change indicates that the gaze patterns were closer to those for the baseline, suggesting that people's experience of the video content is less disrupted by reading the subtitles.

In this analysis, the gaze pattern is considered in terms of dwell time. Thus, for each time slice we calculate, for each box in the grid, the *proportion* of total possible attention for that window. If there are n participants, then the total possible attention (A_{total}) is n times the length of the time slice. The attention received by an individual box (A_{box}) is the sum of the durations of all fixations for all participants that occurred in that box during the time slice. The proportion of attention for the box is therefore A_{box}/A_{total}, and the gaze pattern for a given slice comprises of an attention value for each box in the grid. The sum of these values across the grid will approach 1, but will be less due to time spent on saccades, or fixations of less than 100ms (which were discarded). It may be lowered further if any participants looked away, or the eye-tracker failed to record some data. A fixation that overlaps time slices will contribute its duration to each slice proportionately.

For these results, the 1920×1080 pixel scene was divided into an 8×5 grid (resulting in 40 240×216 boxes), and the 115 second clip into 1s slices. The grid size and slice length were determined by the size and duration of the subtitles (subtitles were visible for a mean time of 2.7s, and the mean length of a subtitle block was 550 pixels) — it was necessary to get enough detail to differentiate between areas of the screen and between subtitles, but have the grid/slice combination coarse enough to capture enough data to make meaningful comparisons.

For each temporal slice, a gaze intensity value was calculated for each box in the grid. The intensity of each box represented the proportion of attention received, as described above. To allow for experimental error in gaze position detection, the contribution from those fixations within 20 pixels (approximately 8% of the length of the box sides) of box edges was divided between boxes in ratios proportionate to the edge proximity.

A metric was calculated to reflect the size of the difference of the overall attention pattern for two segments. To do this, a grid was calculated, with each box containing the difference between the corresponding boxes under the two conditions. This grid was smoothed (Gaussian smoothing over the 8×5 grid, with a radius of 1, meant that a shift of attention between neighbouring boxes had a smaller effect on the metric than between distant boxes) and a root mean square value was calculated; these values were linearly scaled to lie between 0 and 5. The difference values calculated in this manner are based on aggregated data, i.e., the difference was comparing the gaze of all participants in one group with all participants in another. This results in a single difference value for each segment of the clip for each condition.

QUALITATIVE RESULTS
The qualitative data comprises three parts: the first impressions of participants; their overall views after having performed the positioning exercise, and; their responses to a set of questions aligned to the framework (above).

In summary, 5 participants did not like dynamic subtitles (P2, P9, P14, P17, P19), 8 were broadly positive (P0, P3, P11, P15, P20, P21, P22, P23), and 12 were very keen on the idea. Interestingly, the 3 participants who most disliked the dynamic subtitles were ones who did

not totally rely on subtitles: P2 was slightly deaf in one ear, and used subtitles when the young kids' 'toys are out'; P14 had no diagnosed hearing problem, but liked to use subtitles 'as a double check', and; P17 said 'I don't rely on them'.

First Impressions
Overall, the first impressions of people were mixed. Three participants were immediately negative: they felt that they had to 'follow them round' and found them distracting. For example, P14 stated:

> 'I hated them, really hated them, I found them really distracting. Every time one flicked up my eye would flick to it, instead of it just being at the bottom where I would just read it when needed. It made me feel tense waiting to see where they would appear.'

Two were mixed, liking aspects of dynamic subtitles, but not seeing sufficient benefit for them to want to change from the familiarity of traditional subtitles. Seven others were immediately positive. They identified two main benefits to dynamic subtitles: it was possible to spend more time looking at the video content rather than reading subtitles, and; identifying which person was speaking the dialogue in the subtitle was easier. For example:

> 'Loved it. It's there for you, it's next to that person saying it. So you don't need to have the different colours. With this you knew who was talking straight away and you felt more sucked into the television.' (P5)

P18 also found identifying the speaker easier, and noted that he was less likely to miss things in the video:

> 'Yeah, it was really good. ...it gives you a much clearer idea of who is speaking...it's more integrated. I can spend more time on the video content. I feel that with this you can see a lot more of the picture as well, not just the words at the bottom...

The remainder of the participants fell somewhere in between, not quite sure what to make of the subtitles immediately after viewing a 2 minute clip for the first time.

General Comments
After capturing the initial thoughts, participants were asked to comment on 4 pairs of alternative dynamic subtitle positions, then asked: *'What do you think are the advantages / disadvantages of having subtitles positioned in different places on the screen?'*

The two themes of being able to identify speaker more easily, and of missing less of the video were noted by more of the participants. There were also comments about how dynamic subtitles felt more integrated with the programme and 'became part of the story' (P0), and:

> 'They seem really well integrated and its easy to switch between the subtitles and the visuals without feeling like it was disjointed.' (P6)

'It's almost cinema like — you have that feel of being enveloped of it' (P8)

More participants commented on the aesthetics, such as P16, who said it was 'aesthetically pleasing', and P20: 'It seems like a very artistic way of doing it.'

Semi-structured Interview
The questions that formed the basis for the discussion, and the responses to them, are summarised below.

Attention
Were you able to follow both the subtitles and the video content comfortably? How does this compare to when subtitles are placed at the bottom of the screen? Does your attention to the video clip differ?

Responses to these questions were largely positive. 16 participants stated that they were able to follow both video and subtitle content, with many noting that the dynamic subtitles were an improvement on traditionally placed ones. For example, P10 stated:

'With traditional subs you have to split your attention, but with this because it's so near to peoples faces you can also get a lot of the physical body language of what people are saying'

Others were able to follow the content, but found it more difficult than traditional subtitles (e.g., P19 'would rather have them in a predictable place'; also P20). Two participants (P9, P17) were wholly negative: P17 didn't want to read the subtitles, and found them intrusive.

Aesthetics
Did you find the positioned subtitles appealing to look at? How do they compare to traditional subtitles? Did the positioned subtitles add or detract in any way from the aesthetics of the video?

Although 4 participants (P2, P9, P14, P17) thought dynamic subtitles detracted from the overall aesthetics (e.g., P14: 'Because of their position they detracted from the video'), 15 participants thought they were an improvement. For example, P16 stated:

'Compared to traditional subtitles this adds aesthetic value. I'm looking at the whole picture in the few seconds that gives me, but with [traditional subtitles] you have to go down and then back up. This shows you everything that you want to see and is pleasing on the eye. This gives me time to read what is going on and not having to move. I'm just looking straight across.'

P11, also noted how 'I liked them, they were appealing, it reminded me of a comic when you're reading the action and the words'. 4 people (P18, P20, P23, P24) thought that they would detract from the aesthetics of other viewers, as they would be harder to ignore.

Usability
Did you have any problems locating the subtitles? Were you able to follow the subtitles comfortably? Did you have any problems identifying the speaker? How did you cope with the subtitles changing positions on the screen? How do reading subtitles placed dynamically on the screen compare to reading the subtitles at the bottom of the screen?

Several people commented that it took a short period of adjustment before they were used to the subtitles ('like a new pair of glasses' - P11). 3 participants (P8, P9, P20) commented on problems locating the subtitles on one or two occasions, while P17 noted that they were 'too immediate' and difficult to miss. Speaker identification was generally not a problem, although 2 people said that colours could be used to help.

Usefulness
How useful do you find this as a method of displaying subtitles? Do you see any added value in this way of displaying subtitles? Can you think of any instances where having some, or all, of the subtitles displayed like this would be useful or add value? OR equally, any instances where you think they might be unsuitable?

Again, the consensus was that presenting subtitles dynamically was useful, although not necessarily appropriate for all types of programme. Most people thought that it would not be useful for news, which has a relatively static format, although P24 felt that having the words alongside a presenter, if there was space, might be useful. Dynamic subtitles were considered most suitable for drama, or for situations where you have many people talking (e.g., a panel — 'The words can be placed next to the person that owns the speech' — P11). For example, P8 commented that it was:

'Very useful, the added value is that there is less attention processes being spend on just reading... [Normally] I don't know whether the actor has done anything when I've been reading... this time I'm reading and also catching the movement in the same field.'

P0 said, 'The added value for this is that its more dynamic, it raises my attention to the whole piece, it seems like it's more integrated with the images', while P7 said, 'Would be a big plus to have subtitles this way'. Two participants noted the difference between usefulness and overall appeal — P4 said that dynamic subtitles were 'not useful, but preferable', while P2 said 'Yeah it could be useful... but I don't like it how it is there'.

Involvement
Do positioned subtitles have any impact on how engaged you feel with the subtitled text (and your enjoyment of reading the subtitles)? Do positioned subtitles have any impact on how engaged you feel with the overall video (and your enjoyment watching the video)?

The majority of the participants in the experiment felt that the dynamic subtitles meant that they were more engaged with the content, or enjoyed it more. P14 and P19 felt that they detracted from their enjoyment as they were 'more conscious of them' (P19) or 'I was trying to second-guess where the text would appear'. One of the key benefits of dynamic subtitles that participants identified as increasing their involvement was that they were 'more aware of what was going on' (P13) and able to identify small, but important, aspects of the video that would otherwise have been missed. This was specifically picked out by participants 16 and 18:

> 'I wouldn't have caught a lot of the small social cues if I were watching this with traditional subtitles.'

> 'Normally you are looking down at the bottom of the screen and you miss facial expressions, but with this nearer to the mouth it's easier to see everything.'

Familiarity
Does this method of displaying subtitles feel familiar (or strange)? How does this method of displaying subtitles compare to traditional subtitles?

For P14 ('strange and distracting') and P17 dynamic subtitles felt strange, while for some people they felt natural (P4 — 'feels quite natural', P8 — 'first impression was that this is intuitive', P10 — 'because I read comics it felt familiar', P18 — 'It felt happier; it was more natural'). For some it felt unfamiliar, but something that could be got used to, either quickly (e.g., P7: 'It felt a little bit strange, but only for a nanosecond – as quick as that'), or more slowly (e.g., P20 'It felt new, I feel like I would have to concentrate but I think that would disappear over continued use').

Endurability
Do you think you could you watch subtitled content like this for an extended period of time? Would you want or choose to view content with subtitles like this in the future?

The majority of participants who expressed an opinion (12) stated that they could watch dynamic subtitles for longer periods of time, and that they would choose to watch subtitles like this if they had the option. P7 commented that it was less tiring than traditional subtitles:

> 'Reading subtitles can be tiring, so I've got a limited span, I can watch a couple of films and that's about it. I think that this is a lot gentler on the eye.'

Others were unsure about viewing for longer periods, but would like to try. Only P14 and P17 said that they wouldn't want to watch these subtitles again.

POSITIONING SUBTITLES
The overall preferences for each of the four pairs of alternative subtitle positions (version A, in the original position, and B, in the revised position) are summarised in Figure 3. For two subtitles, the participants were split almost equally, while for the other two, they were more likely to prefer the revised subtitle. More interesting than the preferences, however, are the themes that emerged from the discussions about the various placements. These can be classified as follows.

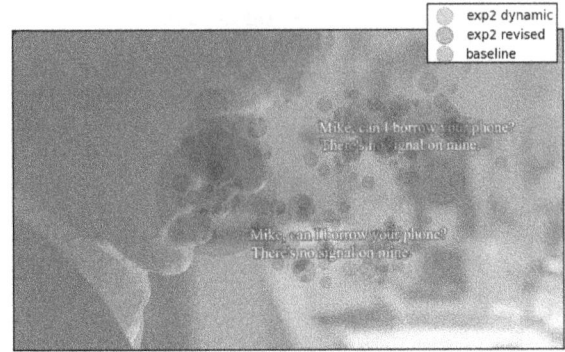

(a) Subtitle 3. Version A is the upper one.

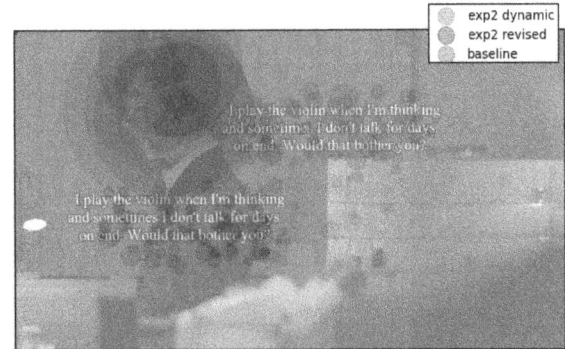

(b) Subtitle 19. Version A is the upper one.

(c) Subtitle 24. Version A is the upper one.

(d) Subtitle 33. Version A is the right one.

Figure 2: Versions A (original) and B (revised) of four subtitles. Overlaid are the fixations made during the lifetime of the subtitle, for people watching with the original subtitle, the revised subtitle, or no subtitle.

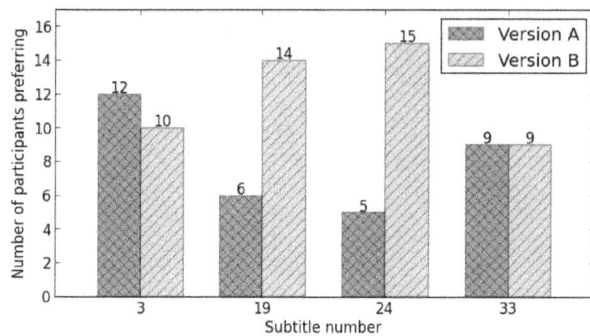

Figure 3: Numbers of participants expressing a preference for the version A (original) or B (revised) of the subtitles.

Speaker identification

One of the key factors in people's preferences was positioning the subtitle so that it could be easily associated with the character who was speaking. This was explicitly mentioned by 8 of the participants. For example P19 and P10 preferred the revised version of subtitle 24:

'I prefer [B] because you can clearly see that it's attached to Sherlock. It's where he is in the screen — it makes more sense with him being there.' (P19)

'Maybe [B] is better, because it's the speech that is linked with his characters so it makes it clearer that it's him that is speaking' (P10)

Five of the participants commented positively on how dynamic subtitles were comic-like or similar to a cartoon, with the text resembling a speech bubble. Although clearly related to speaker identification, the cartoon style is not necessary for it (e.g, the subtitle could be placed over the actor's body), and subtitles presented like speech bubbles seemed to have an intrinsic appeal.

Readability

Although most participants said that the subtitles were usable, the qualities of the background were an important consideration when selecting position. When this was mentioned, people either stated that they liked a position because it was particularly clear, or said that they found a position difficult. A plain, dark background was considered good, e.g., P4 said of subtitle 24B: 'it's easier to read as its against the dark background'. P10 also found subtitle 3A easy to read ('the background is blurred so the words stand out quite well'). In contrast, lighter or more varied backgrounds were more difficult. For subtitle 33A, P0 said, 'It's a bit noisy in the background, there's so much other stuff behind the text, and [B] is a lot easier'.

Obscuring the action

Five people felt that the action was, or could be, obscured, particularly if over the actor. Positive comments were made when subtitles were over the background of the scene, e.g,. 'it's in a place where it's just over a

blurred bit of background so you're not missing much' (P6 on subtitle 19B). Similarly, some people felt that having the subtitles placed over the actor diminished the experience, blocking their view. For example, comments on subtitle 19B included:

P9: 'I don't like how its over him...Its like the subtitles are competing with the actor in the scene.'

P15: I don't like it over his body, it feels like if he starts moving around you don't want to be looking through the writing. You want them to be slightly separate.

This was not an over-riding preference, as these same participants sometimes preferred later subtitles that were placed over the actor (e.g., P15 preferred version B of subtitle 24 'That actually looks quite good down there, which contradicts from my last choice', and P9 preferred 24B and 33B).

On the other hand, some participants clearly preferred subtitles to be placed over the actor, so that the character and subtitles were co-located. P18 stated about subtitle 19B, 'My gaze is naturally on him so it makes sense for them to be together', and P19 said (of the same subtitle), 'I think that this one is possibly better, in that your attention is focused on the left hand side of the screen'. For the last subtitle, P24 wanted to see the subtitle over Sherlock, because that placed the subtitle close to the important action:

'The important thing is to see Sherlock and the action — the director has chosen that shot for a reason. It's the same viewing experience then, it doesn't matter if you look at the subtitles or not, you're still looking at what the director intended.'

General positioning

In more general terms, participants P3 and P7 had a preference for subtitles on the right of the screen. Participant 14, who did not like dynamic subtitles, wanted them placed lower on the screen, where they were less obstructive. P17 felt 'for some reason, the higher it is the more it throws itself at you, so I prefer the more subtle one'. Conversely, P7, P19 and P24 all expressed a preference for subtitles to be placed higher. P10 wasn't keen on the central positioning of 19B, explaining, 'I did photography at college, so I'm thinking about the rule of thirds when I'm going through it'.

There was a slight aversion to subtitles being placed too close to characters, with 7 people commenting on subtitle 19A being too close to Sherlock 'like it's going to hit him in the neck' (P11). P6 and P15 wanted 3B to be placed slightly to the right or lower.

Eye-tracking data

The eye-tracking data was inconclusive when comparing the revised subtitles with the original ones. A grid representing the gaze pattern for each condition over the lifetime of each subtitle was generated, and the difference between each subtitle and the baseline was calculated.

subtitle	original	revised
3	2.1	2.0
19	1.8	2.0
24	2.0	1.4
33	1.5	1.4

Table 1: Difference metric values between the two subtitles and the baseline.

EYE-TRACKING RESULTS

Before full analysis of the data, the difference metric was tested. This was done by comparing the revised and original subtitles; as expected, difference values were low (median difference of 0.9) except when the subtitle positions differed (peaks of 2-3). Having tested the metric, the additional baseline data was combined with the baseline data from Brooks and Armstrong's original work [3], giving usable gaze data for 5 participants watching with each of the traditional and dynamic subtitles (French audio), and 11 participants watching without subtitles. The difference metric was calculated to compare each subtitle condition with the baseline.

Figure 4 plots the differences between each subtitle condition and the baseline across the clip, with the filled line indicating which is closer (below the x-axis indicates that the gaze pattern of dynamic subtitles was less different from the baseline). Looking across all slices, the median difference values are 1.9 for the dynamic subtitles (95% confidence intervals ±0.14) and 2.3 for the traditional subtitles (±0.18). This indicates that, on an average slice, the viewers of dynamic subtitles have gaze patterns that more closely resemble those of un-subtitled content than viewers of traditional subtitles.

Figure 5 summarises the results, showing the difference values for the four conditions: experiment 1 traditional and dynamic subtitles, and experiment 2 original and revised subtitles. This plot shows the median value, and 95% confidence intervals, for the slices in the clip, divided into those slices where subtitles were present (of which there were 87), and those where they were not (28). In this graph, it can be seen that the difference values for segments without subtitles were all relatively low — this is what would be expected, as the stimulus was essentially the same for all participants in these segments (although there will be some effect from people moving their gaze between the subtitle and the video). In those segments containing subtitles, however, the gaze patterns were all more different than the baseline. In particular, it is notable that traditional subtitles resulted in the largest difference, while dynamic subtitles had smaller differences (the median difference values for segments with subtitles in experiment 1 are 2.78 for traditional subtitles and 1.96 for dynamic subtitles).

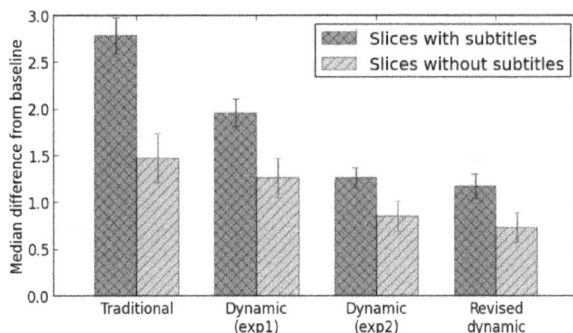

Figure 5: Median difference values for the 1s slices for the different conditions. These are split into values for slices in which subtitles were visible, and those in which there were none.

The results from the second experiment show smaller differences, with no significant difference between the revised and original subtitles. Interestingly, the gaze patterns of viewers watching dynamic subtitles were less different from the baseline in the second experiment than the first. There are two factors that might account for this. First, the viewers in the second experiment were habitual subtitle users; second, participants in the second experiment had the ability (in some cases) to augment their use of subtitles with lip reading and the English audio. These factors may also explain the differences between experiments 1 and 2 for those slices without subtitles — the experienced subtitle users and lip-readers of experiment may revert their gaze to the baseline more quickly than the participants of experiment 1.

CONCLUSIONS

The majority of people who watched dynamic subtitles enjoyed the experience, and wanted to try them further. A number of participants were very keen, and would have liked to convert to dynamic subtitles immediately.

"This is going to spoil subtitles for me now" (P16)

The main reason was that it meant that the viewers were more immersed in the action, and missed less of the video content. Reading the subtitles was a less disjointed experience, and people were more able to follow the action, and pick up non-verbal cues from the actors. The new analysis of the eye-tracking data from the previous experiment supports this (albeit for people who do not normally use subtitles), finding that people who viewed the clip with dynamic subtitles had gaze patterns that were more similar to people who viewed without subtitles than those who viewed with traditional subtitles.

'I wouldn't have caught a lot of the small social cues if I were watching this with traditional subtitles' (P16)

The other major benefit was that dynamic subtitles enabled a more explicit link between speaker and text than using colours on traditional subtitles. Most participants

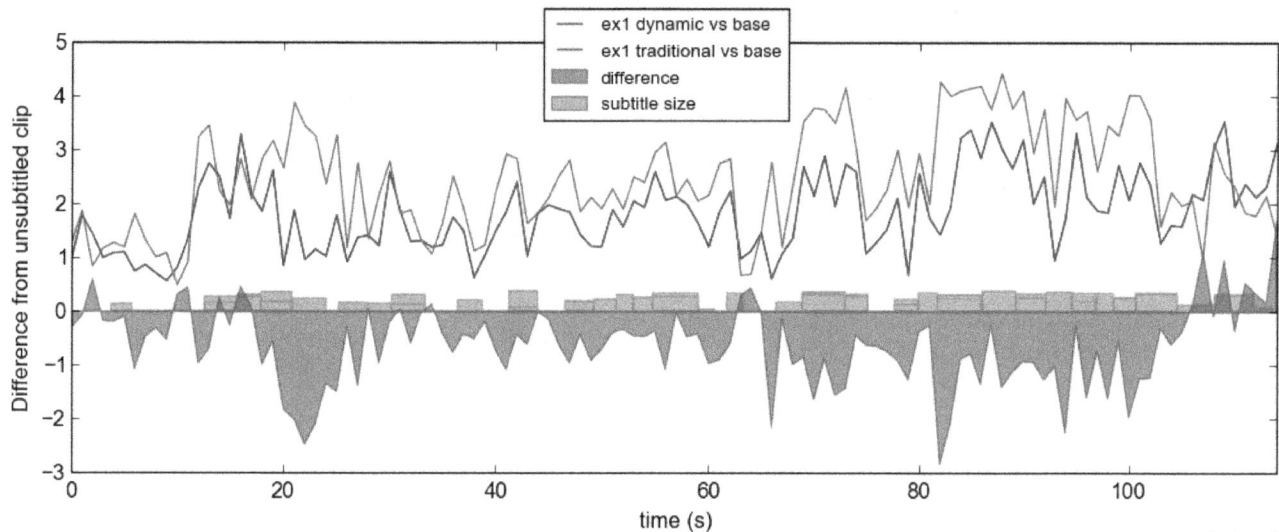

Figure 4: A comparison of how much gaze patterns in the traditional subtitle and dynamic subtitle conditions differed from the baseline. The differences between traditional subtitles and the baseline are shown in green; those between dynamic subtitles and the baseline are in blue. The filled line indicates which was closer: below the x-axis shows that the gaze pattern for dynamic subtitles was closer to the baseline than for traditional subtitles. Red bars indicate when subtitles were visible, with height correlating to the number of characters.

were able to connect subtitles to actor even with all text presented in white, although the additional use of colour should be investigated. One of the major use-cases identified by participants was in situations where multiple people were talking, such as panel shows.

'I think this would have a huge benefit for a lot of people to make more sense of conversations' (P10)

A small number of the participants in this experiment did not like this style of subtitle presentation — 2 were ambivalent and would prefer to use the subtitles they were used to, while 3 really disliked dynamic positioning. Interestingly, these participants were ones who did not totally rely on subtitles. In contrast, those who were most enthusiastic about the subtitles tended to be those who relied more on the subtitles as an access service.

Two of those people who liked dynamic subtitles themselves expressed concern that co-watchers (who did not need subtitles) would find them more disruptive. This suggests that the ideal solution would be to give viewers the option of whether to have subtitles dynamically placed, or placed in the traditional position at the bottom of the screen. Most people also thought that using dynamic subtitles would not be appropriate for all content; the news was identified by many as a genre for which traditional subtitles were more suitable, due to its relatively static nature.

This experiment has also identified some of the factors that need to be taken into consideration when authoring dynamic subtitles. Identifying the speaker is one of the key benefits, so subtitle position needs to reflect this. Positioning the text as a cartoon speech-bubble would

be placed is one option; another is to place the text over the speaker's body. There were divided opinions about this, however, with some people feeling that the subtitle became a barrier in this situation. It should be noted, however, that this tended to be an opinion found among those people who were against the idea in general. In either case, the text should not obscure important action, and should not be placed too close to the speaker, particularly to the face. There is perhaps also an argument for placing the subtitles more towards the right of the screen (it could be hypothesised that this is because, for subtitles on the right, the viewer starts reading in the centre of the screen, which is likely to be closer to their current gaze). Readability is clearly important, so the effect of the background, particularly if light or varied, needs to be considered. It may be worth exploring the use of font effects to improve readability in such situations.

While the participants in this study were positive about the use of dynamic subtitles for Sherlock, and expressed a wish to use them on other content, the conclusions should not be extrapolated too far. The scene contained a maximum of 3 characters on screen at once, and shot-changes were not as frequent as they might be, e.g., in action movies. These factors may well influence the UX of dynamic subtitles, and should be explored further.

In summary, the majority of participants reported that they felt that dynamic subtitles would provide an improvement over traditional subtitles on all aspects of the framework. Some participants (notably those people who were not reliant on the subtitles to follow the dialogue) did not like their first experience of dynamic subtitles, finding them more disruptive than traditionally placed subtitles. It would therefore be desirable for viewers to have the option to revert to traditional subtitles if they, or their viewing companions preferred. For most people, however, it enabled a more immersive experience. They allowed people to relax and enjoy the programme, to follow the dialogue while also picking up more non-verbal cues from the speaker. Speaker identification was improved compared to traditional subtitles, although subtitle location may need supplementing with colours in some situations.

'With traditional subtitles you feel too focused and cant veg out on television, with this it makes it a lot easier to relax and watch television.' (P10)

ACKNOWLEDGEMENTS

The authors would like to thank those who participated in this experiment. In addition, Mike Crabb is support by RCUK Digital Economy Research Hub EP/G066019/1 SIDE: Social Inclusion through the Digital Economy.

ADDITIONAL AUTHORS

James Sandford (BBC R&D, email: james.sandford@bbc.co.uk), Matthew Brooks (BBC R&D, email: matthew.brooks@bbc.co.uk), Mike Armstrong (BBC R&D, email: mike.armstrong@bbc.co.uk) and Caroline Jay (School of Computer Science, University of Manchester, UK, email: caroline.jay@manchester.ac.uk),

REFERENCES

1. Baker, R. G., Lambourne, A. D., Rowston, G., Authority, I. B., Association, I. T. C., et al. *Handbook for Television Subtitlers*. Independent Broadcasting Authority, 1982, 13.

2. Bosworth, R. G., and Dobkins, K. R. The effects of spatial attention on motion processing in deaf signers, hearing signers, and hearing nonsigners. *Brain and Cognition 49*, 1 (2002), 152 – 169.

3. Brooks, M., and Armstrong, M. Enhancing subtitles. In *TVX2014* (2014).

4. Chapdelaine, C., Gouaillier, V., Beaulieu, M., and Gagnon, L. Improving video captioning for deaf and hearing-impaired people based on eye movement and attention overload. *Proc. SPIE 6492* (2007), 64921K–64921K–11.

5. D'Ydewalle, G.and Gielen, I. Attention allocation with overlapping sound, image, and text. In *Eye Movements and Visual Cognition*, K. Rayner, Ed., Springer Series in Neuropsychology. Springer New York, 1992, 415–427.

6. Foerster, A. Towards a creative approach in subtitling: a case study. In *New Insights into Audiovisual Translation and Media Accessibility*, J. Cintas, A. Matamala, and J. Neves, Eds. Rodopi, New York, NY, 2010, 81–98.

7. Hong, R., Wang, M., Yuan, X.-T., Xu, M., Jiang, J., Yan, S., and Chua, T.-S. Video accessibility enhancement for hearing-impaired users. *ACM Trans. Multimedia Comput. Commun. Appl. 7S*, 1 (Nov. 2011), 24:1–24:19.

8. Hu, Y., Kautz, J., Yu, Y., and Wang, W. Speaker-following video subtitles. *ACM Trans. Multimedia Comput. Commun. Appl. 11*, 2 (Jan. 2015), 32:1–32:17.

9. Jensema, C. J., Danturthi, R. S., and Burch, R. Time spent viewing captions on television programs. *American annals of the deaf 145*, 5 (2000), 464–468.

10. Jensema, C. J., El Sharkawy, S., Danturthi, R. S., Burch, R., and Hsu, D. Eye movement patterns of captioned television viewers. *American Annals of the Deaf 145*, 3 (2000), 275–285.

11. Law, E. L.-C., Roto, V., Hassenzahl, M., Vermeeren, A. P., and Kort, J. Understanding, scoping and defining user experience: A survey approach. In *Proceedings of the SIGCHI Conference on Human Factors in Computing Systems*, CHI '09, ACM (New York, NY, USA, 2009), 719–728.

12. Law, E. L.-C., and van Schaik, P. Modelling user experience–an agenda for research and practice. *Interacting with computers 22*, 5 (2010), 313–322.

13. Lee, D., Fels, D., and Udo, J. Emotive captioning. *Comput. Entertain. 5*, 2 (Apr. 2007).

14. O'Brien, H. L., and Toms, E. G. The development and evaluation of a survey to measure user engagement. *Journal of the American Society for Information Science and Technology 61*, 1 (2010), 50–69.

15. Rashid, R., Aitken, J., and Fels, D. Expressing emotions using animated text captions. In *Computers Helping People with Special Needs*, K. Miesenberger, J. Klaus, W. Zagler, and A. Karshmer, Eds., vol. 4061 of *Lecture Notes in Computer Science*. Springer Berlin Heidelberg, 2006, 24–31.

16. Secară, A. R U ready 4 new subtitles? Investigating the potential of social translation practices and creative spellings. *Linguistica Antverpiensia, New Series Themes in Translation Studies 0*, 10 (2013).

17. Vy, Q., and Fels, D. Using placement and name for speaker identification in captioning. In *Computers Helping People with Special Needs*, K. Miesenberger, J. Klaus, W. Zagler, and A. Karshmer, Eds., vol. 6179 of *Lecture Notes in Computer Science*. Springer Berlin Heidelberg, 2010, 247–254.

EnvDASH - An Environment-Aware Dynamic Adaptive Streaming over HTTP System

Stefan Wilk, Sophie Schönherr, Denny Stohr,
Wolfgang Effelsberg
Technische Universität Darmstadt, Germany
{stefan.wilk, sophie.schoenherr, denny.stohr,
wolfgang.effelsberg}@cs.tu-darmstadt.de

ABSTRACT

The recent advances in adaptive video streaming technologies including Dynamic Adaptive Streaming over HTTP (DASH) are capable to adjust video streams to rapidly changing network conditions. Our system, EnvDASH, differs from those standard implementations as it extends DASH with mechanisms that allow sensing the environmental conditions of a device. EnvDASH leverages that users in mobile situations are often distracted from watching a video or that viewing conditions are severely degraded by adapting the video to reduce the generated network traffic. The system senses if the user is interested in watching a video, if the displaying device is held stable and if the ambient noise level allows listening to an audio track of a video. This is especially helpful as mobile devices usually use capped data volume contracts for the network access.

Author Keywords

DASH; Context; Environmental Conditions; Mobile

ACM Classification Keywords

H.5.1 Multimedia Information Systems: Evaluation/ methodology

INTRODUCTION

Dynamic Adaptive Streaming over HTTP (DASH) [13] is a new digital video streaming standard which allows fine-grained video quality adaptation. Existing clients are able to adapt solely based on the current network conditions. But, especially for mobile video streaming the environmental conditions as well as user's interests may vary, too. An example for degraded viewing conditions are shaking smartphones as users are not able to perceive a video stream at full quality. Luckily today's smartphones contain sensors which can be leveraged to sense the device's environment. The proposed work illustrates the combination of adaptive video using DASH and the sensing of a playback device's environment. We leverage DASH as it is a standardized, adaptive

streaming protocol which gains significant support by both industry as well as academia. In contrast to previous approaches, it allows adaptations to be executed by the clients and requires solely a stateless HTTP web server to host different video representations as independent files. To allow adaptation while streaming the video representations are equally segmented. DASH allows to switch the video quality and thus the video representation at the end of a video segment.

Our proposed system, EnvDASH, aims at reducing the network load in situations in which non-optimal viewing conditions exist or the user is distracted from watching a video. Three different forms of influences are investigated: 1) the user's interest in watching a video stream, 2) the instability of the device (shakiness) and 3) the ambient noise level. Additionally, a network adaptation scheme is chosen to tailor the streaming session to available network resources. Our assumption is that in mobile scenarios a context-aware adaptation is beneficial and can lead to significant traffic savings.

Our contributions are twofold:

- The work describes the first DASH-based environmental adaptation scheme respecting the user's interest, ambient noise level and device stability.

- An evaluation is conducted with real world measurements as well as users' feedback.

RELATED WORK

Different approaches exist which try to optimize the adaptation behavior of mobile DASH clients depending on the available network resources, as e.g. proposed by Wang et al. [16]. In contrast to the majority of this previous work, the proposed EnvDASH system leverages sensors in modern mobile devices to adapt video streaming sessions. A related approach is pursued by the MASERATI system [6], which analyzes the location and speed of a device as well as the surrounding humidity level. MASERATI shows that all three attributes have an influence on the performance of network connections and plans video segment requests accordingly. Hao's work [8] uses the GPS in mobile devices to probe bandwidth at different locations, but it is rather limited in terms of novelty compared to MASERATI. Both approaches allow pull-based video streaming clients to plan future video requests depending on the sensed location. Similar approaches for analyzing the geo-location while video streaming and combining it with

TVX 2015, June 3–5, 2015, Brussels, Belgium.
Copyright © 2015 ACM 978-1-4503-3526-3/15/06 ...$15.00.
DOI: http://dx.doi.org/10.1145/2745197.2745205

the planning of video segment requests have been proposed by Wang et al. [17].

Despite sensing the location of a device some approaches exist which leverage other sensor readings to adapt mobile video. Those approaches have in common that they solely focus on one modality, e.g. the acceleration of the device during the playback of a video. In the work of Qi et al. [12] the accelerometer is used in order to scale down the framerate of a video when it is being recorded. The assumption behind this is, that with an increase in motion while recording, the video is going to be shaky and hard to retrieve for a watcher. Decreasing the framerate will lead to larger jumps between frames. But, as the video quality is already impaired due to the shaking, it will not have a major impact on the viewing experience. Hanning et al. [7] try to stabilize a video recorded by a smartphone using rolling shutter cameras by applying a 3D rotational distortion model. By leveraging accelerometer readings they can precisely determine occurring errors and adjust the video. In contrast to their work, Bao's system [2] leverages the camera to sense user reactions to a played back video. It uses the front-facing camera of a mobile device to sense the user's facial expressions. This approach allows to create a summary of the interesting segments of a video.

Our work differs from the related work as we want to monitor and analyze the viewing conditions during video streaming sessions and use the sensed environmental information to adapt a video stream. Our main goal is to reduce the generated network traffic without degrading the perceived quality that mobile users experience.

ENVIRONMENT-AWARE DASH

The EnvDASH system is implemented as an extension to an existing DASH client. We use the DASH Industry Forum reference implementation of a streaming client [4]. EnvDASH builds an additional adaptation layer on top of this client which allows to invoke different quality selection heuristics. Figure 1 illustrates the architecture of the EnvDASH client. Different environmental detectors build a layer for sensing the environment of a device during a streaming session. The adaptation logic leverages the sensed environmental conditions to appropriately fill the streaming buffer of the DASH player. The DASH client itself can be replaced by other players which allow to dynamically adjust the quality of a video stream by the client. Clients which want to support the EnvDASH concepts have to solely offer an adaptation interface including functions to in- and decrease the video representation. We assume that the video and audio representations are demuxed and the manifest lists the video and audio representations with an average bitrate.

The used DASH client uses a buffer-based network adaptation approach to adjust video representations according to the current network speed. The video streaming buffer is divided into zones with different priorities as proposed by Abboud et al. [1]: the critical buffer zone, the normal buffer and the comfort buffer zone. Thresholds define when the critical buffer zone ($T_{critical}$) and the normal buffer zone end (T_{normal}). If the buffer reaches a critical level of $T_{critical}$, a decrease in quality is initiated. In the evaluated EnvDASH version

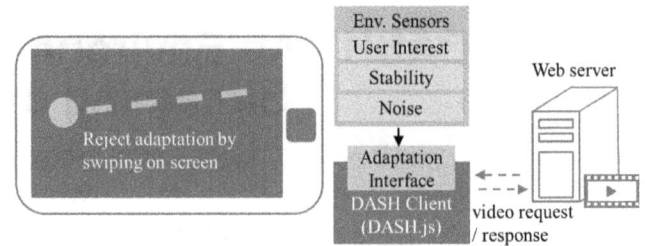

Figure 1. Architecture of our EnvDASH system. The display is indicating gestures used to reject an adaptation.

$T_{critical}$ is set to $1\,segment$ and T_{normal} to $2\,segments$. The available download speed of each video segment is measured and compared to the average bitrate of the next segment. Adaptations are executed based on the highest possible representation which bitrate is below the current download speed. An increase in quality is initiated if the buffer exceeds the threshold T_{normal}. The maximum number of segments the client tries to load is defined as $T_{comfort} = 3\,segments$. This network monitoring component can be replaced with more sophisticated approaches.

In the remaining subsections the different adaptation schemes 1) user's interest, 2) stability of the device and 3) ambient noise level are described.

Adapting to the User's Interest

Especially mobile users will not always concentrate on watching a currently streamed video. In such situations streaming of high quality video representations would waste data volume, which can be costly in today's cellular network contracts. We retrieve the information whether a user is interested in a video stream at a specific point in time by using the front-facing camera of a smartphone in combination with a face detection and tracking algorithm. We assume that if a face can be detected by the front-facing camera, the probability is high that a user is currently interested in watching the video. If no face can be detected for more than T_{UI}, an adaptation is triggered to decrease the video representation index. As long as no face can be detected the quality is slowly decreased. A slow decrease of the video representation means that the DASH representation index is reduced by $\delta r = \delta r + 1$ as long as no user's interest is sensed. δr is reset as soon as user's interest is sensed again. A slow but increasing reduction of the video representation is chosen in order to reduce the impact of short losses of user's interest, but significantly increase the bandwidth savings when users are not watching the video stream over a longer time. We have chosen T_{UI} in order to be adjusted between 1 second and 10 seconds. An increasing threshold value will decrease the risk of false negatives in detecting a face, but will potentially keep high qualities in times when a decrease of network traffic is possible. A threshold of $T_{UI} = 5\,s$ is chosen in order to compensate for situations in which the face detection algorithm is not performing reliable - e.g. brightness changes.

Face Recognition and Detection

EnvDASH integrates a face detection and tracking functionality on the mobile device. Therefore, the front-facing camera is recording a video frame every 0.5s. Note, that adaptations are invoked depending on the segment duration defined in the DASH manifest, which results in multiple sensings available per adaptation decision.

In a first step our, algorithm is detecting a face within a recorded video frame. If a face is detected, we apply a tracking algorithm in the remaining frames. Two different algorithms are leveraged for the face detection and the face tracking phase. Face recognition is done using haar-like feature classifier and detectors as proposed by Viola et al. [14]. Based on a staged classifier of different features including edge, line and surround features, a window is shifted over the video frame. The algorithm states whether a region contains a searched frontal face or not. The applied classifier is scale-invariant to easily detect faces at different sizes. Boosted classifiers are applied at every stage consisting of multiple simple, basic classifiers. Boosting is achieved by applying Adaboost [5].

As such an approach is computationally intensive on a mobile devices a second, less-computational tracking algorithm is implemented. Once the searched face is detected in one frame, the system switches to a low computational tracking based on the MeanShift algorithm [3] for the remaining frames. MeanShift is applied for the next frames until no face can be detected anymore. The algorithm applies a segmentation using colors to track templates. The color of the human skin offers an unique color combination in the HSV and YCrCb color space. We leverage the YCrCb color space and identify a range of the human skin color which is reliable under changing lighting conditions. The Y component is chosen to be $Y \geq 75$ and for the Cr component in the range of $Cr \leq 130$ and $Cr \geq 75$. The respective thresholds of the Cb component are chosen accordingly: $Cb \geq 133$ and $Cb \leq 173$. Chosen values ensure a reliable detection of human skin colors.

To reduce the calculation overhead and still be able to cope with movement of the detected face in a frame i, we detect the centroid of a detected face in a frame at location x_c, y_c and search a potential face candidate at this position in frame $i+1$ and the close proximity. As long as an oval area complying the above mentioned thresholds can be found in the proximity of this centroid the tracking is seen as successfully detecting a face. The proximity is determined in a distance of up to 15 % of the frame size around the last known face's contours. The underlying assumption is that in consecutive, recorded frames the position of a face can only change its position in a very limited range from its previously detected position.

Training the Detector
As users may watch a video stream from different viewing angles, we allow training of watching situations. Therefore, users can generate own haar-like features of their frontal face while watching a test video sequence (see Figure 2). During this test video sequence the user is asked to apply different viewing positions. To reliably detect faces also negative examples are required. Thus, the user is asked to position according situations in which no comfortable viewing is pos-

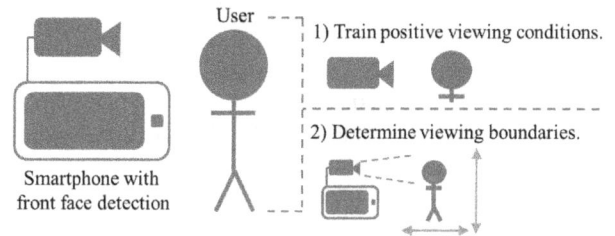

Figure 2. Training of the face tracking classifiers of EnvDASH by giving positive and negative examples.

sible. During the playback of the test sequence a video is recorded, which frames are used to create haar-like features.

Adapting to the Stability of a Device
Video streaming sessions in a mobile setting often lead to unstable viewing conditions of the playback device. E.g. while walking or taking the train or bus smartphones will encounter continuous shaking. A shaking device influences whether a user is able to consume high quality video. Such a shake is handled by our client by triggering a slowly decreasing quality adaptation - reducing the representation index by $\delta r = \delta r + 1$, as previously described. As long as shaking is detected, the device continuously reduces the quality of the next video segment. A slow decrease of the video representations is preferred in contrast to large jumps in order to avoid a high degradation of the perceived quality if the device is shaking for a short time.

A sliding window is used which gathers m samples. Device shakes can be identified within the window by at least two consecutive direction changes, which are measured with the counter c_d. To avoid small shakes to influence the adaptation behavior, the counter is only increased if the absolute impact of the direction changes exceeds the threshold T_{Abs}, which according to previous work [19] is chosen as $T_G = 2\frac{m}{s^2}$. If no movement is measured for the sample size m, the counter c_d is reset. A constant sample rate of four samples per second is set. The resulting algorithm (see Algorithm 1) illustrates how low quality video viewing conditions are detected based on the detection of motion direction changes and the estimated impact on the perceived quality in terms of the Mean Opinion Score (MOS). The MOS represents the subjective video quality ranging from 1 (bad quality) to 5 (excellent quality). Based on our previous work [18] we define the MOS function as $MOS = a_0 + a_{ampl} * x_1 + a_{dur} * x_2 + a_{speed} * x_3$. In this model x_1 is the amplitude of a measured device shaking, x_2 represents the duration of the current shaking and x_3 the velocity of the shaking. We fit the model using the parameters $a_0 = 3.7$, $a_{ampl} - 2.5723$ and $a_{dur} = -0.0494$ and $a_{speed} = -2.412$. These findings were gathered for smartphone shakes during the recording of a video, but can easily be mapped to video watching situations. A threshold of 3.5 is used to distinguish viewing conditions with imperceivable shakes ($MOS \geq 3.5$) from unstable ones ($MOS < 3.5$). If the system encounters viewing conditions worse than this MOS, an intrusive shaking is assumed.

Algorithm 1 Detection of a shaking device.

> **function sgn**(p,q): 3D-Signum-Function - calculates the sign of the difference of p to q for each dimension of a 3D vector and returns a 3D vector.
> **function abs**(p,q): Calculates the absolute difference of p to q and returns a single positive value.
> **Require:** s: Three-dimensional sample array (x,y,z) of size m filled with gravity sensor samples
> **Require:** t: Latest sample index
> **Require:** MOS: Mean Opinion Score for detecting a harmful shaking of a device.
> $c_d \leftarrow 0$: Counter for direction changes
> **if** $s_{t,x} \neq s_{t-1,x}$ **or** $s_{t,y} \neq s_{t-1,y}$ **or** $s_{t,z} \neq s_{t-1,z}$ **then**
>   **for** $i \leftarrow 0..t-3$ **do**
>   **if** $sgn(s_i, s_{i+1}) \neq sgn(s_{i+1}, s_{i+2})$ **and**
> $abs(s_{i+1}, s_{i+2}) \geq T_G$ **then**
> $c_d \leftarrow c_d + 1$
>   **end if**
>   **end for**
>   **if** $c_d \geq 2$ **and** $MOS < 3.5$ **then**
>   **return** $false$
>   **end if**
> **end if**
> **return** $true$
> **Output:** Quality - $true$: good; $false$: degraded by shaking;

Adapting to the Ambient Noise Level

Even though the video track is causing a large proportion of the network traffic, the audio track can be adapted to save network traffic as well. Users of a mobile video streaming system can not retrieve the sound of a video, if the volume of the ambient noise is too high. If the speakers of the smartphone are used to play back an audio track, EnvDASH adapts according to the ambient noise level sensed.

The microphones of the phone senses the ambient noise, which leads to a slow decrease of the audio track quality if the threshold T_{noise} is exceeded. We convert recorded noise segments into the unified and standardized unit of decibel ($dB(A)$). The ISO-standardized approach for noise mapping [9] is used to convert microphone samples into the $dB(A)$ unit. In the proposed standard, noise is measured using the A-weighted equivalent continuous sound pressure level $L_{A,eq}$ as:

$$L_{A,eq} = 10 * log_{10} \frac{1}{T} \int \frac{p^2}{p_0^2} dt \qquad (1)$$

p_A is a reference pressure chosen to be $20\mu Pa$. An open-source implementation for ambient noise level measurement which we used is offered by the NoiseTube project[1].

A threshold is chosen to determine when the ambient noise level is intrusive and does not allow to perceive the sound of the video. The threshold is defined as $T_{noise} = 75\,dB(A)$, as audio of up to $65\,dB(A)$ usually represents the maximum level of a normal conversation in a one meter distance. As

smartphones during streaming sessions usually have a distance to the viewer of less than one meter, the threshold is increased by additional $10\,dB(A)$.

In order to overcome situations in which the ambient noise is a result of the audio track of the streamed video an audio fingerprinting approach is used. Therefore, the existing and evaluated approach for fingerprinting as proposed by Kennedy et al. [10] records an audio probe and generates audio features as explained by Wang et al. [15]. Wang's approach applies a short-time Fourier transform on a given audio segment in order to find local frequency peaks. For a set of frequency peaks, in our case per one second audio segments, one fingerprint is generated by hashing the detected frequency and time values. Identifying whether the ambient noise is influenced by the audio track of the played back video is possible by generating fingerprints for both the sensed noise and the streamed audio segment. An detailed explanation of the conversion from microphone samples to dB(A) can be found in Kennedy's work [10]. In cases, when the sensed ambient noise segments show fingerprints of the played back audio track, EnvDASH slowly (1% of volume per second) decreases the volume. As we sense the ambient noise level periodically, the volume decrease will result in a significantly reduced sensed noise level if it is generated by the video.

USER FEEDBACK ON ADAPTATION

As user's preferences are different and some users may not accept our adaptation or thresholds defined, we allow customization of the adaptation during playback (see Figure 1). An adaptation is always indicated by the front LED. Red illustrates a decrease in quality whereas green illustrates an increase of quality. Adaptations can be rejected by the user. Rejecting an adaptation is achieved by swiping over the display from the right to the left. If, for more than five seconds after invoking, an adaptation is not rejected, it is enforced. Rejecting an adaptation leads for the upcoming DASH segments to a switch to the representation index prior to the adaptation.

EVALUATION

In this section, we describe the overall performance of the EnvDASH system. To evaluate the performance of EnvDASH 18 test subjects[2] were recruited to assess the system in a mobile streaming scenario. All subjects have a university background and know or even use digital video streaming services regularly, but are no video streaming researchers or experts. During this evaluation each user conducted two train rides between the two German cities Darmstadt and Frankfurt. We use the video sequence 'Valkaama' from the DASH dataset [11]. The video sequence is re-encoded in differing framerates (5 and 30 fps), resolutions (from 320x240 to Full HD) and bitrates (75 kbit/s to 7.2 Mbit/s) resulting in multiple representations. The audio tracks are encoded at 64 kbit/s, 96 kbit/s, 128 kbit/s and 256 kbit/s. The segment duration is set to 2 seconds. Every user was trained on how to use EnvDASH on a provided Google Nexus 5 smartphone with a provided mobile data contract. The evaluation generated in total

---

[1] http://noisetube.net/

[2] 13 male subjects participated. The age of the subjects ranged from 18 to 34 years.

20:49:12 hours of video streaming experience by all 18 evaluation subjects. These video streaming experiment without the concepts proposed by EnvDASH would have generated 13.42 GB of network traffic - adapting solely to the network conditions.

Network Load Reduction

Aim of EnvDASH is to reduce the generated network traffic in situations in which a user is either not able to retrieve the full quality of a video stream or is not interested in watching the video. Our collected data of two train rides per user shows that around 8.2% of the aggregated video playback duration can be played back with a lower quality representation. The user's interest algorithm detected in total that for more than 53 minutes that no face has been detected. This results in 1596 adaptations resulting from lack of user's interest. Significant shaking has been detected as well. In total 31:07 minutes of shaking devices have been detected, which led to additional 933 adaptations. For 11 minutes an 51 seconds of video streaming playback the ambient noise detection adapted the audio quality to a reduced quality level. This resulted in a potential of 530 adaptations. Each of the adaptations will lead to a decrease of the video representation and thus generated network load. But, as the saved bandwidth is depending on which representation is currently played back the resulting bandwidth gains may show a different result.

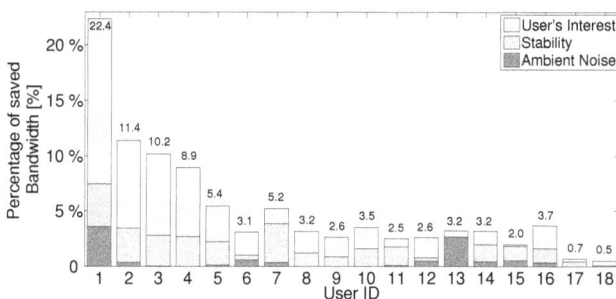

Figure 3. Overview on the percentage of bandwidth saved per user.

In average, the percentage of bandwidth saved over all users accounted for 5.3%. The generated network traffic during the train rides with the enabled EnvDASH concept is thus around 12.7 GB. The network reduction potential is very different from user to user. Some of the streaming users are continuously watching the video stream under good environmental conditions. Thus, the minimum potential lies at only 0.5% of the total watching time. The maximum network reduction achieved lies at 22.4% (see Figure 3). Figure 3 also shows the huge diversity of potential bandwidth savings between different users and between the different adaptation sources - user's interest, device stability and ambient noise level. E.g. user 1 shows the highest potential for bandwidth savings of all users which is to a large amount caused by the loss of user's interest. The sensing of user's interest is also generating the highest bandwidth savings for most other users including user 2, 3, 4, 5, 6, 10, 12 and 16. The lack of user's interest lasts significantly longer and results in the highest bandwidth savings of all investigated adaptation sources. As the dominant source for bandwidth reduction it could save 436 MB of

Table 1. Reliability of the EnvDASH algorithms.

	Accuracy	F-Meas.	Precision	Recall
User's Interest	0.98	0.79	0.81	0.76
Device Shake	0.99	0.96	0.96	0.97
Ambient Noise	0.99	0.82	0.99	0.70

bandwidth in comparison to pure network-based adaptation - around 3.17% of the total network traffic. In comparison, the adaptation source generating the second highest bandwidth savings - the device stability - is accounting for 1.6% of the traffic (224 MB). As the ambient noise level-based adaptation is solely adjusting the audio track, which in comparison to video can be encoded at low bitrates with still high quality, this adaptation source is causing the lowest impact on the saved bandwidth.

Significant network gains can be achieved by degraded viewing conditions or the loss of user's interest which last long. This is a result of our slowly increasing decrease of video representations adaptation scheme: the representation index is decreased by $\delta r = \delta r + 1$, and reset after EnvDASH senses good viewing conditions. And indeed the average adaptation length lasts around 19.1 seconds (around 9 DASH segments) with a median value of 14 seconds (7 DASH segments).

Precision of the Algorithms

Besides gained network savings the reliability and precision of the used algorithms shall be evaluated. To retrieve a ground truth for detecting the user's interest the front-facing camera is used to record a continuous video stream. By manual annotation of this video stream we could determine when a user looked directly at the device display. Additionally, we gathered a continuous stream of gravity sensor readings and the ambient sound level for building a ground truth on device shaking and the ambient noise level. For evaluation purposes those reactions are gathered to determine when an adaptation is accepted by the user and when it is classified as an error. If an adaptation is not rejected by the user, we accept this as correct invocation of an adaptation. The data has been sampled with an interval of two seconds and is provided for further scientific experiments[3].

Table 1 summarizes the accuracy, F-Measure, precision and recall of the different adaptation sources in the gathered dataset. The proposed algorithms show high accuracy and precision, which indicates that the internal sensors in combination with appropriate algorithms are adequate to predict environmental conditions during a streaming session. Non-detected, potential adaptations in the category user's interest are significantly higher compared to other adaptation sources. In some situations a face has been detected, but the ground truth has shown, that the user is not watching the content, e.g. looking away from the screen. The ambient noise level is introducing false hits as well. In many cases, they occur due to highly varying noise levels within the mobile setting, which invokes adaptations too late when the noise level is back on a

---

[3] https://www.dms.informatik.tu-darmstadt.de/research/envdash-dataset/

moderate level. With a F-Measure of 0.82, it's still a reliable source for reducing the network load.

CONCLUSION

This work describes an environment-aware adaptive streaming client based on DASH, which adapts a video stream according to viewing conditions and user's interest. Aim of our EnvDASH system is to leverage the sensed environment to reduce the generated network traffic in situations in which the user is not able to enjoy a high quality video. Therefore, the system uses the front-facing camera of a smartphone to detect the user's interest in a video. Additionally, EnvDASH monitors the ambient noise level and allows to adapt the quality of the audio track according to whether a user is able to retrieve a high quality audio track. A similar approach is taken for the video track of a stream, if the internal sensors notice that the device is not held stable. As shaking devices do not allow to retrieve a full quality video stream EnvDASH decreases the video representation to a low quality version of the video. Our work shows that such a system works reliably and offers potential for network traffic reduction.

One of the major issues is still the battery consumption of such an approach as we implemented the algorithms in software on top of the Android platform. Future smartphones could embed sensors such as efficient face tracking or noise cancellation and perform these operations in more energy conserving ways on hardware chips.

ACKNOWLEDGMENTS
This work has been co-funded by the German Research Foundation (DFG) as part of the projects C03 and B01 within the Collaborative Research Center (CRC) 1053 – MAKI as well as by the Software Campus project LiViU, which is funded by the German Federal Ministry of Education and Research (BMBF) under grant no. 01IS12054.

REFERENCES

1. Abboud, O., Pussep, K., Mueller, M., Kovacevic, A., and Steinmetz, R. Advanced Prefetching and Upload Strategies for P2P Video-on-Demand. In *ACM Workshop on Advanced Video Streaming Techniques for Peer-to-Peer Networks and Social Networking* (2010).

2. Bao, X., Fan, S., Varshavsky, A., Li, K., and Choudhury, R. R. Your Reactions Suggest You Liked the Movie: Automatic Content Rating via Reaction Sensing. In *ACM International Joint Conference on Pervasive and Ubiquitous Computing* (2013).

3. Comaniciu, D., Ramesh, V., and Meer, P. Kernel-based Object Tracking. *IEEE Transactions on Pattern Analysis and Machine Intelligence 25*, 5 (2003), 564–577.

4. DASH Industry Forum Reference Implementation. https://github.com/Dash-Industry-Forum/dash.js, 2014.

5. Freund, Y., Schapire, R., and Abe, N. A Short Introduction to Boosting. *Journal of the Japanese Society For Artificial Intelligence 14* (1999), 771–780.

6. Han, D., Han, J., Im, Y., Kwak, M., Kwon, T. T., and Choi, Y. MASERATI: Mobile Adaptive Streaming

Based on Environmental and Contextual Information. In *ACM International Workshop on Wireless Network Testbeds, Experimental Evaluation and Characterization* (2013).

7. Hanning, G., Forslow, N., Forssen, P., Ringaby, E., Tornqvist, D., and Callmer, J. Stabilizing Cell Phone Video using Inertial Measurement Sensors. In *IEEE International Conference on Computer Vision* (2011).

8. Hao, J., Zimmermann, R., and Ma, H. GTube: Geo-predictive Video Streaming over HTTP in Mobile Environments. In *ACM Multimedia Systems Conference* (2014).

9. International Standardization Organisation. ISO 1996-2:2007 - Acoustics – Description, Measurement and Assessment of Environmental Noise – Part 2: Determination of Environmental Noise Levels, 2007.

10. Kennedy, L., and Naaman, M. Less Talk, more Rock. In *International Conference on World Wide Web* (2009).

11. Lederer, S. and Müller, C. and Timmerer, C. Dynamic Adaptive Streaming over HTTP Dataset. In *ACM Multimedia Systems Conference* (2012).

12. Qi, X., Yang, Q., Nguyen, D. T., and Zhou, G. Context-aware Frame Rate Adaption for Video Chat on Smartphones. In *ACM Conference on Pervasive and Ubiquitous Computing* (2013).

13. Stockhammer, T. Dynamic Adaptive Streaming over HTTP: Standards and Design Principles. In *ACM Conference on Multimedia Systems*, ACM (2011).

14. Viola, P., and Jones, M. Rapid Object Detection using a Boosted Cascade of Simple Features. In *IEEE Conference on Computer Vision and Pattern Recognition* (2001).

15. Wang, A. An Industrial-strength Audio Search Algorithm. In *ISMIR International Conference on Music Information Retrieval (ISMIR)* (2003).

16. Wang, X., Chen, M., Kwon, T. T., Yang, L. T., and Leung, V. C. M. AMES-Cloud: A Framework of Adaptive Mobile Video Streaming and Efficient Social Video Sharing in the Clouds. *IEEE Transactions on Multimedia 15*, 4 (2013), 811–820.

17. Wang, Z., Sun, L., Wu, C., Zhu, W., and Yang, S. Joint Online Transcoding and Geo-distributed Delivery for Dynamic Adaptive Streaming. In *IEEE INFOCOM* (2014).

18. Wilk, S., and Effelsberg, W. The Influence of Camera Shakes, Harmful Occlusions and Camera Misalignment on the Perceived Quality in User-generated Video. In *IEEE Internernational Conference on Multimedia and Expo* (2014).

19. Wilk, S., Kopf, S., and Effelsberg, W. Video Composition by the Crowd: A System to Compose User-generated Videos in Near Real-time. In *ACM Multimedia Systems Conference* (2015).

SAM: Dynamic and Social Content Delivery for Second Screen Interaction

Atta Badii
Marco Tiemann
University of Reading
Reading, UK
atta.badii@reading.ac.uk
m.tiemann@reading.ac.uk

Andreas Menychtas
Christina Santzaridou
Alexandros Psychas
National Technical
University of Athens
Athens, Greece
ameny@mail.ntua.gr
csantz@mail.ntua.gr
alps@mail.ntua.gr

David Tomas
University of Alicante
Alicante, Spain
dtomas@dlsi.ua.es

Stuart Campbell
Juan Vicente Vidagany Espert
TIE Kinetix
Breukelen, The Netherlands
stuart.campbell@tiekinetix.com
juanvi.vidagany@tiekinetix.com

TVX'15, June 03-05, 2015, Brussels, Belgium
ACM 978-1-4503-3526-3/15/06.
http://dx.doi.org/10.1145/2745197.2755511

Abstract

Social media services offer a wide range of opportunities for businesses and developers to exploit the vast amount of information and user-generated content produced via social media. In addition, the notion of TV second screen usage – the interleaved usage of TV and smart devices such as smartphones – appears ever more prominent, with viewers continuously seeking further information and deeper engagement while watching movies, TV shows or event coverage. In this work-in-progress contribution, we present SAM, an innovative platform that combines social media, content syndication and targets second screen usage to enhance media content provisioning and advance the user experience. SAM incorporates modern technologies and novel features in the areas of content management, dynamic social media, social mining, semantic annotation and multi-device representation to facilitate an advanced business environment for broadcasters, content and metadata providers and editors to better exploit their assets and increase revenues.

Author Keywords

Social Media; Content Syndication; Second Screen; Social Communities.

Relevance of TV Second Screen Usage

According to a Nielsen/Yahoo study, mobile devices are increasingly serving as second screens during TV usage, with 88% of respondents using their mobile devices while watching TV [1]. Their top-three activities are to

- find out more about the show they are watching
- retrieve information on the cast of a show
- engage with products featured in ads aired during the program

ACM Classification Keywords

H.3.3. Information Search and Retrieval: Information Filtering; H.3.5. Online Information Services: Web-based services; H.5.m. Information interfaces and presentation: Miscellaneous; I.2.7 Natural Language Processing: text analysis.

Introduction

Social media and the adoption of smart personal connected devices have changed the way users are interacting with media from being passive and unidirectional recipients to proactive and interactive participants. Users can now and frequently do comment on or rate TV shows or search for related information about characters, places or objects appearing in them [1]. They can follow updates of their friends regarding shows, can participate actively and be part of wider social communities in the context of a program. This type of usage is known as second screen usage; forecasts predict dramatic growth and impact rates for it even if the initial usage and facilities of second screen are currently still limited [2].

Currently, there are no second screen software application standards, protocols or common ways in which users can discover and access information related to TV first screen contents on their second screen devices [3]. Users must actively search for information using generic services (e.g. Google, Twitter or Facebook) to start "participating" in a programme, or must access (and install apps for) custom services for each individual show they are interested in. Enterprises that would like to provide second screen services have to develop custom solutions for individual programmes over and over again.

This work presents the Socialising Around Media – SAM Platform [4], an EU co-funded research project that is developing an advanced social media delivery platform. The vision for SAM is based on the idea of fusing second screen and content syndication [5] and on exploiting advances in social media. This is achieved by providing new ways of characterising, discovering and syndicating media assets (e.g. TV series) interactively as part of a unified business-oriented second screen service creation environment, which will provide an integrated and efficient environment for the creation of second screen experiences so that End users will be able to consume and interact with digital assets from different syndicated sources across devices (e.g. connected TVs), thus creating richer experiences around the original media assets. The SAM project extends over a 3-year period from late 2013 to 2016. The project consortium consists of technical partners as well as application partners, including an international TV broadcaster and a media metadata provider as well as affiliates that will carry out an end-user evaluation.

SAM incorporates features for the creation of dynamic social communities related to the user and digital asset context (e.g. user profiles, preferences, devices connected and content usage) in order to enable media content syndication enriched with comments, ratings and recommendations as well as additional programme-related information. The system has been designed around three main pillars that highlight the main research and business directions of this work:

- **Content Syndication:** Based on content syndication techniques, different content providers prepare their assets so that they can be linked to specific media and context. The platform provides mechanisms for asset discovery, association with user activities and delivery in a suitable format.

- **Social Media:** Social interaction around media items will be facilitated through the integration of existing social media platforms and enhanced through dynamic contextual communities, in which users of the SAM Platform may be invited because of shared preferences for programmes, contextual factors such as their location or product preferences, or their attitudes and emotions expressed through social media.

- **Multi-device representation and second screen:** A multi-device representation layer enables the SAM platform to provide syndicated information ready for usage on different types of devices. This approach is used to provide second screen content while a first screen media asset is being viewed.

The remainder of this paper is organised as follows: The next section briefly presents selected related work. Then, the platform key features and platform architecture are set out. The following section identifies validation and evaluation scenarios, and the final section highlights technical innovation and business opportunities and concludes this contribution.

Related Work

As mentioned above, the approach applied in SAM is based on three main pillars, covering a wide range of state-of-the-art technologies, including second screen, content syndication, social mining, sentiment analysis and natural language processing.

In the area of content syndication, Web 2.0 technologies and service-based computing architectures

are driving continuous change: end-user contextual data syndication, service syndication and social syndication are among current industry trends. Several companies specialise in providing the infrastructure necessary for Content Syndication, such as TIE Kinetix [6], Zift Solutions [7] and WebCollage [8].

Social media are a group of Internet-based applications that allow the creation and exchange of user-generated content. They provide users with an easy way to communicate with each other and to act as publishers themselves. The growth of social media over the last decade has significantly changed the way individuals interact and industries conduct business. A number of research areas are associated with this area. Social media mining is one such area, aiming to represent, analyse and extract information from social media [9].

There are many different applications and benefits of social media mining technologies: social conversation monitoring, Twitter network analysis for community detection, social recommendation, influence modelling and sentiment analysis [10]. Another field of research linked to social media is the identification and creation of social communities. A straightforward approach for identifying subgroups within such a graph can then be to apply graph-based clustering methods [11] [12]. Since social network interactions and structures are not static, but change over time, [13] propose a solution for tracing social media communities over time.

The second screen domain is dominated by commercial actors in addition to general social media services such as Twitter. Popular examples of commercial second screen are Beamly [14], i.TV [15], Viggle [16] and Shazam [17].

Key Features and Platform Architecture

The key features of the SAM Platform are derived from the main goals of the platform and user requirements elicited in the SAM project. Figure 1 summarises the key features and relates them to the three technical pillars outlined earlier as well as the important application domain of digital marketing.

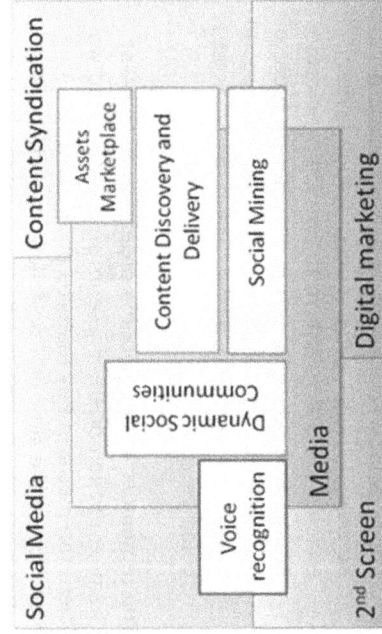

Figure 1: Overview of SAM key features related to the three pillars of SAM and the application domain of digital marketing.

Second Screen and multi-device representation features provide the communication and presentation infrastructure that is required for presenting and interacting with second screen devices; it also includes representation and interaction functions for the TV first screen. **Voice recognition** and voice dialogue interaction features are integrated into the SAM Platform in order to enable voice-driven interaction similar to those available to smartphone users via services provided by smartphone operating system creators for controlling their systems.

Social media and **Dynamic Social Communities** functionalities are integrated into the SAM end user interface. SAM interfaces with existing social media services (e.g. Twitter) that can be accessed directly from within SAM second screen experiences, and dynamic social communities are generated automatically in order to capture sub-communities within a community of media users (e.g. fans of different football clubs watching the same match) and super- or cross-communities not tied to individual media programmes (e.g. viewers generally interested in talent shows).

Content Syndication functionalities include an **Assets Marketplace**, where second screen experience creators can compose second screen experiences using content and services offered by third parties and **Content Discovery and Delivery** mechanisms that automate the personalised and syndicated delivery of content to end users. Content syndication and the creation of second screen experiences are facilitated through a dedicated backend user interface.

Digital marketing in SAM is supported through the integration of state-of-the-art commercial business analytics and improved through **Social Mining** functionalities, including sentiment analysis in order to evaluate emotional reactions of users as expressed via connected social media channels. Social mining functionalities are also used in other components of SAM, in particular Dynamic Social Communities and the Assets Marketplace.

SAM leverages a flexible platform architecture and component-based system that loosely couples system components through a state-of-the-art service

SAM User Interfaces

SAM will provide dedicated user interfaces for business users of the SAM Platform as well as a SAM Dashboard for end users. The Dashboard is a widget-driven UI system displayed on second screen and first screen devices.

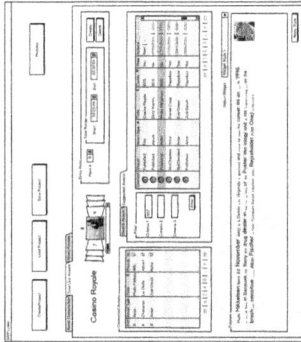

Figure 3: Business UI Example

Figure 3 and Figure 4 depict mockup versions of the two user interfaces above. Larger versions are provided as supplemental material.

Figure 4: Dashboard UI Example

integration bus in order to create the SAM Platform, depicted in Figure 2. All components are implemented using a Service-Oriented Architecture and service composition approach facilitated through the integration bus [10].

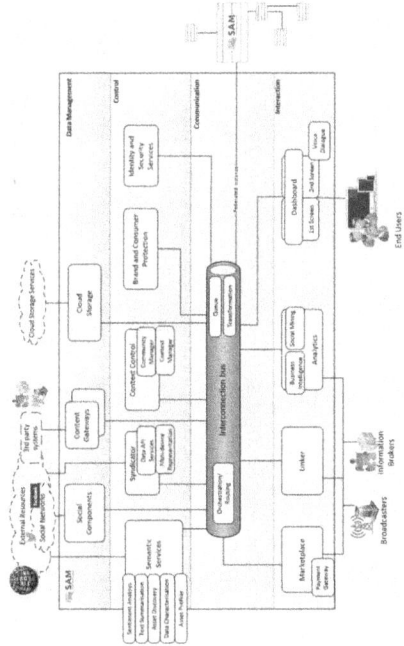

Figure 2: The SAM Platform high-level architecture; a higher-resolution version of this figure is available as supplementary material to this paper.

Validation and Evaluation Scenarios

The developments in the SAM project are being driven by two main use cases that address the creation of second screen experiences and their consumption respectively. Both scenarios will be used for evaluations with both business and end user groups in order to determine the user acceptance of SAM.

Use Case I "Content Syndication and Media enrichment" is concerned with the creation of a second screen experience. This includes the addition of content and services as assets into the SAM Platform, the description and configuration of descriptive and usage-oriented asset metadata including commercial as well as brand and consumer protection configurations. This use case also encompasses the creation of second screen experiences for a TV programme up to the point at which it is made available to the end user.

Use Case II "Social Consumption" is concerned with the usage of and interaction with a second screen experience that is provided through the SAM Platform. Activities within this use case include the interaction with second screen content, user-driven content discovery and basic as well as advanced interactions via social media. Specific sub-scenarios address different activities for "lean forward" users and "lean backward" users of second screen experiences.

Conclusion

This paper has presented an overview and the current status of the SAM project and platform for socialising around media through second screen experiences. The SAM project is currently implementing the described platform, which will be available upon completion of the project at the end of 2016.

Key benefits that will be realised through SAM include personalised and context-aware content delivery of interactive content experiences combined with dynamic social media community integration for end users. Business users will be provided with a central market place infrastructure for providing content and creating second screen experiences without requiring complex and expensive custom development efforts.

Further information on the SAM project is available online at http://www.samproject.eu and via Twitter @SamProjectEU.

Acknowledgements

This work has been partially funded by the European Commission under the Seventh (FP7 - 2007- 2013) Framework Programme for Research and Technological Development through the SAM (FP7-611312) project.

References

1. Second Screen Society. 2014. Second Screen Journal - Advancing the mobile viewing experience. Second Screen Society. Retrieved February 26, 2015 from http://www.2ndscreensociety.com/

2. C. Courtois and E. D'heer. 2012. Second screen applications and tablet users: constellation, awareness, experience, and interest. In *Proceedings of the 10th European Conference on Interactive TV and Video*, 153-156.

3. E. Tsekleves, L. Cruickshank, A. Hill, K. Kondo and R. Witham. 2007. Interacting with digital media at home via second screen. In *Proceedings of the 9th IEEE International Symposium*, 201-206.

4. SAM EU Research Project. 2015. Retrieved February 26, 2015 from http://socialisingaroundmedia.com/

5. N. Heino, S. Tramp and S. Auer. 2011. Managing web content using linked data principles–combining semantic structure with dynamic content syndication. In *Proceedings of the Conference on Computer Software and Applications (COMPSAC)*, 245-250.

6. TIE Kinetix. 2015. TIE Kinetix Website. Retrieved February 26, 2015 from http://tiekinetix.com/

7. Zift. 2015. Content Syndication: Zift Solutions. Retrieved February 26, 2015 from http://www.ziftsolutions.com/products/content-syndication/

8. Web Collage. 2015. Web Collage. Retrieved February 26, 2015 from http://www.webcollage.com/

9. M. Kardara et al. 2014. SocIoS API: A data aggregator for accessing user generated content from online social networks. In *Proceedings of the 15th International Conference on Web Information System Engineering*, Thessaloniki.

10. D. Kyriazis et al. 2011. Interactive Social TV on Service Oriented Environments: Challenges and Enablers. In *Proceedings of the 3rd International IEEE Conference on Games and Virtual Worlds for Serious Applications*, 152-155.

11. B. S. Everitt, S. Landau and L. Morven. 2009. Cluster Analysis. Wiley Publishing.

12. Y. Zhao and G. Karypis. 2002. Evaluation of hierarchical clustering algorithms for document datasets. In *Proceedings of the eleventh international conference on Information and knowledge management*, 515-524.

13. C. Tantipathananandh, T. Berger-Wolf and D. Kempe. 2007. A framework for community identification in dynamic social networks. In *Proceedings of the 13th ACM SIGKDD international conference on Knowledge discovery and data mining*, 717-726.

14. Beamly. 2015. Retrieved February 26, 2015 from http://beamly.com/

15. i.TV. 2015. Retrieved February 26, 2015 from http://i.tv/

16. Viggle. 2015. Retrieved February 26, 2015 from http://get.viggle.com/

17. Shazam. 2015. Retrieved February 26, 2015 from http://www.shazam.com/music/web/productfeatures.html?id=1266

18. S. van Boskirk, C. Spivey Overby and S. Takvorian. 2011. Forrester US Interactive Marketing Forecast, 2011 To 2016.

SensiTV - Smart EmotioNal System for Impaired people's TV

Diana Affi
HumanTech Institute
University of Applied Sciences
Fribourg, Switzerland
diana.affi@hes-so.ch

Joël Dumoulin
HumanTech Institute
University of Applied Sciences
Fribourg, Switzerland
joel.dumoulin@hes-so.ch

Marco Bertini
MICC
University of Florence
Florence, Italy
marco.bertini@unifi.it

Elena Mugellini
HumanTech Institute
University of Applied Sciences
Fribourg, Switzerland
elena.mugellini@hes-so.ch

Omar Abou Khaled
HumanTech Institute
University of Applied Sciences
Fribourg, Switzerland
omar.aboukhaled@hes-so.ch

Alberto Del Bimbo
MICC
University of Florence
Florence, Italy
alberto.delbimbo@unifi.it

Abstract

In this paper, an innovative solution is presented: a smart emotional system for impaired people's TV. It aims to accompany the cognitive information contained in a movie, with the affective content. The affect is then communicated to the movie viewers in ways compatible for people with hearing and/or visual impairments, to let them experience all of the sensations offered by the movie. To do so, emotion recognition techniques are used to classify movie scenes into seven basic emotions. These emotions are then represented, in realtime, while the movie is playing, to the viewers, using environmental lights, emotional subtitles and a second screen application that integrates vibrations, emoticons and background music.

Author Keywords

Smart TV; Affective Computing; Emotion Recognition

ACM Classification Keywords

H.5.1 [Information interfaces and presentation (e.g., HCI)]: Multimedia Information Systems—video; K.4.2 [Computers and society]: Social Issues—Assistive technologies for persons with disabilities; H.5.3 [Image Processing and computer vision]: Feature Measurement—Feature representation; I.5.2 [Pattern recognition]: Design Methodology—Classifier design and evaluation,Feature evaluation and selection

TVX'15, June 03-05, 2015, Brussels, Belgium
ACM 978-1-4503-3526-3/15/06.
http://dx.doi.org/10.1145/2745197.2755512

Introduction

People suffering of hearing or visual impairments are not being able to enjoy a movie in all of its aspects, and the percentage of these people cannot be neglected. Some solutions already exist to provide these people with the semantic content of the video, using for instance subtitles for the hearing impaired, and audio-description for the visually impaired. But solutions that bring them the emotions contained in the movies are not so common yet. Even though the current solutions help the hearing and visually impaired people to understand the content of the corresponding movie, they deliver raw and static cognitive information lacking all the affective level which is one of the essential factors in delivering the desired TV experience: *a)* by enhancing the ability to process and comprehend the language[1] *b)* and by immersing the viewer in the movie and helping him identify himself with the actors[11]. Finding a way to introduce empathic TV experiences in visually and hearing impaired people's living rooms will bring them the missing information in the current way of consuming visual media: the emotions.

Related work

This work focuses on two research aspects: emotion recognition in audio-visual content, as well as exploring different communication modalities that can be used to translate these emotions to the viewers. In both aspects some work has already been done.

Most of recent works on video analysis have focused on the extraction of video semantics, while the recognition of affective information is less explored. Emotion recognition in audio has dealt with music and with emotion recognition in prosody, leading to the development of toolkits such as OpenSMILE [8]. The linguistic content of speech has also been used for emotion recognition [3] as well as the accom-

panying text (subtitles, tags, comments etc.) of images [2]. Visual features have also been subject to emotion recognition researches, specially the facial expressions [7]. In this paper's case emotions are detected from movie scenes, which contain visual objects, audio aspects, as well as cinematographic techniques that do contribute in defining the global contained emotion. Hanjalic et al. [10] proposed to extract and model the affective content of the video using both audio and video features, and called this approach *Affective content analysis*. Studies followed Hanjalic, using multiple classification techniques (hidden Markov Models, Partial Least Squares, Support Vector Machines etc.). In [14] an accuracy of 50.37% have been obtained by using both audio and advanced visual features (deep learning) applied on faces and classified using Partial Least Squares.

Concerning the hearing and visually impaired, the approaches currently used to provide them the emotional information conveyed in a movie, rely on audio description and subtitles. [15, 9] have dealt with possible ways to deliver emotions to impaired people through different techniques relying on their complementary functional senses. The limitation of these techniques is that *i)* they rely on the presence of emotional meta-data related to the videos - that are not commonly available - and *ii)* they are not applied in home environments.

SensiTV concept

After going through the state of the art of affective data retrieval from audio-visual content and the study of emotion communication techniques to people with hearing or visual impairment, it was clearly revealed that there is some considerable work to add. SensiTV is developed in order to fill these shortcomings. The system will contain two main modules: a module for emotion recognition from audio-visual content as well as a module for communicating these de-

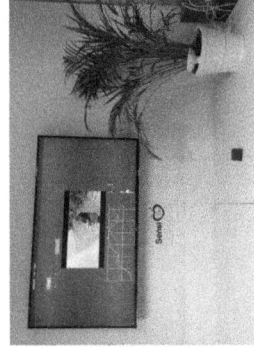

(b) Light projection from over the plant for positive emotions

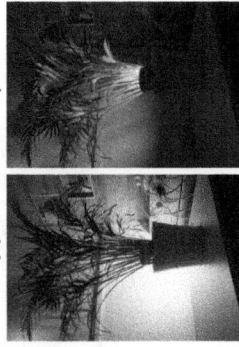

(a) Sensi TV setup

(c) Light projection from under the plant for negative emotions

Figure 1: Emotion communication via light. SensiTV setup

tected emotions to the viewers in realtime while they are watching the concerned video.

Emotion recognition in movies

Feature extraction

It has been proven that both audio and visual content are important when trying to depict the affective content of a specific scene. The cinematographic techniques, used to awaken certain emotions, are also the guide in finding adequate features but they represent high level features that are hard to detect programmatically (ex. filming from behind the character). In the following we will describe the extracted features in our system for emotion classification.

Audio features: The audio features are extracted using OpenSMILE[8] which enables specifying the framing and windowing over an audio file, as well as it gives the possibility to apply functions on the retrieved features. The audio features extracted are inspired of the ones used in the INTERSPEECH 2010 paralinguistic challenge [16]. Over these features the following functions are applied over a window of one second: Linear regression, Range, Skeweness, Kurtosis, Standard deviation, Minimum, Maximum, Mean and Delta regression.

Visual features: One frame per second is used to extract the following visual features: brightness, shot cut density, edges, color histogram, arousal and the biconcept[1].

After the feature extraction process, the audio and visual features are concatenated, normalised and a Linear Discriminant Analysis (LDA) is applied on them in order to reduce their dimensionality.

---

[1] The biconcept is a feature vector of size 1200, each dimension is associated to an adjective-noun couple expressing sentiment, developed in the visual sentiment ontology study [2].

Classification

Support Vector Machines (SVM) have proven their capabilities for emotion features classification from audio-visual content as seen in the state of the art. This led the choice of an SVM to be used for classification. In our case, we need to classify seven emotions so we are using the one-to-one approach for multi-class classification. This approach tends to train one classifier for each pair of classes. The SVM is based on an *RBF* kernel in order to treat nonlinear data.

Communicating emotions

Once the movie is affectively annotated, its progress is tracked while the user is watching it, and all the emotion communication modalities are synchronised with it: at each second of the movie, a command for expressing the corresponding emotion is sent to the chosen modalities detailed in the following section.

Implemented Modalities

The implemented modalities are inspired by communication techniques used by hearing and visually impaired people as well as by studies related to emotion and its expression through different cues. The main constraint is that the chosen modalities cannot be intrusive and should be applicable in the home environment.

Lights: The lights have been always used to set the mood in houses, concerts, restaurants etc. using three modalities: light intensity, light projection and colours. We have profited from these findings by controlling two Philips hue LEDs and one Philips strip led. The setup of SensiTV is shown in Figure 1. It shows the strip LED attached to the borders of the TV as well as the Philips hue lights that are placed one aiming to lighten up the plant from above and the other from below in order to differentiate between negative and posi-

Emotion	Vibration pattern
Anger	
Disgust	
Fear	
Happiness	
Sadness	
Surprise	

Figure 2: Vibration patterns for each emotion

tive emotions using colours and light projection type (see Figure 3).

Vibrations: Touch has been shown to be an alternative communication technique with both hearing and visually impaired people[12]. From this logic came the idea of using mobile phone vibrations for conveying emotions to these viewers. Vibrations are conceptualised to play the role of stimuli that will notify the viewers about an uprising emotion. They trigger the viewers attention and try to give hints about the current emotion by using a different vibration pattern for each emotion. In Figure 2 they are presented in a morse code way.

Emoticons: Emoticons are world widely known to convey emotions when using text messaging solutions. We display emoticons corresponding to the movie affective state on the mobile application as well. The viewer can check his second screen to know the current emotion.

Background mood music: We have added to the mobile application a module responsible for playing the corresponding mood music to the current emotion. The music's volume is very low so the viewer can still enjoy his movie and listen to the speech.

Subtitles: We chose the subtitles as an emotion communication modality due to their minimal intrusion level since they are widely used and already accepted by the viewers. The main idea is to personalise the font, the colour, and the size of the subtitles' text according to the emotion associated with the current movie scene (see Figure 5).

Preliminary results
Preliminary tests are conducted to verify the feasibility of the system and to provide a basis for the choice of emotion communication modalities. The user experience related

tests (importance of audio-visual content in movies and communication modalities tests) are conducted using an online survey on people not suffering from any impairments. Since the visually and/or hearing impaired do convey and recognise emotions in similar ways as non impaired people [13], but with some delays[6], tests on people not suffering from any impairments are relevant to find emotion communication modalities and easier to organise. The survey was taken by 126 men and 87 women majorly from Switzerland and Lebanon, which ages are spread between 17 and 60 (avg=24,δ=3).

Importance of audio-visual content in movies
A test was conducted to explore the importance of the two dimensions of a movie (audio and video), in the viewer's perception. Movie clips are shown to viewers who are asked to select the corresponding emotion between anger, disgust, fear, happiness, sadness, surprise and neutral. The viewer is showed several video clip types: *i*) normal movies, *ii*) movies with a muted sound; and *iii*) audio clips from movies. The survey comes in three formats in order to shuffle the movie presentation type for each viewer.

The results of emotion recognition accuracy by viewers are shown as confusion matrices (see Figure 4) where the diagonal line of the confusion matrix is best seen when the movie is presented fully to the viewers, which means that both audio and video streams are important in emotion transmission. Also, these results show that the video has more relevance than audio in distinguishing emotions.

Emotion recognition tests
For training and testing we have used the Acted Facial Expression in the Wild (AFEW) dataset [4, 5]. It consists of two separated movie clip sets: training data and test data. It contains short movie scenes (three seconds) showing a

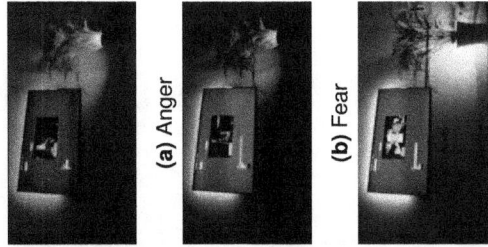

(a) Anger

(b) Fear

(c) Happiness

Figure 3: Emotion communication via lights and colours

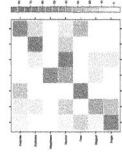

(a) Full Movies

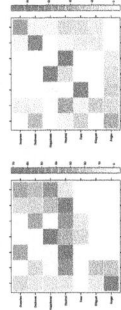

(b) Only audio   (c) Only video

Figure 4: Confusion matrices of emotion recognition by viewers

specific emotion among the following emotions: anger, disgust, fear, happiness, sadness, surprise and neutral.

The tests are performed using different features' combinations, and for each test, GridSearch is used to test all possible combinations of SVM's parameters in order to find the best solution. The best found estimator is an SVM with an *RBF* kernel, a *penalty parameter of the error term* (C) equal to 1000 and a *kernel coefficient* (Gamma) equal to 0.0001. The combination of audio and visual features have proven to be the best specially when dimensionality reduction techniques are applied such as LDA (number of components = 6) or SVD (number of components = 45). The first results are indicating that the biconcept visual feature is not adapted for this dataset. The confusion matrix associated with the best classification results is shown in Figure 6.

Communication Modalities Tests

The tests were conducted by displaying some of these modalities during the online survey and asking people to guess which emotion corresponds to which encoding.

One of the tested modalities was the colour. People were asked to select a colour from a list of predefined colours (red, green, blue, grey, yellow and purple) to represent the basic emotions. Results are shown in Figure 7a. Anger,

sadness and disgust show a unique response from the users as can be seen. Concerning the other emotions, *fear* will be associated with *blue* since the *grey* is more dominant for the *sadness* emotion. *Happiness* and *surprise* are tricky since both *purple* and *yellow* are associated to them.

Another test was performed to make sure the used emoticons were a universal standard. Results from the survey part concerning the emoticons can be seen in Figure 7b. The results have assured that the emoticons are a very straightforward modality for emotion communication.

Future work

First of all, user experience tests will be conducted on the target audience (visually and/or hearing impaired) to gather their feedback and adjust the system for their needs. According to the results, improvements and adjustments will be done regarding the emotion communication part. Some new channels will as well be considered in a later step, through smart objects for instance, like animated paintings or vibrating seats, in order to provide an even more intense experience. As for the classification part, it will be continuously improved, by adding new features (mainly visual), by enhancing the features selection, and by using more advanced classification techniques (e.g. deep learning).

Conclusion

This paper presented and analysed the problem related to the empathic TV experience of people with hearing and/or visual impairments. To this end, a solution to fill this gap is proposed, by implementing a complete system covering the emotion recognition from movies, as well as the communication of these emotions to TV viewers. The empirical results of emotion classification show high accuracy for some emotion classes and low for others, while the communication process rely on some well proven modalities in

(a) Anger

(b) Disgust

(c) Happiness

(d) Surprise

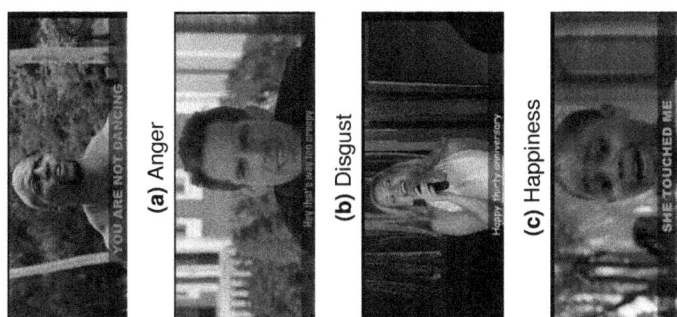

Figure 5: Showing emotions through subtitles

(AV_LDA)	Anger	Disgust	Fear	Happiness	Neutral	Sadness	Surprise
Anger	53%	12%	6%	8%	11%	5%	5%
Disgust	24%	10%	3%	30%	20%	5%	8%
Fear	23%	4%	23%	13%	20%	9%	7%
Happiness	18%	13%	4%	30%	30%	1%	4%
Neutral	9%	13%	3%	26%	37%	9%	3%
Sadness	4%	15%	6%	29%	29%	13%	4%
Surprise	9%	11%	4%	31%	27%	9%	9%

Figure 6: Confusion matrix for emotion recognition (AV-LDA: audio visual features with LDA applied)

emotion expression. Both of these modules will be objects to enhancements for better performance and better user experience.

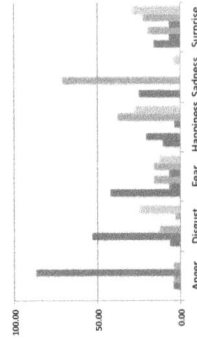

(a) SensiTV survey: association of colours with emotions

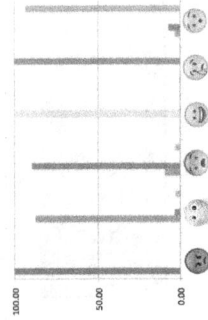

(b) SensiTV survey: association of emoticons with emotions (red: anger, green: disgust, blue: fear, yellow: happiness, grey: sadness, pink: surprise)

Figure 7: Communication modalities survey test results

References

[1] C. Becker, S. Kopp, and I. Wachsmuth. 2001. Why emotions should be integrated into conversational agents. (2001).

[2] D. Borth, R. Ji, T. Chen, T. Breuel, and S.-F. Chang. 2013. Large-scale visual sentiment ontology and detectors using adjective noun pairs. In *Proc. of ACM MM*. ACM Press, 223–232. http://dl.acm.org/citation.cfm?doid=2502081.2502282

[3] J. De Silva and P. S. Haddela. 2013. A term weighting method for identifying emotions from text content. In *Proc. of IEEE ICIIS*. 381–386.

[4] A. Dhall, R. Goecke, J. Joshi, and T. Gedeon. 2014. Emotion Recognition In The Wild Challenge 2014 : Baseline, Data and Protocol Categories and Subject Descriptors. (2014).

[5] A. Dhall, R. Goecke, S. Lucey, and T. Gedeon. 2012. Collecting large, richly annotated facial-expression databases from movies. *IEEE Multimedia* 19, 1 (2012), 34–41. DOI:http://dx.doi.org/10.1109/MMUL.2012.26

[6] M. J. Dyck, C. Farrugia, I. M. Shochet, and M. Holmes-Brown. 2004. Emotion recognition/understanding ability in hearing or vision-impaired children: do sounds, sights, or words make the difference? *Journal of Child Psychology and Psychiatry* 45, 4 (2004), 789–800. DOI:http://dx.doi.org/10.1111/j.1469-7610.2004.00272.x

[7] P. Ekman. 2003. *Emotions Revealed*.

[8] F. Eyben, F. Weninger, F. Gross, and B. Schuller. 2013. Recent Developments in openSMILE, the Munich Open-Source Multimedia Feature Extractor. In *Proc. of ACM MM*. 835–838. DOI:http://dx.doi.org/10.1145/2502081.2502224

[9] S. Firdus, W. Fatimah, W. Ahmad, and J. B. Janier. 2012. Development of Audio Video Describer Using Narration to Visualize Movie Film for Blind and Visually Impaired Children. In *Proc. of IEEE ICCIS*. 1068–1072.

[10] A. Hanjalic, L. Xu, C. D. Delft, A. Park, M. Heath, and I. Ip. 2001. User-oriented Affective Video Content Analysis. In *Proc. of IEEE CBAIVL*. 50–57.

[11] A. Hanjalic and L.-q. Xu. 2005. Affective Video Content Representation and Modeling. 7, 1 (2005), 143–154.

[12] M. J. Hertenstein, D. Keltner, B. App, B. a. Bulleit, and A. R. Jaskolka. 2006. Touch communicates distinct emotions. *Emotion (Washington, D.C.)* 6, 3 (Aug. 2006), 528–33. DOI:http://dx.doi.org/10.1037/1528-3542.6.3.528

[13] R. Hiraga, N. Kato, and T. Yamasaki. 2006. Understanding emotion through drawings comparison between hearing-impaired people and people with normal hearing abilities. In *Systems, Man and Cybernetics, 2006. SMC '06. IEEE International Conference on*, Vol. 1. 103–108. DOI:http://dx.doi.org/10.1109/ICSMC.2006.384366

[14] M. Liu, R. Wang, S. Li, S. Shan, Z. Huang, and X. Chen. 2014. Combining Multiple Kernel Methods on Riemannian Manifold for Emotion Recognition in the Wild. In *Proc. of ICMI*. 494–501.

[15] J. Ohene-djan and R. Shipsey. 2006. E-Subtitles : Emotional Subtitles as a Technology to assist the Deaf and Hearing-Impaired when Learning from Television and Film. In *Proc. of ICALT*. 2–4.

[16] B. Schuller, S. Steidl, A. Batliner, F. Burkhardt, L. Devillers, M. Christian, and S. Narayanan. 2010. The INTERSPEECH 2010 Paralinguistic Challenge. In *Proc. Interspeech*. 2794–2797.

A Second-Screen Meets Hypervideo, Delivering Content Through HbbTV

Toni Bibiloni

Universitat de les Illes Balears
Departamento de Matemáticas e Informática
Laboratorio de Tecnologías de la Información Multimedia, LTIM
Palma, Illes Balears, Spain
toni.bibiloni@uib.es

Miquel Mascaró

Universitat de les Illes Balears
Departamento de Matemáticas e Informática
Laboratorio de Tecnologías de la Información Multimedia, LTIM
Palma, Illes Balears, Spain
mascport@uib.es

Pere Palmer

Universitat de les Illes Balears
Departamento de Matemáticas e Informática
Laboratorio de Tecnologías de la Información Multimedia, LTIM
Palma, Illes Balears, Spain
pere.palmer@uib.es

Antoni Oliver

Universitat de les Illes Balears
Departamento de Matemáticas e Informática
Laboratorio de Tecnologías de la Información Multimedia, LTIM
Palma, Illes Balears, Spain
antoni.oliver@uib.es

Abstract

In this paper two improvements for the Hypervideo platform, used to represent augmented reality on Interactive TVs thanks to the hypervideo concept, are presented: the introduction of a second-screen application to the platform, enabling the user to obtain the additional information on its handheld device and delivering the video track through the broadcast channel, thanks to the HbbTV capability.

Author Keywords

Hypervideo; Augmented Reality; HbbTV; Second-Screen Application.

ACM Classification Keywords

H.5.1 Information interfaces and presentation (e.g., HCI): Multimedia information systems—Artificial, augmented, and virtual realities.

H.5.4 Information interfaces and presentation (e.g., HCI): Hypertext/Hypermedia—Architectures, Navigation.

Introduction

A hypervideo, or "video with hyperlinks" [1] is an interactive video stream in which the user is able to interact with the content through hyperlinks, leading to non-linear navigation, searching, sequence skipping, etc. with the purpose of improving the access to the information and bringing the viewer from a passive to an active state [2].

When the hypervideo concept is applied to real images recorded in a video product, augmented reality can be experienced, when this indirect view of the real world is combined with virtual elements, creating a mixed reality.

This paper follows the work from previous papers [3, 4] and demo [5], where a hypervideo platform capable of creating and delivering an AR experience to the viewer through current generation Interactive TV solutions, such as HbbTV, Android TV or Samsung Smart TV was presented.

Two of the improvements proposed in the testing of that prototype are the object of study in this paper: enabling a second-screen device to connect to the application in order to get the additional information in a handheld device and using the capability of HbbTV of representing the broadcast video.

In the first section, the previous work is reviewed to introduce the platform to the reader. Then the second-screen companion application is introduced in the hypervideo platform. Finally, we discuss how this improvement enables the platform to deliver the video through the broadcast channel.

Previous work

The hypervideo solution
The hypervideo format chosen in this project has three dimensions:

- An audiovisual track, which represents the PoIs and is the base for the whole product. In previous work it was delivered via streaming and now is intended to be played through the broadcast channel.

- The points of interest (PoIs), plus their additional information, which can be textual, visual and complementary.

- The markers that represent these PoIs on the video track that enable the user to identify them (*hot-spot* role) and access its additional information (hyperlink role).

This format was proven to be understood by audiovisual producers in previous work and was used to create functional demos.

The hypervideo platform
The hypervideos are created and viewed thanks to the hypervideo platform. The proposed architecture for the platform is shown in Figure 1, consisting in two modules which interact with a server in the middle.

The creation module comprises the tools needed to create a hypervideo, starting by managing the audiovisual repository and inserting new data in the PoI catalogue.

Once these steps have been completed, PoIs are linked to the media through the positioning of the markers that represent them with the aid of an interactive tool.

This module has been developed as a Javascript web application hosted in the server.

The visualization module is a hypervideo player application, with the ability to playback the audiovisual

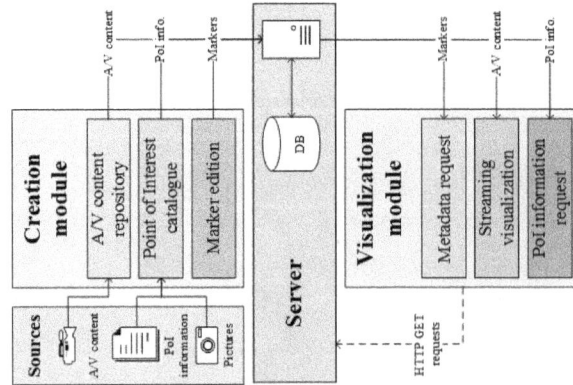

Figure 1. Diagram of the architecture of the hypervideo platform

track, represent the markers over it and show the additional information of the PoIs requested by the viewer.

A multiplatform development has been followed, being implemented in HbbTV, Android TV and Samsung Smart TV technologies, using HTML and Javascript.

Finally, the hypervideo server is the agent between both modules. It serves the creation module as a web application, and the creation module for the HbbTV and Android TV platforms, as they use a web-based approach.

The server also stores all the data related to the hypervideos and handles the requests from the modules.

Second-Screen companion application

One of the most commented future work proposals in the previous work was the inclusion of a second-screen companion application to enable the user to access the additional information in a separate, personal device.

As stated in [6], a common trend among Interactive TV applications is the introduction of a second-screen companion application. In [7] several insights from the perspective of both the user and the creators of this type of application.

The reasons to introduce a second-screen companion app in the hypervideo platform were:

- The need to pause the video playback to obtain the additional information breaks the intended storytelling and forces other viewers to pause their

experience, having or not interest in the PoI which additional information is being obtained.

- Displaying the additional information on the same screen as the audiovisual track, hiding it, can distract the viewer from the video track.

Having a second-screen companion application, many features related to obtaining additional information from the PoIs can now be carried within the personal device, such as:

- selecting the hypervideo to playback;

- selecting a PoI to obtain additional information from it, whether it is visible at the moment or not;

- navigating that additional information, including text and pictures;

- accessing the complementary information of the PoI, such as their website or location within a map;

- sharing the additional information of the PoI to social networks;

- marking a PoI (and its related information) as "read later", so the user can focus on the audiovisual content;

- sending the additional information to other second-screen devices or to the TV application, so as to share the experience to the other viewers;

- seeking the audiovisual content to the moment when a PoI appears.

To enable the communication between the visualization module and the new second-screen application, a few key changes were made to the first and a Second Screen Server was introduced to intermediate between the second-screen application and the visualization module.

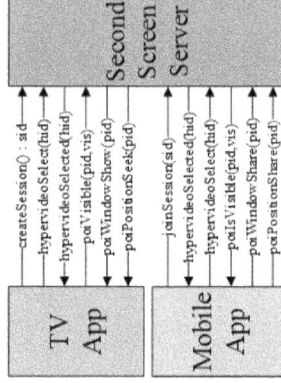

Figure 2. Diagram of the communication protocol between the visualization module, the second-screen app and the Second Screen Server

TV App — createSession() : sid → / hypervideoSelect(hid) → / hypervideoSelected(hid) → / poiVisible(pid,vis) → / poiWindowShow(pid) → / poiPositionSeek(pid) → Second Screen Server

Mobile App — joinSession(sid) → / hypervideoSelected(hid) → / hypervideoSelect(hid) → / poiIsVisible(pid,vis) → / poiWindowShare(pid) → / poiPositionShare(pid) → Second Screen Server

Communication protocol

Many interactive TV platforms have begun to propose their own second-screen framework, such as Samsung's [8] or LG's [9]. Besides, HbbTV 2.0 will include support for second-screen apps [10]. To avoid this mix of different techniques and frameworks, a simple, HTML5-based communication protocol is proposed using the WebSocket protocol [11], already implemented in most of Interactive TVs.

The purpose of the Second Screen Server is to act as the target of the communication by both clients, TV application and mobile app. It runs a socket server implemented in Javascript, using the Node.js runtime [12] in a Linux environment, thanks to einaro's ws WebSocket server implementation for Node.js [13].

The purpose of this server is to coordinate events between the TV application and the mobile applications associated to a single TV application. Therefore, it waits for a TV application to start a session, creating a unique session ID (sid), used by the second-screen applications to join it.

Once the link between TV and mobile application is done, the Second Screen Server bounces the events shown in Figure 2 from one application to the other(s), taking into account that more than one mobile application can simultaneously connected to a single TV application.

Changes made to the visualization module

A new second-screen option is shown in the visualization module on the TV. Once the user selects it, the TV application creates a WebSocket connection and requests a session ID to the Second Screen Server

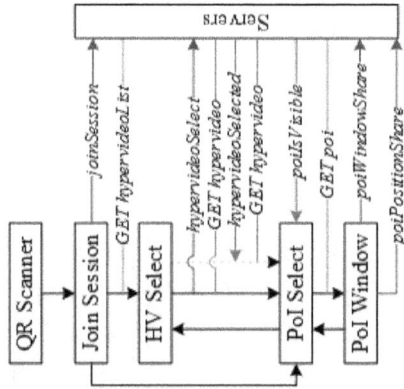

Figure 3. Detailed diagram of the relation between second-screen app states and communication protocol

and displays it encoded in a QR-code, to be scanned by the second-screen device(s), joining the session started by the TV application.

The TV application can fire these events:

- *createSession*, explained above;
- *hypervideoSelect*, fired when a hypervideo is selected to be played in the Visualization Module;
- *poiVisible*, fired when a PoI becomes visible or it leaves the screen.

The TV application listens for these events:

- *hypervideoSelected*, making the Visualization Module change the hypervideo being played;
- *poiWindowShow*, making the application display the additional information of a PoI;
- *poiPositionSeek*, making the TV application seek the audiovisual content to the next occurrence of a given PoI.

The second-screen companion app

The companion app is being developed as an HTML5 application, available through URL or inside a native app for Android devices (smartphones and tablets).

Following the same idea as the previous application, the companion app syncs with the TV app thanks to the Second Screen Server, and gets the needed hypervideo data from the Hypervideo Server. In Figure 3, sync messages sent from the app are shown as a right arrow, sync messages sent to the app as a left arrow and data requests without any arrow.

The application has a QR-code scanner built in, that enables it to join a session with the TV. (scanning the code outside the app would trigger opening it), sending the *joinSession* command to the Second Screen Server.

After doing that, the companion app gets the hypervideo ID being currently played (if any). Depending on this, the hypervideo selection window (no hypervideo is being played) or the PoI selection window (a hypervideo is being played) are displayed in the companion app.

In the hypervideo selection window, the list of hypervideos is received from the Hypervideo Server and displayed, allowing the user to select a hypervideo. When doing so, the event *hypervideoSelect* is fired and the data related to that hypervideo is requested. If another user selects a hypervideo, the event *hypervideoSelected* is received and the hypervideo data is requested too.

In the PoI Select state, the hypervideo is being played in the TV application, and the event *poiIsVisible* is received when a PoI enters or leaves the screen, as explained in the previous section.

The user can choose any PoI in the list, visible at that time or not, and request their additional information to the Hypervideo Server.

Finally, in the PoI Window state, the user can browse the additional information of a given PoI, as shown in Figure 4, and access its web page and location through the native apps in their device. Additionally, the user can emit two messages to the Second Screen Server: *poiWindowShare*, to bring that additional information window to the TV screen, and *poiPositionShare*, to

Figure 4. Prototype of the second-screen application, showing the additional information of a Point of Interest

make the visualization module seek for the next appearance of that PoI in the media played.

Finally, in the PoI Window state, the user can browse the additional information of a given PoI, and access its web page and location through the native apps in their device. Additionally, the user can emit two messages to the Second Screen Server: *poiWindowShare*, to bring that additional information window to the TV screen, and *poiPositionShare*, to make the visualization module seek for the next appearance of that PoI in the media played.

Content delivery through HbbTV

As introduced before, HbbTV is one of the present-day Interactive TV technologies to develop applications on. An interesting feature offered by this technology is the ability to interact with the broadcast emission.

This feature enables the Hypervideo platform to deliver the audiovisual track through the broadcast channel, instead of via streaming through the broadband channel.

The main obstacle of doing so was the need to pause the video in order to select a PoI and get their additional information, but with the introduction of the second-screen application, there is no need of doing so.

When playing the audiovisual track through the broadcast channel it is possible that the user starts the application in the middle of the program, so a synchronization mechanism is needed. This can be achieved thanks to the introduction of DSM-CC Stream Events to the HbbTV specification [14], section 8.2.1.

This way, the hypervideo ID and current position in time can be transmitted to the visualization module.

Conclusion

Two improvements for the Hypervideo platform have been introduced, which are still under development.

The addition of a second-screen application to the Hypervideo platform introduces a whole set of new opportunities to the user, permitting multiple viewers to obtain different information simultaneously.

A "faire mode" is being studied, so as not to permit the viewers to interfere each other by changing the video, or seeking the video track: they would only be able to obtain additional information in their devices.

To obtain additional information when playing audiovisual content through the broadcast channel, it could not be paused, and another technique was needed. The second-screen application proves to be adequate for this purpose.

References

1. Shawhney, N., Balcom, D., Smith, I. Hypercafe: Narrative and Aesthetic Properties of Hypervideo. In *Proc. Hypertext 1996*, ACM (1996), 1-10.

2. Landow, G., Kahn, P. Where's the Hypertext? The Dickens Web as a System-Independent Hypertext. In *Proc. Hypertext 1992*, ACM (1992), 149-160.

3. Bibiloni, T., Mascaró, M., Palmer, P., Oliver, A. Realidad Aumentada en HbbTV: Implementación de una plataforma Hypervideo para la Televisión Digital Conectada. In Proc. CISTI 2014, AISTI (2014), 743-748.

4. Bibiloni, T., Mascaró, M., Palmer, P., Oliver, A. Hypervideo: Augmented Reality on Interactive TV. In Proc. jAUTI 2014, ACM (2014).

5. Bibiloni, T., Oliver, A. Augmented Reality on HbbTV: An Hypervideo approach. In Demo Proc. TVX 2014, ACM (2014).

6. Courtois, C., D'heer, E. Second screen applications and tablet users: constellation, awareness, experience and interest. In Proc. EuroITV 2012, ACM (2012), 153-156.

7. Geerts, D., Leenheer, R., De Grooff, D., Negenman, J., Heijstraten, S. In Front of and Behind the Second Screen: Viewer and Producer Perspectives on a Companion App. In Proc. TVX 2014, ACM (2014), 95-102.

8. Samsung. Multi-Screen SDK. http://www.samsungdforum.com/Guide/?FolderName=d30&FileName=index.html

9. LG. Connect SDK. http://connectsdk.com

10. HbbTV Consortium. HbbTV 2.0 FAQ. https://www.hbbtv.org/pages/news_events/pdf/HbbTV%202.0%20FAQ.pdf

11. Fette, I., Melnikov, A. The WebSocket Protocol. RFC 6455. IETF (2011).

12. Joyent, Inc. Node.js. http://nodejs.org

13. Stangvik, E. ws: a node.js websocket implementation. http://einaros.github.io/ws

14. ETSI. TS 102 796 v1.1.1. Hybrid Broadcast Broadband TV. http://www.etsi.org/deliver/etsi_ts/102700_102799/102796/01.01.01_60/ts_102796v010101p.pdf

Design Requirements for PT-tv (Play Therapy with TV): An Observational Study on Play Therapy and TV Viewing

Kyoungwon Seo
Imagine Lab.
Hanyang University, Korea
cseo@hanyang.ac.kr

Garam Han
Imagine Lab.
Hanyang University, Korea
hangaraming@naver.com

Hyunju Lee
Dept. of Pediatrics, Hanyang
University Medical Center, Korea
2102069@hyumc.com

Hokyoung Ryu
Imagine Lab.
Hanyang University, Korea
hryu@hanyang.ac.kr

Jieun Kim
Imagine Lab.
Hanyang University, Korea
jkim2@hanyang.ac.kr

TVX'15, June 03-05, 2015, Brussels, Belgium
ACM 978-1-4503-3526-3/15/06.
http://dx.doi.org/10.1145/2745197.2755514

Abstract

Television (TV) is hard to be separated from our daily lives. Many infants and toddlers are in perpetual contact with TV and/or video content. Recent studies have focused on what characteristics of TV content would affect children's language development. We are interested in the developmental play therapy performed by pediatricians and how this can be translated into the TV content design to enhance their language development. An observational study was conducted for three weeks at the Infants Care Center. The behavioral patterns during the play therapy and TV viewing were compared and the design requirements for the play therapy with TV (PT-tv) were proposed.

Author Keywords

PT-tv; design requirement; developmental play therapy; TV viewing; infant and toddler; language development.

ACM Classification Keywords

H.5.m. Information interfaces and presentation (e.g., HCI): Miscellaneous.

Introduction

Since the first television (TV) content aired from the NBC studio in 1936, a large number of TV contents for infants and toddlers were created (e.g., BabyEinstein®,

Brainy Baby®, and Sesame Beginning®). These TV programs convinced many parents that the learning experience with TV could be not only educational but also entertaining. Recent research outcomes supported this belief. For example, Linebarger and Walker [7] argued that well-designed TV contents with the correct language uses and coherent narrative structure would contribute to positive language development.

Conversely, the American Academy of Pediatrics (AAP) recommends to be distant from the screen media as much as the children can, especially younger than 2 years [1]. Another evidence [10] also suggests a negative relationship between children's language development and the TV contents. These mixed results, along with the proliferation of various visual media in our daily lives, lead us to question if how TV content design could be bridged with child's cognitive development, in particular, their language development.

The joint-play with TV content is recently hailed by young parents [12] where infants and toddlers read interactive fairy tales on iPad™. Therefore, unless we can separate the children from TV, a key is how to design this new electronic experience being more beneficial and less harmful for children's language development. Here, it is noted that the developmental play therapy has long focused on children's cognitive development, and the studies of the play therapy might shed light on how to design TV viewing experiences better. In this regard, the aim of this article is to introduce the design requirements of new TV (or video) experiences for fostering children's cognitive development (especially, in this study, language). In so doing, several observational studies of the play therapy

were firstly carried out, and how TV (or video) viewing experience can borrow the characteristics of the play therapy for language development was considered.

Related Studies

A first comparative research on the relationship between the TV and the children's language development was carried out by Anderson [2]. He claimed that infants and toddlers learn more from a real-world experience with adults rather than they do it from TV viewing, and the term 'video deficit' was firstly proposed. Many experimental studies supported this video deficit phenomenon [e.g., 10].

However, as sketched out in Ron Suskin's book "Life, Animated", under a certain circumstance this video deficit effect disappears and TV (or video) viewing itself may strengthen children's cognitive and language development. In more academically-thorough experimental settings, for example, Barr et al. [4] demonstrated that repetitive TV viewing helped to improve learning for 12 to 18 months old children. In a similar vein, Krcmar [6] also presented positive effects of TV for 6 months old infants.

More recent studies, instead, focus on what factors or characteristics of the TV contents would make such effects. According to Okuma and Tanimura [9], the number of scenes with virtual characters that are directly facing TV viewers would be critical for children's development, and further on this, frequent scene changes might be significantly detrimental to children's speech development. In a similar vein, Richert et al. [10] emphasized the crucial role of parental interventions on TV (or video) viewing, to purport successful learning of words.

Behavior	Description
Keep direct eye contact	Try to keep a direct eye contact with children during play therapy
Incite curiosity	Before offering a new toy, incite children's curiosity about it
Allow exploration phase	After offering a new toy to children, let them explore and examine that toy for enough time
Provide playful experience	Let children enjoy a playful experience (e.g., provide a song which children love to sing)
Repeat for imitation	Repeat specific learned behavior by children for further imitation
Give positive feedback	After playing with a complex toy, give positive feedback like applause
Stimulate multimodal interaction	Provide various types of sensory interaction for carrying out a developmental play therapy

Table 1. The coding scheme from the developmental play therapy.

In sum, in order to provide successful children's language development with TV viewing, future TV content should have (i) appropriate design guidelines for fostering children's language development; and (ii) essential requirements for parental interactions while seeing TV. Reflecting on the issues briefly discussed above, Imagine Lab. and Hanyang University Medical Center worked together for children's language development procedure with TV contents. In this article, what the current therapies are performed by pediatricians for cognitive development are studied.

Methods

An observational study was conducted for three weeks at the Infants Care Center, Hanyang University Medical Center, where provides both the developmental play therapy and the TV educational program for premature infants. The aim of this clinical program is to educate caregivers about how to enhance children's cognitive abilities with play therapy and/or TV viewing at home. We observed each treatment (i.e., developmental play therapy and TV educational program) performed by pediatricians and therapists (see Figure 1). This observational study was designed to identify children's different behaviors between the play therapy and the TV viewing, by which to examine what aspects are in need of effective TV UX (User eXperience) design.

A written consent form was provided to the parents before conducting the observational study. The children with significant disabilities (e.g., intelligence) were excluded. A total of eight children (age: 6.13±3.76 months; three females) participated and the whole sessions were recorded (play therapy: 28.45±5.56 minutes; TV viewing: 7.50±1.03 minutes). To prevent any impact caused by the video recording, the video

was hidden from the children's UFOV (useful field of view).

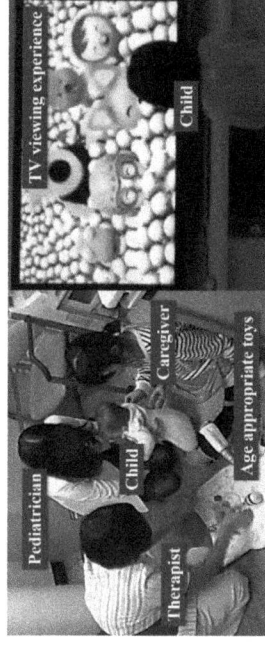

Figure 1: Developmental play therapy (left) and TV viewing experience with 'Pororo the Little Penguin' (right).

There is no predefined coding scheme to describe children's behaviors during the play therapy and TV viewing, so an exploratory analysis was first applied by two independent researchers. A workshop session was conducted with this result (by one pediatrician and two therapists) and derived the coding scheme of frequent behavioral patterns (see Tables 1 & 2). Based on this coding scheme, after one researcher conducted a behavior analysis, the other researcher independently rated the same subject with commercial behavior analysis software (ObserverXT 12). The inter-rater agreement between two researchers was then tested (k=0.83). The time proportion of each behavioral pattern was then interpreted.

Results

As shown in Table 3, the frequent behaviors during the play therapy and the TV viewing were different. The independent samples t-test showed that critical behaviors during the play therapy were 'keep direct eye contact' (56.58%), 'allow exploration phase' (45.16%),

Behavior	Description
Keep direct eye contact	Characters in TV contents show direct eye gaze to infants and toddlers
Incite curiosity	Incite children's curiosity about content's scenario
Allow exploration phase	Before progressing scenario, let children explore and examine what will be happening
Provide playful experience	Let children enjoy a playful experience (e.g., provide a song which children love to sing)
Repeat for imitation	Repeat specific learned behavior by children for further imitation
Give positive feedback	When children accomplish a certain task in content, give positive feedback
Stimulate multimodal interaction	Provide various types of sensory interaction while progressing TV content scenario

Table 2. The coding scheme from the TV educational program.

and 'repeat for imitation' (63.29%). In particular, 'repeat for imitation' most frequently occurred, such as children's repetitive actions like 'rolling over', 'clapping hands' and 'babbling'. In a stark contrast, most significantly repeated behaviors from TV viewing experience were 'provide playful experience' (89.11%) and 'stimulate multimodal interaction' (73.33%).

Behavior coding scheme	Play therapy (%)	TV viewing experience (%)
Keep direct eye contact	**56.58**^{**}	6.22
Incite curiosity	16.37	21.78
Allow exploration phase	**45.16**^{**}	9.56
Provide playful experience	12.81	**89.11**^{**}
Repeat for imitation	**63.29**^{**}	10.89
Give positive feedback	22.52	15.78
Stimulate multimodal interaction	56.58	**73.33**^{**}

Table 3: Time proportion of behavior coding scheme on play therapy and TV viewing experience (^{**} p<0.05).

Considering the different behavior revealed in the play therapy and TV viewing, we further interpreted 'keep direct eye contact', 'allow exploration phase', and 'repeat for imitation' that are mainly employing children's language development.

Discussion

Keep direct eye contact

First, "keep direct eye contact" was one of the most crucial behaviors in the play therapy (56.58%), but not observed in TV viewing (6.22%). In the play therapy, the pediatrician, the therapist, and the caregiver tried to induce an eye contact with children by voice cues,

interesting gestures, and cooperative motions like high-five (see Figure 2). On the contrary, the TV viewing provides only a short period of time for keeping a direct eye contact between virtual characters and children.

Recent studies supported the importance of this direct eye contact for cognitive development. For instance, Urakawa et al. [11] investigated the infant's cerebral hemodynamic responses and eye tracking movements in response to social play with the partner's direct gaze. They showed that the partner's direct eye contact shifts an infant's attention to the partner's eyes for interactive communication, and specifically activates the brain region which is essential for social interaction, by which we can readily screen some developmental disorders, e.g., autistic spectrum disorder.

Allow exploration phase

Second, while playing with children, the behavior like "allowing exploration phase for children" often occurred in the play therapy (45.16%), compared to TV viewing (9.56%). In the play therapy program (see Figure 3), the pediatrician and therapist promote children's intentional exploration with various environments and objects (e.g., put a toy in mouth, spill water, and throw a remote control). This is deliberate to give the children a chance of divergent thinking, so creative usages with the objects are to be examined (note that functional fixedness of an object can be demonstrated in 6 to 7 years old [5]).

The exploration phase draws much attention from recent studies. Whipple et al. [13] focused on parental supportive behaviors in the context of infant's exploration and found them to be linked to 'security of attachment' which is conceptualized as an infants'

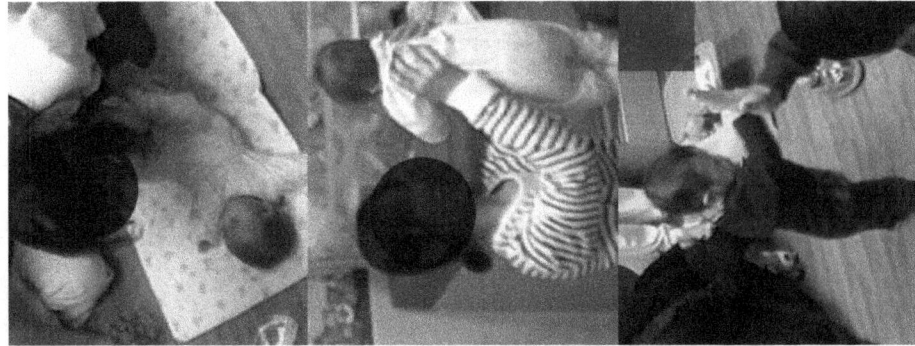

Figure 1: Eye contact with child during the developmental play therapy.

attachment to the real world objects being detached from their closest person (i.e., mum). Okuma and Tanimura [9] found that the passive TV contents give no time for children to explore and detach (and attach) with the objects from the contents. This might lead delayed speech development problems.

Repeat for imitation

Third, *"repeat for imitation"* takes place most frequently in the play therapy (63.29%). While watching TV contents, children usually become a passive viewer (10.89%). There exist only a few chances to imitate virtual character's behavior and/or songs. On the contrary, as shown in Figure 4, during the play therapy, the pediatrician and therapist deliberately ask the children to copy and utter simple syllables or words, behavior (e.g., build a block toy), action (e.g., bang the table), and expression (e.g., imitate a smiling face).

Many studies emphasized the imitation as the most important developmental stage in language development. For instance, through repetitive imitations, children can recognize having their actions imitated by others (i.e., parallel play) and this kind of interpersonal communication (i.e., proximity play) promotes feelings of affinity and a sense of emotional connection to others. This mutual imitation is also an important aspect of social-cognitive development, further, for social language development derived from this skill [3, 8].

Conclusion & Future Direction

The three behaviors briefly discussed above suggest that the current TV viewing experience is far from effective support of children's language development. Hence, to make beneficial TV viewing for children, rich

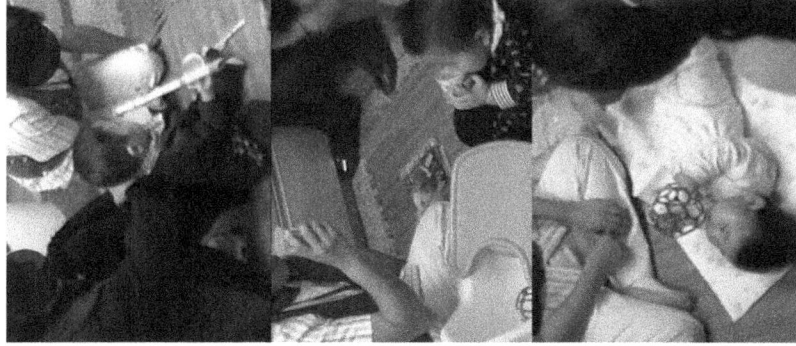

Figure 3: Promoted exploration phase during the developmental play therapy.

behaviors presented in the developmental play therapy need to be translated into the TV/video content design.

Behavior	Design requirement
Keep direct eye contact	Big enough characters for children's eyesight
	A virtual character's direct gaze
Allow exploration phase	Parent's support and encouragement
	Enough time for exploring and examining
Repeat for imitation	Repeated character's behavior
	Parent's imitation of children's behaviors

Table 4: Critical behavior for cognitively beneficial TV viewing experience and its design requirements.

Table 4 summarizes some design requirements for the TV UX designer to develop TV viewing experiences for children. First, increasing a direct eye contact while watching TV contents is important. Though it is a common sense that TV viewing would provide a higher level of visual attention, we found that our participating children (note 6 months to 10 months infants participated in this study) had less direct eye contact with the characters on TV. Perhaps this is because the virtual characters on the TV content were not big enough (*Big enough characters for children's eyesight*), and they did not act like the real world characters (*A virtual character's direct gaze*).

Second, to promote language development, children's exploration phase should be intentionally inserted into the TV content. In this regard, the TV content 'Blue's

Clues' is noted because it intentionally asks the children to search out some objects at home (e.g., balls, scissors, apples and so forth), and even give some time break to find such objects. To enhance such exploratory TV experiences, how to promote children's curiosity about various elements should be considered and encouraged by parental supportive behaviors (*Parent's support and encouragement*). In a similar vein, TV contents itself need to provide sufficient time for children (*Enough time for exploring and examining*).

Finally, the repeat for imitation should be considered in TV experience. Of course, as one can see from 'Blue's Clues' or 'Teletubbies', the same TV content is repeated twice. However, what we are suggesting here is the repetition of a certain behavior by TV characters for promoting children to copy and utter simple syllables or words, behavior, and actions (*Repeated character's behavior*) [7]. Moreover, parents need to copy children's behaviors while watching TV contents (*Parent's imitation of children's behaviors*). Through this mimicry by the parents, children have feelings of affinity and a sense of emotional connection [8].

In future work, more observational study will be conducted. Also, based on the derived design requirements, we are now developing a provocative prototype of TV content. This will be installed in the Infant Care Center for validation of the design requirements proposed in this study.

References

1. American Academy of Pediatrics. Policy statement on media education. *Pediatrics 126,* (2011), 1-7.

2. Anderson, D.R., & Pempek, T.A. Television and very young children. *American Behavioral Scientist 48,* 5 (2005), 505-522.

3. Bandura, A. *Social learning theory.* Prentice Hall Press, Upper Saddle River, NJ, USA, 1997.

4. Barr et al. The effect of repetition on imitation from television during infancy. *Developmental Psychobiology 49,* 2 (2007), 196-207.

5. German, T.P., & Defeyter, M.A. Immunity to functional fixedness in young children. *Psychonomic Bulletin & Review 7,* 4 (2000), 707-712.

6. Krcmar, M. Can social meaningfulness and repeat exposure help infants and toddlers overcome the video deficit? *Media Psychology 13,* 1 (2010), 31-53.

7. Linebarger, D.L., & Walker, D. Infants' and toddlers' television viewing and language outcomes. *American Behavioral Scientist 48,* 5 (2005), 624-645.

8. Meltzoff et al. *Developmental Perspectives on Action Science: Lessons from Infant Imitation and Cognitive Neuroscience.* The MIT Press, Cambridge, MA, USA, 2013.

9. Okuma, K., & Tanimura, M. A preliminary study on the relationship between characteristics of TV content and delayed speech development in young children. *Infant Behavior and Development 32,* 3 (2009), 312-321.

10. Richert et al. Word learning from baby videos. *Archives of pediatrics & adolescent medicine 164,* 5 (2010), 432-437.

11. Urakawa et al. Selective medial prefrontal cortex responses during live mutual gaze interactions in human infants: An fNIRS study. *Brain topography,* (2014), 1-11.

12. Wartella, E.A., & Lauricella, A.R. Should babies be watching television and DVDs?. Pediatric Clinics of North America 59, 3 (2012), 613-621.

13. Whipple et al. Broadening the Study of Infant Security of Attachment: Maternal Autonomy-support in the Context of Infant Exploration. *Social Development 20,* 1 (2011), 17-32.

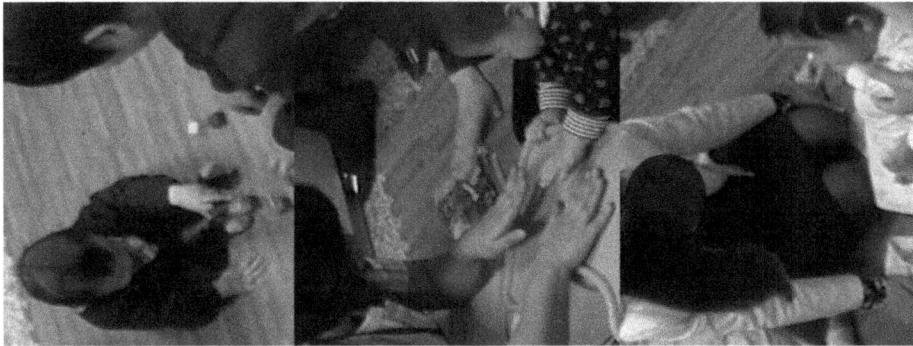

Figure 4: Repeat for imitation during the developmental play therapy.

Learning Lessons for Second Screen from Board Games

Rinze Leenheer

CUO | Social Spaces, iMinds /

KU Leuven

Parkstraat 45 Bus 3605

Leuven, 3000 Belgium

rinze.leenheer@soc.kuleuven.be

David Geerts

CUO | Social Spaces, iMinds /

KU Leuven

Parkstraat 45 Bus 3605

Leuven, 3000 Belgium

david.geerts@soc.kuleuven.be

Jeroen Vanattenhoven

CUO | Social Spaces, iMinds /

KU Leuven

Parkstraat 45 Bus 3605

Leuven, 3000 Belgium

jeroen.vanattenhoven@soc.kuleuv
en.be

TVX 2015, June 3–5, 2015, Brussels, Belgium.
ACM 978-1-4503-3526-3/15/06.
http://dx.doi.org/10.1145/2745197.2755515

Abstract

This paper identifies important requirements for second
screen (game) companion apps. Participants were
invited to create their own (board) game to play
alongside a TV show. Afterwards they were interviewed
about their experience. Analyses of the games and
interviews lead to some valuable insights in what
contributes to an engaging 'TV game'. Lessons learned
include: using events on the TV show to influence the
game, and striking the right balance between luck and
skill elements.

Author Keywords

Interactive TV; Second Screen; User Experience; Board
Games

ACM Classification Keywords

H5.1 [Information Interfaces and presentation]:
Multimedia information systems – audio, video; H5.m
[Information Interfaces and presentation (e.g., HCI)]:
Miscellaneous

Introduction

Second screen companion apps have featured in many
different types of shows and offer different
functionalities [2]. One of these functionalities is
enriching the show by offering additional content and
interaction. Quiz and game shows are a popular format

to add interaction to. In previous research we looked at the way people interact with their second screen [3]. This resulted in a set of requirements to take into account when developing second screen applications. This paper will try and do the same for quiz and game apps specifically.

Related Work

Second screen game companion apps

There has been quite a lot of research on the topic of quiz and game related companion apps and the way people interact with them. Villegas et al [6] tried to establish a profile for the 'Remote Contestant', a person who actively participates while watching a TV show. Similarly Pifarre et al [4] try to establish the profile of the 'remote contestant'. The main findings are that 'the remote contestant' wants fast and simple interaction combined with smooth synchronisation. Almeida et al [1] created an application that "combines some social games characteristics with iTV features". Results showed participants are strongly motivated to continue using this type of application with their friends. Results also showed the potential of this type of applications to engage viewers more with the content on TV. Sperring and Strandvall [5] investigated 'Enigma', "the first Finnish TV game show with fully integrated, synchronized interactivity". Similar to the other research they found that the interactivity had added value to participants and made their experience more exciting. At the same time however they reported the interactivity took away a great deal of time and attention from the video.

These papers show, that participants generally like the added interaction of second screen game companion apps. However concerns are still there about attention

and engagement. This paper tries to identify ways to make these apps more engaging by taking a step back and looking at what kind of games groups of viewers create themselves when asked to create a game to play alongside a TV-Show.

Board games

People have been playing board games for generations. They are often enjoyed with family or friends and people tend to get quite competitive and engaged by them. There is almost no scientific literature to be found dealing with board games (as opposed to video games) so the element classification used in the rest of this paper is from the authors' own review of popular board game elements.

Methodology

Ten groups of users (three groups of two, four groups of three and three groups of four) were recruited. There were couples, groups of friends, and families that knew each other well and watched TV together at least occasionally. The age range was between 10 and 52 (M=26.1 stdev=10,6) years old. The groups were invited to our living lab which is setup to resemble a living room see **Figure 1** for an impression.

Participants were told that they would watch an episode of The Voice of Holland. The Voice is an audition show, in which candidates sing a song in front of a jury of four, who cannot see them. If a jury member thinks the candidate is good enough they can press a button and turn around. If one jury member turns the candidate goes to the next round on that jury members' team. If more then one jury member turns around, the candidate can pick between them. We chose the Voice because it is a well-known entertainment format. We

Figure 1. Living lab setup.

did not choose a game or quiz show because we felt it would incite participants to just play along with the questions on the show and limit their creativity in creating their own type of game. We chose an episode of the Voice of Holland because it is broadcasted on a Dutch channel that is not regularly available in Belgium (all participants were Dutch speakers so there was no added language barrier). This would minimize the risk that any of our participants had already seen the specific episode and indeed no one had seen it.

Before they would start watching the episode, participants were asked to create a game that they could play while watching the Voice and they would all participate in. To help them create a game, they were offered a selection of attributes. See **Figure 2** for an overview.

The attributes included items to facilitate timing, score keeping, representation, and chance elements. When they were done creating their game they were asked to explain it to the researcher. Then the episode was started and the participants were instructed to simply watch the show and play their game. After about an hour of watching the show and playing the game, the research leader stopped the show and interviewed the participants on their experience.

Data Analysis

First the interviews were transcribed. The researcher singled out all relevant quotes and observations from the data and turned them into snippets (individual notes). These snippets were then grouped according to their content. The emerging groups were given a name, which resulted in a number of categories. When all

snippets were allotted to a category the categories were reviewed and renamed where appropriate.

Results

First the games that were created by the groups will be briefly discussed. In the second part the categories that emerged from the interviews will be presented. Two groups created a game that was unrelated to the TV show. This was not explicitly forbidden but we felt these unrelated games created a very different experience for the players. This in itself is a very interesting finding but not one we feel we can explore thoroughly without more groups playing unrelated games. So we left these groups out of the analysis for the current paper and may revisit the concept in a follow up paper.

The Games

All the remaining groups created a game that was closely related to the audition part of The Voice. Either the choice of the candidate for a jury member or the jury members for the candidate (or both) was central to the way the game was played. All but one of them did this by having the players predict the candidate or jury choice. Players who made the right prediction were rewarded with points or play money. Players in the last group chose a jury member at the start and would score points according to that jury member's choices throughout the rest of the game. There was one more group that linked themselves to a particular jury member but they could still make prediction on what their jury member would do. The games from these two groups also featured a board game that allowed for an element of progress (the position on the board) other then pure score. In three games there was an element of gambling involved where players could influence the amount of points they could win or lose per prediction

Figure 2. Attributes participants could use to create their games.

by betting a certain amount of play money. Three others involved a chance element where the role of a dice would determine the amount of points that were scored. Finally one group added consequences other then winning or losing to the game by means of punishments they could buy for others with there winnings. These punishments included things like doing pushups for a minute or watching the next song upside down on the couch.

The interviews

The interview served to question the participants about the 'why' of their games and their experience. From the interview data different clusters emerged that will be discussed below. The clusters are illustrated with quotes from participants. The participants group number and if they were male/female is noted between brackets at the end of the quote.

INTEGRATING THE SHOW AND THE GAME

As mentioned in the "Games" paragraph, all groups used elements from the shows' auditions to 'power' the game i.e. the events on the show influenced the game. What people like about this is that it feels natural to use elements from the show you are already watching to 'power' an accompanying game. The games all took the audition moment and following jury/candidate decision as a part that influenced their game in a certain way.

"The choices are the most interesting thing of the show and now something is linked to that. You are always involved with the show about who will turn around and now there

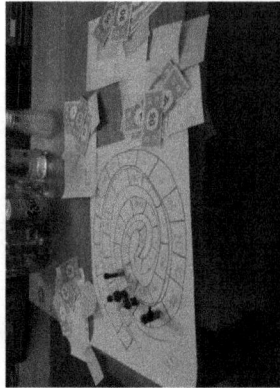

Figure 3. Game created by group 1.

is something connected and its more fun to see who will turn." (G4, M1)

Viewers identify with the people they see on the show. This can also be seen in the games where two games had the players assume the role of jury members.

"That's what you do in computer games link yourself to an avatar. You personify with a jury member you almost want to press the button yourself. You feel more involved." (G3, M)

DISTRACTION VS. ENGAGEMENT

Closely related to this is the concept of distraction vs. engagement. The game is an extra activity besides viewing the show and can lead to players being somewhat distracted from the show. However a number of players also feel that they are more involved with the show. Because they feel paying attention to the show could increase their chance of winning, they claim it actually increases their engagement to the show.

"I wasn't really good at it but it was fun to do it also makes it more exciting. Normally it is just watching them sing and now you are really listening well and everything they say before they start to sing can be important so you listen to it more carefully." (G2, F1)

Three groups added an hourglass to the game they all used it to limit the time they got to make a choice in predicting jury decisions. Besides the added action element, two groups mentioned this also made the periods outside these 30 seconds more relaxed.

"Otherwise you would be stressing throughout the song should I still make a choice?" (G8, M) "Yes after the 30seconds you know the choice has been made." (G8, F1)

SKILL VS. CHANCE

One of the main debates between the participants is the one between skill and chance factors determining the outcome of the game. Some prefer chance to be the main determinant because it makes for a level playing field.

"Because it is not about being smarter to win but you all have the same chance to win. Nobody is disadvantaged to win." (G6, M)

Others prefer skill to be the main determinant because it gives them a feeling of control and it feels like more of an accomplishment if they end up being the winner.

"Then it is in your own hands. If you think it will be four and the dice shows one that's terrible. (G2, F2) "I think it gives more satisfaction when you guess correctly." (G2, M1)

There are also players that prefer to have a combination of the two. In two games, skill affected if

you would get points but chance determined how many. This gave the feeling that you always had a chance to catch up even after a few wrong answers if you rolled a high number on the dice.

All in all it seems best to create a game that has enough chance involved so that anyone can win and you won't be out of the game after just a few 'misses' but also put in enough of a skill factor so participants feel in control and accomplished when they win.

GOALS AND CONSEQUENCES

All of the games included a scorekeeping element, which was used to determine a winner at the end of the game. The main reason to keep score was to have the goal of winning included in the game, to have something 'at stake'. Most participants claimed this lead to more excitement.

"I thought it was very important that there were points so you could see at the end who was the best. Because then you have a goal in the game and not just a game." (G7, F)

One of the groups took it a bit further and included a form of punishments to add to the excitement and the fun (being afraid of punishment and the joy of handing them out).

SOCIAL INTERACTION

A big part of the enjoyment seemed to come from the interaction between the people playing the game. Sharing laughs commenting to each other and the competitive feeling of wanting to beat the others. All our participants knew each other well and this seems

List of Requirements for Competitive Applications

Let elements of the show directly influence the rules of the second screen game.

Have the game increase identification of viewers with people from the show.

Let occurrences on the show have a(n) (perceived) impact on the game to focus viewer attention.

To lessen distraction, confine the games decisive moments to brief periods.

Have enough (perceived) skill elements to make a victory feel rewarding.

Have enough chance elements so that anyone can win and comebacks are possible.

Have something at stake; at the very least have points and a winner.

Focus on competition between people who know each other.

an important factor in the enjoyment of playing and watching together.

"That you have fun with friends. That you sat together and shared laughs, that is also part of watching TV. You can also watch alone but with others its more fun you also comment to each other, you sit together with friends you laugh and have a fun evening." (G4, M1)

The lessons taken away from each of these clusters lead to a list of requirements that are listed in the sidebar.

Conclusion

By having players create their own game from board game elements, valuable lessons were learned towards creating an engaging second screen companion app. These requirements combined with the more general requirements from our previous research will help create an app that will be evaluated with a group of testers. These testers will be able to play the game at home during regular broadcast. This is part of the TV-Ring project (www.tv-ring.eu). These requirements should also prove useful to others creating second screen apps that offer the user a play along game experience.

Acknowledgements

The research leading to these results was carried out in the TV-Ring project (EC grant agreement ICT PSP-325209).

References

[1] Almeida, P., Ferraz, J., Pinho, A., & Costa, D. (2012, July). Engaging viewers through social TV games. In *Proceedings of the 10th European conference on Interactive tv and video* (pp. 175-184). ACM.

[2] Cesar, P., Bulterman, D. C., & Jansen, A. J. (2008). Usages of the Secondary Screen in an Interactive Television Environment: Control, Enrich, Share, and Transfer Television Content. In *Proc. of the 6th European Conf. on Changing Television Environments* (pp. 168-177). Berlin, Heidelberg: Springer-Verlag.

[3] Geerts, D., Leenheer, R.A., De Grooff, D., Negenman, J., Heijstraten, S. (2014) In Front of And Behind The Second Screen: Viewer and Producer Perspectives on a Companion App. *TVX 2014*

[4] Pifarre, M., Villegas, E., Fonseca, D., Redondo, E., Navarro, I., Al-Mousa, M. M., ... & Alade, F. O. (2012). Applying user experience methods on TV quiz shows interaction design. *Ubiquitous Computing and Communication Journal, 7(1)*.

[5] Sperring, S., & Strandvall, T. (2008). Viewers' experiences of a TV quiz show with integrated interactivity. *Intl. Journal of Human-Computer Interaction, 24(2)*, 214-235.

[6] Villegas, E., Pifarré, M., & Fonseca, D. (2011, July). Exploring new interaction systems on quiz shows. In *Multimedia and Expo (ICME), 2011 IEEE International Conference on* (pp. 1-6). IEEE.

Small-Scale Cross Media Productions. A Case Study of a Documentary Game

Oliver Korn
University of Stuttgart, VIS
70569 Stuttgart, Germany
oliver.korn@acm.org

Adrian Rees
Korion GmbH
71640 Ludwigsburg, Germany
adrian.rees@korion.de

Uwe Schulz
Stuttgart Media University
70569 Stuttgart, Germany
schulz@hdm-stuttgart.de

TVX'15, June 03-05, 2015, Brussels, Belgium
ACM 978-1-4503-3526-3/15/06.
http://dx.doi.org/10.1145/2745197.2755516

Abstract

With major intellectual properties there is a long tradition of cross-media value chains – usually starting with books and comics, then transgressing to film and TV and finally reaching interactive media like video games. In recent years the situation has changed: (1) smaller productions start to establish cross media value chains; (2) there is a trend from sequential towards parallel content production.

In this work we describe how the production of a historic documentary takes a cross media approach right from the start. We analyze how this impacts the content creation pipelines with respect to story, audience and realization. The focus of the case study is the impact on the production of a documentary game. In a second step we reflect on the experiences gained so far and derive recommendations for future small-scale cross media productions.

Author Keywords

Cross media production; 360-degrees content; gaming

ACM Classification Keywords

I.6.8 [**Types of Simulation**]: Gaming; Animation; K.8.0 [**General**]: Games; D.2.9 [**Management**]: Productivity; Programming teams

Introduction

When dealing with cross media productions, a common approach for a long time was to have a main medium as the starting point. From there, several spin-offs contributed to the story by offering additional perspectives or extra content. *Batman* is a good example for a classical intellectual property (IP) which transgressed into a broad range of cross media content. Based on the long history of comic book publications, the story of *Batman* transcended into a proto-text [1] all subsequent productions could draw from. The famous example *Tomb Raider* marked a turning point: in this case a video game became the proto-text for commercially successful mainstream movies, books and comics.

With the small cross media production *Conquest of the Seven Seas* (Figure 1) we try to pass the restraints of the established concepts of primary and secondary content. Instead we establish a production cycle that consciously targets each aspect of a transmedia development process. We identified a set of requirements that could be helpful for the success of future small-scale cross media productions.

State of the Art

The term cross media refers to the adaptation of the same text, or proto-text in different media: as "progressive or contemporary adaptations on different channels" [1]. For most TV productions, until recently, the creation of additional content for other channels or platforms usually started after the main production was completed or well established [11]. As Jenkins [8] explains, there were attempts of co-operation between TV and gaming early on – however, it was difficult to align the different production cycles and establish a

suitable production strategy: "These relationships were difficult to sustain, since all parties worried about losing creative control, and since the time spans for development and distribution in the media were radically different" [8].

These structural differences probably result from the traditional media characteristics: while TV productions often involve a long-term storyline that necessarily results in a longer production time, games usually are produced in a concentrated effort.

This is why Murray distinguishes between primary and secondary content [11] where the main storyline is almost exclusively told in the primary content. More recently this has changed to a production strategy where both streams of content are produced simultaneously, e.g. the first episode of a TV series along with the first entries of a web diary and a mobile game – or even a companion app like HBO Go for Game of Thrones which provides annotations synchronized with the video feed. However, the biased classification remains – and often it produces results where the secondary content stays behind the originality and quality of the primary medium.

The amount of companion apps for *Game of Thrones*, registered on Google Play and other mobile marketplaces shows that there is a high interest in cross media strategies. Yet many companion apps just contain a series of trivia questions or, in the case of *Game of Thrones*, do not provide enough information to bring new viewers up to speed on the highly complex story world of the primary medium.

Figure 1: Still from the trailer of Conquest of the Seven Seas. The ship was modeled in 3D and used in all platforms: TV, video game and web log.

The rising interest in cross media strategies has arrived in the games industry [7]. Yet the resulting games often still have the typical flaws of "secondary content": they use a generic gameplay mechanism – often puzzle games – and merely decorate it with visual elements [11] from the primary content.

While the TV series *Lost* aroused great involvement of fans, who tried to discover parts of the backstory on their own (resulting in an online encyclopedia with broad user participation), the accompanying video game was considered dissatisfactory by these fans because of the "poor imitation of the original cast [...] and confusions it created over which non-broadcast story elements were 'canonical' and part of the central storyworld and which were just throw-away riffs on similar situations" [11].

Interestingly, the first major commercial film based on a game as primary content was not well received by critics: Turan from the *Los Angeles Times* called *Tomb Raider* "almost completely lacking in genuine thrills" and Morgenstern from *Wall Street Journal* described it as "remarkably joyless" [6]. Yet the movie was a highly successful production featuring the actress Jolie in the main role and generating about $270 million in sales worldwide with a budget of just $115 million [5].

These examples indicate that IPs with established names, brands and a well-known storyworld can sometimes afford to have generic productions in their cross media mix and still be able to generate production value. While this might work as a strategy for large IPs, small productions with on new or unfamiliar intellectual properties need to employ different strategies.

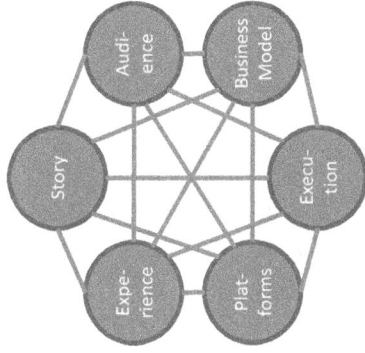

Figure 2: Transmedia Development Process as described by Pratten [13].

Case Study

In our case study we took the approach of going cross media from the start in a transmedia development process (Figure 2) as described by Pasman [12] and Pratten [13]. The proto-text of *Conquest of the Seven Seas* is based on the actual historic events of the explorations of Ferdinand Magellan and Francis Drake. They are known to most people, at least to some extent, with a long history of precedent productions each trying to convey different parts of the stories, altering and romanticizing them to a certain degree.

This makes most historical events ideal topics for cross media adaptations and especially for small-scale productions: without having to establish settings and characters in a long story arc, well-known historical subjects offer a convincing story while still at the same time surprising moments or new insights previously unknown to most viewers can be introduced. The story is brought to life in three intertwined productions:

- A two part TV documentary for the TV-channel arte. Here, two contemporary researches try to unveil the political and strategic calculations of the monarchs of that time.

- The strategy game *Conquest of the Seven Seas*, released in parallel to the documentaries. In the game the player meets one of the protagonists, Sir Francis Drake. However, the narrative point of view is different as the player is his antagonist.

- The interactive weblog called *The Secret Captain's Log* where each chapter covers a different waypoint of Magellan's journey. The aim is to let users explore the daily life of sailors on board of those ships and get insights of their thoughts and motivations.

Production and Audience

The production's film part consists of two 52 minutes documentaries with narratives, reenactment scenes and interviews. The visual style (Figure 4) is a "comic-like virtual world with real actors operating in a CGI universe" [4]. This approach bridges the production's different content types.

Figure 4: The documentaries' reenactment scenes feature a specific comic-look which bridges the boundary to the other cross media elements.

"By retaining the strong emotive capacity of real characters and combining this with the endless possibilities of the digital world, we are able to employ an entirely new and innovative approach to the visualization of historical documentaries." [4]

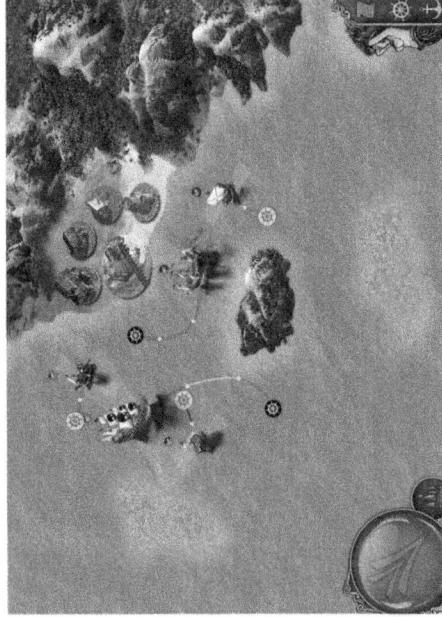

Figure 5: The strategy game is browser-based and uses the classic isometric perspective of old-school strategy titles. The fights are turn-based to generate a feeling of control.

The turn-based strategy game can be played in a browser, since it was developed in HTML-5. In the fight view it uses an isometric perspective (Figure 5) to produce a 3D impression while staying in a 2D environment [9]. In the explorer view the player navigates through maps based on historic originals. While a 3D look looks was important to build a bridge towards the documentary films, the historical maps encompass the production's historical authenticity.

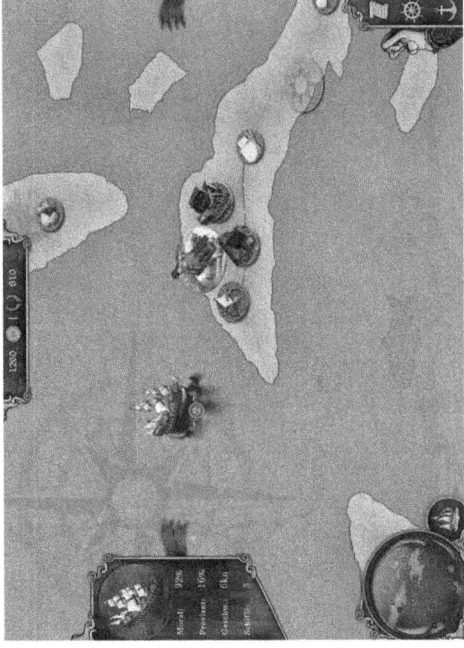

Figure 6: The game's strategy view is based on historic maps.

The interactive logbook is a web application consisting of several chapters, one for each waypoint of Magellan's journey. It features film sequences, 2D animation as well as original entries out of Magellan's logbook.

In a transmedia development process special attention has to be paid on how each platform supports different perspectives, so various narrative approaches are used accordingly. As audiences can be classified into types according to the amount of involvement they are willing to devote [1], the ideal cross media production should be designed to address all of them. The coverage of different reception types allows the audience to switch between the media according to mood, level of interest or time budget.

In our cross media production we tried to achieve this completeness as follows:

- the TV documentary addresses the users preferring a 'Lean Back Experience' (Figure 4)
- the strategy game requires more interaction in a 'Lean Forward Experience' (Figures 5, 6)
- the web log mixes both types and adds historical depth for interested users.

This freedom of choice for the user was not only a paradigm between the three productions – it also was a goal within each one of them. In the game the user was allowed to choose the level of detail of the historical background. The story is told through different characters, who grant optional access to a deeper story level. Thus we avoid offering unnecessary information to an audience interested in special aspects of the user experience. For example the player is told by his advisor (Figure 7), that Drake seized one of his ships and left a note on the mast, mocking his opponents. This historically accurate message can optionally be accessed by a link to a story module, where all game events are put into the historical context.

Recommendations

Pasman states that in smaller cross media productions the design process will most likely be a "pragmatic mix of the principles and characteristics of the design disciplines that constitute the individual platforms, such as web design, mobile design, game design, or graphic design" [12].

However, during the production according to the transmedia development process we noticed several issues not covered. We describe these and provide three recommendations (Rec 1–3) for future small-scale cross media productions.

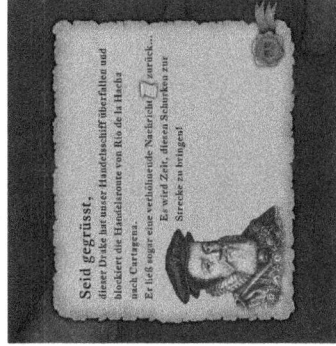

Figure 7: The advisor explains the relevant story elements and offers optional historical content for inclined players.

Recommendation 1:
The proto-text must be made transparent before production start to all stakeholders.

Recommendation 2:
Legal issues regarding the copyright of assets have to be clarified before the production starts.

Recommendation 3:
All assets should be shared on a repository accessible by all stakeholders. Within the repository generic and platform-specific content has to be clearly separated.

The first thing we noticed is that in a small cross media production it is essential that all stakeholders are familiar with the proto-text (Rec 1). For IPs with a historical background we found that it is mandatory to invest some time in research; if not this knowledge is missing during the production and there are issues like graphic designers developing ship models which are historically inaccurate. The content production then needs to establish a design process that covers the main user experience and links the various media platforms on the story level. The individual platforms like film, web or games can then can be considered as means to express these ideas in different ways for different types of audiences.

In our case study the VFX production company for TV had completed a substantial part of the 3D work before the production cycle of the game part could start. However, several assets could not be used because of legal issues. Even in small-scale productions such issues have to be clarified in advance (Rec 2) so various teams within the different companies can work together on a functional level. Another challenge was that the distributed contributors had to make sure to stay in consistency not only with the overall vision (see Rec 1) but also with each other. No artist or engineer enjoys to copy or "adapt" the work of a colleague: so if a common repository for assets is established in the production process (Rec 3) the teams usually have no problems sharing to avoid doing work twice. A repository has synergetic effects leaving more time both for generating platform-specific content and optimizing the content generic to all platforms. To achieve this, however, recommendation 1 has to be taken into account very early in the production process.

Work in Progress

TVX 2015, June 3–5, 2015, Brussels, Belgium

154

Conclusion

Based on an overview of the state of the art in cross media productions we introduced a case study on a small-scale production with documentary films, a strategy game and a web log. We described how the differences between the media platforms can be used to appeal to different audiences.

During our production we faced challenges related to small-scale productions not covered by the current transmedia development process. Based on these experiences we derived three recommendations for future productions.

When story designers, graphic artists and programmers work together early in the project and are not held back by legal issues, the media platforms specifics can be used to create more and better content. Moreover it is possible to generate a synergistic effect between the creation of generic and platform-specific content if these are shared and aggregated in a common repository.

References

1. Ciancia, M. Transmedia phenomena: new practices in participatory and experiential content production. In *Proc. EuroITV 2013*, ACM Press (2012), 41-44.
2. Conquest of the Seven Seas - Captain Ferdinand Magellan´s interactive logbook. http://magellan.arte.tv/en/
3. Conquest of the Seven Seas – The Crossmedia Experience. http://www.conquestofthesevenseas.com/index.php?Langue=en
4. Filmtank GmbH. Conquest of the Seven Seas Docudramas.
5. Internet Movie Database. Box office / Business for Lara Croft: Tomb Raider. http://www.imdb.com/title/tt0146316/business.
6. Internet Movie Database. Lara Croft: Tomb Raider (2011). *Critic Reviews*. http://www.imdb.com/title/tt0146316/criticreviews?ref_=tt_ov_rt
7. Jegers, K. Elaborating eight elements of fun: Supporting design of pervasive player enjoyment. *Computers in Entertainment (CIE) - SPECIAL ISSUE: Media Arts and Games (Part II)*. Volume 7 Issue 2 (June). Article No. 25. ACM Press (2009).
8. Jenkins, H. Convergence Culture: Where Old and New Media Collide. New York University Press, New York, NY, USA, 2006.
9. Krikke, J. Axonometry: A Matter of Perspective. In *IEEE Computer Graphics and Applications*. Volume 20 Issue 4 (July). IEEE Computer Society Press, Los Alamitos, CA, USA (2000), 7-11.
10. Lindt, I., Ohlenburg, J., Pankoke-Babatz, U., Ghellal, S. A report on the crossmedia game epidemic menace. In *Computers in Entertainment (CIE) - Interactive entertainment archive*. Volume 5 Issue 1 (January). Article No. 8. ACM Press (2007).
11. Murray, J. H. Transcending transmedia: emerging story telling structures for the emerging convergence platforms. In *Proc. EuroITV 2012*, ACM Press (2012), 1-6.
12. Pasman, G. Lost in transition: issues in designing crossmedia applications and services. In *Proc. SIGDOC 2011*, ACM Press (2011), 175-180.
13. Pratten, R. Getting started in Transmedia Storytelling. A practical guide for beginners. Create Space, USA, 2011.

Making Second Screen Sustainable in Media Production: the BRIDGET Approach

Alberto Messina
RAI – Radiotelevisione Italiana
Via Cavalli, 6 – Torino, IT
alberto.messina@rai.it

Francisco Morán Burgos
Univ. Politécnica Madrid
Madrid, ES
fmb@gti.ssr.upm.es

Marius Preda
Institut Mines-Telecom
Evry, FR,
marius.preda@it-sudparis.eu

Skjalg Lepsoy
Telecom Italia S.p.A.
Via G. Reiss-Romoli, 274 –
Torino, IT
skjalg.lepsoy@telecomitalia.it

Miroslaw Bober
CVSSP, University of Surrey
Guildford, Surrey, GU2 7XH, UK
m.bober@surrey.ac.uk

Davide Bertola
CEDEO.net
10040 Villar Dora, IT
davide@cedeo.net

Stavros Paschalakis
Visual Atoms
The Surrey Technology Centre
40 Occam Road
Guildford, Surrey GU2 7YG, UK
s.paschalakis@visualatoms.com

Abstract

This paper presents work in progress of the European Commission FP7 project BRIDGET "BRIDging the Gap for Enhanced broadcasT". The project is developing innovative technology and the underlying architecture for efficient production of second screen applications for broadcasters and media companies. The project advancements include novel front-end authoring tools as well as back-end enabling technologies such as visual search, media structure analysis and 3D A/V reconstruction to support new editorial workflows.

Author Keywords

Second screen applications; Multimedia linking; MPEG-4 BIFS; 3D A/V reconstruction; Visual Search; Content analysis and structuring.

ACM Classification Keywords

H.3.1 Content Analysis and Indexing: Indexing Methods. H.5.1 Multimedia Information Systems: *Artificial, augmented, and virtual realities*. I.5 PATTERN RECOGNITION: I.5.4 Applications: Computer Vision

Introduction

Current companion screen applications let user enjoying broadcast programs access related information on other – typically internet-connected – devices. Although several services are already available in the consumer domain, especially in commercial and advertising arenas, the problem of ensuring sustainability of such applications in the media production domain and for generic program formats still remains vastly unsolved. The most relevant challenges to be tackled in this area are: 1) it is essential that the production costs related to enriched content are affordable for the broadcasters, e.g., the enrichment process should not constitute a barrier in terms of additional human resources; 2) second screen presentation must be ergonomic and functional, and links should include rich and exciting content (e.g., 3D models) to ensure a differentiating factor for the quality of user experience; 3) since enriching content is result of an editorial decision, authors and editors must be supported by efficient authoring tools, which must also be easily integrable in existing workflows.

BRIDGET works to address these issues by providing an advanced architecture for authoring and consumption of second screen content and demonstrating the viability of the approach through field trials and user evaluations. BRIDGET aims to develop innovative functionalities for enjoying multimedia content by connecting it to other related content, augmenting it with virtual information of interest, and allowing navigation of the 3D reconstruction of the scene.

BRIDGET has developed the namesake notion of a bridget: a link from the program being watched to (combinations of) external interactive media elements such as web pages, images, audio clips, different types of video (2D, multi-view, 3D free viewpoint) and synthetic 3D models. Bridget are more than just URLs.

Bridgets are links which exist because of some inherent semantic relationship between content items. As such, they can be products of an editorial decision, taken by someone inspecting (manually or automatically) content items, or they can be objects of a workflow which involves different roles taking care of finding, organizing and crafting the data that constitute them.

In order to facilitate the bridget creation, the project develops: a) advanced visual search tools that help locate semantically related images and video segments in archives; b) advanced media structure analysis and content annotation tools that help identify candidate content segments to be enriched and offer quick and efficient navigation through content; c) advanced A/V 3D reconstruction tools to provide new content types to enrich the main content; d) efficient authoring tools integrating the above technologies in the production workflow.

Related Work

The project brings a number of innovations beyond the current state-of-the art. Firstly, it defines a common, open format for the generic link between the media elements, which will enable entire eco-system of creation, distribution, use and re-use of bridgets. Currently the closest open specification is the HbbTV standard (https://www.hbbtv.org/). Although HbbTV is based on HTML-5 it requires hardware support in the receiver. Conversely, BRIDGET format is generic, device independent and supports content linking between any media elements, for example between two video segments available in a library. Secondly, the project advances Content Search technologies beyond what is currently possible [4][5], in terms of search speed and robustness by introducing novel descriptors,

feature aggregation and geometric verification tools. Finally, we also introduce sophisticated algorithms for media structure analysis (e.g., outperforming approaches as [7]), and 3D A/V scene reconstruction from unstructured data. In fact, although 3D scene reconstruction algorithms based on Structure-from-Motion (SfM) techniques have been deeply investigated in order to reduce their computational complexity [8], the progressive fusion of new information into pre-existing models has received so far little attention.

Enabling Technologies

Visual Search

The BRIDGET visual search engine is an extension of MPEG's Compact Descriptors for Visual Search (CDVS) specification, which reached the Final Draft International Standard (FDIS) status in December 2014 [1], further augmented by the state-of-the-art tools developed within the project. All media assets available as end-points are pre-processed off-line and compact visual descriptors are extracted and indexed in a database. The bridget creators can then pose a visual query by selecting an object of interest (e.g. a building or a book cover), entire frame (e.g. a scene) or a video segment (e.g. a shot of an interior of a museum). The search process will return all available content in the database that is linked by visual similarities to the query. **Figure 1** shows the current descriptor extraction pipeline. It detects scale-invariant local key-points in the image and selects a subset of robust features that will be used to create image representation. Subsequently, SIFT local descriptors are extracted and compressed using the Transform and Scalar Quantization Coding (TSQC) method, which offers a scalable, high-performance compression with ternary representation.

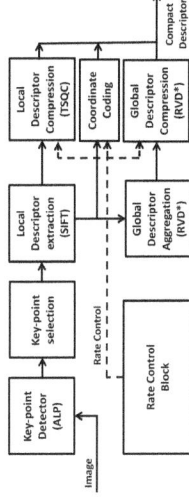

Figure 1: Processing pipeline for extraction of Image Descriptors for Visual Search

Global (frame level) descriptors are computed using a novel aggregation method called RVD*, which significantly improves search capabilities and speed [2]. The image coordinates of the key-points are also stored and used during the search process to reject false matches and to localize the match spatially within the image.

For what concerns geometry consistency of the matches, in BRIDGET we propose a novel method that integrates evidence over several frames, whenever local features are present either in the query, in the candidate, or both. This method promises to be superior to late fusion techniques (e.g., [6]) for single-frame comparisons. For search involving videos as queries, two approaches are currently investigated – one based on reference frames obtained by temporal sampling of the video segment and another where local descriptors are aggregated spatially and temporally.

3D A/V Scene Reconstruction

Bridgets may point to synthetic 3D objects or scenes, either manually created by artists, or automatically reconstructed from sets of real-world images. Thanks to 3D reconstruction, the user can choose to be placed, via the 2nd screen, inside a virtual model of the 1st

represent potentially significant interest points for bridgets. Such audio-visual sequences carrying semantic information inferable from the automatic analysis of the content editorial rules are termed computational scenes (CSs), and can be used as is or as segmentation boundaries between logical units of content. Examples of CSs include dialogs, regular anchors and monologues. The division of long programs into such diverse program structures aims to increase the efficiency of the visual search tools and the quality of the content produced by the authoring tools by helping editors quickly segment content. The specific challenge in this area is to specify media structure analysis tools that allow implementations which are much faster than real-time or any existing system (e.g. processing an hour of video in just a few seconds) so that they may be effective in enhancing the operation of the visual search and authoring tools.

The media structure analysis results make it possible to quickly navigate bridget source and destination content through multi-modal storyboards, organized around a hierarchical shot/scene structure, or around the people which appear in different segments, and so on. This approach improves the efficiency of the authoring tool since the operator applies the same action, e.g. creating a bridget and associating content to it, to many portions of the program in one single action.

Applications

The BRIDGET Authoring Tool lets an editor search for relevant images or shots of a given program to become source content, search for destination content by using the visual search tools described previously, and create/edit bridgets. The Program Player (**Figure 2** – (a)) allows the bridget author to manually select shots

screen scene and experience it by freely navigating beyond what dictated by the program creator.

BRIDGET's 3D scene reconstruction tools target multi-view 3D A/V media generation and encoding at the service provider's side, as well as decoding and rendering at the end user's side. This enables the content creator to run a semi-automatic extraction of 3D scene information from archived (and, typically, previously broadcast) 2D/3D A/V content captured from several viewpoints. After its efficient transmission, the virtual or augmented 3D scene is decoded and rendered according to the user-selected viewpoint.

In 3D A/V scene reconstruction, coding and rendering, the scientific challenges addressed by BRIDGET include: 1) progressive refinement of the 3D model initially extracted through SfM techniques with additional material (images, videos, sounds) captured from yet other viewpoints, possibly harvested on the internet thanks to VS; 2) w.r.t. the visual part of the 3D synthetic scene, hybrid modeling with both triangle meshes and point clouds; w.r.t. its audio part, use of 3D audio source localization methods for reconstruction purposes; 3) efficient coding of mixed/augmented 3D scenes with both natural and synthetic content; 4) realistic rendering of augmented reality, free-viewpoint 3D scenes

Media Structure Analysis

The media structure analysis tools provide different segmentations types, e.g. according to shots, scenes, faces, interior/exterior settings, etc. and different kinds of summarizations, e.g. according to shot or speaker clusters or more complex repetitive structural patterns. The latter can pertain to more than one modality and

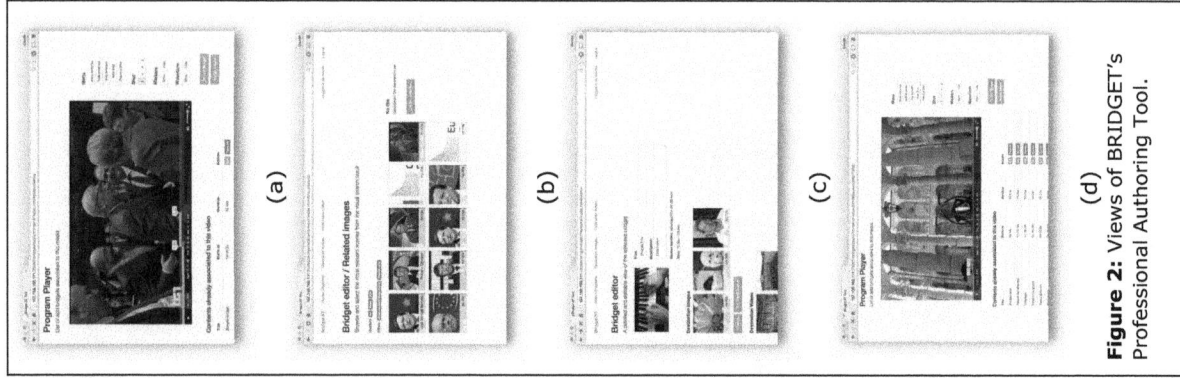

(a)

(b)

(c)

(d)

Figure 2: Views of BRIDGET's Professional Authoring Tool.

candidate for bridget enrichment. The Program Player can also present shots that are automatically detected in the current program. The bridget author who has decided that the shot or an image drawn from the shot should become the source content starts the creation of a bridget (**Figure 2**-(b)). Destination content can then be selected manually or by calling the CDVS-based visual search (**Figure 2**-(c)). The author can select one or more items and include them as bridget destination contents. **Figure 2**-(d) shows the result of an enriched program. At the bottom it is possible to see all the bridgets and the time at which they will become active.

The way in which such functionalities are presented to the user on the second screen (e.g., a tablet) represents one of the differentiating factors for the quality of experience. The user attention has to be alternatively dedicated to the first and second screens so it is necessary to carefully design how and when the content on the second screen is displayed. For example, the experiences on the second screen should be short enough in order to allow the user resynchronize with the main story.

The transformation of the traditional linear experience of consuming TV content is illustrated in Figure 4. Here, one single bridget is illustrated: S_1 is the start time and E_1^1 the end time if the user is not interacting with the content. If there is interaction, then the bridget end time can be any of E_1^n (n>1). One may observe that selecting the starting time (S_1) is fundamental for a proper experience, and this can be done by the content designer. The same situation occurs for E_1^1, however for E_1^n (n>1) the content designer has no direct control. However, he can design the bridget in such a manner that E_1^n (n>1) will be in a certain range. The

situation may be much more complicated in real cases, mainly because when several bridgets are designed overlapping may occur. We derived a first set of rules for designing bridgets: 1) each bridget should start with one screen synthetically presenting the main topic; 2) if the bridgets are interactive – details are made available "on click"; 3) bridgets have a life time; 4) a special view should indicate which bridgets are available at the current time.

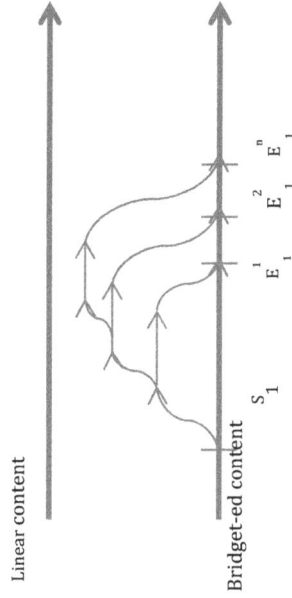

Figure 4: Linear vs. bridget-ed consumption experience.

The result of the authoring is a data format describing the interactive experience, which can be exported in MPEG-4 BIFS and played by a standard MPEG-4 BIFS player. The current BRIDGET player, based on GPAC open source, is supporting representation of all data types required by rich media applications, composition of synthetic and natural objects, access to remotely/locally stored audio, video and graphics. The player supports user interaction and server generated scene changes as well as management of the physical context, either captured by a broad range of standard sensors or affected by a broad range of standard actuators. **Figure 3** illustrates the BRIDGET player.

Figure 3: BRIDGET player executed on the 2nd screen.

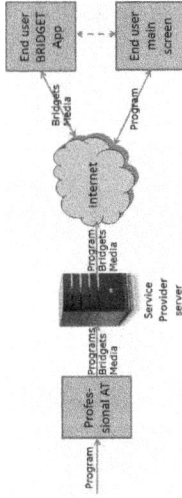

Figure 5: Bridgets in a purely internet scenario.

In an Internet delivery scenario (**Figure 5**), bridgets and destination media are both stored in the service provider server and the three content types are all delivered via the internet. In this case synchronization is provided by the service provider, however the accuracy of synchronization between 1st and 2nd screens may depend on the protocols used to deliver program and destination media. **Figure 6** shows a possible implementation of this approach in a mobile app player.

Conclusions & Future Work

This paper reports work-in-progress of BRIDGET, an European project making second screen applications a sustainable process in professional media production. This is achieved through the employment of advanced technologies like visual search, 3D A/V reconstruction and media analysis integrated in an authoring environment specifically designed for the task. Some of the BRIDGET technologies are being standardized in ISO by consortium partners, in the MPEG working group. One of these is ARAF (Augmented Reality Application Format), a collection of MPEG tools selected to create powerful yet simple data formalism to represent rich augmented reality experiences [3]. The second is a proposal for a new Part of MPEG-A, named MLAF (Media Linking Application Format) with the aim of standardizing both the representation and presentation formats of bridgets.

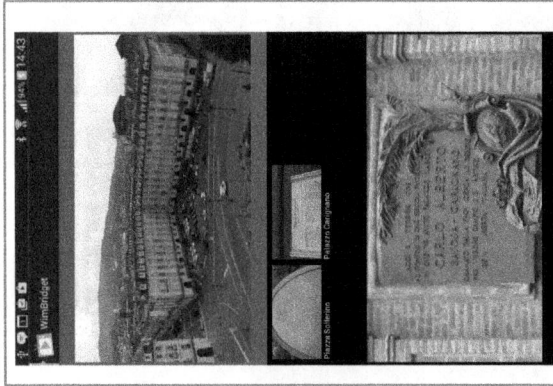

Figure 6: Mobile app player example (pure internet scenario). The video in the window above corresponds to the 1st screen, the icons below are bridgets that pop up whenever the appropriate time comes, while the window below shows the destination content (another video in this case). When a user taps a bridget, the corresponding video starts in the window below and the audio of the video above is muted. When the user taps the window above, the audio of the video below is muted but still plays. By tapping again the video below the audio of the video above is muted again and the audio of the video below is restored.

Acknowledgements

This work has received funding from the European Commission under Grant Agreement 610691.

References

1. ISO/IEC FDIS 15938-13, *Information technology – Multimedia content description interface (MPEG-7) – Part 13:Compact descriptors for visual search*, ISO, Dec. 2014.

2. S. Husain and M. Bober, "Robust and scalable aggregation of local features for ultra large scale retrieval," in IEEE Int. Conf. on Image Processing, Paris, France, Oct. 2014.

3. ISO/IEC 23000-13:2014, *Information technology – Multimedia application format (MPEG-A) – Part 13: Augmented reality application format (ARAF)*, ISO, May 2014.

4. Girod, B. et al , "Mobile Visual Search", Signal Processing Magazine, IEEE vol. 28: 4 , pp 61-76

5. H. Jegou, F. Perronnin, M. Douze, J. Sanchez, P. Perez, and C. Schmid, "Aggregating local image descriptors into compact codes," IEEE Trans. on Pattern Analysis and Machine Intelligence, vol. 34, no. 9, pp. 1704–1716, Sep. 2012

6. X. Zhou, A. Depeursinge: "Information Fusion for Combining Visual and Textual Image Retrieval", IEEE Int. Conf. on Pattern Recognition (ICPR), 2010, pp. 1590-1593.

7. P. Antonopoulos, N. Nikolaidis, I. Pitas, "Hierarchical Face Clustering using SIFT Image Features", IEEE Symposium on Computational Intelligence in Image and Signal Processing, pp. 325-329, 2007

8. C. Wu, "Towards linear-time incremental structure from motion", IEEE Int. Conf. on 3D Vision, p. 127-134, Seattle, WA, USA, June 2013.

Interactive Design Documentary as a Method for Civic Engagement

David Green

Culture Lab,
Newcastle University,
Newcastle-Upon-Tyne, UK
d.p.green@ncl.ac.uk

Clara Crivellaro

Culture Lab,
Newcastle University,
Newcastle-Upon-Tyne, UK
c.crivellaro@ncl.ac.uk

Jimmy Tidey

Royal College of Art,
London, UK

TVX 2015, June 3–5, 2015, Brussels, Belgium.
TVX'15, June 03–05, 2015, Brussels, Belgium
ACM 978-1-4503-3526-3/15/06.
http://dx.doi.org/10.1145/2745197.2755518

Abstract

We present a method for civic engagement that uses interactive video documentary to capture discourses within focused settings (eg workshops or focus groups) and translocate them to public spaces (via interactive vox-pops) and online spaces (via an interactive web-based tool). Our method aims to facilitate encounters and the exchange of perspectives between communities across these spaces. We describe how the method was developed through five stages, beginning with a workshop and culminating in a prototype design tool and offer preliminary insights into its potential benefits. We argue that a key strength of this method lies in its potential to support situated encounters and build connections between researchers, designers, institutions and members of the public, with potential benefits in the areas of user-centered research and design. Finally, we outline directions for future development, including a model for lightweight civic engagement that uses an "interactive design documentary" as a central component.

Author Keywords

Civic Engagement, Video, Vox-pops, Documentary, Design, Interactivity, Participation, Methods

ACM Classification Keywords

H.5.m. Information interfaces and presentation (e.g., HCI): Miscellaneous.

Introduction

Documenting everyday life has now become a common activity, as high-quality digital video-making equipment becomes ever more affordable and easily available. Likewise, distribution channels such as YouTube allow a much broader range of topics to connect with audiences through video. In this more accessible, less exclusive landscape, innovative new forms of video documentary are beginning to thrive, particularly in online environments, as new production methods and distribution systems blur the formal qualities of 'the documentary' into different forms [8].

Of these new forms, the concept of the *design documentary* has the potential to play a critical role in research and design activities. Design documentaries aim to capture unique insights into real-life scenarios by "leaving the erratic, elusive fabric of the everyday intact". They have been shown to aid the process of discovery that informs user-centered design [13]. That this 'fabric of the everyday' is a desirable perspective for designers is perhaps obvious, but one may look to YouTube, for example, for instances of documentary video where 'the fabric of the everyday' is intact, but translating this into information useful to designers is still relatively challenging. Dovey et al, alluding to enormous quantities of (often poor-quality) user-generated video content online, describe a "sea of data", from which it is sometimes difficult to extract meaningful information [4, see also 1]. This sea of data suggests documentaries that embrace user-participation still require a level of directorial

intervention to maintain coherence and narrative legibility. Indeed, Rajmakers et al suggest the neutral 'fly-on-the-wall' approach to documentary is less useful than more 'dialectical', 'interventional' or 'performative' approaches [13]. We suggest that these latter approaches can also be used to facilitate encounters between different communities' discourses – by framing them around the same topic and embracing heterogeneity (as in Gaudenzi's concept of the 'living documentary' [6] and utilizing aspects of Kester's "dialogical aesthetic" [10] (particularly a "resistance to fixity" (p2)). Thus, rather than aiming for narrative coherence, we suggest that interactive design documentaries could be a useful tool for focused engagement with (and across) academics and the public. Our hypothesis is that a repeatable production model could be a useful tool for researchers and designers to use to obtain a variety of perspectives on a subject in a minimally-interventional, accessible and lightweight manner.

Background and Related Work

The transmedia art project, *Question Bridge* used a chain of responses and questions to "facilitate a dialogue between a critical mass of black men from diverse and contending backgrounds" [15]. By subverting a staple technique of documentary-making (the subject interview), the artists effectively 'crowdsourced' interview questions from the subjects themselves. By relinquishing a degree of control over the topic covered, the result is a meandering narrative, whereby each 'question bridge' leads to new avenues of thought and the narrative emerges only through a combination of the collective whim of the participants and the particular actions of the spectator. *Photostroller* [7] employs a form of 'semantic drift' more explicitly, within a fixed dataset, to allow users to physically 'tune in' (with varying degrees of precision) to specific categories from a large image database. In doing so, they allow "a relatively small set of initial terms to give access to a larger, and potentially serendipitous, range of images". In the context of the design documentary, we might consider how interactivity, participants' whim or serendipity could potentially be usefully harnessed to negotiate the space between the infinite "sea of data" and the specificity of a directorial vision. Joshua McVeigh-Shultz's work provides an insight on the role of interactive platforms in relation to questions of public representation. In his redesigned model of *Vox Pop Live Online*, users contribute questions for on-street interviews, in doing so, re-configuring concepts of *the user* and public intervention in public spaces and giving *the user* a central role within a media production landscape [11]. Techniques such as those outlined here demonstrate the potential for new configurations of roles for audiences/users of interactive systems. They also suggest how interactive documentaries might be appropriated as sites for civic engagement by de-centralising authorial/directorial roles and representing multiple perspectives, rather than striving for singular, coherent narratives. In the following case study, we describe our production method and process, which attempts to realise some of this potential.

CASE STUDY

In this study we set out to explore the use of a neologism ('digital public space') in an academic context and how discourses around this term had constructed particular yet multiple perspectives. We describe how we transitioned from this abstract 'concept' to tangible design ideas through the

---

development and application of a 5-stage production model (see left panel).

Context – 'Digital Public Space'
The term "Digital Public Space" was coined by Tony Ageh (Controller of Archive Development at the BBC) to describe an "arrangement of shared technologies, standards and processes that will be collaboratively developed and commonly applied" [9]. It was adopted as the title for the annual Future Everything conference in 2013 [*ibid*] and secured academic investment through the AHRC-funded Creative Exchange (CX) Knowledge Exchange hub, which aims to build on the concept and, "create new products, experiences and business opportunities which empower anyone, anywhere to access, explore and create with the newly accessible collections of media, public information and data trails which form the Digital Public Space." [9]. The question of how to synthesize insights from across CX is one of its central reflexive questions. However, first-hand accounts of impressions of the term 'digital public space' from the variety of creative practitioners and academic researchers in CX had – at the beginning of this project – yet to be documented.

Development of the 5-Stage Method

1 – Workshop
This Case Study began with – and was inspired by – an existing series of three 45-minute workshops at a CX symposium in Newcastle-upon-Tyne, UK, in July 2014. The workshops aimed to, "facilitate a general exploration of the idea of 'digital public space' in as open a way as possible." [3] These workshops revealed diverse impressions of "digital public space" (across approximately 25 PhD students and 12 full-time

---

The 5 Stage Model

1 - Workshop
Small co-located groups

2 - Discourse Analysis
Conducted in-situ at the workshop and presented as a summary to workshop participants

3 - Interviews
Interviews with workshop participants, each participant responding to the previous response.

4 – Vox Pops
Street-based interviews; responding to tablet app.

5 – Web-Based Design Tool
Online tool containing all of the above video data and facilitating online responses.

academic staff) who were all existing members of the CX project. Each workshop took the form of a round-table discussion with between six and eight participants (plus two facilitators, who were present at all three discussions). Several specific ideas and topics emerged during the workshops, which were identified and noted by the facilitators.

fig 1 – workshop in progress

2 – Discourse Analysis

Next, the workshop coordinators conducted a discourse analysis [14] on the workshop data, which was then presented to the attendees in the form of a summary. Discourse analysis was specifically chosen to encourage reflection on the ways particular versions and perspectives were being created through discourses around "digital public space".

3 – Interviews

After the presentation of the discourse analysis, we conducted filmed interviews with 16 workshop participants. The first interviewee was asked to "define *Digital Public Space*" in under one minute, using a visible countdown and buzzer. Inspired by the "Question Bridge" method, subsequent participants were then first shown the video of the previous

respondent then asked to '*improve upon*', '*expound upon*' or '*ignore and re-define* "digital public space*" in response. Again, a time limit of 1 minute was imposed. Once all 16 members of the workshop had provided a response, we edited the responses into a back-to-back sequence, resulting in a 15-minute documentary. All participants consented to their responses being used.

4 - Vox Pops

Using the video interview materials, we produced an app that presented the 'talking heads' in the form of a clickable grid, with each face linking to the corresponding ⬜1-minute video.

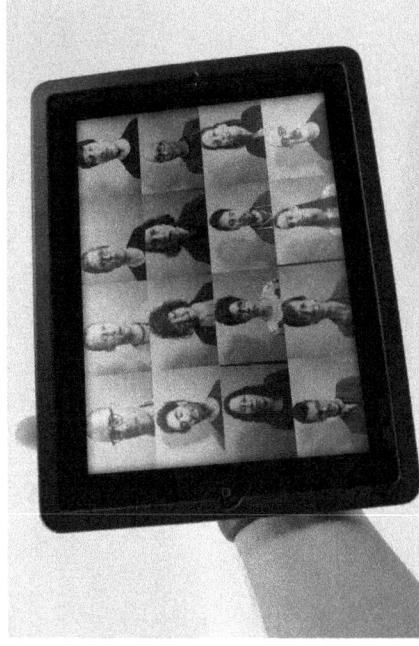

fig 5 – vox pops interface.

Over 2 days, this was presented on a tablet device to a total of 28 members of the public and introduced as a 'game' in which the participant was invited to choose one (or more) faces, watch the video(s) and then guess what the individual was talking about. Most participants chose one before responding; some chose two. The

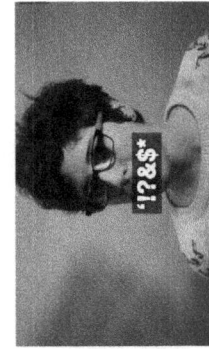

fig 2 (top) – Edited interview clip.

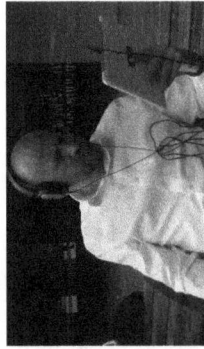

fig 3 (middle) – Participant using Vox Pop app

fig 4 (bottom) – Vox pop with participant after using the app.

responses ranged in duration from a few seconds to several minutes. To disguise the topic, each video had been 'bleeped' and a `!?&$*` graphic superimposed over the mouth where participants had mentioned the 'Digital Public Space' by name. Following their guess about the topic, the researchers revealed the answer and enquired what they might interpret from the term. Their responses were recorded in the style of a 'vox pop'. Participants we de-briefed, given an information sheet to take away with details about the project, and consent was obtained to include their responses in the next stage of the project.

5 – Web-Based Design Tool (prototype)

Finally, we constructed a prototype web-based platform in HTML5, using JQuery and CSS to style the interface. The platform allows users to view each of the talking heads; both the workshop participants and the public vox-pops. By clicking on a head icon, users can view the video of that participant, as well as link to the video(s) that they responded to (to the left) or that responded to them (to the right). Users can also view a 45s trailer (the ! icon), an information page about the project (the ? icon), or add their own response (the + icon). User responses are currently text-based, but the aim is to develop a method that enables users to activate their webcam to submit their own time-limited talking head response. At the time of writing, this has yet to be implemented.

Discussion

The prototype method we have described – and the resulting prototype tool – was both *inspired by* and *about* the "digital public space". Thus, two of the design outcomes from the early stages of the process were actually implemented in stages 4 and 5 of the method

(the 'vox pops app and the 'web-based tool'). However, as well as these emergent outcomes, the method also revealed specific design ideas, which will inform the next stages of the development for stage 5. For example, we have identified another possible application area for this tool in town planning, where a public body-to-public connection could be facilitated (rather than the academic-to-public connection described here).

So far, the method we have presented yielded promising outcomes. By using processes that traversed different spaces and user-groups, we (as designers) identified themes relating to 'public perceptions of the ivory towers of academia', 'transparency and public liability', 'synthesizing multiple perspectives' and 'data privacy and consent' that fed into the development of the later stages. We successfully connected academic workshop participants (stages 1-3) with members of public (stage 4) and used this dialogue to inform design specifications. With this being a work in progress, we acknowledge that further work is necessary to make any substantive claims about the efficacy of this method in other contexts. However, while the "digital public space" remains an enigmatic term, we suggest that by taking academic discourses to the streets, we have demonstrated a method by which academic conduct can be made accountable and preoccupations might be cross-checked with real issues facing everyday people. Future developments could enable the discussions to come full-circle, with the academics provided a 'right to reply' in stage 5 and vox-pop participants given further opportunities to learn more and contribute further. With additional development, there is scope for the processes to be synchronized and/or iterated through multiple passes.

fig 6 (top) – Web-based tool. "What is the Digital Public Space?" as of 2nd March 2015 at http://www.dpgreen.info/idocs/dps

fig 7 (middle) – Individual video clip playing – previous clip (left) and subsequent clips (right).

fig 8 (bottom) – The current state of the user-feedback mechanism (at time of writing). Integration of video feedback is earmarked for future development.

Summary

We have described how a method was developed as means of supporting the video capture of heterogeneous perspectives, with influences derived from several different documentary traditions, and new platforms developed to facilitate civic engagement in the context of a specific research challenge. We propose that the method we outline offers a novel structure for a production model for lightweight "interactive design documentaries". The next steps will be to verify the feasibility of translating this process into a usable design method, by conducting a further study, ideally addressing a more focused / less reflexive design challenge.

Acknowledgements

This research was funded by the AHRC Creative Exchange Knowledge Exchange Hub. Many thanks also to the individuals who participated in the interviews.

References

1. Alluvatti, G. M. et al., "User Generated (Web) Content: Trash or Treasure?", Proc' IWPSE-EVOL '11, Szeged, Hungary. pp 81-90. 2011.

2. Bhimani, J. et al., "Vox Populi: Enabling Community-Based Narratives through Collaboration and Content Creation". In Proc' EuroITV '13. ACM, New York, NY, USA, 2013. 31-40.

3. Bowers, J. and Stewart, H. CX KE Symposium Workshop Plan - unpublished

4. Dovey, J. et al. "We're happy and we know it: Documentary: Data: Montage". Studies in Documentary Film. vol 6. no 2. pp. 159-166, June 2012.

5. Fruchtman, S., "Question Bridge: Black Males Socially Engaged Art and the Politics of Dialogue", in The Arbutus Review, Vol. 3, No 1 (2012)

6. Gaudenzi, S., "The Living Documentary: from representing reality to co-creating reality in digital interactive documentary". PhD Dissertation. Goldsmiths, University of London, UK, 2013.

7. Gaver, W., et al., 2011. "The Photostroller: supporting diverse care home residents in engaging with the world". In Proceedings of the SIGCHI Conference on Human Factors in Computing Systems (CHI '11). ACM, New York, NY, USA, 1757-1766.

8. Green, D., et al., "Beyond Participatory Production: Digitally Supporting Grassroots Documentary", In Proc. of CHI'15, ACM, Seoul, Korea, 2015.

9. Hemmet, D. et al. (eds), Digital Public Spaces, online, http://futureeverything.org/wp-content/uploads/2014/03/DPS.pdf

10. Kester, Grant H. "Dialogical aesthetics." in Conversation Pieces Community + Communication in Modern Art (2004): 82-123.

11. McVeigh-Schultz, J. "Redesigning the Vox Pop: Civic Rituals as Sites of Critical Reimagining, in Ratto, M., and Boler M''., in DIY Citizenship Critical Making and Social Media, MIT Press, 2014

12. Milne E-J. et al. (eds.), Handbook of Participatory Video. Altamira Press: Plymouth, 2012.

13. Raijmakers, B., Gaver, W. and Bishay, J., 2006. "Design documentaries: inspiring design research through documentary film". In Proceedings of the 6th conference on Designing Interactive systems (DIS '06). ACM, New York, NY, USA, 229-238.

14. Wodak, R., Krzyzanowski, M. Qualitative Discourse Analysis in the Social Sciences, Palgrave Macmillan Press, 2008.

15. Question Bridge, http://questionbridge.com/

A Game of Thrones Companion: Orienting Viewers to Complex Storyworlds via Synchronized Visualizations

Pedro Silva
Yasmin Amer
William Tsikerdanos
Jesse Shedd
Experimental Television Lab
Georgia Institute of Technology
Atlanta, GA 30308, USA
pedrosilva@gatech.edu
yamer3@gatech.edu
gth684f@gatech.edu
jbshedd13@gatech.edu

Isabel Restrepo
Hipertropico
Universidad de Antioquia
Calle 67 Número 53 – 108
Medellín, Antioquia, Colombia
isabelr27@gmail.com

Janet Murray
Experimental Television Lab
Georgia Institute of Technology
Atlanta, GA 30308, USA
janet.murray@lmc.gatech.edu

TVX'15, June 03-05, 2015, Brussels, Belgium
ACM 978-1-4503-3526-3/15/06.
http://dx.doi.org/10.1145/2745197.2755519.

Abstract

The merger of television and digital technology allows TV producers to author increasingly complex narratives, which pose new challenges for modern audiences. The prototype presented here is targeted at viewers of HBO's Game of Thrones and utilizes manipulatable, tightly synchronized spatial visualizations to concretize complex character relationships. A preliminary user study was conducted, utilizing the less tightly synchronized, non-diagramatic HBO Go application as an experimental control. Results show that users were able to more accurately identify character relationships after watching segments of the TV drama with the companion app prototype.

Author Keywords

Second screen companion design; narrative; agency; interactive television.

ACM Classification Keywords

H.5.2 Information interfaces and presentation: User Interfaces; User-centered Design.

Figure 1: Upon appearing, character portraits arrange themselves across two concentric circles; characters physically present in the scene line the inner circle, while characters who are alluded to in dialogue line the outer ring. These rings are further divided into sectors, each representing a familial house (e.g., Targaryen, Stark, etc.). The size of a character's portrait signifies his/her status as major or minor character, with major characters' portraits appearing larger than those of minor characters.

Introduction

The integration of television and digital technology affords designers the tools to cultivate a more synchronized, immersive experience for viewers [21, 22]. The proliferation of on-demand streaming services such as Netflix and Hulu continue to shape the habits of TV viewers. Once firm delineations between serial and episodic narratives begin to blur [13]. Viewers prioritize narrative consistency, as back-to-back viewing--or "binge watching"--renders failures of continuity especially apparent. It is common for contemporary television shows to feature a dozen or more frequently recurring characters, and plots that arc across multiple seasons [14]. If viewers are to successfully follow narrative developments from episode to episode, contemporary storyworlds demand close attention.

Jenkins [11, 12] remarks on the possibilities of interactive television for enrichment and sharing, citing examples of media convergence where content is "spreadable" and consistent across mediums and platforms, while remaining open to fan participation. Mittell [15] countervails Jenkins' "spreadability" with his own term, "drillability". Whereas highly spreadable media prioritizes shallow engagements that appeal to broad audiences, highly drillable media encourages a mode of "forensic fandom", a vertical probing of the text's complexities. Murray [16] calls this testing of the narrative world as "active creation of belief," and has predicted such increased participatory, immersive viewing as a result of the convergence of television and computation.

That viewers are attracted to narrative complexity is not surprising. Cognitive science has established that In order to better comprehend the real world, humans build cognitive structures that represent the events of their

lives via models similar to those encountered in narrative [2]. Narrative form in media is increasingly understood as an extension of cognitive schema building [10, 23]. Thus the ability to abstract and retain story patterns is requisite to experiencing the pleasures afforded by these dense storyworlds: their encyclopedic [16], ergodic [1, 5] and immersive [19] qualities, their demand for nontrivial effort, and the subsequent reward of additive comprehension [11]. Character relationships are of particular importance, as cognitive scientists have shown that audiences rely on the intentions behind characters' actions as a means of comprehending narrative [7, 8].

Second screen devices provide an already widely adopted platform for disseminating synced, contextualized information without obstructing the primary media [18]. Likewise, viewers already engage in sites of community participation, where fans author their own summaries of plot points, hold debates and self-police to a careful standard of accuracy [15]. Viewers utilize digital devices to more closely engage with these storyworlds, to browse through catalogs of characters, locations and plot points. Cesar and Bulterman [3] categorize four major uses for second screen interaction with television: to control, enrich, share, and transfer conventional television content. However, design guidelines usually focus on expanding TV's social accommodation [6, 9]. The prototype presented here aims to explore the potential of second screen companions for enhancing retention and narrative comprehension of character relationships, in order to identify design issues and guidelines for creating companion apps that support complex storyworlds.

Previous Work

Historically, discussions of interactive television often reference a tension between "lean back" and "lean

Figure 2: Sansa's portrait sits at the circle's origin. Characters present or alluded to in the current scene surround her, mostly enemies and nearly all loyal to house Lannister. The scene depicts Sansa's interrogation by Joffrey, sadistic king and murderer of Sansa's father.

Technical Implementation:
GoTC was developed using HTML5, CSS3 and JavaScript. All animations were handled through the support of the Kinetic.js library. To sync playback across first and second screens, *GoTC* utilized Node.js and http sockets. Timing information was stored as JSON objects. Synchronization was achieved by utilizing the timecodes of the TV drama's streaming playback, allowing the prototype to fit any synchronization technique.

forward" experiences. Expanded interaction poses an attractive endeavor for industry leaders, who see opportunities for additional revenue and increased audience engagement. Yet, evidence suggests that viewers prefer modes of interaction that do not require mastery and are therefore less susceptible to user error [4]. Network-affiliated applications have thus favored single button interactions, usually in the form of multiple choice trivia with immediate feedback. Designers employ synchronized second screens as a means of eliciting user input through polls, expressions of character allegiance and guesses at future developments [4, 20].

The *HBO Go* second screen application focused on *Game of Thrones* provides viewers with text and image annotations synchronized with particular moments within a television drama, including condensed character bios, related plot points, and behind-the-scenes anecdotes. Viewers may choose to pause the show and examine these annotations, or watch the show uninterrupted and review the annotations separately. Despite the potential for added context available through synchronization, character descriptions remain decontextualized, lacking any anchor to the particular episode or dramatic moment. Additionally, the frequent foregrounding of production information (e.g., set-design, actor commentary) presents a breach of the fourth wall.

Our past work [17] found that a companion app for the long-form television show *Justified* enhanced comprehension for new viewers and supported their understanding of character relationships. User responses to the *Justified* prototype led to several design recommendations, including minimizing interruptions, focusing on characters, and synchronizing the application to the show's current context. The prototype presented

here, *Game of Thrones Companion* (*GoTC*), expands our inquiry to another storyworld, HBO's *Game of Thrones*, in order to assess the generalizability of second screen companions across genres and at a much higher level of narrative complexity. Secondly, this study incorporates the *HBO Go* app as a control during usability testing. This study also compares the effectiveness of second screen companions for both naive and experienced viewers.

A Game of Thrones Companion

The design of *GoTC* aims to support the retention of character relationships for both naive and experienced users. HBO's *Game of Thrones* was selected as our target due to the rich complexity of its storyworld: indeed, the Wikipedia entry for *Game of Thrones* lists 38 major characters, all of whom reappear throughout show's current five seasons; by contrast, *Breaking Bad* includes 11 major characters, whereas *Justified* includes 8.

Also, *Game of Thrones*' Westeros presents itself as eminently "drillable" [15], rewarding attentive fans with a wealth of cohesive, consistent narrative details. *Game of Thrones* exemplifies Jenkins' and Rose's conception of convergence, and unsurprisingly, engenders a forensic fervor among fans, a hunger to drill into the details of Westeros. The *Game of Thrones Wiki* hosts 2,611 fan-created articles at the time of this writing. Crucially, *Game of Thrones* exhibits the encyclopedic capacity required to reward fans' engagement. Narratively speaking, *Game of Thrones* foregrounds character relationships. Characters organize into houses, debate familial lineages and negotiate carefully detailed, often conflicting allegiances. In Westeros, personal betrayals motivate armies.

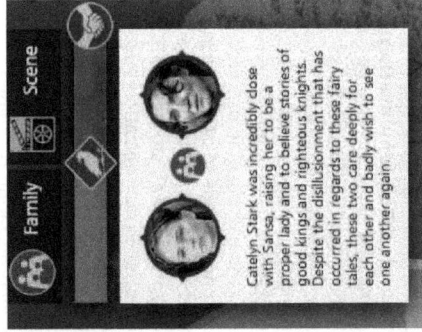

Figure 3: A user explores Sansa's relationships with disabled family and scene filters, and the relationship slider narrowed to characters considered neutral, friends and allies.

Design Considerations

GoTC utilizes an iPad as a second screen device. It presents synchronized visualizations of character relationships in a highly legible arrangement. Ideally, these visualizations should orient users "at a glance," be ignorable when not required, and allow users to drill down or to shift attention to follow story threads across the series' wealth of characters. In order to meet these aims, the GoTC app exploits tight temporal synchronization to focus users' attention on the characters and relationships most relevant to the current scene. As characters are introduced into the scene, their respective portraits appear on the second screen. To maximize legibility, information is mapped onto spatial dimensions (see figure 1).

At any time, users may drag a major character's portrait to the circle's center, which shifts focus onto the selected character. The concentric circles merge into one, character portraits surround the focal character, and the circle's "house" sectors shrink and grow according to the new arrangement. Here, a character's distance from the center signifies the tenor of his/her relationship with the focus character. These relationships are composed of a single abstracted value, which categorizes relationships into five types. From most amiable to most antagonistic, they are: ally, friend, neutral, rival, and enemy. The characters whom the focal character considers allies are positioned closest to the center, while those considered enemies are positioned farthest. Finally, icons are used to highlight key relationships such as betrothal and parentage.

Since well-constructed storyworlds invite users to drill down in pursuit of encyclopedic narrative pleasure, GoTC includes filters for exploring the story structure without

being overwhelmed. The *scene filter* (on by default) narrows the presented characters to those present or alluded to in the current scene. The *house filter*, when enabled, narrows presented characters to those belonging to the *focal character's* house. The *relationship slider* allows users to narrow presented characters to those within a desired relationship range. These filters may be toggled on and off in any configuration (see figure 3).

Preliminary Usability Testing

The preliminary user study involved 26 participants, each with varying degrees of familiarity with Game of Thrones. Participants watched four scenes from the fourth episode of season two, Garden of Bones, with each scene chosen for its diversity of characters and dramatic appeal. Each participant was provided with either the GoTC or the HBO Go app to utilize during testing. To allow users a chance to peruse their respective apps for further information, two-minute breaks were provided between each scene. After watching the four scenes, participants were asked to complete a 20-question questionnaire.

The questionnaire focused on: (1) gauging participants' familiarity with Game of Thrones; (2) measuring participants' ability to identify which major and minor characters were present in a given scenes, as well as the nature of those characters' relationships; and (3) obtaining evaluations of the apps' usefulness for enhancing understanding and recall. Based on their self-reported familiarity with Game of Thrones, participants were divided into naïve and experienced groups. These groups were further divided into a GoTC and HBO Go group, for a total of four test cases: naïve and experienced GoTC users, and naïve and experienced HBO Go users (see table 1).

Test Cases	n
Exp. GoTC	5
Naïve GoTC	10
Exp. HBO Go	6
Naïve HBO Go	5

Table 1: Distribution of participants across four test cases.

For both sets of experienced users, retention was strong when identifying major characters' presence across the four scenes; though, experienced *GoTC* users accurately identified the presence of a greater number of minor characters. In contrast, naïve *GoTC* users had significantly better recall across all four scenes when compared to naïve *HBO Go* users. Naïve *GoTC* user's recall of major characters was just as effective over all 4 scenes as our experienced user testing groups. During the first scene, for example, naïve *GoTC* users were better able to comprehend the relationship between Sansa Stark, a protagonist, and Joffrey Baratheon, sadistic king and fiancé to Sansa. Participants ranked their understanding of the relationship average of 4.4 out of 5, as compared to an average of 1.2 for *HBO Go* users. In another case, when asked which character posed the greatest challenge to Joffrey, naïve *GoTC* users provided answers that more closely reflected those of the experienced groups, with Tyrion being the most popular answer. Lastly, only *GoTC* users were able to identify Robb Stark, who is mentioned though never physically present in the first scene. Our group also wanted to determine when users were likely to use the given application. Users could choose any combination of answers, which included "during the show", "after the show", "during breaks" and "would not use". Again, the biggest difference was also between naïve *GoTC* users and naïve *HBO Go* users with 4 of 10 (i.e., 40%) *GoTC* users and naïve *HBO Go* users responding that they are likely to use the application both during the show and during breaks and only 1 of 5 (i.e., 20%) naïve *HBO Go* users giving the same answer. Furthermore 2 of 5 naïve *HBO Go* users said they would not use the application at all compared with 0% of *GoTC* users.

Design Observations and Future Work

When developing the prototype, several design considerations surfaced. First, visualizations should prioritize spatial arrangement. The design of *GoTC* mapped the scene's most salient information onto the spatial dimension. Character portraits appear as they arrive on scene. Major and minor characters are delineated by portrait size. To shift focus onto a character, users drag a portrait into the center; friends huddle around their ally; enemies disperse. These spatial arrangements capitalize on users' understanding of visual language. For parts of the design that strayed from spatial cues, participants suggested shorter character descriptions. Secondly, maintaining visual consistency between first and second screens allows for more seamless transitions between screens.

Matters of spatial arrangement and abstraction present rich possibilities for future research. Synchronized visualizations may be applied to discrete narrative threads or geographical settings. Social TV apps offer unique social affordances that have yet to be integrated into narrative-focused apps. Lastly, these visualizations offer equally rich potential for non-fictional material such as televised news and historical documentaries.

References

1. Aarseth, E. J. Cybertext: perspectives on ergodic literature. JHU Press (1997).
2. Bruner, J. S. Acts of Meaning. Harvard University Press (1990).
3. Cesar, P., Bulterman, D. C., & Jansen, A. J. Usages of the Secondary Screen in an Interactive Television Environment: Control, Enrich, Share, and Transfer Television Content. *Changing Television Environments* (2008). 168–177

15. Mittell, J. Sites of Participation: Wiki Fandom and the Case of Lostpedia. *Transformative Works and Cultures*, 3 (2009)

16. Murray, Janet. Hamlet on the Holodeck: The Future of Narrative in Cyberspace. The Free Press. New York, NY (1998).

17. Nandakumar, A., & Murray, J. (2014, June). Companion apps for long arc TV series: supporting new viewers in complex storyworlds with tightly synchronized context-sensitive annotations. In *Proceedings of the 2014 ACM international conference on Interactive experiences for TV and online video* (pp. 3-10). ACM.

18. Nielsen Company. Living Social: How Second Screens are Helping TV Make Fans (2014).

19. Rose, F. (2012). The art of immersion: How the digital generation is remaking Hollywood, Madison Avenue, and the way we tell stories. WW Norton & Company.

20. Simon, H., Comunello, E., & Von Wangenheim, A. Enrichment of Interactive Digital TV using Second Screen. *International Journal of Computer Applications* (2009), 64(22), 58–64.

21. Simons, N. Television Audience Research in the Age of Convergence: Challenges and Difficulties. In *Proceedings of the 9th International Interactive Conference on Interactive Television* New York, NY, (2011). (pp. 101–104).

22. Tsekleves, E., Whitham, R., Kondo, K., & Hill, A. (2011). Investigating Media Use and the Television User Experience in the Home. *Entertainment Computing* (2011), 2(3), 151–161.

23. Turner, M. (1998). The literary mind: The origins of thought and language. Oxford University Press.

4. Cox, D., Wolford, J., Jensen, C., & Beardsley, D. An Evaluation of Game Controllers and Tablets As Controllers for Interactive Tv Applications. In *Proceedings of the 14th ACM International Conference on Multimodal Interaction (2012)*. New York, NY. 181-188.

5. Dena, C. Transmedia Practice: Theorising the Practice of Expressing a Fictional World across Distinct Media and Environments. University of Sydney (2010).

6. Geerts, D., & De Grooff, D. Supporting the Social Uses of Television: Sociability Heuristics for Social TV. In *Proceedings of the SIGCHI Conference on Human Factors in Computing Systems* (2009). New York, NY. ACM. 595–604.

7. Gerrig, R. J. Experiencing Narrative Worlds: On the Psychological Activities of Reading. Yale University Press, New Haven (1993).

8. Graesser, A., Lang, K. L., & Roberts, R. M. Question Answering in the Context of Stories. *Journal of Experimental Psychology* (1991). 254-277.

9. Harboe, G., Metcalf, C. J., Bentley, F., Tullio, J., Massey, N., & Romano, G. Ambient Social TV: Drawing People into a Shared Experience. In *Proceedings of the SIGCHI Conference on Human Factors in Computing Systems* (2008) New York, NY. ACM. 1-10.

10. Herman, D. Story logic: Problems and possibilities of narrative. University of Nebraska Press (2004).

11. Jenkins, H. *Convergence Culture: Where Old and New Media Collide*. NYU Press (2006).

12. Jenkins, H., Ford, S., & Green, J. *Spreadable Media: Creating Value and Meaning in a Networked Culture*. NYU Press (2013).

13. Mittell, J. Complex TV: The Poetics of Contemporary Television Storytelling. MediaCommons Press (2015).

14. Mittell, J. Narrative Complexity in Contemporary American Television. The Velvet Light Trap. University of Texas Press (2006). 58(1), 29-40

173

United Universe: A Second Screen Transmedia Experience

Dillon Eversman
Experimental Television Lab
Georgia Institute of Technology
Atlanta, GA 30308, USA
nollid45@gmail.com

Timothy Major
Experimental Television Lab
Georgia Institute of Technology
Atlanta, GA 30308, USA
tmajor3@gatech.edu

Mithila Tople
Experimental Television Lab
Georgia Institute of Technology
Atlanta, GA 30308, USA
mithila.tople@gatech.edu

Lauren Schaffer
Experimental Television Lab
Georgia Institute of Technology
Atlanta, GA 30308, USA
la.schaffer@gatech.edu

Janet Murray
Experimental Television Lab
Georgia Institute of Technology
Atlanta, GA 30308, USA
janet.murray@lmc.gatech.edu

TVX'15, June 03-05, 2015, Brussels, Belgium
ACM 978-1-4503-3526-3/15/06.
http://dx.doi.org/10.1145/2745197.2755520

Abstract

United Universe is a second screen transmedia experience aimed at supporting understanding of a complex storyworld presented across media artifacts. Using the highly interconnected and allusive Marvel Cinematic Universe as a primary example, *United Universe* abstracts a story into the fundamental elements of characters, events, items, and locations, and presents them in a "glanceable" manner to the interactor. As significant story elements are referenced, the application provides explanatory information on the second screen. Drawing from the larger story world made up of multiple comic books, movies, games, and television shows, *United Universe* aims to provide clarity and background for the novice, and depth and engagement for more knowledgeable viewers.

Author Keywords

Second screen; transmedia; television; film; cinematic universe; interactive television; media evolution.

ACM Classification Keywords

H.5.2. Information interfaces and presentation: User Interfaces; User-centered Design

Introduction

Transmedia storytelling is defined by Henry Jenkins as "a process where integral elements of a fiction get dispersed systematically across multiple delivery channels" and creating a connected and coordinated entertainment experience. [10]. The Marvel Cinematic Universe (MCU), in particular, is a highly expansive and intricately woven transmedia storyworld, extending from comic books to cinema and television, both of which challenge viewers by referencing story elements that cross mediums. Currently, the MCU consists of ten films, with twelve more announced for release between February 2015 and July 2019. In addition, two MCU television shows are airing on ABC, and there are five MCU-based Netflix shows planned to release over the next two years. The films in the cinematic universe have grossed over seven billion dollars worldwide, and the *Agents of S.H.I.E.L.D.* television show averages 8.3 million viewers per episode [1, 13].

Television often provides an entire social world to viewers, including the emotional and empathetic reactions of the human experience, provoking highly active engagement in fictional worlds [10, 15]. Comic book fans have well-known appetites for sharing extensive knowledge, engaging in fan fiction to prolong and intensify their engagement with these alternate worlds. New York ComicCon, the largest comic convention in America, brings in over 150,000 fans annually [3]. There is clear interest from fans to become immersed in the storyworld in ways that expand beyond the classic television screen.

According to The Nielsen Company, 70% of tablet owners and 68% of smartphone owners say that they use their devices while watching television. With this tendency to multitask, there are many opportunities to integrate users' second screens into their viewing experiences, but users are not satisfied with existing aids [11]. This research, along with our user studies,

suggests that users can increase their engagement with long-form narrative television content by using second screens to seek more contextual information.

Previous Work

Other researchers have identified uses for second screen devices that include "learning and content selection." [4, 8] Users can view more information about specific items or repeat information they may have missed. In addition, users may personalize that information by organizing it in a way that enhances their experience with the main content. This led us to develop a prototype that allows viewers to navigate through information about *United Universe* characters, events or items they choose. This can serve both new viewers by prompting them of references they may not otherwise catch as well as existing viewers by serving as a reminder and exploratory tool.

Television shows oftentimes present concepts to viewers that require knowledge of previous episodes or seasons. Second screens are a potential way to close the information gap as long as they are designed in a minimally-interruptive fashion. Cruickshshank et al. point out two major advantages in employing a second screen: 1) the device's mobility and 2) the ability to reduce clutter on the main screen. [6] While the authors focused on reducing visual clutter on the main screen, we believe this is also an opportunity for the second screen to reduce content clutter.

Other approaches to contextual information with a second screen have primarily focused on the exploration of character relationships. *Story Map*, a second screen experience developed at Georgia Tech's Experimental Television Lab, is a system developed for the television show, *Justified*, and focuses on

What do you hope to learn about when consulting outside sources? (Multiple answers allowed)

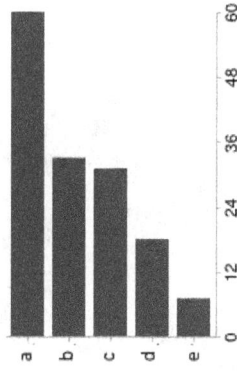

a. *More details about the show/movie's fictional universe: 67.4%*

b. *How the movie/TV show was made:37.1%*

c. *Clarification about what happened in the program: 34.8%*

d. *I don't use any additional sources: 20.2%*

e. *Other: 7.9%*

Figure 1:

Survey responses show that 67% (60 participants) of those who looked up information on a second screen while watching a TV show or film are "seeking further information on the storyworld," followed by "how the show was made," "clarification about what just happened," "I don't use additional sources," and "other."

synchronously informing the viewer of character relationships and referenced events [7]. Although the content is timely, it is not easy to take in at a glance. Navigation requires precise actions which divert the viewer's attention away from the television screen. Our objective is to create a second screen that responds quickly to a limited set of targeted touchscreen gestures, keeping the viewer focused on the show. *United Universe* includes character and event information, but goes beyond *Story Map* by expanding the coverage to locations and fictional items.

Many official Marvel applications have been designed for smart phones and tablets as well, including capacious compilations of Marvel comic lore and large-scale games [12]. In addition, there are various unofficial, fan-made apps for *Agents of S.H.I.E.L.D.* and other stand-alone storylines. However, this content is heavily focused on comic books, and there is currently no app that integrates live viewing of media with the expansive knowledge one might desire as significant story elements are referenced across mediums.

User Research

In the early stages of development for *United Universe*, we conducted user needs research through an online survey. This survey focused on television viewing habits and second screen behaviors, alongside experiences with films or television shows within the MCU.

From the survey, 63% of viewers stated that they utilize a second screen device while watching Marvel content. Although results showed mixed responses as to what the second screen was used for, we believe this is partially a result of existing solutions failing to

support the "glanceability" a second screen should provide.

If additional content within the MCU is desired by the viewer, more than 67% of individuals would seek more information specifically about the storyworld (see Figure 1). Based on these findings, it was important not to extend the MCU information to non-diegetic elements of the TV shows/films (i.e. "Behind the Scenes") and to provide an unobtrusive, passive experience for the viewer while engaged in a show. Additionally, the survey results supported the need for a system that provides additional information to accompany the viewing of a single piece of media in the MCU. In response to these findings, we framed the following research questions to build our prototype: 1) How do you provide contextualized information for a dense transmedia storyworld without overwhelming the viewer? 2) How do you explore connections between heterogeneous narrative components?

United Universe
Overview

In order to orient viewers to a storyworld that runs across multiple media artifacts, we drew on abstract descriptions of story elements proposed by the branch of literary criticism known as narratology [5]. We identified four story element categories that helped define the fictional landscape and link the comic books, films, and television series to one another: events, locations, items, and characters. In *United Universe*, these four categories of story elements, called "blips," are interactive, coin-shaped data sources (color coded by category), and are indicated by a marker that appears on the main screen video to indicate synchronized content on the tablet screen.

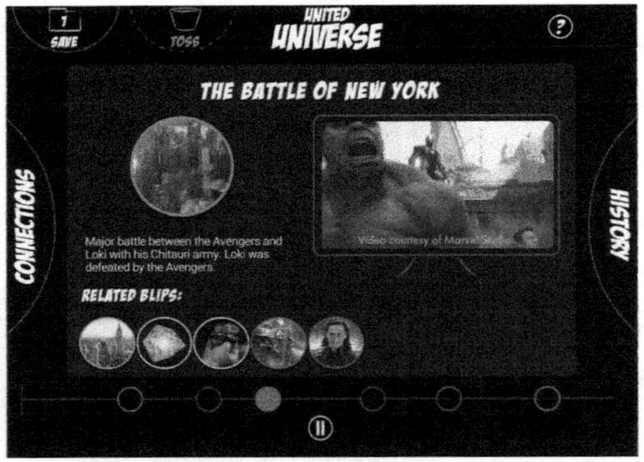

The MCU is explored by dropping blips into "buckets" marked as Connections, History, Save, and Discard. These buckets are placed along the sides of the tablet, providing rapid and deliberate actions that do not require precise movements from the interactor.

For our prototype, *Agents of S.H.I.E.L.D.* was chosen as the media source. It is the first television show connected to the MCU, and the ties between this show and previous Marvel films are extensive. For example, the "Battle of New York" is a climactic final fight in *The Avengers*, and it is referenced more than four times within the first two episodes of the show. Additionally, the Tesseract and a Chitauri Neural Link – two key items in the "Battle of New York" – are referenced throughout early episodes. S.H.I.E.L.D., the organization on which the show is based, is a law-enforcement agency in the MCU that deals with paranormal and superhuman threats. In this fictional world, they protect the public from the knowledge and use of items such as the Tesseract and Chitauri Neural Link. Items like these are the reason why S.H.I.E.L.D. exist, but any viewer of the show who has not seen *The Avengers* would be overwhelmed by several unexplained references.

Features

DETAIL VIEW AND TIMELINE

Detail View is the default screen in *United Universe*. It displays the featured blip with a brief description, a 6 second edited supporting video, and a list of blips directly related to it. All

A timeline runs across the bottom of the second screen app and updates the tablet screen with the Detail View of a blip as it is referenced in the main screen video (see Figure 2). To avoid spoilers, there are no images on the timeline – only the color to let the interactor know what type of blip will be triggered. To access a timeline blip before it appears on the screen, the interactor may tap to view it in Details View.

CONNECTIONS VIEW AND HISTORY VIEW

The primary views to contextualize blips within *United Universe* are the Connections View and the History View. These two views augment the viewer's understanding of a blip by visualizing its relation to other story elements.

Connections View extends the "related blips" section of Detail View and allows the interactor to explore extensive relationships between story elements of all types. This answers key questions regarding character relationships with one another, key characters involved in significant events, where important items have been used, etc.

To interact with Connections View, the user may tap on a blip for its name (and alias, if applicable). If there are multiple instances of the same blip within Connections View, each instance will be highlighted on the tablet (see Figure 3). In addition, the interactor may tap on the lines connecting blips to view a brief description of their relationship. If the interactor wants to update Connections View with a new blip, they may drag their selection from its initial position to the center.

History View is a way for the interactor to understand the storyline of a particular blip (see Figure 4). All

Figure 2: Detail View (center) with featured blip, description, edited supporting video, and related blips; Timeline (bottom) synced with main screen video.

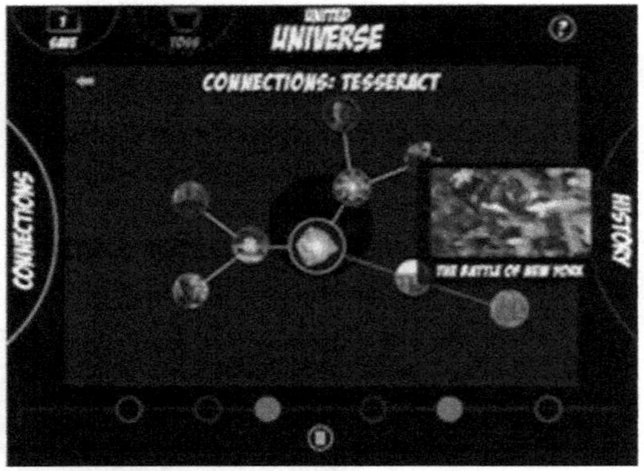

Figure 3: Connections View after selecting a blip to view its connection to the "Tesseract."

events associated with the selected blip are presented chronologically on a timeline, and allow the interactor to watch or read its path throughout the MCU.

SAVE AND DISCARD

A save feature preserves information without requiring immediate interaction from the viewer. If the interactor would like to remember a particular blip, s/he may drop it into the top left bucket and it will be added to a list. Unlike the timeline which only displays blips that are referenced in the main screen video, the saved folder can store all blips within the MCU. Furthermore, the interactor may drop a blip into the "Toss" bucket, removing

undesired blips from the timeline and main screen.

TECHNICAL IMPLEMENTATION

United Universe was developed using HTML5, CSS3 and JavaScript, with animation developed using the Velocity.js library. To sync playback across screens, the system incorporated Node.js. Timing information from the main screen video was stored and referenced by the server, which then signaled events to the iPad.

Blip data was modified from the MCU Wiki, a community site dedicated to all MCU films, TV shows, and story elements associated with them [14]. This blip information was custom structured into a json format.

United Universe was designed with a modular layout that is easily customizable for development beyond the MCU. In our initial prototyping phase, we also utilized *United Universe* for ABC's *Once Upon a Time* storyworld which deals with complex character relationships and intertwined storylines across parallel worlds.

Figure 4: History View with blip description.

Testing

A formative evaluation was conducted in December 2014 with five individuals in the television industry to assess both the design of the system and the abstraction of story elements into blips. Participants were asked to perform a specific set of tasks and provide their reflective opinions about the system afterward. In addition, a heuristic evaluation following the same structure was performed with 6 Human-Computer Interaction graduate students to further refine the structure of the interface.

Feedback from participants validated the taxonomy of the storyworld, since the questions participants had about the excerpted TV show were answered with the *United Universe* prototype.

Testing also surfaced a UX Design problem with the metaphor of "buckets." Initially, participants interpreted the buckets as "panels" or "buttons" that would slide out from each direction of the screen. As a result, we redesigned the interface and added animations that reinforced the metaphor of placing the coin-like blips into bucket-like areas of the screen. The bucket design was modified to be more circular in addition to animating outward if a blip was dragged on top, providing a clearer visual indicator of user affordances. Animated transitions between views were also added to reinforce the system's current state.

Future Work

We continue to develop the UX Design of *United Universe*, ensuring that users learn about the MCU while reading minimal text. We also plan to acquire information from the Marvel comics which could help the interactor understand how MCU story elements compare to the comic book counterparts on which they are based. We received feedback suggesting use of the framework for educational applications, which we are considering in the context of television news coverage.

Conclusion

With the rise of transmedia storytelling in the entertainment industry, there is an increasing need to curate this content into a contextualized format. The *United Universe* prototype is a way of exploring the design issues raised by the challenge of maintaining coherence while encouraging exploration of densely interconnected narrative worlds.

Acknowledgements

We thank all the Experimental Television Lab members who provided helpful comments on the prototype and the previous versions of this document.

References

1. Agents of S.H.I.E.L.D. Ratings. 2015. Retrieved February 27, 2015 from http://tvbythenumbers.zap2it.com/tag/marvels-agents-of-s-h-i-e-l-d-ratings/

2. Alt, Eric. Why Marvel Works: A Scholarly Investigation. October 7, 2014. Retrieved February 25, 2015 from http://www.fastcompany.com/3036710/why-marvel-works-a-scholarly-investigation

3. Bricken, Rob. Holy Crap, New York Comic-Con Is Bigger Than San Diego Comic-Con. October 14, 2014. Retrieved February 26, 2015 from http://io9.com/holy-crap-new-york-comic-con-is-bigger-than-san-diego-1646158769.

4. Cesar, P., Bulterman, D. C., & Jansen, A. J. Usages of the Secondary Screen in an Interactive Television Environment: Control, Enrich, Share, and Transfer Television Content. *Changing Television Environments* (2008). 168–177

5. Chatman, S. Story and Discourse: Narrative Structure in Fiction and Film. Ithaca, Cornell University Press. 1980.

6. Cruickshank et al. Making interactive TV easier to use: Interface design for a second screen approach. The Design Journal, 10 (3) (2007), pp. 41des

7. Experimental Television Lab: Story Map (2013) Retrieved February 27, 2015 from etv.gatech.edu/storymap

8. Fallahkhair, S., Pemberton, L., Griffiths, R.: Dual device user interface design for ubiquitous language learning: Mobile phone and interactive television (iTV). In: WMTE 2005: Proceedings of the IEEE International Workshop on Wireless and Mobile Technologies in Education, pp. 85–92 (2005)

9. Herman, D. Story Logic: Problems and Possibilities of Narrative, Nebraska University Press. 2002.

10. Jenkins, Henry. 2007. Transmedia Storytelling 101. Retrieved February 23, 2015 from http://henryjenkins.org/2007/03/transmedia_story telling_101.html

11. Koenig, Steve. The Rise of TV's Second Screen. March 25, 2014. Retrieved February 25, 2015 from http://www.ce.org/i3/Grow/2014/March-April/The-Rise-of-TV's-Second-Screen.aspx

12. Marvel Apps. 2015. Retrieved February 22, 2015 from http://www.marvel.com/mobile.

13. Marvel Cinematic Universe. 2015. Retrieved February 27, 2015 from http://boxofficemojo.com/franchises/chart/?id=ave ngers.htm

14. Marvel Cinematic Universe Wiki. 2015. Retrieved August 2014 – February 2015 from marvelcinematicuniverse.wikia.com

15. Singer, J. L. (n.d.). The Power and Limitations of Television: A Cognitive-Affective Analysis. In The Entertainment Functions of Television. 1997. (pp 50–51).

Engaging Citizens with Televised Election Debates through Online Interactive Replays

Brian Plüss
Knowledge Media Institute
The Open University
Milton Keynes MK7 6AA, UK
brian.pluss@open.ac.uk

Anna De Liddo
Knowledge Media Institute
The Open University
Milton Keynes MK7 6AA, UK
anna.deliddo@open.ac.uk

Abstract

In this paper we tackle the crisis of political trust and public engagement with politics by investigating new methods and tools to watch and take part in televised political debates. The paper presents relevant research at the intersection of citizenship, technologies and government/democracy, and describes the motivation, requirements and design of Democratic Replay (Figure 1), an online interactive video replay platform that offers a persistent, customisable digital space for: (a) members of the public to express their views as they watch online videos of political events; and (b) enabling for a richer collective understanding of what goes on in these complex media events.

Author Keywords

Online Video; Interactive Visualisations; Televised Election Debates; eDemocracy; Instant Audience Feedback

ACM Classification Keywords

H.5.3 [Information interfaces and presentation (e.g., HCI)]: Group and Organization Interfaces.

General Terms

Online Video, Visualisations, Democracy, Politics, Engagement

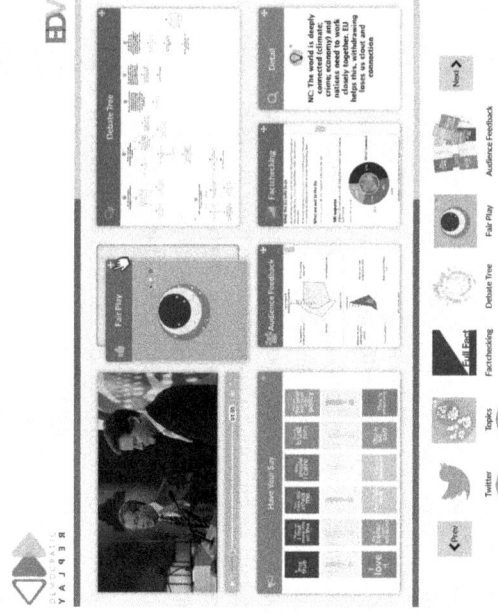

Figure 1: Mockup of Democratic Replay: an online interactive election debate replay. Copyright of debate still owned by the BBC.

TVX'15, June 3–5, 2015, Brussels, Belgium.
ACM 978-1-4503-3526-3/15/06.
http://dx.doi.org/10.1145/2745197.2755521

Introduction

The Internet and mobile computing devices are changing how viewers experience political media events like televised election debates [1, 18]. Streams of complementary information originating from mainstream media and other viewers are now available. We present research to address four challenges: (a) the lack of organisation between information streams and media events, which can confuse viewers; (b) the low levels of engagement with politics, which creates a divide between citizens and candidates; (c) a need for citizens to communicate their views in meaningful ways knowing that these views are heard; and (d) the inherent complexity of in-depth analyses of these events, which makes interpretation difficult to most viewers.

Televised General Election debates were first introduced in the UK in 2010, were greatly appreciated by the public, and energised first-time voters [3]. With negotiations underway for 2015 Election debates, we envisage a future in which these events are enriched by a range of information channels that, brought together coherently in an online debate replay with advanced analytics and visualisations, would turn viewing into a rich learning experience.

Four Requirements for Online Interactive Election Debate Replays

Our work sits at the crossroads of research in television and the Internet, political communication, collective intelligence, and hypermedia. We identify four high-level requirements for online interactive debate replays related to these areas.

Television and the Internet

Information technologies and social media are turning TV consumption into a participatory experience often involving thousands of viewers [1, 12]. Programme-specific apps can organise and deliver enhancements, both inbound by

channelling streams of information from the Internet to the viewers [13], and outbound by giving viewers access to comment channels and social media [1, 12], or to special-purpose audience feedback tools [10]. Still, these changes present new challenges. Secondary information streams introduce distractions [15] and can prevent viewers from focusing on contents [12, 13]. New media can alienate individuals and social groups who are not 'tech-savvy', e.g. those not involved in social media [6]. This leads us to the first requirement for online interactive replays:

Requirement 1. The technology has to be non-intrusive and accessible to as wide a range of citizens as possible. This calls for a free and open platform in which access to contents is not limited by fees, memberships or proprietary licenses: e.g. an open data, open source web application, independent of device-specific technologies and existing social media platforms. Information channels must be non-trivial, relevant and synchronised with the video [13].

New Media and Live Political Events

The same holds for citizen engagement with political media events [3, 18, 19]. Online media open the possibility of more direct political representation [5], especially among young people [19]. The challenges of making events accessible, engaging and informative also hold [6], coupled with common impediments of democratic participation: e.g. failures in civic education, apathy, and a disconnect between citizens and politicians [21]. Coleman identifies requirements on televised debates for democratic citizenship: 'being informed…; being free to participate…; feeling engaged in the processes that affect their lives…; and experiencing a subjective belief that they have at least some chance of making a difference in the world' [6, p. 10]. We aim to address these, specifically:

Requirement 2. The technology has to increase citizen

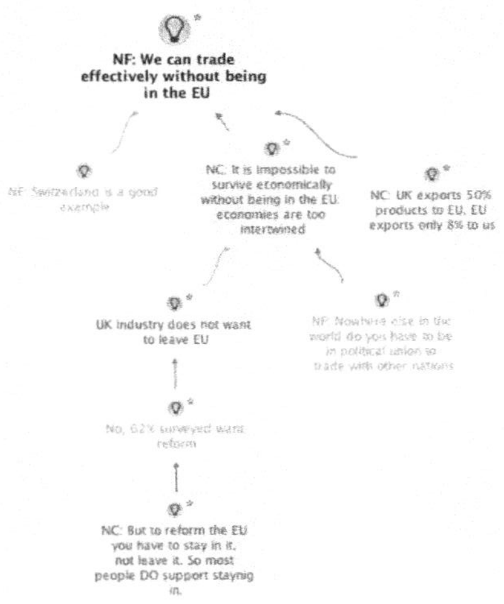

of audience feedback analytics that are shown back to viewers or used later as assessments of the candidates' performances and of the debate as a media event [10].

Hypervideo for Enhanced Televised Debates

By analogy with hypertext, hypervideo refers to video that can be navigated non-linearly via timed links. Technologies for deploying hypervideo on the Web include Popcorn.js[1] and the HTML5 video tag[2]. They allow for video replay manipulations and functional links with hypermedia annotations. Tools for dynamic, interactive visualisation of hypervideo annotations include Advene [2] and Compendium [24], although they are desktop applications with no support for delivery of visualisations on the Web. Further, the potential of web hypervideo tools, such as WebCHM [23] and Popcorn.js, to deliver interactive hypervideo visualisations is yet to be explored. These shortcomings lead us to the final:

Requirement 4. Complementary information has to be presented in ways that are consistent, non-intrusive and accessible. This involves developing techniques for turning annotations into meaningful visualisations, coupling hypervideo technologies like Popcorn.js, with dynamic data visualisation libraries like D3.js[3].

Democratic Replay

In order to meet these requirements, Democratic Replay uses in-depth analyses which are made freely and openly available online as synchronised, dynamic and interactive visualisations. We currently focus four analyses: 1. argumentation visualisation, 2. debate rule compliance, 3. instant audience feedback, and 4. factchecking.

―――――――――
[1] http://popcornjs.org/
[2] http://www.w3schools.com/html/html5_video.asp
[3] http://d3js.org/

engagement in political debates. It must address the reasons for disengagement: e.g. lack of trust in politicians' communication strategies [3], difficulties in understanding and evaluating political arguments [17], feelings that policies do not relate to citizens' lives [3, 6, 7]. This calls for a 'slowing down' of the debates, letting viewers play them at their own pace, with synchronised visualisations of in-depth analyses and non-trivial knowledge curation.

Citizen Participation and Collective Intelligence

In the 2010 debates, broadcasters polled undecided voters with 'the worm': a line going up and down when viewers respectively liked or disliked what candidates said. The method has been criticised due to small viewer samples [16] and because it can affect independent judgement if shown during broadcasts [9]. Twitter sentiment analysis has been used to map the changing mood of tweets during political media events [1, 18]. But uncovering the reasons why Twitter users feel positive or negative is difficult and researchers have challenged the soundness of inferences drawn form social media data [22]. De Liddo et al. [10] propose a method to engage the audience in televised election debates by eliciting aware, rich and meaningful feedback through a set of statements on coloured flashcards. The method builds on *contested collective intelligence* [11], capturing people's interpretations to support deep reflection and understanding. Still, it does not scale: reactions are captured with paper flashcards that must be physically delivered to viewers and require onerous manual annotation. Thus, we aim to address the following:

Requirement 3. The technology has to provide effective means for viewers to participate in the debate experience. This involves digital participatory channels for citizens to express their views as they watch the event, ensuring that the views are attended to [7]. We developed visualisations

Figure 2: A partial issue map for a debate between Nick Clegg and Nigel Farage on EU-UK relations (BBC, 2 April 2014), showing the issues under discussion (black), connected with claims supporting (green) or challenging (red) the issue or one another.

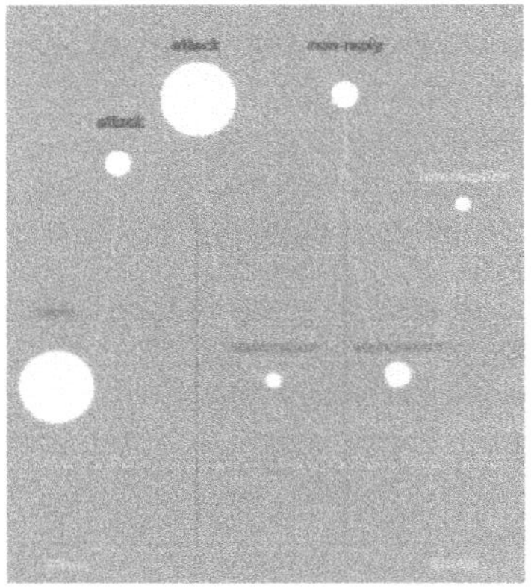

Figure 3: Visualising rule compliance in political debates.

Work in Progress

Figure 4: Deck of flashcards for eliciting instant audience feedback to televised election debates.

Computer Supported Argumentation Visualisation (CSAV)
Political issues are often inherently complex, resulting in arguments that are beyond the grasp of many citizens. This causes citizens to feel excluded from the event and leads to disengagement. CSAV helps to make sense of complex arguments using information technologies [4]. Argument maps make crucial elements of arguments visually explicit: e.g. 'showing' how the candidates are addressing key issues, the claims they make, whether they offer evidence for these claims, and how their arguments relate to each other. We use Issue and Dialogue Mapping as techniques [8] and Compendium [24] as a tool to build and visualise arguments (see Figure 2 for a partial debate issue map). Dialogue Mapping captures verbal exchanges in real-time and was used to map the 2010 UK Election debates[4].

Debate Rule Compliance Assessment
Candidates in election debates agree on a series of implicit and explicit rules: e.g. they are expected to answer questions, stay on topic, respect turns and avoid personal attacks[5]. When they break the rules, e.g. avoiding questions or attacking each other, they violate this agreement, hindering communication in pursuit of egoistic goals. Following Plüss [20], we automatically analyse manually-annotated debate transcripts, yielding markers when rules are broken. These markers are visualised on a timeline (see Figure 3) and aggregated into scores that show the extent to which a debater complied with the rules. Candidates' actions can thus be measured against the rules agreed by broadcasters and the parties, or against the citizens' democratic expectations. We hypothesise that exposing violations will help viewers to scrutinise politicians' rhetoric and detect manipulative communication strategies.

Instant Audience Feedback
Democratic Replay incorporates visualisations of the feedback method proposed by De Liddo et al. [10], which consists of 18 statement cards (see Figure 4) in three dimensions: information need (blue), trust (yellow) and emotion (red). During the live broadcast of the 2015 UK Election debates, 400 citizens will use Democratic Reflection: a web application which allows them to select reaction statements as they watch the debate. Choices, linked to user identifiers and timestamps, will be recorded as hypervideo annotations and visualised, giving a rich understanding of the audience's reactions to the debaters' performances (see the spider diagrams on Figure 5 for an example and [10] for details).

Factchecking
This is the verification of claims against objective evidence [14]. In political debates, factcheckers contrast debaters' claims with publicly available evidence, determining whether they are factually true, false, etc. The UK independent factchecker Full Fact[6] checked in real-time the truthfulness of claims in the 2014 Clegg-Farage EU debates[7]. We are currently liaising with them to incorporate their analyses as hypermedia visualisations in Democratic Replay.

Platform Overview and Front End Prototype
Figure 6 shows the ecosystem behind Democratic Replay. *Data Sources* are imported into a *Hypermedia Repository*. *Analytics and Visualisations* of the data are added to the repository as hypermedia annotations, packed with the video on the *Curator Dashboard* and published in *Democratic Replay*. These can also be exported as *Open Data*[8] for reuse and dissemination. Figure 7 shows the front

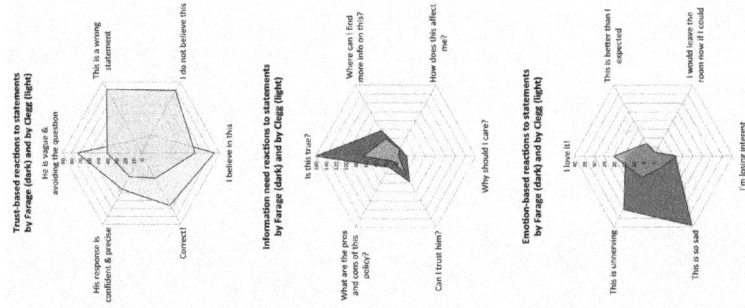

Figure 5: Spider diagrams visualising audience responses to a debate between Nick Clegg and Nigel Farage on EU-UK relations (BBC, 2 April 2014).

---

[4] See a partial video-linked map at http://youtu.be/WPF64UXFER0 and dialogue maps for the first two 2010 debates at http://bit.ly/1DV9ukC.
[5] See the 2010 debate rules at http://bit.ly/2010debaterules.

[6] https://fullfact.org
[7] http://bit.ly/198jfjP
[8] http://opendefinition.org/od/

instant feedback tool? Are citizens satisfied with the available options? Were there obvious missing statements? Did it change their experience of the debate? Did it empower them? 4. How intuitive, informational, meaningful, and timely were the visualisation? Did they have a positive or negative impact on the viewing experience? Future efforts also include the development of more visualisations (e.g. topical analysis, integration with Twitter sentiment analysis; see Figure 6), and making hypervideo annotations and visualisations available as reusable open data.

Acknowledgements

This research is part of the Election Debate Visualisation project, funded by the UK Engineering and Physical Sciences Research Council. We gratefully acknowledge our project partners from the University of Leeds (UK): Prof Stephen Coleman (PI), Dr Giles Moss and Dr Paul Wilson.

References

[1] N. Anstead and B. O'Loughlin. 2011. The Emerging Viewertariat and BBC Question Time: Television Debate and Real-Time Commenting Online. *The International Journal of Press/Politics* (2011).

[2] O. Aubert and Y. Prié. 2007. Advene: an open-source framework for integrating and visualising audiovisual metadata. In *Proceedings of the 15th International Conference on Multimedia.* ACM, 1005–1008.

[3] J. G. Blumler and S. Coleman. 2010. Voters' responses to the Prime Minister debates: A rock of (future?) ages. Leaders in the Living Room: the Prime Ministerial debates of 2010: evidence, evaluation and some recommendations, 35–54.

[4] S. Buckingham Shum. 2003. The roots of computer supported argument visualization. In *Visualizing argumentation.* Springer, 3–24.

[5] S. Coleman. 2005. New mediation and direct

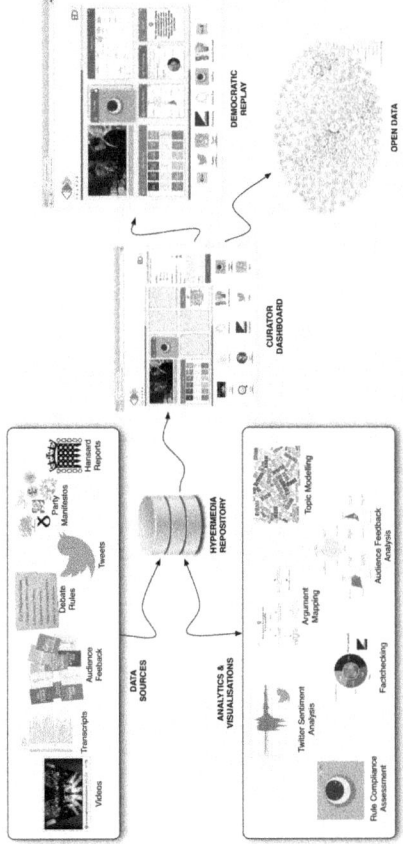

Figure 6: Overview of the election debate replay platform.

end prototype, built as a grid of widgets using gridster.js[9] and YouTube's JavaScript Player API[10]. We are building the back end to serve contents to D3.js visualisations.

Conclusions and Future Work

We presented Democratic Replay: an interactive video replay aimed to help citizens engage with televised election debates. We identified high-level requirements from gaps in research in on television and the Internet, political communication, collective intelligence and hypermedia; and described the platform's architectural drawing and four in-depth analyses and interactive visualisations.

We will test Democratic Replay on data from the 2015 UK General Election debates. This includes a robust evaluation around the requirements above to answer questions like: 1. How accessible is the technology for users from different backgrounds and with levels of digital literacy? Where does the platform stand in terms of organisation, usability and functionality? Was it helpful or intrusive? 2. What is the impact on users' engagement with the debate, the election, the politicians and politics in general? 3. How useful is the

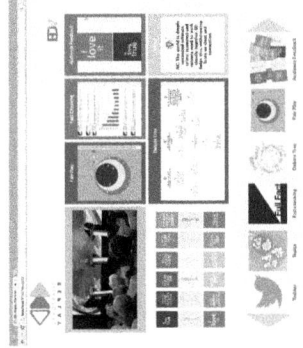

Figure 7: Democratic Replay front-end prototype. Copyright of debate still owned by the BBC.

---

[9]http://gridster.net/

[10]//developers.google.com/youtube/js_api_reference.

183

representation: reconceptualizing representation in the digital age. *New Media & Society* 7, 2 (2005), 177–198.

[6] S. Coleman. 2013. Debate on Television The Spectacle of Deliberation. *Television & New Media* 14, 1 (2013), 20–30.

[7] S. Coleman and G. Moss. 2015. Rethinking Election Debates: What Citizens Are Entitled to Expect. (2015). Unpublished Manuscript.

[8] J. Conklin. 2006. *Dialogue mapping: Building shared understanding of wicked problems.* Wiley Chichester.

[9] C. J. Davis, J. S. Bowers, and A. Memon. 2011. Social influence in televised election debates: A potential distortion of democracy. *PloS one* 6, 3 (2011).

[10] A. De Liddo, B. Plüss, and P. Wilson. 2014. Gauging Audience Engagement with Televised Election Debates Through Instant, Nuanced Feedback Elicitation. (2014). Submitted for publication.

[11] A. De Liddo, Á. Sándor, and S. Buckingham Shum. 2012. Contested Collective Intelligence: Rationale, technologies, and a human-machine annotation study. *Computer Supported Cooperative Work (CSCW)* 21, 4–5 (2012), 417–448.

[12] E. D'heer and C. Courtois. 2014. The changing dynamics of television consumption in the multimedia living room. *Convergence: The International Journal of Research into New Media Technologies* (2014), 1–16.

[13] D. Geerts, R. Leenheer, and D. De Grooff. 2014. In Front of And Behind The Second Screen: Viewer and Producer Perspectives on a Companion App. In *Proceedings of the ACM International Conference on Interactive Experience of Television and Online Video.*

[14] L. Graves and T. Glaisyer. 2012. The Fact-Checking Universe in Spring 2012. *New America* (2012).

[15] M. E Holmes, S. Josephson, and R. E. Carney. 2012. Visual attention to television programs with a

second-screen application. In *Proceedings of the Symposium on Eye Tracking Research and Applications.* ACM, 397–400.

[16] House of Lords Select Committee on Communications. 2014. *Broadcast General Election Debates - HL171, 2nd Report of Session 2013-14.* The Stationery Office.

[17] P. A. Kirschner, S. Buckingham Shum, and C. Carr. 2003. *Visualizing argumentation: Software tools for collaborative and educational sense-making.* Springer Science & Business Media.

[18] M. S. McKinney, J. B. Houston, and J. Hawthorne. 2014a. Social Watching a 2012 Republican Presidential Primary Debate. *American Behavioral Scientist* 58, 4 (2014), 556–573.

[19] M. S McKinney, L. A Rill, and E. Thorson. 2014b. Civic Engagement Through Presidential Debates Young Citizens' Political Attitudes in the 2012 Election. *American Behavioral Scientist* 58, 6 (2014), 755–775.

[20] B. Plüss. 2013. *A Computational Model of Non-Cooperation in Natural Language Dialogue.* Ph.D. Dissertation. The Open University, Milton Keynes, UK.

[21] K. Rostiashvili. 2012. Information Society and Digital Democracy-Theoretical Discourse. *Journal in Humanities* 1, 1 (2012), 11–15.

[22] D. Ruths and J. Pfeffer. 2014. Social media for large studies of behavior. *Science* 346, 6213 (2014), 1063–1064.

[23] M. Sadallah, O. Aubert, and Y. Prié. 2012. CHM: an annotation-and component-based hypervideo model for the Web. *Multimedia Tools and Applications* 70, 2 (2012), 869–903.

[24] A. Selvin, S. Buckingham Shum, M. Sierhuis, J. Conklin, B. Zimmerman, C. Palus, W. Drath, D. Horth, J. Domingue, E. Motta, and G. Li. 2001. Compendium: Making meetings into knowledge events. In *Knowledge Technologies.* Austin, Texas.

Designing TV Recommender Interfaces for Specific Viewing Experiences

Jeroen Vanattenhoven

Centre for User Experience
Research

KU Leuven - iMinds

Parkstraat 45 bus 3605

3000 Leuven

jeroen.vanattenhoven@soc.kuleuv
en.be

David Geerts

Centre for User Experience
Research

KU Leuven - iMinds

Parkstraat 45 bus 3605

3000 Leuven

david.geerts@soc.kuleuven.be

TVX'15, June 03-05, 2015, Brussels, Belgium
ACM 978-1-4503-3526-3/15/06.
http://dx.doi.org/10.1145/2745197.2755522

Abstract

In this paper we report upon our prototyping and
design efforts aimed at supporting specific viewing
experiences or situations. In our previous studies we
gathered insights into which types of viewing situations
occur in the home based on the group of viewers, the
mood, the type of content, and time-related factors.
Based on these situated experiences we now aim to
support these experiences via specific user interface
designs. The focus is mainly on presenting the right
content in the right way for the specific viewers in each
situation. The explored interfaces vary by look & feel,
content selection, and interaction possibilities. By going
through different prototype evaluation sessions we aim
to increase our understanding of each situation's user
requirements. Ultimately, viewers should save
considerable time when choosing content.

Author Keywords

Design; prototyping; user experience; context;
recommendations.

ACM Classification Keywords

H.5.m. Information interfaces and presentation (e.g.,
HCI): Miscellaneous.

Introduction

Today, the TV and video consumer is spoiled by the sheer number of options available for watching any kind of content on many different devices. At the same time however this also causes many problems: some programs are only available on one service, consumers have to switch between many devices at home (PVR, cable, Smart TV applications...), and people have to find the right content in a maze of services and an enormous amount of possibilities. To be able to help the consumer with making a suitable choice between the many items in a collection recommender systems offer an important part of the solution. These systems take factors such as personal taste, viewing history, group composition, and sometimes, contextual factors into account in order to filter out unsuitable options.

However, the algorithms in the back-end cannot form a complete solution. Churchill points to the difference between "outcome personalisation" and "process personalisation" [3]. Whereas the first is about calculating the right items (as in traditional recommender systems research), the latter is about optimising the process or the interaction with the system. It is on the latter aspect of "process personalisation" that we focus in this paper. Our goal is to design different interfaces for providing content in each kind of viewing experience in the home.

Viewing experiences at home

If we are to match interfaces to specific viewing experiences, the first question then is: what are typical viewing situations in the home? In [6] a study was carried out to understand how certain contextual queues determined viewing situations. These archetypical viewing situations were: quality time, opportunistic planning, sharing space but not content, and opportunistic self-indulgence. We have further studied these issues in [8]. Our investigations were inspired by the work of [2] that derived the important factors that determine how people choose what to watch via a survey in Portugal. They found that genre, state of mind at the moment, being alone or accompanied, and available time, were the most important factors. To continue with our study conducted in [8], our aim was to understand how genre (or content properties in general), the viewers, time (available time, time of day, meaning of certain moments), and mood determined different viewing situations. We focussed on how to describe the different viewing situations and to determine the influence of the household type (families, couples, singles etc.).

The viewing situations we determined in [8] are described in **Table 1**. We mention this information here since we want to support each of these situations via a specific interface design.

Viewing Situation	Description of Contextual Factors
Weekend mornings	Children are watching programs for children or music programs, and are in a happy, cheerful and fun mood; at the same time they are relaxed because they are still waking up.
When the children are sleeping	Parents are usually watching video on demand or recorded programs when they have the living room to themselves. Then they want to relax by viewing drama on TV, movies or soaps.
Family quality time	After or during supper the whole family is watching TV; being together is more

Viewing Situation	Description of Contextual Factors
	important than what is on TV. Usually, this means lighter genres (comedy, reality TV…)
Relaxing after school	When children come home from school they like to relax and watch programs for children (shows about animals).
A free moment	This situation mostly involved mothers in our sample, and occurs when there is a free moment during the day. Then, they watch drama series, reality TV, and movies sometimes.
Men and sports	Mostly men and boys watch sports and want to relax (in our sample). There are specific weekly programs about sports news, and live sporting events.
Lazy afternoons	In the weekend or during a day of (bank holidays), we noticed many households sometimes have and take the time to watch movies, sports, recorded programs. This is time to relax and to socialize.

Table 1: An overview of typical viewing situations and the respective descriptions using contextual factors, adapted from [8].

Designing user interfaces for viewing situations

A number of researchers have focussed on novel interfaces for that offer TV/video content or recommendations. In [1] a novel interface was created to help people decide what to watch. Based on their earlier work on insights surrounding viewing behaviour [2] they designed an interface that allows users to select their mood, the intended audience, and the genre. Our approach is different in that we first want to support each viewing situation separately via an

interface, and then find ways to provide navigation to go from one screen to another, or to determine the right context via the system and automatically show the right interface for that specific situation. Wheatley investigated the viewing practices of children in different age groups, designed and evaluated prototypes that varied for each age group [7]. The interfaces varied on interaction, trick play, media content, content choice, and personalisation. Finally, we briefly mention YouTube that just released a video app specifically designed for children [4].

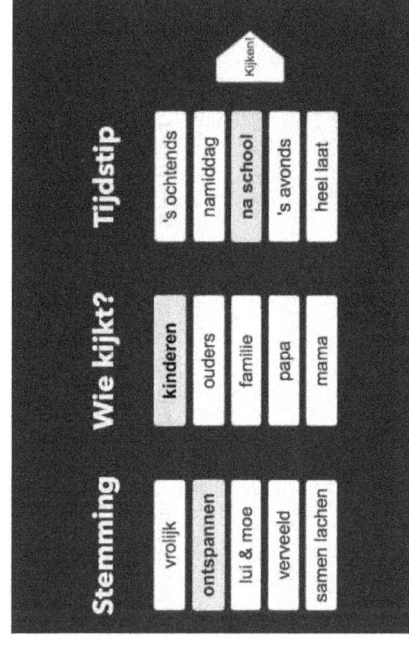

Figure 1. Selector screen: first column with different moods, second column with different viewers, and third column with different times. This example illustrates the pattern of children wanting to relax after school.

First prototype evaluation

In a first prototype evaluation [5] session we gathered reactions on six interfaces. This session was conducted in a design room in our research centre, where a set up was made for participants to sit in front of a laptop-controlled flat screen. First, they were asked to confirm an

the scenarios or situations that we obtained from the co-design session (see **Table 1**). Therefore, we asked them to provide feedback on a paper that contained a written-out version of the scenarios. Then, we presented the participants with the selector interface (see **Figure 1**), and asked them to use it in each of the seven scenarios to evaluate whether this way of interacting made sense. Finally, we presented participants with the different interface designs for different situations, one-by-one (One such example is shown in **Figure 2**), and asked them to indicate with which scenarios each interface would fit. In this final exercise, they would indicate an item to watch, and the researcher would then start that item on the flat screen via the laptop in order to increase the realism.

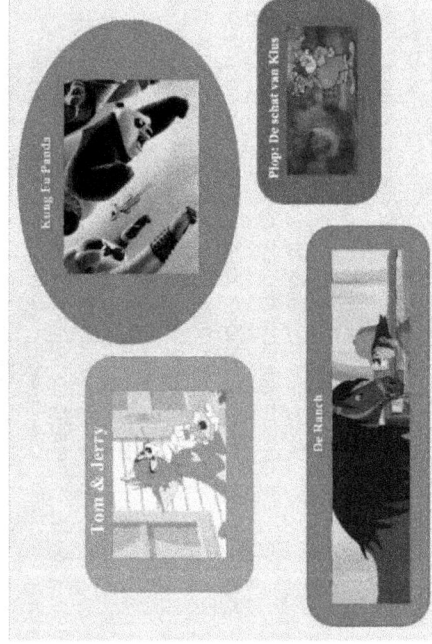

Figure 2. This interface is designed for children via specific content, look & feel, and simple interaction.

Unfortunately, the recruiting was difficult, and three families cancelled participation for the prototyping

sessions. Therefore, only one family (a mother with her two boys) participated in this first session.

Firstly, the scenarios were confirmed mostly. In this family, one scenario did not take place, namely "relaxing after school" in which children watch some TV to relax after school. In this family the children were not allowed to watch TV during the week. For the first scenario, "weekend mornings", in which children watch TV on weekend mornings while their parents are still sleeping or getting up, there was still some doubt after the co-creation session. The issue was that sometimes participants indicated an active mode of viewing, while others indicated a more relaxed mode of viewing, or in other words, the children were still wakening. The feedback now showed that this active/passive distinction is very difficult to make; they are very active and still a bit drowsy in the morning at the same time. After dinner, the family watches TV together; this was also confirmed. One family noted that at this time, the programs are chosen by the children. Concerning the "lazy afternoon" scenario, participants added that they often watched recorded content, in order to catch up with shows that could not be watched at the time of broadcast.

Secondly, the selector interface concept was found to be clear. Moreover, the selections that were made concerning mood, viewers, and time, were in line with the results from the co-design workshop (see **Table 1**). The main difficulty here remains mood: participants use several moods, sometimes seemingly contradicting moods, at the same time to describe their mood for one viewing situation. For example, relaxed, tired and lazy go together. But also relaxed and laughing together. After participants used the selector for the seven scenarios, they confirmed that they understood the concept. The main benefit as stated by the participants was "saving time", especially, when the application would pre-fill the characteristics of time, mood, viewer, based on historical TV usage.

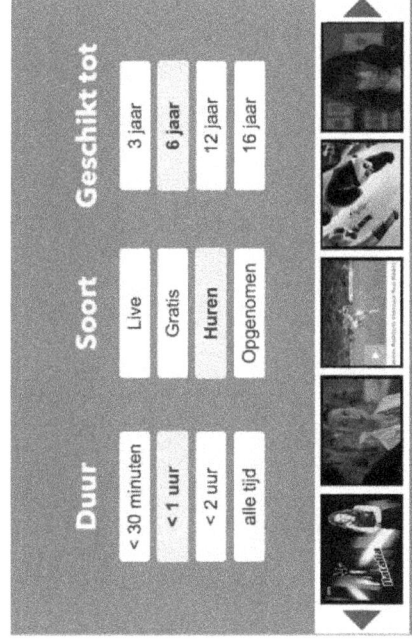

Figure 3. Active, dynamic viewing mode interface with filter options: duration, type, and suitability for different ages.

Finally, different versions of the recommender interface were explored and used to select an item to watch. Participants would also indicate for which scenarios each interface could be used. The interface for children was found suitable for scenarios 1, 3, and 7; participants related the sports interface to scenarios 6 and 7.

Then, we explored two opposite interfaces for finding what to watch: one supporting active viewing with many filtering options for content (see **Figure 3**), and one supporting more relaxed viewing involving minimal interaction (see **Figure 4**). An insight of the prototyping session was that the active viewing

interface was not liked because participants found that there were too many buttons on it.

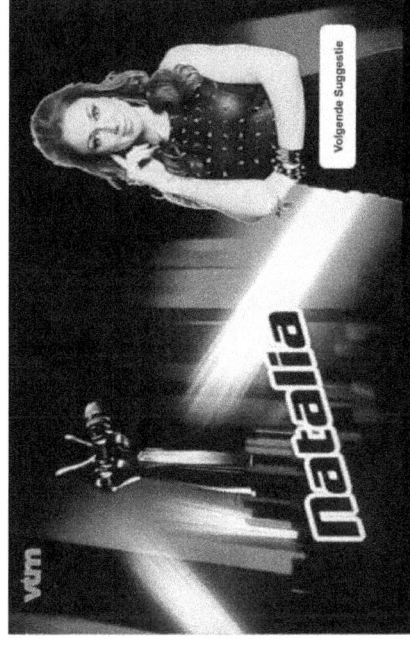

Figure 4. Interface for relaxed viewing mode, with only one button to receive another recommendation.

On-going prototyping sessions

At this moment we are organizing new prototyping sessions to investigate further which look & feel variations, how many content items, which interaction possibilities and which content types fit best in each viewing situation. We foresee two half days that consist of three phases: validating the viewing situations (see Table 1) and evaluating different interfaces for different situations. For both workshops we aim to involve three larger families with children, three seniors or senior couples, three singles and three younger couples.

Another issue we will try to tackle in these sessions will be the reduction of the number of interfaces. It is be unlikely that seven different interfaces will be usable. For this reason, and the request of the research partner with whom we are working, we currently have reduced the number of interfaces to three: one supporting long form content, one supporting short form content, and one specifically for children.

Conclusions and future work

The results of this limited prototyping session and the preceding investigation into the different viewing situation indicate that designing interfaces that support the finding and discovery of suitable content related to specific viewing situations is promising. These efforts are aimed to fill the gap between the advanced recommender algorithms in the back-end (outcome personalisation) and the user. We hope to gain insights into what content users would like in each situation and into the best way of offering this via interaction with the system by manipulating content selection, look & feel, and interaction options.

Acknowledgements

The research leading to these results was carried out in the TV-Ring project (EC grant agreement ICT PSP-325209).

References

1. Abreu, J., Almeida, P., and Teles, B. TV discovery & enjoy: a new approach to help users finding the right TV program to watch. *Proceedings of the 2014 ACM international conference on Interactive experiences for TV and online video*, ACM (2014), 63–70.

2. Abreu, J., Almeida, P., Teles, B., and Reis, M. Viewer Behaviors and Practices in the (New) Television Environment. *Proceedings of the 11th European Conference on Interactive TV and Video*, ACM (2013), 5–12.

3. Churchill, E. Putting the person back into personalization. *Interactions 20*, 5 (2013), 12–15.

4. Della Cava, M. YouTube unveils new app for kids. *USA TODAY*, 2015. http://www.usatoday.com/story/tech/2015/02/19/youtube-for-kids-new-android-app-out-feb-23/23707819/.

5. Houde, S. and Hill, C. What do prototypes prototype. *Handbook of human-computer interaction 2*, (1997), 367–381.

6. Mercer, K., May, A., and Mitchel, V. Designing for video: investigating the contextual cues within viewing situations. *Personal and Ubiquitous Computing 18*, 3 (2014), 723–735.

7. Stefanidis, K., Shabib, N., Nørv\aag, K., and Krogstie, J. Contextual recommendations for groups. *Proceedings of the 2012 international conference on Advances in Conceptual Modeling*, Springer-Verlag (2012), 89–97.

8. Vanattenhoven, J. and Geerts, D. Contextual aspects of typical viewing situations - a new perspective for recommending television and video content. Conditionally accepted for *Personal and Ubiquitous Computing*, Special Issue: Interactive Experiences for Television and Online Video (2015).

9. Wheatley, D.J. Design and evaluation of a children's tablet video application. *Proceedings of the 2014 ACM international conference on Interactive experiences for TV and online video*, ACM (2014), 79–86.

HbbTV goes Cloud: Decoupling Application Signaling and Application Execution in Hybrid TV

Alexandra Mikityuk
Technical University Berlin
Security in
Telecommunications
alex@sec.t-labs.tu-berli.de

Oliver Friedrich
New Media
Telekom Innovation
Laboratories
oliver.friedrich@telekom.de

Randolph Nikutta
New Media
Telekom Innovation
Laboratories
randolph.nikutta@telekom.de

Abstract

The cloud-based execution of the User Interface has already begun to disrupt the TV domain. Indeed, in European Hybrid TV Standard - Hybrid Broadcast Broadband (HbbTV) - the signaling of applications is terminated by special libraries on the client. Therefore, the cloud-based UI execution does directly affect the HbbTV. This work presents an architecture that enables the shift of HbbTV functionality into the Cloud. This is based on the decoupling of HbbTV application signaling and application execution on the client side. The shift is executed by defining new interfaces for HbbTV-to-cloud and cloud-to-device. This work describes possible approaches for such architectures, relevant open issues and corresponding challenges.

Author Keywords
Hybrid TV; HbbTV; Red-Button Signaling; UI Cloud execution; Cloud-based HbbTV

ACM Classification Keywords
H.3.4 [Systems and Software]: Distributed Systems—*Decoupling of application execution and signaling;* H.3.5 [Online Information Services]: Web-based services—*Cloud-based HbbTV*

Introduction

The Web sets the pace for developments in the TV broadcast and broadband domain. Web browsers have become a powerful cross-platform technology for the deployment of User Interfaces (UI). As part of this, the native execution of the UI in TV Platforms has migrated to browser runtime environments. This refers to browsers running locally or on virtual appliances in the Cloud. The first deployments of UIs, which are entirely streamed from the Cloud, have already taken place. Cablevision Systems, Ziggo and some of the European operators have already deployed cloud-based UIs.

The ubiquity of Cloud Browser runtime environments does directly affect the Hybrid Broadcast Broadband (HbbTV) Standard. In Europe and in some other countries, HbbTV has become a major standard for Digital TV. Most of the TVs available on the European market support the HbbTV functionality [8].

The HbbTV 1.0 was specified in 2010 [4]. The specification of the application signaling is provided by Digital Video Broadcasting (DVB) [2]. Application signaling in HbbTV is called Red-Button signaling. HbbTV combines web-based technologies with DVB-based video delivery. HbbTV defines a web browser as a standard execution environment for HbbTV applications. Web browsers in the TV domain have to support all the HbbTV specifications to support the HbbTV standard.

Problem statement: With regard to UI execution in the Cloud, the browser capability is shifted from the Set-Top Box (STB) to the Cloud. In HbbTV standard Reb-Button signaling is terminated by the DVB stack on the STB of the end user. The applications are also executed on the STB by the HbbTV Browser, which

supports the HbbTV standard. With the release of the HbbTV 2.0 specification [5] in mid February 2015, a step towards the convergence of W3Cs HTML5 specification and HbbTV was made. Still, references to cloud-rendered browser-based services are missing in both organizations' specifications. Therefore, the shift of the browser into the Cloud completely disrupts the classical HbbTV approach.

Contribution: In this paper, we present an approach for the Cloudification of HbbTV. We propose to accomplish this through decoupling the application signaling and the application execution functionalities, and subsequently shifting them into the Cloud. To enable the decoupling and the shift into the Cloud, we define new interfaces between the STB, the Cloud and the HbbTV. To the best of our knowledge, this is the first work to present a decoupling of the HbbTV functionality from the STB.

Related Work

The HbbTV Specification Working Group has begun to work on the specification of Independent Application Discovery. This work is supported by NPO (Netherlands Public Broadcasting). They address the scenario, in which application signaling does not reach the HbbTV terminal. Currently the scenario where broadcasters must signal a special server ID is preferred. This ID is used by the terminal to resolve the server that then serves the Application Information Table (AIT). However, it is still unclear whether the broadcasters will accept it or not.

Another important initiative, which is the first step on the way to decoupling of DVB functionality, is DVB integration into RDK [7]. The RDK is an initiative driven by cable operators in order to standardize STB middleware. They develop and specify a common framework to power STBs and other end-client TV devices.

Kienzle et al. explore [6] the possibilities for integrating of cloud-enabled Service Delivery Platforms (SDP) into HbbTV delivery. They show, that such SDP is a proven foundation to address the challenges of HbbTV. However, they also highlight the fact that the most preferable cost-driven approach here would be the implementation of cloud-enabled SDPs.

Cloud-rendered UI

Cloud-rendered UI is a concept that enables the shift of the browser from the STB into the Cloud. Therefore, the rendering of the content/ User Interface happens in the browser in the Cloud. The UI is then delivered to the STB in the H.264 MPEG-TS stream. The STB runs a lightweight client that handles video decoding and the key events. Operators has already begun to deploy CloudTV services [3].

Cloud HbbTV Architecture

Two steps in the shift of HbbTV into the Cloud are presented here:

Cloud HbbTV Execution: describes the decoupling of the signaling and execution of applications. Only the HbbTV browser is shifted to the Cloud. The signaling logic stays on the client side.

Cloud HbbTV Signaling and Execution: the complete HbbTV functionality is virtualized.

Cloud HbbTV Execution

In this architecture, we have decoupled the DVB stack and the HbbTV functionality on the client side.

However, the DVB Logic still resides on a client side (see Figure 1). This architecture can address scenarios where the STBs do not support an HbbTV-enabled browser.

To enable this shift of the HbbTV Browser into the Cloud we have defined the following required interface. Interface STB-CL: must be used for communicating between the STB and the Browser/ the Middleware in the Cloud. Over this interface, Red-Button signaling is forwarded by the STB towards the Cloud. In this case, the STB plays the role of a gateway, which terminates the DVB application signaling. The STB must have both broadband and broadcast interfaces.

1: The DVB signal is terminated by the STB in its DVB Logic - the DVB stack. The DVB data containing the AIT is extracted from MPEG-2 TS by the DEMUX and is afterwards processed to filter the Red-Button signaling data. After the data is extracted, the new XML syntax is created and is then sent to the Cloud.

2: The Digital Storage Media Command and Control (DSM-CC) provides broadcasters with file system like functionality and is used to signal and to deliver the Red-Button applications. At this point, the STB must forward the signaling data to the Cloud. Therefore, STB translates DSM-CC data into an http request. The signaling data include the name of an object, e.g. button, and its properties, e.g. red, and additional data:

```
"button": "red", "data": {channel id,
            session id, app url, }
```

where channel id and session id are the IDs of the

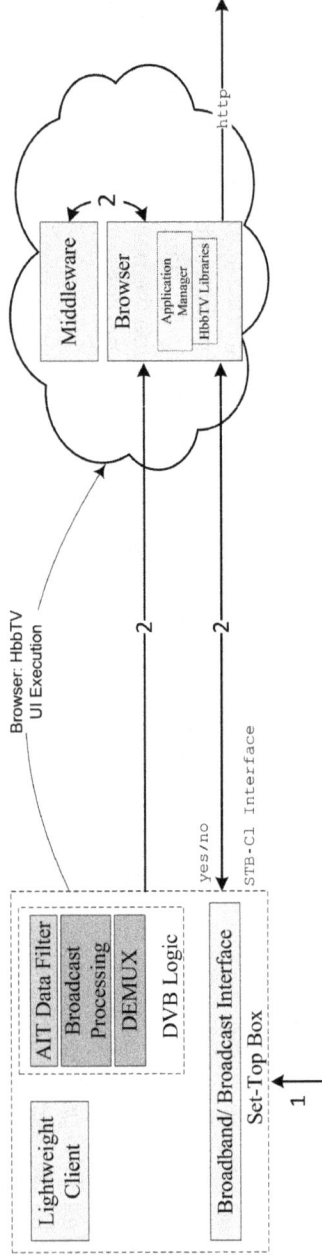

Figure 1: The shift of HbbTV Browser into the Cloud

channel and the session, `app url` is the URL of the HbbTV application.

This request will trigger the Red-Button event in the Browser. The Browser in turn must contact the Middleware to adjust the User Interface by inserting a red button into the UI. The adjusted UI is sent back to the client and is then presented by its Lightweight Client.

After the user presses the red button, the Browser in the Cloud can start to request the received before `app url` over http. The component responsible for handling the application is the Application Manager. HbbTV Libraries and the Application Manager are part of the HbbTV profile of the HbbTV-enabled Browser. The application in this architecture can only be requested via http, assuming that the Cloud does not terminate the DSM-CC. This case would be considered in Section Cloud HbbTV Signaling and Execution.

Cloud HbbTV Signaling and Execution
In the next step, the whole DVB and HbbTV signal termination and execution are shifted to the Cloud. In this approach the classical DVB broadcast scenario is disrupted. The STB is not required to have the Broadcast interface. Therefore, this approach can address scenarios, where the STBs does not have broadcast interfaces, e.g. mobile scenarios.

To enable the shift of DVB and HbbTV functionality the following interfaces are required. Interface `CL-STB:` must be used for communication between the Browser/ the Middleware in the Cloud and the STB. The STB must have a broadband interface. Interface `Hbb-Cl:` The HbbTV/DVB logic is now responsible for the termination of the Red-Button signaling. This component must have a broadcast interface.

The scenario sequence is then as follows:

3: The DVB signal is now terminated and the DVB data is extracted from MPEG-2 TS by the HbbTV/DVB logic in the Cloud. The extraction of the data and its translation occurs as described in 1 in Section Cloud HbbTV Execution.

4: The Red-Button signaling information is sent to the Browser/ Middleware in the Cloud by the HbbTV/ DVB Logic. The further request/response execution is analogue to 2 in Section Cloud HbbTV Execution.

5: However, the whole DSM-CC logic is now within the DVB stack and is part of Cloud functionality. The HbbTV applications can now also be delivered over DSM-CC. The Application Manager redirects the app url to the HbbTV/DVB logic. This URL points to the DSM-CC object that is then delivered over the DSM-CC object carousel.

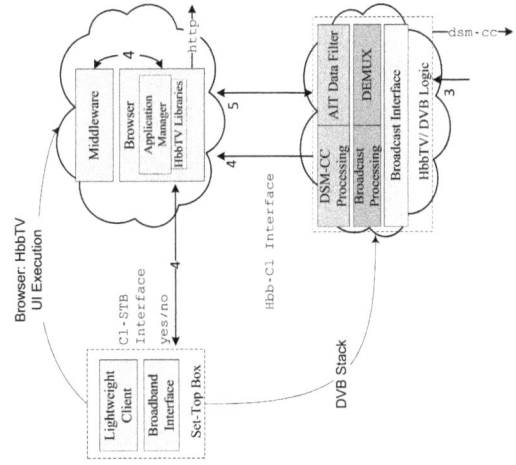

Figure 2: The shift of HbbTV Browser and the DVB logic into the Cloud

Challenges

The shift of HbbTV functionality into the Cloud requires more complex application management on the server side. The AIT tables, which were described earlier, are sometimes different depending on the geo location of the user. Therefore, the client STB must also inform the server about its geo location. According to this information, the client would get the corresponding AIT.

Another issue would be content synchronization between the server and the client side. In current implementations, the broadcasters update the AIT tables rather infrequently. They update it so that the operator can refresh it every 24h without any loss of information. However, if the broadcasters would update it more often, invalid structures in the stream events of the operator could sometimes come up.

For scenarios where the Red-Button signaling is terminated on the STB the integrity of the signal must be ensured. Assuming that an attacker can compromise the STB and insert malicious data in the signal, the STB must also be authenticated.

Open issues

OipfDRMAgent defines the Javascript API towards the DRMAgent. No specific DRM solution is mandated by HbbTV. The DRM technology for HbbTV is a legacy technology and is available only for embedded domain.

The integration of DRM hooks into browser environments resulting in huge disruption of how DRM works. Desktop browsers like Chrome, Firefox and Internet Explorer already support the HTML5 Encrypted Media Extensions (EME) standard [1]. However, they are all limited to one single DRM (Chrome-Widevine; Adobe-Firefox, Internet

Explorer-PlayReady). This disrupts a classical DRM approach. In contrast, for the embedded Domain, namely Set-Top-Box and Connected TVs no final decisions have been made. Therefore, the main challenge for the Cloud HbbTV concept is a possible adaptation of HbbTV DRM technologies in combination with Cloud browsers and W3Cs HTML5 EME specification.

Furthermore, the role of CA and its integration into HTML5 technology and the HbbTV specifications must be clarified. Possible handover scenarios between CA and DRM for multi-device scenarios must also be taken into consideration.

The question of which role the broadcaster assumes in such scenarios also remains open. The regulations and industry will also decide whether or not the operator is allowed to intercept the Red-Button signaling.

Conclusion

The HbbTV standard does not address cloud-rendered browser-based services. To enable this we have proposed two steps on the path toward enabling Cloud HbbTV in this work. First we proposed the decoupling approach where the signaling and execution functionalities are separated. The HbbTV browser, which is responsible for the execution, is shifted to the Cloud. In the next step we presented a completely Cloud-enabled architecture for HbbTV. Here the DVB logic is also shifted into the Cloud. Furthermore, we

discussed challenges and open issues for both approaches. In our future work we will present these approaches and their implementation in more detail.

References

[1] David Dorwin, Adrian Bateman and Mark Watson. W3C Editor's Draft - Encrypted Media Extensions., 2014.

[2] DVB. *Signalling and carriage of interactive applications and services in Hybrid broadcast/broadband environments (TS 102 809 V1.1.1)*, Jan. 2010.

[3] EUROMEDIA Magazine. STB and Home Gateway Survey. `http://irdeto.com/documents/Articles/art_euromedia-magazine_JulAug_2014.pdf`, 2014.

[4] European Broadcasting Union. *Hybrid Broadcast Broadband TV (DVB); Technical Specification (TS 102 796 V1.1.1)*, June 2010.

[5] HbbTV. *Hybrid Broadcast Broadband TV (DVB); Technical Specification 2.0*, Feb. 2015.

[6] Kienzle, M., Brooks, L., and Schaffa, F. *Smarter TV - Linking Broadcast and Broadband Television Through a Service Delivery Platform in the Cloud.* Hawthorne, USA.

[7] Reference Design Kit Alliance. `http://rdkcentral.com/`, 2015.

[8] SevenOne Media. Connected TV. `https://www.sevenonemedia.de/hbbtv1`, Mar. 2014.

Gesture Interfaces, Ambient Intelligence, and Augmented Reality for the Interactive TV

Radu-Daniel Vatavu
University Stefan cel Mare of Suceava
13 Universitatii
Suceava 720229
Romania
vatavu@eed.usv.ro

This course is structured into three chapters that will introduce participants to (1) ambient intelligence principles applied to home entertainment, (2) augmented reality applications, and (3) gesture interaction design. Relevant examples from research and industry will be discussed.

Author Keywords: augmented reality; gestures; ambient intelligence; course; interactive TV.

ACM Classification Keyword: H.5.1 Multimedia Information Systems: Artificial, augmented, and virtual realities. H.5.2. User Interfaces: Input devices and strategies.

1 Introduction: What Happened to the TV Set? (15 minutes)

Participants will be reminded of today's technology that found applications for home entertainment. Relevant examples will be presented to participants to make them

aware of the benefits, but also the pitfalls of adapting new technology to existing systems, *e.g.*, gesture interfaces may not work for all user categories.

2 Augmenting Reality: New TV Installations that Dissolve within Living-Rooms (30 minutes)

The fundamental principles of designing augmented reality applications will be presented, and examples from research and industry will be provided to participants in the context of the interactive TV. Specifically, the mixed-reality Around-TV system [3] will be used to pinpoint aspects of designing AR apps for the interactive TV.

3 Intelligent Ambient and Smart TVs (30 minutes)

The fundamental principles of ambient intelligence will be presented to participants in the context of designing home entertainment systems and applications. As ambient installations are context-aware, personalized, adaptive, and anticipatory of their users' demands, integrating the TV into such application scenarios puts similar demands on applications running on the TV set. Participants will be presented with practical ways of making that happen by discussing custom content delivery, user identification, and intent recognition.

4 Gesture User Interfaces (60 minutes)

The main technologies available today to acquire human gestures will be presented. Advantages of each approach will be discussed in the context of the home entertainment environment. The Nintendo Wii remote,

Course history

Part of this course was offered at EuroITV'12 (the 10th European Conf. on Interactive TV and Video) under the title "Designing Gestural Interfaces for Future Home Entertainment Environments", where it was well received by attendees. For example, one participant appreciated the tutorial "*quite comprehensive and included a lot of background information. This is how a tutorial should be*". The 2013 version was delivered at EuroITV'13 with updated references and case studies. In 2014, a course was offered at TVX'14 (the ACM Int. Conf. on Interactive Experiences for TV and Online Video) with focus on ambient intelligence and augmented reality for iTV. The plans for TVX'15 are to reach a wider audience of researchers and practitioners by adopting an integrative approach of augmented reality, ambient intelligence, and gesture interface design principles for prototyping our future home entertainment experience.

Course Overview

Target attendees

Researchers and practitioners working in Human-Computer Interaction, user interfaces, and design of the home entertainment user experience. A mixture of participants from research and industry is ideal. No previous knowledge about gesture interface design, ambient intelligence, or augmented reality is required.

Teaching methods

The instructor will employ topics presentation, working with examples, discussions and collaboration to actively involve the auditory.

"All the theoretical and technical developments in which I have been involved have the ultimate goal to understand the user. Understanding fundamental human characteristics and designing for those characteristics are the most worthy goals I can imagine as a researcher in the Human-Computer Interaction field of study."

Microsoft Kinect sensor, and the Leap Motion controller will be highlighted to participants as easy-to-use, low-cost technologies for rapid prototyping of gesture interfaces. Simple and efficient techniques for recognizing gestures will be presented. Design criteria for gestures, such as learnability and fit-to-function will be explained and exemplified to participants.

5 Take-Aways: A Summary of Design Guidelines for Home Entertainment Environments (20 minutes)

Practical guidelines will be extracted for participants from case studies in which gestures, ambient intelligence, and augmented reality have been integrated into iTV and home entertainment scenarios.

Instructor

Radu-Daniel Vatavu, Ph.D., works in Human-Computer Interaction with focus on designing novel interactions for new usage scenarios. He is particularly interested in designing for the home environment with a specific concern toward human aspects and the way technology can enhance everyday human-human interactions.

Teaching experience

Radu-Daniel Vatavu holds an Associate Professor position at the Computer Science Department of the University "Ștefancel Mare" of Suceava, where he has been teaching Algorithms Design, Pattern Recognition, Advanced Programming, and Advanced Artificial Intelligence for undergraduate and graduate students since 2008. He has delivered tutorials and courses on gesture interaction during EuroITV'12, EuroITV'13, and TVX'14.

References

[1] Vatavu, R.D., Zaiți, I.A. 2014. Leap gestures for TV: insights from an elicitation study. In *Proc. of the 2014 ACM Int. Conf. on Interactive experiences for TV and online video (TVX '14)*, 131-138

[2] Vatavu, R.D., Mancas, M. 2014. Visual attention measures for multi-screen TV. *TVX '14*, 111-118

[3] Vatavu, R.D. 2013. There's a world outside your TV: exploring interactions beyond the physical TV screen. In *Proc. of the 11th European Conf. on Interactive TV and video (EuroITV '13)*, 143-152

[4] Vatavu, R.D. 2013. A Comparative Study of User-Defined Handheld vs. Freehand Gestures for Home Entertainment Environments. *J. Amb. Intell. and Smart Env., 5(2)*, 187-211

[5] Vatavu, R.D. 2012. User-defined gestures for free-hand TV control. *Proc. of the 10th European Conf. on Interactive TV and video (EuroITV '12)*, 45-48.

[6] Vatavu, R.D. 2012. Point & Click Mediated Interactions for Large Home Entertainment Displays. *Multimedia Tools and Applications, 59(1)*, 113-128

[7] Vatavu, R.D. 2012. Nomadic Gestures: A Technique for Reusing Gesture Commands for Frequent Ambient Interactions. *J. Amb. Intell. and Smart Env., 4(2)*, 79-93

[8] Vatavu, R.D., Pentiuc, S.G. 2008. Interactive Coffee Tables: Interfacing TV within an Intuitive, Fun and Shared Experience. In *Proc. the 6th European Interactive TV Conference (EuroITV '08)*, 183-187

[9] Vatavu, R.D. 2013. The Impact of Motion Dimensionality and Bit Cardinality on the Design of 3D Gesture Recognizers. *International Journal of Human-Computer Studies, 71(4)*, 387-409

[10] Vatavu, R.D., Anthony, L., Wobbrock, J.O. 2012. Gestures as point clouds: a $P recognizer for user interface prototypes. In *Proc. of the 14th ACM Int. Conf. on Multimodal interaction (ICMI '12)*, 273-280.

Multi-Sensory Media Experiences

Marianna Obrist

School of Engineering &
Informatics
University of Sussex
Chichester 1
BN1 9QJ Brighton
m.obrist@sussex.ac.uk

Abstract

The way we experience the world is based on our five senses, which allow us unique and often surprising sensations of our environment. Interactive technologies are mainly stimulating our senses of vision and hearing, partly our sense of touch, and the sense of taste and smell are widely under-exploited. There is however a growing international interest of the film, video, and game industries in more immersive viewing and gaming experiences. This course will engage researchers and practitioners in a discussion on why and how we should think about touch, taste, and smell for future media experiences. The aim of this course is to introduce participants to the field of multi-sensory research and examine the opportunities and challenges for TVX.

Author Keywords

Multi-sensory interaction; User experience; Interaction design; Sensory integration; Media experiences; TV.

ACM Classification Keywords

H.5.m. Information interfaces and presentation (e.g., HCI): Miscellaneous. H.1.2 User/Machine Systems.

Introduction and Goals

Designers of interactive systems, such as TV and online video systems, know how to design for depth and distance perception in visual user interfaces to augment people's experiences. Vision is however not always enough to create compelling viewing experiences.

Course Overview

Finding the right combination between the different sensory stimuli could enable us to create, for instance, tactile emotional experiences matching the visual content [2] or the use of scents could enhance media experiences through creating anticipation [3] such as it is done through sound (e.g., thrilling soundtrack).

In the 20th century there was a demand for a controllable way to describe colours that initiated intense research on the descriptions of colours and substantially contributed to advances in computer graphics, image processing, photography and cinematography. Similarly, the 21st century now demands an investigation of touch, taste, and smell as sensory interaction modalities. This course will put to the fore the key questions we need to think about within the TVX community. We will examine related work in the field of human-computer interaction and multimedia research (e.g., [1,2,3,4,5,6]).

The ambitious goals of this course are:

- To provide an introduction and overview on previous and current approaches for designing multi-sensory experiences relevant for TVX.
- To present insights into the three under-exploited senses: Touch, Taste, and Smell.
- To discuss challenges and opportunities for creating multi-sensory media experiences.

Participants will be presented with an interdisciplinary and thought-provoking introduction into the field of multi-sensory research and design coupled with an interactive discussion of specific practice examples.

Course Instructor

Marianna Obrist is a Lecturer in Interaction Design at the University of Sussex, at the School of Engineering and Informatics, UK. The focal point of her research is to create a rich understanding on users experiences with various interactive systems. She specifically investigates the design spectrum for touch, taste, and smell experiences (http://www.multisensory.info/).

Acknowledgments

This work is supported by the EC within the Horizon2020 programme through the European Research Council (Starting Grant Agreement 638605).

REFERENCES

1. Ghinea, G., Ademoye, O. (2012). The sweet smell of success: Enhancing multimedia applications with olfaction. *ACM Trans. Multi. Comput. Commun. Appl.* 8(1), Article 2, 17 pages.

2. Obrist, M., Subramanian, S., Gatti, E., Long, B., and Carter, T. (2015). Emotions Mediated Through Mid-Air Haptics. *Proc. ACM CHI'15*.

3. Obrist, M., Tuch, A., Hornbæk, K. (2014). Opportunities for Odor: Experiences with Smell and Implications for Technology. *Proc. CHI'14*, 2843-2852.

4. Obrist, M., Comber, R., Subramanian, S., Piqueras-Fiszman, B., Velasco, C., Spence, C. (2014). Temporal, Affective, and Embodied Characteristics of Taste Experiences: A Framework for Design. *Proc. CHI'14*, 2853-2862.

5. Obrist, M., Seah, S. A., Subramanian, S. (2013). Talking about tactile experiences. *Proc. CHI '13*, 1659-1668.

6. Ranasinghe, N., Karunanayaka, K., Cheok, A.D., Fernando, O.N.N., Nii, H., Gopalakrishnakone, P. (2011). Digital taste and smell communication. *Proc. BodyNets*, 78-84.

To Hack or Not to Hack: Interactive Storytelling in the 21st Century

Sandra Gaudenzi

Digital Cultures Research Centre,

UWE, Bristol, UK

sgaudenzi@yahoo.com

@sgaudenzi

Abstract

This course aims at introducing notions of user-centered design in the realm of interactive storytelling. After reviewing how software methodologies like hacks and agile development have been used in the context of storytelling prototyping, the course will provide a hands-on workshop aimed at putting the user at the center of the story from day one of the production process.

Author Keywords

Interactive storytelling; interactive documentary; hack; hackathon; POV hacks, Tribeca hacks; Popathon; Learn Do Share; user; user experience; user-centered design; design thinking; workshop.

ACM Classification Keywords

H.5.2 User Interfaces: User-centered design; theory and methods; Prototyping.

Introduction

In the past few years software development methodologies such as hackathons and agile development are permeating the narrative realm. Tribeca Hacks, POV Hackathons and Popathons are all events that want to put together storytellers, coders and designers in the hope that new methodologies of collaborative work can emerge.

Is this the way forward for interactive storytelling production, or is it just a moment of disruption? Are the rules of storytelling really changing for good? What are the tensions that are emerging from this changing of paradigm?

Participants:

This course is opened to all. No specific technical knowledge is required. Previous viewing of existing interactive documentaries is a plus.

Structure:

1st part (30 min):

The first part of the course will be a lecture that will present evidence of some new methodologies of production in storytelling. The Learn Do Share (Lance Weiler), Tribeca Hacks (TFI), POV Hackathons and Popathons (Philo Van Kemenade, Gilles Pradeau) will be

explained, and for each of those case studies will be presented. Examples of projects such as *Priyas' Shakti*, *Do Not Track* and *Empire* that emerged from hacks will be shown.

2nd part (2 hrs):

A brief workshop will be proposed to the participants. They will have to apply the design thinking process (dSchool, Stanford University) to the creation of an interactive story: empathize, define, prototype, test and start again.

3rd part (30 min):

A discussion time will be allowed in this course so to accommodate both some feed-back on the workshop and a debate on the new types of methodologies that could be applied to interactive storytelling.

Acknowledgements

I'd like to thank the Digital Cultures Research Centre, and Tribeca Hacks, POV Hackatons, Popathons and Learn Do Share for sharing information about their activities with me.

References

[1] Do Not Track.
http://donottrack-doc.com/en/.

[2] Empire.
http://www.pbs.org/pov/empire/.

[3] Institute of Design at Stanford.
http://dschool.stanford.edu/.

[4] Learn Do Share.
http://www.learndoshare.net/.

[5] Priya's Shakti.
http://www.priyashakti.com/.

[6] Popathon.
http://popathon.org/.

[7] POV Hackathons.
http://www.pbs.org/pov/hackathon/.

[8] Tribeca Hacks.
https://tribecafilminstitute.org/programs/%20detail/tribeca_hacks.

3rd International Workshop on Interactive Content Consumption (WSICC'15)

Rene Kaiser
JOANNEUM RESEARCH
Graz, Austria
rene.kaiser@joanneum.at

Britta Meixner
Passau University, Passau
Germany
meixner@fim.uni-passau.de

Joscha Jäger
Merz Akademie, Stuttgart
Germany joscha.jaeger@merz-akademie.de

Katrin Tonndorf
Passau University, Passau
Germany
katrin.tonndorf@uni-passau.de

Omar A. Niamut
TNO, Delft, The Netherlands
omar.niamut@tno.nl

David Marston
BBC, London, UK
david.marston@bbc.co.uk

TVX'15, Jun 03-05, 2015, Brussels, Belgium
ACM 978-1-4503-3526-3/15/06.
http://dx.doi.org/10.1145/2745197.2745700

Abstract

The third edition of the WSICC workshop aims to bring together researchers and practitioners working on novel approaches for interactive multimedia content consumption. WSICC has established itself as a truly interactive workshop at EuroITV'13 and TVX'14 with two successful editions. The aims and scope of WSICC'15 have been sharpened based on the results from previous workshops. New technologies, devices, media formats and consumption paradigms are emerging that allow for new types of interactivity. All these recent advances have an impact on the user's experience – therefore, discussions during the workshop based on the participants' contributions will consider this aspect with particular emphasis. The workshop's program, further details and documentation about all WSICC editions is available on the http://wsicc.net website.

Author Keywords

workshop; multimedia; content consumption; interaction; HCI; user experience;

ACM Classification Keywords

H.5 [Information Interfaces and Presentation]: [Multimedia Information Systems]

Workshop Aims and Scope

WSICC's objective is to provide a highly interactive discussion forum that allows capturing a comprehensive view on the research area it addresses. During the workshop, an overview on new content interaction concepts, research activities and future challenges in this area will be concluded and documented. An interdisciplinary view on the topic is compiled by contributions from technical research, conceptual work, user-centric studies, industry developments, as well as experimental showcases. In other words, the workshop aims to examine and evaluate new forms of content interaction by discussing the field along three axes:

- Recent technological advances that enable new forms of audiovisual content interaction;

- User-centric studies that evaluate new types of audiovisual content interaction, especially in the realm of societal trends and media consumption paradigm shifts;

- Studies from industry considering and evaluating user needs and the impact of advances in this area.

As another way to look at the workshop's scope, in previous workshop editions, the research landscape was characterized along 4 dimensions (see Figures 1 and 2): Enabling Technologies, Content, User Experience, and User Interaction. The following taxonomy defines the workshop's scope by examples:

Enabling Technologies: This dimension searches for technology and tools for the consumption and the authoring of interactive content, especially:

Figure 1: Mindmap result of WSICC'13.

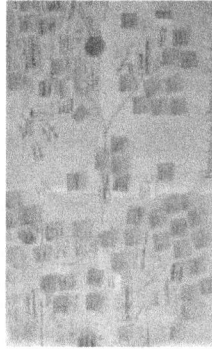

Figure 2: Mindmap result of WSICC'14. Available in better resolution on the website. Both mindmaps are currently being digitized by the organization team to be further analyzed for scientific publication of the workshop results.

- Techniques for content adaptation, rendering and converting for a wide variety of devices and delivery channels.

- Approaches for interactive personalization and recommendation.

- Research on interactive content delivery.

- Studies on immersive devices, such as VR goggles, wearables, and cyber-physical systems.

- Novel approaches in content production technology (object-based or format-agnostic).

User Experience: The user experience dimension explores research on quality of user experience (QoE) theory and evaluations, the impact and effects of interaction on perceived quality, the role of the audience, and the role of social context. It investigates the effect of increased interactivity and user engagement, empowerment but also overload and distraction, e.g.:

- Studies and foundations from the social sciences.

- Evaluation of user needs regarding personalized content consumption.

- Research on collaborative and community-based multimedia consumption and creation.

- Exploration of immersive audio.

- Approaches for inclusion and improved accessibility (e.g. automatic content enhancement for special needs).

User Interaction: This dimension analyzes novel interaction approaches, concepts and paradigms. Thereby, interactivity might be interpreted both as computer mediated communication as well as human computer interaction. Interest lies in:

- Research on natural interaction techniques.
- Experiments on multi-modal interaction and social signal processing, especially gesture control and speech recognition.
- Studies on social interaction during content consumption and mobile content consumption.
- Methods of feedback for user control, including visual, acoustic and tactile interaction.
- Studies on lean-forward interaction trends and joint interaction of larger groups.
- Studies on the balance between active (lean forward) and passive (lean backward) content consumption.

Content: The content dimension researches new types and forms of interactive content, such as:

- Content from gaming or the mobile and VR domains.
- Live and recorded materials.
- Data representation formats for interactive content.
- Adaptable content and content of variable length.
- High-quality and ultra-high definition content.

Figure 3: Fishbowl discussion at WSICC'13.

Figure 4: Fishbowl discussion at WSICC'14.

- Content captured by novel types of sensors (e.g. 3D or panoramic video).

Beyond these four areas, the workshop welcomes discussion on best practices, future challenges and research road-mapping.

In contrast to previous WSICC editions, WSICC'15 will emphasize one of the above dimensions, the *user experience*. Technology and content characteristics will not be discussed for their own sake only, but also in their role as factors that lead to certain user experiences.

Interactively shaping the process of content consumption is often associated with positive outcomes and experiences like higher engagement with the content, participation in the content creation, user empowerment, etc. But also negative aspects may be considered, for example what happens when users dont have the resources to deal with increased interactivity (e.g., knowledge about the media offering, meta-cognitive skills). The need to constantly make decisions and to actively control the information flow can lead to negative consequences like overload, or sub-optimal content usage behavior. Discussion during WSICC may also engage in the consequences of content consumption that go beyond the immediate usage experience like the development of information bubbles because of selective exposure practices. This road may lead to more normative discussion of the impact of changing media practices on individuals but also on the society.

Workshop Format

WSICC has developed a workshop format to stimulate both networking and knowledge transfer among the participants. The full day workshop will be an active

Interactive Media: Technology and Experience in Springer's Multimedia Tools and Applications (MTAP) journal. The CfP is available on Springer's website[2].

WSICC'15 will consist of the following sessions:

- Welcome, introduction to the workshop format, and presentation of workshop aims.
- Interactive participant introduction in Barcamp style (name, affiliation, role, 3 keywords/hashtags).
- Invited keynote with focus on the experience aspect, in order to establish a common understanding among the participants.
- A _madness_ session to kick start the poster/demo session. Each contribution is presented by a short pitch á 2min.
- The poster and demo session. Posters are based on short paper contributions. Technical demos are regarded an essential part of the workshop as they allow discussion upon hands-on experience. This session shall establish an understanding of everybody's work, focus and interest.
- Three research paper based talks. In line with the informal atmosphere, questions will be allowed during the talks.
- Two sessions in _fishbowl_ discussion format, around aspects raised during WSICC. In a nutshell, there is a limited number of active seats. If you want to say something, you have to take an empty seat or wait for one to become available. This format of a dynamically changing working panel proved to work well for discussions among experts on concrete questions. The fishbowl format has been

[2] http://static.springer.com/sgw/
documents/1494253/application/pdf/
SpecialMTAPIssueInteractiveMultimediaDeadlines.pdf

---

forum to discuss research challenges, methodologies and results in a field that maintains relevance in an ever-changing landscape of new device types, content forms, and growing technical infrastructure. Both media consumption needs and habits are constantly evolving.

More than half the time is reserved for discussion. The chairs will establish an informal atmosphere, inspired by the basic principles of the Barcamp format[1]. In an active moderating role, they will make sure the workshop's underlying questions will be discussed, answered as far as possible and documented. Nevertheless they will allow some flexibility in order to meet the interest of the audience spontaneously, as appropriate.

In contrast to the WSICC editions in 2013 and 2014, the scope of this workshop is considerable more narrow, as described above. However, the methodology of both organizers and participants collecting inputs on large flip charts along multiple question dimensions throughout the day will be kept. Throughout the day, the audience will be encouraged to contribute, and especially to comment existing inputs (_I'd love to collaborate on this!... This has already been solved in my project!_). The outcome of the workshop will be summarized on a poster for the presentation at the main conference, based on the inputs on the flip charts. A publication summarizing the workshop results will be considered.

Further, the WSICC organization team is currently processing inputs from previous editions (mind maps) to process the results for the scientific community. In another activity stemming from the workshop series, authors from all three WSICC editions are invited to submit to a Special Issue on WSICC's scope named

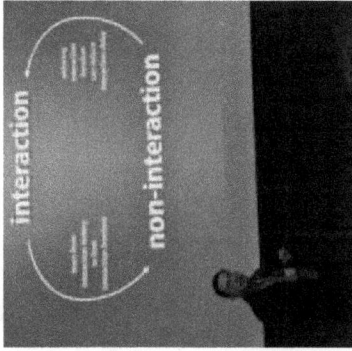

Figure 5: WSICC'13 keynote by Wei Tsang Ooi.

Figure 6: WSICC'14 keynote by Marian F. Ursu.

[1] See http://en.wikipedia.org/wiki/BarCamp

understood very well and quickly in the past by WSICC participants.

- Concluding session. The group will revisit what has been collected throughout the day. Conclusions will be summarized. A best paper award will be given to the contribution with the highest review scores regardless of its type.

Organizing Committee

The following presents short bios for the organization team, which in line with the workshop's target audience represents technical research, social sciences research, and industry. Team members complement each other well and are dedicated to contribute to the research community by conducting this activity. They are taking care about workshop results after the workshop day, as indicated above. Results will be openly accessible through the website, and ultimately in a scientific publication. The team will continue to stimulate discussions within the community, using social media platforms.

The workshop is supported by several research projects as indicated below. Some of the results from previous editions are accessible via the workshop website[3] which already contains the 2014 proceedings[4] (2013's were part of the adjunct EuroITV proceedings[5]) and visual impressions[6] [7].

Figure 7: Group photo at WSICC'13.

Figure 8: Group photo at WSICC'14.

Rene Kaiser is a key researcher for JOANNEUM RESEARCH and has been involved in a number of European projects dealing with automation of content production such as NM2, APOSDLE, FascinatE, TA2 and Vconect. His research focus is on *Virtual Director* software, on automating shot selection through cinematographic behavior models. Rene is a PhD student at TU Graz and head of the Knowledge Management Forum Graz. Rene has co-organized the first edition of WSICC at EuroITV 2013 and its second edition at TVX 2014. He also organized the Interactive and Immersive Entertainment and Communication Special Session at MMM'12. He is part of a group hosting the annual PhD cooperation workshop at the i-KNOW conference, active member and E-Letter chair of IEEE STCSN, and co-organizer of the Barcamp Graz, a yearly 3-day *unconference* which is an interactive and open discussion format.

Britta Meixner is a researcher at Passau University. She received a diploma in computer science and a state examination for lectureship at secondary schools from the University of Passau, Germany, in 2008. She made her PhD degree in computer science at the Faculty of Computer Science and Mathematics of the University of Passau, in 2014. Her PhD thesis has the title "Annotated Interactive Non-linear Video - Software Suite, Download and Cache Management". Further she is interested in hypervideo on mobile devices, collaborative hypervideo creation, and decision rules in hypervideo. Britta is a member of the BMBF research project "mirKUL" that investigates application scenarios of interactive non-linear video. Britta is a reviewer for the Multimedia Tools and Applications Journal (Springer) and was a member of the program committee of the 1st International Workshop on Interactive Content Consumption at EuroITV 2013 and an

---

[3]http://wsicc.net/
[4]http://wsicc.net/2014/Proceedings-WSICC-2014.pdf
[5]https://sites.google.com/a/euro-itv.org/2013/program/proceedings
[6]https://www.flickr.com/photos/49520289@N04/sets/72157634457839167/
[7]https://www.flickr.com/photos/49520289@N04/sets/72157645061214918/

Figure 9: Technical demo at WSICC'13.

Figure 10: Poster discussion at WSICC'14.

organizer of the 2nd International Workshop on Interactive Content Consumption at TVX2014.

Joscha Jäger is a researcher at Merz Akademie Stuttgart and founder of filmicweb - Hypervideo Interface Design. His research covers Web-based hypervideo technology, time-based interaction, and semantic video search interfaces. Joscha has a strong focus on film as information architecture, collaborative editing systems for non-linear film, and user-driven annotation systems. He is interested in finding new ways of distributed interaction with open video technologies and interfaces on the web. He was an organizer of the 2nd International Workshop on Interactive Content Consumption at TVX2014.

Katrin Tonndorf is a researcher at Passau University. She received a magister degree in media studies from the Technical University Braunschweig and the Braunschweig University of Arts in 2010. Currently, she is working towards a PhD degree in communication studies at the Faculty of Arts and Humanities at University of Passau. She is conducting research in the area of online and social media communication practices. Furthermore she is interested in the use of interactive audiovisual content for learning and support purposes. Katrin is also a member of the BMBF research project "mirKUL".

Omar Aziz Niamut is a senior research scientist at TNO. He has a background in the coding and transport of digital signals. His PhD research included the development of universal audio coding algorithms. He advised the European Parliament on the harmonization of mobile TV and was editor of the technology report on mobile TV in the European Commission — assigned European Mobile Broadcast Council. He participated in ETSI TISPAN standardization with over 200 contributions on interactive services for next-generation IPTV and advised the

Singapore government on the use of IPTV standards. His current focus is on social and interactive media services over next-generation networks and immersive media delivery. He is the author of academic papers and articles in the fields of audio coding, interactive IPTV services and immersive media. Omar holds over 15 patents and has contributed a chapter to a book on Social TV. He has been a member of the EuroITV TPC, for the Systems and Enabling Technologies track.

David Marston is a senior R&D engineer for the BBC's Research and Development department. He is a part of the audio team which specialised in various areas of broadcast related audio research work, including the latest developments in object-based audio. Among Dave's responsibilities is standardisation work and is chairman of the EBU FAR-BWF group and a ITU-R WP6B rapporteur group both working on file formats for future audio. Dave is also project manager for the BBC's part of the EU-funded ICoSOLE collaborative project (JRS being one of the project partners), which includes work on immersive and interactive audio to enhance the audience experience.

Acknowledgements

The workshop is supported by the European Commission under the contract FP7-287760, "Vconect – Video Communications for Networked Communities" and FP7-610370, "ICoSOLE – Immersive Coverage of Spatially Outspread Live Events". Further the workshop is supported by the German Federal Ministry of Education and Research (BMBF) under contract 03V0633.

People, Context, and Devices: Defining the New Landscape of TV Experiences

Isha Dandavate
User Experience Researcher
Youtube
San Bruno, CA
ishad@google.com

Jennifer Milam
User Experience Designer
Youtube
San Bruno, CA
jmilam@google.com

Jeanne Allen
User Experience Producer
Youtube
San Bruno, CA
jeanneallen@google.com

Christiane Moser.
Thomas Kargl
Manfred Tscheligi
Center for HCI,
University of Salzburg
{firstname.lastname}@sbg.ac.at

Jeroen Vanattenhoven
CUO | Social Spaces, iMinds -
KU Leuven
jeroen.vanattenhoven@soc.kuleu
ven.be

Lilia Perez Romero
CWI: Centrum Wiskunde &
Informatica
l.perez@cwi.nl

Fabian Schiller
IRT,
schiller@irt.de

Joost Negenman
Dutch Public Broadcast, NPO
joost.negenman@npo.nl

Abstract

Modern technologies (e.g., tablet, smartphone, large public displays) remove many of the constraints that define the scope of what television is or can be, but we often define it based upon our prior TV experiences with broadcast and cable television. This one-day workshop at TVX 2015 will address design challenges and opportunities (e.g., of video streams, social TV apps, second screens) in order to consolidate existing knowledge to describe the changing landscape of TV experiences. It's time to redefine what we think of when we say "television," and this workshop will engage participants in that process.

Author Keywords

Television; Video; Online Video; Social TV; Second Screen; User Experience; Frameworks;

ACM Classification Keywords

H.5.m. Information interfaces and presentation (e.g., HCI): Miscellaneous.

Introduction

Since the introduction of the TV, the user experience has evolved from a single use case involving groups surrounding a single set, viewing limited programming on 2-3 channels, to ever more complex systems involving competing and complementary technologies, devices, services, programming, inputs and

Workshop Summary

interactions, contexts, and expectations which are further convoluted by the ecosystem of user, programmer and advertiser intentions.

Modern users consume programming and services in a wide variety of scenarios. They now have the ability to watch in co-located and/or geographically dispersed groups; can simultaneously engage with several displays, devices, channels, people, and services; and can consume content on demand, freeing them from programming schedules. In addition to the added flexibility in viewing habits, there is also an ever-increasing amount of programming options coming from a variety of content creators, allowing for more niche content options. Those designing modern and future TV experiences must consider disparate or related programming, social engagement, varying degrees of user attention and interaction, and use-cases involving a wide variety of locations, and contexts and time.

One emerging focus area, the usage of second screens, is often not directly related to the presented TV content, though a lot of recently developed applications pair the TV screen with a second screen. Challenges emerging from the interaction with second screens are, for example, the tension between lean-forward content and lean-back consumption, the loss of immersion due to a fragmentation of the video frame, and the tension between multiple and single users [3]. Additionally, social TV applications have become increasingly important and enable social interactions around TV content (e.g., by combining it with social media on a second screen in order to share favorite television programs or get recommendations) [2].

Researchers and practitioners often face challenges when designing for new TV experiences due to restricted understandings. Designing for this richer landscape of experiences requires the development and organization of knowledge around these complex ecosystems of technology and humans behaviors. We will focus on a few emerging areas of knowledge development to support future innovation.

Aim

This workshop aims at exploring the changing landscape of the television experience. We will explore the impact of devices, context and social interactions on users' television watching behaviors. The day will be divided into two portions led by different organizations:

1. Members of the University of Salzburg and KU Leuven, in collaboration with three industry practitioners, will lead a discussion about lessons learned through practice or research, and best practices.

2. Members of the YouTube User Experience team will lead an interactive working session to enumerate and characterize key facets of the developing landscape of TV experiences, culminating in the creation of a framework that will inform and foster innovation.

Scope

This workshop is for academics and professionals who have experience in TV UX. It encourages inter-disciplinary discussions and aims to include researchers and practitioners in the fields of content creation, interaction design, user interface design, computer science, psychology, cognitive science, and sociology, etc. Through this two-part workshop, we aim to bring together experts to discuss lessons from previous work, and articulate and challenge existing assumptions.

Workshop Format

Before the Workshop

The workshop organizers will promote the workshop with a website. The call for participation will be distributed via HCI, TV and entertainment related mailing lists as well as specialized ones (e.g., ACM SIGCHI). Furthermore, the organizers will reach out to industry contacts to attract submissions.

During the Workshop

09:00 – 09:10 INTRO TO WORKSHOP TOPIC
Introduction by both teams of workshop organizers to review the day's agenda.

09:10 – 10:30 WORLD CAFE INTRO
Participants will be invited to share short anecdotes and stories on challenges or opportunities. Afterwards, organizers present summarized highlights and common themes of the submitted papers in order to facilitate formation of groups for the world café.

10:30 – 11:00 COFFEE BREAK AND DEMOS
During coffee breaks the participants will have the opportunity to try out selected demos of TV applications.

11:00 – 12:30 WORLD CAFÉ
The groups will participate in a world café [1] and discuss opportunities and lessons learned for second screen and social experiences, highlights of which will be documented on a poster for the afternoon session.

12:30 – 13:30 LUNCH BREAK

13:30 – 13:45 WORLD CAFÉ SUMMARY
The table hosts (organizers) will summarize the findings as starting point for the next phase.

13:45 – 14:00 INTRO TO DOUBLE DIAMOND PROCESS
Workshop organizers from YouTube will introduce the process, which involves two phases of broadening ideation followed by scope refinement.

14:00- 14:30 PHASE 1: DIVERGE
In this phase, we will conduct a series of timed, fast-paced brainstorming sessions, each of which will aim to collect answers to a different facet of how we think about the video watching experience. This process will result in a collective "brain dump" of TV-related knowledge.

14:30 – 15:00 COFFEE BREAK

15:00 – 15:30 PHASE 1 (CONT): CONVERGE
In the "convergence" phase of the workshop, participant groups will be assigned to one of the themes from the divergent phase, and attempt to surface clusters and patterns. This process will inform the next step in which participants will apply the clusters to developing a framework.

15:30- 16:00 PHASE 2: DIVERGE & CONVERGE
The workshop organizers will moderate a conversations in which participants will surface relevant patterns and collectively distill a final framework that captures the best aspects of the day's work.

16:00-17:30 CLOSING NOTES

After the Workshop

Following the workshop, the organizers will produce a final poster for the TVX 2015 poster session.

Participation

Interested participants must submit a 2 to 4-page position paper discussing their existing work in the TV space and their background via email to ishad@google.com and christiane.moser@sbg.ac.at. Insightful papers fostering an interdisciplinary perspective are welcomed. Participants will be selected based on their position papers and CV to ensure a variety of viewpoints and expertise are represented.

Deadlines

March 9th, 2015: Workshop submission deadline.
April 2nd, 2015: Notification deadline.
May 2nd, 2015: Camera-ready version deadline.
June 3rd, 2015: Workshop at TVX2015.

Organizers' Background

YOUTUBE TEAM

Isha Dandavate is a User Experience Researcher working on TV experiences for YouTube. She holds a Master's degree in information management and systems at the UC Berkeley School of Information. Prior to joining YouTube, Isha was a researcher at SonicRim, a global design research consultancy based in San Francisco, where she worked on developing frameworks through exploratory qualitative research and co-creation workshops. At YouTube, her research focuses on living room experiences, which include multi-device experiences, on-screen keyboard interactions, search experiences in the context of short-form videos, and social watching behaviors.

Jennifer Milam is a User Experience Designer imagining new video ads experiences for YouTube. Prior to joining YouTube, she designed user experiences for Apple and IBM. Jennifer holds an M.S. in Human-Computer Interaction/Computing from Georgia Institute of Technology, and a B.S. in Applied and Computational Math from University of Washington, Seattle. Much of her research and design has focused on video and immersive experiences, including collaborative video annotation, video-mediated negotiations, bio-signals as virtual reality game input, and mobile augmented/mixed reality experiences. She explores rich media experiences as a medium to entertain, inform, and persuade.

Jeanne Allen is a User Experience Producer working to support the strategy and creation of the YouTube user interface across the device ecosystem. Prior to joining YouTube, she was a member of the Xbox UX team at Microsoft where she focused on the design and development of the platform UI. This included the creation of gestural and voice UI for Kinect. Her career focus has revolved around the evolution of how people consume entertainment across time and place in meaningful ways.

Second Screen and Social Experiences team

Christiane Moser is a research fellow the ICT&S Center of the University of Salzburg and working in an international research project which develops advanced interfaces for special user groups using TV and tablet. She has been involved in EU research and innovation projects on social media. She organized workshops at IDC2011, MobileHCI2011, FnG2012, CHI2013, ACE2013, and CHIPLAY2014.

Thomas Kargl is research fellow the ICT&S Center of the University of Salzburg and working in international research projects, where he designs the user interface for the TV and tablet platform.

Manfred Tscheligi is full professor for HCI & Usability at the ICT&S Center of the University of Salzburg and is directing CURE in Vienna. He is directing the Christian Doppler Laboratory on Contextual Interfaces. He was involved in several conferences (e.g., co-chairing CHI2004, ACE2007, EuroITV 2009, and AUI2011) and co-organizing workshops and SIGs (e.g., CHI2008, IDC2011, INTERACT2011, AmI2011, CSCW2012, CHI2013, MobileHCI2014, and NordiCHI2014).

Jeroen Vanattenhoven is senior researcher at the Centre for User Experience Research of the interdisciplinary research institute iMinds and the University of Leuven. He has been involved in Flemish and EU research and innovation projects on social media, Social TV, second-screen for more than 8 years. Currently he is working in the TV-RING project focusing on social and contextual recommendations, and second-screen applications for TV, via the HbbTV technology. He is work-in-progress chair for TVX2015.

Lilia Perez Romero is designer and Professional Doctorate in Engineering in the area User System Interaction. She is PhD candidate in computer science at CWI in the Netherlands. She designs and researches second screen applications for web-enriched broadcast video within the context of the European research project LinkedTV.

Fabian Schiller was working in the industry before joining the Institut für Rundfunktechnik, a research and development institute of ARD, ZDF, DRadio, ORG and SRG/SSR. He is engaged in international research projects related to second screen and HbbTV. He is an active member in the HbbTV Testing Working Group.

Joost Negenman is the Senior Policy Advisor R&D at NPO - Dutch Public Broadcast. His scope is Connected/ Hbb TV, 2nd Screen, Mobile - and Broadband content delivery. He strongly believes added value for viewers can only be achieved by accessible and seamlessly integrated platforms. He is the pilot leader at EU TV Ring project and EBU TVP – BBN member.

Acknowledgements

This workshop and research was enabled by the GeTvivid project (funded by AAL JP, AAL-2012-5-200) and TV-Ring project (EC grant agreement ICT PSP-325209).

References

[1] Basapur, S., Mandalia, H., Chaysinh, S., Lee, Y., Venkitaraman, N., and Metcalf, C. 2012. FANFEEDS: Evaluation of Socially Generated Information Feed on Second Screen As a TV Show Companion. In *Proceedings of the 10th European Conference on Interactive Tv and Video*, ACM, 87–96.

[2] Cesar, P. and Geerts, D. 2011. Past, present, and future of social TV: a categorization. In *Consumer Communications and Networking Conference (CCNC), 2011 IEEE*, 347-351.

[3] Pérez Romero, L., Traub, M.C., Leyssen, M.H.R. and Hardman, L. 2013. Second Screen Interactions for Automatically Web-enriched Broadcast Video. In *Workshop proceedings of EuroITV 2013*, Como, Italy.

Media Synchronization Workshop

Hans Stokking
TNO
The Netherlands
hans.stokking@tno.nl

Pablo Cesar
CWI
The Netherlands
p.s.cesar@cwi.nl

Fernando Boronat
UPV
Spain
fboronat@dcom.upv.es

Mario Montagud
CWI
The Netherlands
M.Montagud@cwi.nl

TVX 2015, June 3–5, 2015, Brussels, Belgium.
ACM 978-1-4503-3526-3/15/06.
http://dx.doi.org/10.1145/2745197.2745699

Abstract

The Media Synchronization workshop, in its third
edition, brings together an active community around
the topic of media synchronization, attracting relevant
researchers in this area. The objective of the workshop
is to further built this community and set the research
agenda on the topic of media synchronization. We will
do this by sharing our current research in short
presentations, and by having an active session in the
afternoon. We will be working in subgroups on key
problem areas, present our work to the whole group as
a starting point for an active discussion on the most
relevant research to be carried out in the coming years.

Author Keywords

Media synchronization; distributed systems; media
delivery; standards

ACM Classification Keywords

H.5.1 [Information interfaces and presentation]:
Multimedia Information Systems

Introduction

The main objective of our workshop series is to create
an active community around the topic of media
synchronization. In this community we can share ideas
and research agendas, we can collaborate in new
projects, and bring new solutions to the industry. The
goal in the workshops themselves is mainly to discuss
the research agenda, to help us focus our work for the

coming years. The lively discussions in the previous workshop editions have really helped set the agenda, both inside our community but also in the industry.

We have organized two previous editions of this workshop series [1], in 2012 and 2013. Both workshops attracted about 30 people: from European projects and national projects, from standardization, from the conference we co-located it with, and from our own contacts. The two previous editions had the format of presentations, with a long (panel) discussion at the end. The discussions were mostly about future research needed in the media synchronization domain. We now will run the third edition at the ACM International Conference on Interactive Experiences for TV and Online Video (ACM TVX2015), with a more interactive afternoon session. The goal is still to discuss relevant and emerging research challenges in the area of media synchronization.

Background

Media synchronization has been a challenge in A/V transmission for quite some time. Over the years, many techniques to achieve intra- and inter-media synchronization in various network conditions have been developed. In many cases, synchronization between different media is crucial for a satisfying perceived Quality of Experience (QoE). Currently, many new media synchronization issues arise. On the one hand, novel media technologies such as HTTP streaming protocols, media encoders and HDTV often require new synchronization techniques. On the other hand, new patterns in media consumption often introduce specific synchronization issues. For example, internet applications evolving around broadcast TV content may need synchronization between the

application and the broadband stream. Synchronization between different TV receivers may be needed in Social TV (inter-destination media synchronization).

SIMPLY EXPLAINED

DO YOU LOVE ME?

WHY DON'T YOU ANSWER ME? IS THERE ANOTHER MAN?

YES

geek & poke

WHAT DO YOU MEAN? OF COURSE NOT!!!

LATENCY

Geek and Poke, Simply Explained [2]

In some interactive TV cases synchronization between handheld devices and the TV screen may be needed. Moreover, novel 3D technologies for TV broadcasting and tele-presence (e.g., 3D tele-immersion) may require the adoption of several of these synchronization techniques to achieve a satisfying quality of user experience (QoE). Additionally, the deployment of applications that integrate, and synchronize inputs across all senses including the tactile, olfaction, and gustatory senses, apart from inputs for audio and visual senses, is currently a reality. The integration of such multiple sensorial effects into multimedia applications, or mulsemedia (multiple sensorial media) applications, also requires research on new media synchronization techniques, aligning rich data from multiple human senses, to provide a truly enriched and immersive experience. This workshop proposal addresses all the above synchronization issues and requests contributions from different perspectives.

Scope and Goal

The scope of the workshop is media synchronization in all its facets: architecture, protocols, algorithms, simulations, implementations, standardization, user experience studies, business models, etc. The goal of the workshop is to determine the most relevant research aspects of media synchronization in the coming years. Much research has been done in this area, as said, but many researchers involved in media synchronization have the feeling that they have not finished their job just yet. In this workshop, we want to concretely identify the most relevant research topics in the area of media synchronization that will require our effort in the coming years.

Format

We will follow an interactive format, using a subgroup working structure. From the submissions, we will determine the 3 most relevant topics for future research. On these topics, we will define short cases. These cases may be use cases, they may be major

technical problem areas, they may be user experience issues, etc. We will divide the participants into 3 subgroups, and assign each of the subgroups one of the cases. The subgroups will be asked to work out the case, and provide a solution direction, or a clear insight into the problem. We will ask the subgroups to make 1 poster each on their work, which they will present to the whole group afterwards. These posters will be the input for a group discussion on the future of media synchronization research.

Program

The Media Synchronization Workshop 2015 (https://sites.google.com/site/mediasynchronization/mediasync2015) will be held in conjunction with the ACM TVX on June 3rd, 2015, in Brussels, Belgium. The most pertinent contributions have been selected for inclusion in the workshop's agenda. These include seven papers:

1. A Test Bed for Hybrid Broadcast Broadband Services

2. An Automatic Media Synchronizing Mechanism with TV Programs

3. Leveraging Audio Fingerprinting for Hybrid Content Radio Synchronization

4. Multi-device Linear Composition on the Web, Enabling Multi-device Linear Media with HTMLTimingObject and Shared Motion

5. Time-Awareness for Media-Synchronisation– Opportunities & Challenges

6. NERstar: New Approaches to Improving the Quality of Audiovisual Media Services

7. Review of Media Sync Reference Models: Advances, Inconsistencies and Open Issues

The workshop includes as well five demos, one keynote, and interactive sessions. The demos are (apart from the ones showcasing paper 1 and 6):

- Merge and Forward – Self-Organized Inter-Destination Multimedia Synchronization

- Synchronization and Customization of Subtitles in Web-based Main-Screen and Multi-Screen Scenarios

- A customizable open-source framework for measuring and equalizing e2e delays in shared video watching

The draft schedule looks like this:

9.00 Welcome by the organizers

9:10 Keynote presentation

9.50 Short presentations

11.00 Break

11.15 Discussion about the topics and demos

12.30 Lunch

14.00 Work in subgroups

15.45 Short break

16.00 Presentations of the sub-groups, discussion

17.00 End

Workshop Organization

The workshop is organized by TNO, CWI and UPV. The main organizers are Hans Stokking (TNO), Pablo Cesar (CWI) Prof. Fernando Boronat (UPV), and Mario Montagud (CWI). We would like to thank the Technical Program Committee that helps shaping the program of the workshop: Cyril Concolato, (Telecom ParisTech), Davy Van Deursen (EVS), Luiz Fernando Gomes Soares (PUC-RIO), Jack Jansen (CWI), Tim Stevens (UK), Christian Timmerer (Klagenfurt University), and Ishan Vaishnavi (Huawei).

Bios

Hans Stokking is a Senior Scientist and inventor at TNO in the field of Information and Communication Technology. His focus is on integrating various fields of study, and as such, Hans is active in the area of IPTV solutions, content distribution networks and home networks. His main focus is in 'how to get services across networks' and he has consulted a wide range of customers on a range of services and networks: from consumer and business VoIP services to Internet services to P2P networks and inter-business messaging networks. Hans is (co-) author of over 20 popular and scientific papers, is (co-) inventor of more than 40 patent applications and has prepared many standardization contributions over the years. He is also a TPC member for the yearly ICIN conference, and is (co-) organizer of the international Media Synchronization Workshop series.

Dr. Pablo Cesar leads the Distributed and Interactive Systems group at Centrum Wiskunde & Informatica (CWI) in Amsterdam, the Netherlands. He obtained his PhD from the Helsinki University of Technology, in Finland, in 2005. He has participated and lead very successful EU-funded project like REVERIE, Vconect, TA2, iNEM4U, and SPICE. Pablo has (co)-authored over 70 articles about multimedia systems and infrastructures, social media sharing, interactive media, multimedia content modelling, and user interaction. Several of his publications have won the best paper award at a number of high-quality events such as ACM MMsys (2013), ACM HT (2011), EuroITV (2008) and ACM MM (2008). He has given tutorials about multimedia systems in prestigious conferences such as ACM Multimedia, CHI, and the WWW conference. He is (co-) organizer of the international Media Synchronization Workshop series. Webpage: http://homepages.cwi.nl/~garcia/

Prof. Fernando Boronat studied Telecommunications Engineering at the Polytechnic University of Valencia (UPV), in Spain. After working for several Spanish Telecommunication Companies, in 1996 he moved back to the UPV, where he is an Assistant Professor in the Communications Department at the Gandia Campus. He obtained his PhD degree in 2004 and his main topics of interest are Multimedia Systems, Multimedia Protocols and Media Synchronization. He is IEEE Senior member (M'93, SM'11) and is involved in several IPCs of national and international journals and conferences. Webpage: http://personales.upv.es/fboronat/Research/index_investig_en.html.

Dr. Mario Montagud (@mario_montagud) was born in Montitxelvo (Spain). He studied Telecommunications Engineering at UPV (Polytechnic University of Valencia), in Spain, and obtained the PhD degree from the same university in 2015. Since then, he is a postdoc researcher at CWI (The National Research Institute for Mathematics and Computer Science in the Netherlands). His topics of interest include Computer Networks, Interactive and Immersive Media, Synchronization and QoE (Quality of Experience). Mario is (co-) author of over 30 research and teaching publications, and has contributed to standardization with the IETF (Internet Engineering Task Force). He is also member of the Technical Committee of several international conferences and of the Editorial Board of international journals. Webpage: https://sites.google.com/site/mamontor/

Acknowledgments

Fernando Boronat would like to thank the funding from the following project: GROUP_HYBSYNC (Hybrid and Inter-Destination (IDMS) Synchronization to enable enriched, personalized, inmersive and shared media experiences); MINECO, Ministerio de Economía y Competitividad of Spain (Ref. TEC2013-45492-R).

References

[1] Media Synchronization Workshop series, see https://sites.google.com/site/mediasynchronization/

[2] Geek and Poke, see http://geek-and-poke.com/geekandpoke/2012/12/9/simply-explained.html

Multi-Sensory Media Experiences

Marianna Obrist
University of Sussex, UK

Abstract

The way we experience the world is based on our five senses, which allow us unique and often surprising sensations of our environment. Interactive technologies are mainly stimulating our senses of vision and hearing, partly our sense of touch, and the sense of taste and smell are widely under-exploited. There is however a growing international interest of the film, video, and game industries in more immersive viewing and gaming experiences. In the 20th century there was a demand for a controllable way to describe colours that initiated intense research on the descriptions of colours and substantially contributed to advances in computer graphics, image processing, photography and cinematography. Similarly, the 21st century now demands an investigation of touch, taste, and smell as sensory interaction modalities to enhance media experiences.

ACM Classification

H.5.1 [Information Interfaces and presentation]: Multimedia information systems – audio, video

Author Keywords: Multi-sensory interaction; User experience; Interaction design; Sensory integration; Media experiences; TV

Short Bio

Marianna Obrist is a Lecturer in Interaction Design at the University of Sussex, UK. She is leading the SCHI Lab (Sussex Computer Human Interaction) integrated in the Creative Technology research group established within the School of Engineering and Informatics. Prior to joining Sussex, she was a Marie Curie Fellow at Culture Lab at the School of Computing Science in Newcastle University and before she worked as an Assistant Professor for Human-Computer Interaction at the Department of Computer Science at the University of Salzburg, Austria. Her current research focuses on the systematic exploration of touch, taste, and smell experiences for human-computer interaction. She has been recently awarded €1.5Mk by the European Research Council for a five-year project to expand the research into 'Sensory Experiences for Interactive Technologies' (SenseX). Marianna has published widely in the fields of human-computer interaction and user experience, and is currently Vice Chair for the ACM TVX steering committee.

TVX 2015, June 3–5, 2015, Brussels, Belgium.
ACM 978-1-4503-3526-3/15/06.
http://dx.doi.org/10.1145/2745197.2783433

Author Index

www.ingramcontent.com/pod-product-compliance
Lightning Source LLC
Chambersburg PA
CBHW061412210326
41598CB00035B/6187